LEVANT SUPPLEMENTARY SERIES
VOLUME 1

NEOLITHIC REVOLUTION

NEW PERSPECTIVES ON SOUTHWEST ASIA IN LIGHT OF RECENT DISCOVERIES ON CYPRUS

Edited by

Edgar Peltenburg

and

Alexander Wasse

Papers from a conference organized by the
Council for British Research in the Levant
in collaboration with the
Department of Antiquities, Cyprus

20th to 23rd September 2001
Drousha Village, Cyprus

OXBOW
BOOKS

EDINBURGH UNIVERSITY LIBRARY

WITHDRAWN

Published by
Oxbow Books, Park End Place, Oxford OX1 1HN

© The individual authors, 2004

ISBN 1 84217 132 1

A CIP record for this book is available from the British Library

This book is available direct from
Oxbow Books, Park End Place, Oxford OX1 1HN
(Phone: 01865-241249; Fax: 01865-794449)

and

The David Brown Book Company
PO Box 511, Oakville, CT 06779, USA
(Phone: 860-945-9329; Fax: 860-945-9468)

or from our website

www.oxbowbooks.com

Printed in Great Britain by
Antony Rowe Ltd, Chippenham

Contents

List of Figures

List of Tables

Notes on contributors

Sue Colledge is AHRB Research Fellow at the Institute of Archaeology (UCL) working with Professor Stephen Shennan and Dr James Conolly on a project entitled "The origin and spread of Neolithic plant economies in the Near East". Her interests include Near Eastern archaeobotany and quantitative methods in archaeobotany.
Address: Institute of Archaeology, University College London, 31-34 Gordon Sq, London WC1H OPY, U.K.
Email: s.colledge@ucl.ac.uk

Anna Eirikh-Rose is a PhD student at the Hebrew University, having recently finished her MA degree with the thesis entitled "Sha'ar Hagolan Pottery, it's cultural aspects and spatial distribution". For many years she participated in Sha'ar Hagolan Excavations, and was responsible for Sha'ar Hagolan pottery and ground tool analyses. She currently works for the Israel Antiquities Authority and participated in the Motza excavation project. Her main interests include the Levantine Chalcolithic and Neolithic in general, the beginning of pottery in the Near East, early pottery production of the region, processes of Neolithization in it's social and cultural aspects, ritual and symbolic expressions, Neolithic/Chalcolithic transformation.
Address: Institute of Archaeology, Hebrew University, Jerusalem 91905, Israel.
Email: analexrose@hotmail.com

Bill Finlayson is the Director of the Council for British Research in the Levant, based in Amman, Jordan. His research has concentrated on late Pleistocene/early Holocene hunters and gatherers, the beginnings of sedentism and the transition to agriculture. He is currently excavating at the PPNA sites of Wadi Faynan 16 and Dhra', and working on the conservation and presentation of the Natufian/PPNB site of Beidha, all in southern Jordan.
Address: CBRL Amman, PO Box 519, Jubaiha, Amman 11941, Jordan.
Email: b.finlayson@cbrl.org.uk

Ehud Galili is a marine archaeologist and the Director of the Marine Archaeology Branch of the Israel Antiquities Authority. Research interests include submerged prehistoric settlements, sea level changes, coastal displacement and ancient seafaring, fishing technologies, and the management and preservation of the underwater archaeological heritage.
Address: Israel Antiquities Authority, Marine Archaeology Branch, P.O.B. 180, Atlit 30350, Israel.
Email: Udi@israntique.org.il

Yosef Garfinkel carries out research on the proto-historic era, that is the Pottery Neolithic and Early Chalcolithic periods of the ancient Near East. Three main aspects are involved: field work (large-scale excavations at Neolithic Ashkelon and Sha'ar Hagolan), material culture studies (mainly Neolithic and Chalcolithic pottery) and Neolithic art, cult and dance. Published books include *The Pottery Assemblages of Sha'ar Hagolan and Rabah Stages from Munhata (Israel)*, Association Paléorient: Paris (1992), *Sha'ar Hagolan Vol 1 - Neolithic Art in Context* (with M. Miller), Oxbow Books: Oxford (2002) and *Dance at the Dawn of Agriculture*, Texas University Press: Austin (2003).
Address: Institute of Archaeology, Hebrew University, Jerusalem 91905, Israel.
Email: Garfinkel@h2.hum.huji.ac.il

Avi Gopher is an archaeologist and fulltime professor at the Institute of Archaeology, Tel Aviv University. Research interests include the study of mainly Epi-Paleolithic and Neolithic communities in the Levant and of flint quarrying in the Levant.
Address: Institute of Archaeology, Tel Aviv University, Ramat Aviv 69978, Tel Aviv, Israel.
Email: agopher@post.tau.ac.il

Maya Haïdar-Boustani, currently research assistant at the Musée de Préhistoire Libanaise, belongs to a young team trying to revive prehistoric research in Lebanon after the pioneers, the Jesuits. Her chief interest is the Neolithic period, especially of the Beqa` valley. She collaborates in archaeological surveys in Lebanon.
Address: Research Assistant Musée de Préhistoire Libanaise, Faculté des Lettres et des Sciences Humaines, Université Saint-Joseph, Rue de l'Université Saint-Joseph B.P. 17-5208 Mar Mikhael, Beirut 1104 2020, Lebanon.
Email: maya.boustani@usj.edu.lb

Hitomi Hongo carries out research in zooarchaeology, especially domestication of ungulates and the spread of domestic animals in Turkey, and generally in Southwest Asia and East Asia. His recent publications include H. Hongo, R.H. Meadow, B. Öksüz, G. Ilgezdi (2002) The process of ungulate domestication in Prepottery Neolithic Çayönü Southeastern Turkey. Pp. 153-165 in H. Buitenhuis, A.M. Choyke, M. Mashkour and A.H. Al-Shiyab (eds.) *Archaeozoology of the Near East V*. ARC-Publication: Groningen.
Address: Primate Research Institute, Kyoto University, Kanrin, Inuyama-City, Aichi 484-8506, Japan.
Email: hitomi@pri.kyoto-u.ac.jp

Liora Kolska Horwitz is a freelance archaeozoologist and associate curator of Zoology Collection of Mammals, Hebrew University of Jerusalem. Research interests include the study of the origin and development of animal domestication, the economy of complex societies and bone taphonomy.
Address: Department of Evolution, Systematics and Ecology, Hebrew University, Berman Building, Givat Ram, Jerusalem 91904, Israel.
Email: lix100@excite.com

Carole McCartney is a freelance archaeologist based at the Lemba Archaeological Research Centre, Cyprus and currently an Honorary Fellow of the University of East Anglia, Norwich. Research includes the documentation of chipped stone industries on Cyprus from the island's colonization through the threshing sledge industry of recent history. Participation in a number of projects, in Cyprus, Jordan and Syria, has led to broader discussions of artefact variability including assemblage diversity, craft specialization as well as diffusion and social identity as defined by material culture.
Address: Lemba Archaeological Research Centre, 8260 Lemba, Cyprus.
Email: carole@spidernet.com.cy

A.M.T. Moore's archaeological research has concentrated on understanding the transition from foraging to farming in western Asia and the spread of this new way of life to the rest of Asia, Europe and Africa. Moore has documented the inception of farming at Abu Hureyra in Syria, research that has recently been published (with G. C. Hillman and A. J. Legge) in *Village on the Euphrates* (2000). In his latest project Moore is investigating the economy of Neolithic villages on the Dalmatian coast in Croatia. Moore is a Professor of Anthropology and Dean of the College of Liberal Arts at the Rochester Institute of Technology.
Address: Office of the Dean, College of Liberal Arts, Rochester Institute of Technology, 92 Lomb Memorial Drive, Rochester, NY 14623-5604, U.S.A.
Email: ammgla@rit.edu.

Edgar Peltenburg is Professor of Archaeology at the University of Edinburgh. His research interests include social dynamics within small-scale societies, and structural transformations in the growth of complex, state-like societies. He is Director of the Lemba Archaeological Research Centre in the Paphos District of Cyprus and he also conducts investigations at the site of Jerablus Tahtani beside Carchemish in Syria. His most recent edited publication is *The Colonisation and Settlement of Cyprus*. Studies in Mediterranean Archaeology 70:4 (2003).
Address: Archaeology, SACE, University of Edinburgh, Old High School, Edinburgh, EH1 1LT, Scotland-UK, and Lemba Archaeological Research Centre, 8260 Lemba, Cyprus.
Email: e.peltenburg@ed.ac.uk

Baruch Rosen is a Lecturer at the Institute of Archaeology of the Tel-Aviv University, and at the Faculty of Agriculture at the Hebrew University of Rehovot. Research interests include mainly ancient and pre-modern subsistence systems.

Address: Israel Antiquities Authority, Marine Archaeology Branch, P.O.B. 180, Atlit 30350, Israel.

David Rupp (Ph.D. Bryn Mawr College), Professor of Mediterranean Archaeology and Art in the Department of Classics at Brock University has done archaeological fieldwork in Canada, the United States, Italy, Greece, Cyprus and Israel. In Cyprus his research interests range from archaeological survey methods and practice, the Early Prehistoric period, Iron Age state formation and the economy, Hellenistic/Early Roman settlement patterns to Late Roman mosaics at Kourion. His fieldwork has focused on the Paphos District with an extensive archaeological survey (Canadian Palaipaphos Survey Project) and an excavation (Western Cyprus Project at Prastio - Agios Savvas tis Karonis Monasteri).

Address: Department of Classics, Brock University, St. Catharines, ON L2S 3A1 Canada.

Email: drupp@spartan.ac.brocku.ca

Alan H. Simmons is a Professor in the Department of Anthropology and Ethnic Studies at the University of Nevada, Las Vegas. He has worked extensively with early Neolithic societies in North America, the Near East and Cyprus. In Jordan, he directed or co-directed excavations at the Pre-Pottery Neolithic B "mega-sites" of 'Ain Ghazal and Wadi Shu'eib, and at Ghwair I, a spectacularly preserved PPNB village. In Cyprus, he directed excavations at Akrotiri-*Aetokremnos*, and subsequently at the Khirokita Culture site of Kholetria-*Ortos*. Currently, he is principal investigator for interdisciplinary studies at Ais Yiorkis, a late Cypro-PPNB site near Paphos.

Address: Department of Anthropology & Ethnic Studies, University of Nevada, Las Vegas, 4505 Maryland Parkway, Box 455003 Las Vegas, Nevada 89154-5003, U.S.A.

Email: simmonsa@unlv.nevada.edu

Sarah Stewart is completing her dissertation at the University of Toronto on landscape and settlement in the Aceramic Neolithic of Cyprus. She received her MA in Archaeology from the University Calgary and BA from the University of Toronto. She is currently co-director (with Margaret Morden) of the Idalion Survey Project in Cyprus, and was a survey crew leader and associate lithic analyst on the Canadian Palaipaphos Survey Project in Cyprus. Her research interests include survey, landscape theory, ethnoarchaeology and lithic analysis. Her most recent publication, in the *Journal of Archaeological Science* (with A. Hawkins and E. B. Banning) examines interobservor bias in survey data.

Address: Department of Anthropology, 100 St. George Street, University of Toronto, Toronto, Ontario, M5S 3G3, Canada.

Email: salstew@sympatico.ca

Eitan Tchernov, until his decease in December 2002, was a full professor in the Faculty of Life Sciences at The Hebrew University of Jerusalem, Israel. He was an international authority on Near Eastern fauna and published widely on a broad spectrum of topics concerning their biogeography, biochronology and biodiversity. Eitan's interest in the Cypriot faunal record stemmed from his seminal research on sedentism and domestication in the Levant and his interest in island biogeography.

Trevor Watkins is Emeritus Professor of Near Eastern Prehistory at the University of Edinburgh, where he taught for more than thirty years. He worked in Cyprus in the 1960s and early 1970s, excavating the pottery Neolithic site of Philia-Drakos A and surveying the aceramic Neolithic site of Kataliontas-Kourvellos. He has also directed excavation projects in Syria, Iraq and Turkey. His current research interest is in the emergence of village life among hunter-gatherers in southwest Asia, and the elaboration of symbolic architecture and material culture at the beginning of the Neolithic. He has a book in press with Routledge on 'The Neolithic Revolution'.

Address: Archaeology, SACE, University of Edinburgh, Old High School, Edinburgh EH1 1LT, Scotland-UK.

Email: T.Watkins@ed.ac.uk

Acknowledgements

The idea for this conference grew out of discussions amongst Near Eastern prehistorians who felt that the time was ripe to take a fresh look at the Neolithic of the Levant, especially in light of striking discoveries made recently on the island of Cyprus. The discussants formed a Steering Committee, consisting of Douglas Baird, Andy Gerrard, Bill Finlayson, Edgar Peltenburg and Alan Simmons, to put the plan into action. An end-result of that initiative is evident here in the publication of the conference proceedings.

It is a pleasure for us to thank warmly the diverse group of scholars who took the time to trek to a small village in the western uplands of Cyprus in order to exchange views on some of the new discoveries within the Neolithic of the Levant from the unorthodox perspective of a Mediterranean island. The programme of talks and discussions was interleaved with visits to the sites that are yielding this new evidence and to museums where unpublished material was stored, so there was a real sense of participation in re-writing early prehistory, one that led to a camaraderie amongst participants that was a memorable aspect of the conference.

Neolithic Revolution was made possible by generous support form the Council for British Research in the Levant. Staff of its Amman office, including the Director, Dr. Bill Finlayson, and Samantha Dennis, deserve particular mention. Dr. Sophocles Hadjisavvas, Director of the Department of Antiquities in Cyprus, encouraged the idea of the conference and facilitated its organisation. We are grateful to his staff who provided timely assistance, especially Dr. Despo Pilides and the curators of the local museums at Episkopi, Palaepaphos and Polis. The reception at the Polis Museum was a most welcome and memorable occasion. Prof. Maria Iacovou, who welcomed us with a most stimulating Opening Address, represented the Archaeological Research Unit, Department of History and Archaeology, University of Cyprus, and Dr. Robert Merrillees the Cyprus American Archaological Research Institute. Vathoulla Moustoukki, Administrative Assistant of the Institute, was unstinting with guidance whenever it was needed.

We benefited enormously from the expertise of those who led us on site and museum visits: Prof. Jean Guilaine at Parekklisha-*Shillourokambos*, Dr. Paul Croft at Kissonerga-*Mylouthkia* and Dr. Alan Simmons at Akrotiri-*Aetokremnos* and Krittou Marottou-*Ais Yiorkis*. Dr. Carole McCartney also led a workshop on the intricacies of studying Cypriot chipped stone. The visit to Akrotiri was made possible by Sqn. Ldr. G. Bolton and the help of the Sovereign Base Archaeology Society, particularly its Vice Chairman, David Neville, and Secretary, Frank Garrod. Phillipos Drousiotis and the Staff at Dhrousha Heights Hotel were unflagging in their efforts to make us welcome.

We would also like to acknowledge the help of two Edinburgh graduates: Lindy Crewe for her perceptive advice and expertise in the preparation of the papers for publication, and Adam Jackson for illustrations. Cover photo courtesy Ian A. Todd.

Introduction: a revised Cypriot prehistory and some implications for the study of the Neolithic

Edgar Peltenburg

The beginnings of sedentism and food production are widely acknowledged to be developments that brought about profound and enduring changes in human society and in the environment (e.g. Bar-Yosef 2000, Bender 1978, Douglas Price and Gebauer 1995, Harris 1996, Smith 1995). One of the earliest and most intensively studied zones where these transformations took place is in Southwest Asia during the Late Pleistocene and Early Holocene. Gordon Childe (1934) was the first to present a detailed case for what he termed the Neolithic Revolution in this region, and while his influential model has been significantly refined and modified, researchers have continued to expand their investigations in that region, especially along the hilly flanks that arc round Mesopotamia. It embraces the modern countries of Iran, Iraq, Turkey, Syria, Israel, The Palestine Authority and Jordan. The offshore Mediterranean island of Cyprus was considered to lay well outside the region that witnessed these seminal developments. In September 2001, a group of scholars gathered together in the western village of Dhrousha on Cyprus in order to evaluate an insular Neolithic Revolution, the startling new evidence that has re-cast the island's prehistory and prompted a fresh assessment of current narratives for the Neolithic of Southwest Asia.

cal BC	1960s AD	Cyprus 1980s AD	1990s AD	Mainland Levant
4500–		Sotira Culture	Late Neolithic	
5000–	Neolithic IB (ceramic)	?	?	
5500–	Neolithic IA (aceramic)	?	?	Pottery Neolithic
6000–		Khirokitia Culture		
6500–		?	Khirokitian	Final PPNB/PPNC
7000–			Cypro-LPPNB	LPPNB
7500–			Cypro-MPPNB	MPPNB
8000–			Cypro-EPPNB	EPPNB
8500–			?	
9000–				PPNA
9500		Akrotiri Phase	Akrotiri Phase	
10000–				

Little/no evidence for inhabitants

Table 1 *Table showing the recent marked increase in evidence for early human settlement on the island of Cyprus*

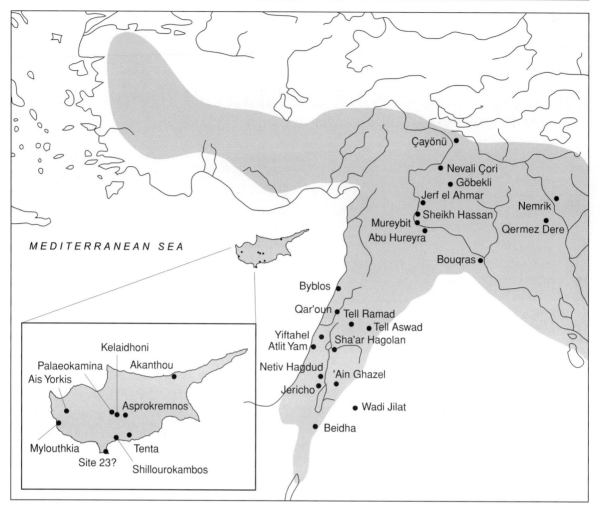

Figure 1 *Map of Cyprus and the Near East showing selected Pre-Pottery Neolithic A and B sites. Shaded area: extent of Pre-Pottery Neolithic B (according to Bar-Yosef 2001a: 144, Figure 5, with the addition of Cyprus)*

Until recently, Cyprus did not figure in debates about formative junctures in the epi-Palaeolithic and early Neolithic because human settlement was believed to have existed there only several millennia after continental break-throughs. It only merited attention in the context of present distributions of wild barley (Zohary and Hopf 1993: 61), one of the founder crops that were to play such a fundamental role in the development of agriculture. Just over a decade ago, in studies on early instances of *Néolithisations*, it was possible to state authoritatively that "there is no clear evidence of human presence in Cyprus before the sudden appearance, at the beginning of the 6th millennium, of a civilization of farmers" (Le Brun 1989: 95).

The situation has changed dramatically since then. Table 1 summarizes how evidence of the island's earliest prehistory has expanded back in time over the last decade. In particular, we now see occupation in the late 9th millennium calibrated BC (4th column), one that shows that the island was inhabited by farming communities when key 'neolithic revolution' changes were taking place in supposed core areas to the east. Since there is clear evidence for close interaction with the mainland at this stage, these findings encourage new directions in research strategies, ones that impact closely on our appreciation of the character of developments in the ancient Near East and on the nature of changes in staple procurement in general. What led to such a radical and belated revision of Cypriot prehistory?

Before the mid-1980s, there was a consensual view that claims for pre-neolithic occupation were ambiguous at best (see Cherry 1990: 151,

152; Simmons *et al.* 1999: 21–25). They were based largely on undiagnostic chipped stone scatters or individual pieces recovered by systematic or, more often, casual survey (e.g. Vita-Finzi 1973; Adovasio *et al.* 1975). But the problem of Khirokitia remained. Here was a large aceramic Neolithic site, C^{14}-dated to *ca.* 6500–5500 BC, that had all the developed characteristics of a highly distinctive culture, yet it lacked formative precursors. Its pioneering excavator, Porphyrios Dikaios, postulated that earlier stages of the same culture existed on the island, and his suggestion was taken up by others in what became known as the "antecedent hypothesis" (Dikaios 1962: 193; e.g. Watkins 1973). In 1977, Stanley Price proposed an alternative, "colonization hypothesis", which assumed Khirokitia was a settlement of the earliest colonisers of the island. To account for its unique character, he outlined two colonising processes: a loss in transmission of certain cultural features and an elaboration of other features (cf. founder effects). Demographic stress on the Levantine mainland was the trigger for migration to Cyprus, and the idea was couched in terms of a 7th–6th millennium calibrated BC settlement regression model. The debate has many ramifications on how archaeologists perceive culture change and colonising processes, but it lacked sound empirical evidence.

The antecedent hypothesis received some support in the mid-1980s when Ian Todd published 21 dates from the aceramic site of Kalavasos-*Tenta* (Todd 1987: 174–6) (see Figure 1 for this and other sites). They included some surprisingly early dates, but they were not easily correlated with his site phasing. Nonetheless, it was felt that, together with calibrated dates from Khirokitia and Cape Andreas, there was now enough evidence available to push back the start of the Khirokitian, perhaps by a millennium. Still earlier dates from *Tenta* Periods 2 and 5 were regarded as insufficient to conclude that the island was inhabited in the earlier 8th millennium BC (see Table 1, 3rd column).

In the late 1980s, Akrotiri-*Aetokremnos* started to yield controversial data about pre-Neolithic human occupation on the island (Simmons *et al.* 1999). As Simmons describes in this volume, the site comprises a decomposed cave cut into the side of cliffs some 40 m above the sea on the south coast of the island. The excavators discerned two major strata, basal Stratum 4 with an immense concentration of pygmy hippopotamus bones and, above, Stratum 2 with more cultural material and, notably, bird bones and shellfish. Controversy surrounds the security of the association of anthropogenic data with the bones in Stratum 4 (see debate in *Journal of Mediterranean Archaeology* 9: 1996), but the intact nature of Stratum 2 seems assured. Some 31 dates were obtained from Akrotiri and they indicate the presence of hunters and foragers in the early 10th millennium BC. According to Simmons, they utilised rather than colonised Cyprus, and after Stratum 2 they left the island (Simmons *et al.* 1999: 323). As shown in recent chronological charts, this reconstruction resulted in a chronological and occupational gap from *ca.* 9500 to 7000/6500 calibrated BC in the island's prehistory (Table 1, 3rd column).

It was during the 1990s that the gap was substantially closed, at least in outline, so finally confirming the antecedent hypothesis. Already in 1989, the first of many deep wells belonging to this period was excavated at the western site of Kissonerga-*Mylouthkia* (Peltenburg *et al.* 2003: 1–103). Its early date was only fully realised in 1994–6 when other wells with indisputably pre-Khirokitian evidence (naviform cores, much obsidian, AMS dates from domestic-type charred seeds) came to light. Together with the remnants of a curvilinear sunken posthole structure, they belong to the 9th – 8th millennium calibrated BC. Amongst the prolific well fills were human crania, secondary burials associated with a polished stone macehead and numerous unbutchered caprine carcases, a surprisingly early package of domestic 'founder crop' cereals (einkorn, emmer and barley), the introduced animals caprines, deer, pig, cat and fox, and many smaller rodents, raptors and birds, hundreds of stone bowl fragments accompanied by hammerstones and pounders, material with PPNA–B (Pre-Pottery Neolithic A and B) analogies in Syria and SE Anatolia, and obsidian from the central Anatolian source of Gollü Dag.

Three other investigations during the 1990s provided much more detail for these precociously early developments on the island. First and foremost was the elucidation of a rich sequence of occupations at Parekklisha-*Shillourokambos*. Excavations at this major site began in 1992 and, as at Mylouthkia, continue today (Guilaine *et al.* 1995, 1998, 2000, 2001, 2002; Guilaine and Briois 2001; Guilaine and Le Brun 2003). Its 9th–8th millennium BC chronology, based on some 13 charcoal-derived radiocarbon dates, underpin site phasing: Early Phase A and B, Middle Phase and Late Phase. Early Phase A comprises wells, pits, post hole alignments, and palisade trenches that form an enclosure. The multi-entry trapezoidal 76 m² enclosure may have functioned as a stockade for animals. Penning of animals, most of which were still morphologically wild, provides an insight, however poorly understood, into the mechanics of 9th millennium BP animal management. One well (23) was re-used for a large collective burial, similar to that at Mylouthkia (well 133). Early Phase B includes a plaster(?) figurine, pits, abundant faunal and lithic remains, together with circular stone architecture that may have started earlier and certainly continues into the Khirokitian. One of the strengths of Shillourokambos is the detailed evidence it provides on animal introductions, including cattle (Vigne *et al.* 2000). Chief amongst the ideographic material is a feline head from Early Phase A with parallels at Jerf el Ahmar, Göbekli and Nevali Çori (Guilaine 2001; Stordeur in press: Figure 7). It epitomizes the strength and direction of foreign contacts at this time and, in its subtle, minimalist rendering, a distinctive insular style that flourished later, in the Khirokitian. Other symbolic items include female figurines, phalli, a quadruped, batons and incised stones, especially picrolites with cross-hatched decoration.

Second was the discovery of yet other sites that could be attributed to this hitherto unknown period. One of these is still poorly known, but may prove critical (Sevketoglu 2002). Akanthou lies opposite Cilicia where the Göksu valley and tributaries of the Ceyhan lead respectively to the Konya plain in the west and Cappadocian obsidian sources in the east. The significance of its strategic position is made clear by reports of prodigious amounts of obsidian imported from Central Anatolia, where a radiocarbon dated obsidian workshop was in operation at Kömürcü-Kaletepe (Greaves and Helwing 2003: 77), and decorated picrolite which must have

been obtained from central or south Cyprus. The association of these exotics on the same coastal site potentially renders it a gateway community. Elevated quantities of obsidian in Cyprus may be a marker of late 9th – early 8th millennium BC occupation, equivalent to the later part of ECA (Early Central Anatolian) I. In addition, McCartney (1998; this volume) argues that chipped stone assemblages point to the existence of inland sites of the period. Ais Yorkis with its dated cattle bone may be one of these (Simmons and O'Horo 2003). Stewart's paper also underlines the wealth of information that exists in island chipped stone scatters, a potential that is only now beginning to be effectively realized.

Third was the re-consideration of the chronological status of Tenta (Peltenburg *et al.* 2001: 41–42). The first of two projected final volumes of results dealt solely with architecture (Todd 1987). In the forthcoming second volume, McCartney demonstrates that most of the diagnostic chipped stone associated with buildings fits pre-Khirokitian stages. Such a conclusion supports the validity of the early radiocarbon dates for Periods 2 and 5, a dating which the excavator did not rule out, even though he preferred a lower chronology. Virtually all the other C¹⁴ assays post-date extant architecture. One important result of this reappraisal is that we may date the nearly complete plan of a hierarchically organised settlement to the pre-Khirokitian period, perhaps equivalent with the Late PPNB on the mainland.

In sum, there is compelling evidence now that the island was inhabited by food producers from at least the later 9th millennium calibrated BC, some 1500/2000 years earlier than was recently thought to be the case (Table 1, 4th column). Their presence proves awkward for reconstructions based on the premise that farming societies were rare and restricted to the mainland then, and that Neolithic dispersals occurred only much later in the PPNB (e.g. Cauvin 2000). The ramifications of these discoveries are starting to be recognised by investigators working outside the island. Bar-Yosef (2001b: 115), for example, perceives that they have "numerous implications for our understanding of continental assemblages", in particular for the "need to revise our views on animal and plant domestication and picture them as a result of a long process of human intervention". This raises core-periphery issues since George Willcox (2002: 137) suggests that domestication may have taken place independently on Cyprus. Hans Georg Gebel (2002: 314) highlights the revisions together with other evidence from the Sahara and Yemen to call for a review of research traditions on Near Eastern Neolithization. And using them as a model, Kuijt and Goring-Morris (2002: 429) note how they raise important questions about the nature of PPN relations between other parts of the ancient Near East, some as bereft of information as was Cyprus until recently.

And yet, most new discoveries are only just being analysed and published, so it is important to acknowledge current limitations of this emerging evidence and to draw inferences cautiously. There is still no consensus amongst archaeologists working on Cyprus on a terminology for the period. The old "Neolithic 1A" for the Aceramic Neolithic of Khirokitia (Table 1) and 1B for part of the Pottery Neolithic will clearly no longer suffice. Proposals for an Early, Middle and Late (=the Khirokitian) Aceramic Neolithic (*cf.* Peltenburg *et al.* 2003: 87, Table 11. 3 and McCartney in this volume) begs the question of what is to be done when the likely Neolithic predecessors of the "Early" are located. Use of the term Cypro-PPNB (Peltenburg *et al.* 2000, 2001) meets this potential difficulty, but those for whom "PPNB" represents an archaeological culture in the Childean sense, rather than a lithics-framed interaction zone, baulk at its introduction (e.g. Le Brun 2001: 259). The term at least has the merit of recognizing the regional characteristics of the PPNB phenomenon.

The Dhrousha Conference aimed to begin to assess the wider effects of a revised Cypriot prehistoric sequence , to take a fresh look at the Khirokitian in its Levantine context (papers by Eirikh-Rose, Stewart and Rupp) and to present mainland evidence that could impinge on the rapidly evolving Cypriot picture (Ha dar-Boustani and Garfinkel). Of the 15 papers given at Dhrousha, 13 are published here, together with the addition of Andrew Moore's paper. During thematic discussions and conference's visits to museum collections and sites, several themes with implications for general Neolithic studies recurred: Neolithization processes, the strikingly

early dates of some of the Cypriot evidence, lack of 9th millennium BC sites between the northern Levantine corridor and the Mediterranean and impressive pre-Khirokitian obsidian occurrences, to name but a few.

A major issue addressed in several papers concerned the conditions of such early Neolithization. It was generally agreed that the earliest C^{14} dated Neolithic sites are likely to have island precursors. McCartney's detailed lithic analysis here bolsters these general assumptions. The intriguing question that arose was: when did visitors who utilised the island become settlers who resided there permanently? The process may have been lengthy, with intergenerational oscillations dependent on the success of augmenting restricted island food resources to the point that it became feasible to remain there. Simmons suggests that the Akrotiri visitors who abandoned it passed on knowledge of the island (but elsewhere he leaves open the possibility that they were the colonisers: Simmons 2001: 14) so implying that settlers were moderately well-informed newcomers. Were they in possession of the animal management and farming practices that we see ca. 8000 cal BC, or, as Watkins advocates, were they complex hunter-gatherers who closely interacted with mainland cousins, and gradually appropriated an agro-pastoral economy piecemeal? In an earlier assessment, Bar-Yosef would seem to favour both by indicating a series of movements from mobile forager terrain near Öküzini in Natufian times, succeeded by influxes from a mixture of zones, including the Aegean, in the PPNB and later (Bar-Yosef 2001a: 136, Fig. 3, 144, Fig. 5).

In general terms, these narratives addressed the often-rehearsed alternatives of acculturation and migration for Neolithization. Acculturation, however, is normally constructed in terms of appropriations by hunter-gatherers from proximate farmers, whereas the 70–100 km separation of the island from the adjacent landmass means that the former were constantly interacting over significant distances, with all that that means for planning, decision-making and travel organisation. Such distances puts a different light on Hayden's (1990) argument that "complex hunter/gatherer societies are primed for agriculture and its actual appearance is dependent merely on the availability of suitable plants for cultivation and of animals to domesticate." Finlayson's paper, on the other hand, encourages us to revise notions that overseas travel necessarily presented a barrier, and to consider the sea as a facilitator of integration. In this scenario, optimal foraging islanders may have been so involved with domestication processes that we may have to think less of acculturation than of pro-active participation in the transformations.

Key to the debate is the absence of evidence for indigenous hunter-gatherers between the time of Akrotiri and sites like Shillourokambos. A number of participants recalled how, in earlier reconstructions of the Cypriot Neolithic, the absence of evidence for occupation on the island in pre-Khirokitian times gave rise to the antecedent and colonising models described above. The recent discovery of a pre-Khirokitian sequence confirmed the antecedent model, so alerting researchers to be wary of the current lack of pre-Shillourokambos and pre-Mylouthkia evidence. But the situation is different in at least one critical respect. Unlike the *sui generis* Khirokitian when few secure contacts or material culture parallels existed abroad, the late 9th–early 8th millennium BC Cypriot record is characterised by evidence for varied contacts, followed by a decline in the importation and adoption of mainland traits. Do contact peaks like this represent markers for initial phases of Neolithic dispersals by migration?

Resolution of the issue of acculturation and/or migration is needed in order to address the broader question of the motivation for Neolithic dispersals. An indigenous dynamic would put the islanders at the forefront of developments, thus challenging the notion of a limited Southwest Asiatic core area, and the chronology of plant domestication especially. Colonisation by farmers has implications for chronology, location and the speed of the spread of founder crops. The discrete Cypriot evidence, therefore, may well contribute to the domestications debate: rapid spread pre-empting independent domestications (Diamond 2002), or multiple pathways to the origins and dissemination of agriculture, as suggested by some DNA research (Jones and Brown 2000; *cf.* Willcox 2002). As Colledge shows in Chapter 5, the directly dated domestic-type Mylouthkia wheats are

very early in relation to the earliest on the continent. This and other evidence suggests that yet earlier examples existed in the Levant and were diffused in some manner, since at the moment it is believed the founder crops were not native to the island (barley excepted). Taking the seed assemblage as a whole, some later 9th millennium Cypriot communities possessed a well established farming tradition in contrast to the northern mainland where it would seem farming was only in the process of consolidation (Garrard 1999; Willcox 2002; *cf.* Bar-Yosef 2000). Was this a special case, prompted by adaptive strategies on the island, or should we infer that there are gaping holes in our distributions of where the earliest farming communities existed on the mainland?

While motivation for introductions is currently regarded in functionalist terms, whether it be stocking the island as larders, as Horwitz *et al.* argue here, or as part of movements due to loss of favoured palaeocoastlines (Peltenburg *et al.* 2000, 2001), we should not forget social factors such as the emergence of a colonising ethos, of taming localities within the landscape and of concepts of territorial acquisition (Gebel 2002), or the symbolic importance of islands (Erdogu 2003). Indeed, the surprising variety of translocated animals supports Frame's contention that we need to focus on the manner in which animals were articulated with the social relations within the community (*cf.* wealth, bride price, pets) and not solely on calories (Frame 2002). Whether Vigne's term 'predomestic' for the animals involved in this phase of man-animal relations is appropriate and practical is another issue emerging from these novel assemblages (Vigne *et al.* 2000), but clearly, re-evaluation and public assessment of criteria in each faunal report, as Baird (1997: 378–9) advocates in another context, and Moore supports in more general terms here, is required. The spectrum of late 9th–early 8th millennium Cypriot faunal introductions and the equivocal character of conclusions from traditional faunal assessments supports moves towards defining new criteria to characterise the nature of human-animal relations during this seminal period. It calls for finer scale research into subregions and our conceived boundaries between hunter-gatherers and food producers.

Another issue brought to the fore by conference was the lack of contemporary sites on or near the adjacent mainland, since evidence for Neolithic settlement there only begins much later, in the LPPNB. The nearest relevant sites with parallels to the Cypriot data are far away, in the northern part of the "Levantine corridor", a situation that has prompted queries about homelands of putative colonists or introduced foodstocks (e.g. McCartney and Peltenburg 2000). The spatial gap, therefore, highlights a pressing need to reframe assumptions about the nature of the archaeological, faunal and floral records that established the idea of the corridor and to prioritise search and excavation of early, non-tell sites in Syro-Cilicia. Mazurowski's (pers comm) discovery of PPNA settlement stratified beneath Early Bronze Age deposits at Tell Qaramel just north of Aleppo is one example of what innovatory fieldwork may reveal in what is virtually PPNA–B *terra incognita*. Preliminary study of lithics from basal levels at Tell Ain el-Kerkh in the Rouj basin in NW Syria and Tell aux Scies near Beirut suggest it is only a matter of time before this westerly region is better known (Arimura 2002). While too early to be of direct relevance, the Upper Palaeolithic cave on the Mediterranean coast at Üçagızlı Magarası, opposite the tip of the Karpass Penninsula, nonetheless points to the probable existence of a coastal tradition of animal exploitation that was very close to the one introduced later into Cyprus: goat, deer (roe and fallow), cattle, pig, as well as dog, fox and cat (Güleç *et al.* 2002: 262, Table 3). The high proportion of deer is particularly relevant to questions of contact and origins, since deer play such an important role in the Cypriot economy, but are barely evident in the wider northern Levantine corridor that has supplied material culture parallels (*cf.* von den Driesch and Peters 2001).

The early dates of several other aspects of recovered insular data also call for adjustments to current perceptions of developments on the mainland. For example, the highest proportions of obsidian from Gollü Dag on Cypriot sites occur in the late 9th–early 8th millennium (Briois *et al.* 1997; Peltenburg *et al.* 2003: 30–34). This contrasts with the meagre occurrences of Cappadocian obsidian on sites in the middle Euphrates valley region and elsewhere at that time (Cauvin, M.-C. *et al.* 1998). Obsidian exchange, therefore, was more varied than eastern statistics alone might suggest, and we need to determine the causes for this inter-regional variation. Cyprus, of course, could be a special case in which obsidian provides a tracer for the origins of colonists, given that during initial stages of colonisation there is a tendency for raw materials to be transported over considerable distances. Alternatively, such long-distance trade may be a signal of more intense interaction that accompanied the development of agriculture (*cf.* Sherratt 1999). Detailed studies are now required to test inferences drawn from what is still sketchy data. It could also be argued that most of the obsidian brought to the island comprised colonists' possessions, and that, being rare, it was assiduously curated.

These are but some of the myriad implications raised by the expansion of chronological horizons on Cyprus. It would seem that its earliest prehistory is so embedded in continental developments that neither can be fully appreciated without reference to the other. The island should now be considered as another regional component of the major socio-economic changes that occurred in southwest Asia during the early Holocene rather than an unconnected entity on the periphery. Indeed, study of insular adaptations, or anomalies according to Galili *et al.* in their paper, may sharpen our understanding of the character of Neolithic developments on the mainland, as Peltenburg attempts to demonstrate here in a comparison of spatial organisation in settlements. Island visitation, exploitation and colonisation should now be regarded as an integral part of epi-Palaeolithic and early Neolithic Near Eastern interactions and of the more general process of wild and diverse animal and crop experimentation that characterises the period. While the proceedings of two other recent conferences on these discoveries primarily provide much needed information on adjustments to the internal record of the island (Swiny 2001; Guilaine and Le Brun 2003), papers collected here represent an explicit initial attempt to contextualise the data within Near Eastern prehistory. It seems safe to state that there will be many more such attempts.

References

Adovasio, J., G. Fry, J. Gunn and R. Maslowski 1975
Prehistoric and historic settlement patterns in western Cyprus (with a discussion of Cypriot Neolithic stone tool technology). *World Archaeology* 6: 339–364.

Arimura, M. 2002
Tell Ain el-Kerkh, site PPNB ancien dans le nord-ouest de la Syria? Etudes préliminaire du matériel lithique des couches les plus anciennes. *Orient-Express* 2002/4: 103–108.

Baird, D. 1997
Goals in Jordanian Neolithic Research. Pp. 371–81 in H. Gebel, Z. Kafafi and G. Rollefson, *The Prehistory of Jordan II. Perspectives from 1997. Studies in Early Near Eastern Production, Subsistence, and Environment 4.* Ex oriente: Berlin.

Bar-Yosef, O. 2000
The impact of radiocarbon dating on Old World Archaeology: past achievements and future prospects. *Radiocarbon* 42: 23–35.

Bar-Yosef, O. 2001a
The World Around Cyprus: From Epi-Paleolithic Foragers to the Collapse of the PPNB Civilization. Pp. 129–164 in Swiny 2001.

Bar-Yosef 2001b
Review of Cauvin 2000. *Cambridge Archaeological Journal* 11: 105–122.

Bender, B. 1978
From Gatherer-Hunter to Farmer: A Social Perspective. *World Archaeology* 10: 204–22.

Briois, F., B. Gratuze and J. Guilaine 1997
Obsidiennes du site Néolithique Précéramique de Shillourokambos (Chypre). *Paléorient* 23: 95–112.

Cauvin, J. 2000
The Birth of the Gods and the Origins of Agriculture. Cambridge University Press: Cambridge.

Cauvin, M.-C. *et al.* 1998
L'obsidienne au Proche et Moyen Orient. British Archaeological Reports, International Series 738. Oxford.

Cherry, J. 1990
The First Colonisation of the Mediterranean Islands: A Review of Recent Research. *Journal of Mediterranean Archaeology* 3: 145–221.

Childe, V. G. 1934
New Light on the Most Ancient East. The Oriental Prelude to European Prehistory. Kegan Paul: London.

Diamond, J. 2002
Evolution, consequences and future of plant and animal domestication. *Nature* 418: 700–707.

Douglas Price, T. and A. Gebauer (eds.) 1995
Last Hunters, First Farmers: New Perspectives on the Prehistoric Transition to Agriculture. School of American Research Press: Sante Fe.

Dikaios, P. 1962
The Stone Age. *Swedish Cyprus Expedition* IV.1A: 1–204. The Swedish Cyprus Expedition: Lund.

Erdogu, B. 2003
Visualising Neolithic landscape: the early settled communities in western Anatolia and eastern Aegean islands. *European Journal of Archaeology* 6: 7–23.

Frame, S. 2002
Island neolithics: animal exploitation in the Aceramic Neolithic of Cyprus. Pp. 233–238 in W. Waldren and J. Ensenyat (eds.) *World Islands in Prehistory. International Insular Investigations. V Deia International Conference of Prehistory.* British Archaeological Reports, International Series 1095. Oxford.

Garrard, A. 1999
Charting the Emergence of Cereal and Pulse Domestication in South-west Asia. *Environmental Archaeology* 4: 67–86.

Gebel, H. 2002
The Neolithic of the Near East. An essay on a "Polycentric Evolution" and other current research problems. Pp. 313–324 in A. Hausleiter, S. Kerner and B. Müller-Neuhof (eds.) *Material Culture and Mental Spheres. Rezeption archäologischer Denkrichtungen in der Vorderasiatischen Altertumskunde. Internationales Syposium für Hans J. NISSEN, Berlin, 23.–24. Juni 2000.* Alter Orient und Altes Testament 293. Ugarit-Verlag: Münster.

Greaves, A. and B. Helwing 2003
Archaeology in Turkey: The Stone, Bronze, and Iron Ages, 2000. *American Journal of Archaeology* 107: 71–103.

Guilaine, J. 2001
Tête sculptée dan le Néolithique pré-céramique de Shillourokambos (Parekklisha, Chypre). *Paléorient* 26 : 137–43.

Guilaine, J. and F. Briois 2001
Parekklisha Shillourokambos. An Early Neolithic Site in Cyprus. Pp. 37–53 in Swiny 2001.

Guilaine, J. and A. Le Brun (eds.) 2003
Le Néolithique de Chypre. Actes du colloque international organisé par le départment des antiquitiés de Chypre et l'Ecole française d'Athénes, Nicosie 17–19 mai 2001. Bulletin de Correspondance Hellénique Suppl. 43.

Guilaine, J., F. Briois, J. Coularou and I. Carrère 1995
L'Etablissement néolithique de Shillourokambos (Parekklisha, Chypre). Premiers résultats. *Report of the Department of Antiquities of Cyprus*: 11–32.

Guilaine, J., F. Briois, J. Coularou, J.-D. Vigne and I. Carrère 1998
Les débuts du Néolithique à Chypre. *L'Archéologue* 33: 35–40.

Guilaine, J., F. Briois, J.-D. Vigne and I. Carrère 2000
Découverte d'un Néolithique précéramique ancien chypriote (fin 9e, début 8e millénaires cal. BC), apparenté au PPNB ancien/moyen du Levant nord. *Earth and Planetary Sciences* 330: 75–82.

Guilaine, J., F. Briois, I. Carrére, E. Crubézy, T. Giraud, S. Philibert, J.-D. Vigne and G. Willcox 2001
L'habitat néolithique pré-céramique de Shillourokambos (Parekklisha, Chypre). *Bulletin de Correspondance Hellénique* 125: 649–654.

Guilaine, J., F. Briois, J.-D. Vigne, I. Carrére, E. Crubézy, C.-A. de Chazelles, J. Collonge, H. Gazzal, P. Gérard, L. Haye, C. Manen, T. Perrin, G. Willcox 2002
L'habitat néolithique pré-céramique de Shillourokambos (Parekklisha, Chypre). *Bulletin de Correspondance Hellénique* 126: 590–597.

Güleç, E., S. Kuhn and M. Stiner 2002
2000 Excavation at Üçagızlı Cave. *Kazı Sonuçlari Toplantısı* 23.1: 255–264.

Harris, D. (ed.) 1996
The Origins and Spread of Agriculture and Pastoralism in Eurasia. UCL Press: London.

Hayden, B. 1990
Nimrods, Piscators, Pluckers, and Planters: the Emergence of Food Production. *Journal of Anthropological Archaeology* 9: 31–69.

Jones, M. and T. Brown 2000
Agricultural origins: the evidence of modern and ancient DNA. *The Holocene* 10.6: 769–776.

Kuijt, I. and N. Goring-Morris 2002
Foraging, Farming, and Social Complexity in the Pre-Pottery Neolithic of the Southern Levant: A Review and Synthesis. *Journal of World Prehistory* 16: 361–439.

Le Brun, A. 1989
La néolithisation de Chypre. Pp 95–107 in O. Aurenche and J. Cauvin, *Néolithisations*. British Archaeological Reports, International Series 516: Oxford.

Le Brun, A. 2001
Colloque International, Le néolithique de Chypre, Nicosie, 17–19 mai 2001. *Centre d'Etudes Chypriotes Cahier* 31: 258–260.

McCartney, C. 1998
Preliminary Report on the Chipped Stone Assemblage from the Aceramic Neolithic Site of Ayia Varvara Asprokremnos. *Levant* 30: 85–90.

McCartney, C. and E. Peltenburg 2000
The Colonization of Cyprus: Questions of Origins and Isolation. *Neo-lithics* 1/0: 8–11.

Peltenburg, E, S. Colledge, P. Croft, A. Jackson, C. McCartney and Mary Anne Murray 2000
Agro-pastoralist colonization of Cyprus in the 10th millennium BP: Initial Assessments. *Antiquity* 74: 844–53.

Peltenburg, E., S. Colledge, P. Croft, A. Jackson, C. McCartney and M. Murray 2001
Neolithic Dispersals from the Levantine Corridor: a Mediterranean Perspective. *Levant* 33: 35–64.

Peltenburg, E. *et al.* 2003
The Colonisation and Settlement of Cyprus. Investigations at Kissonerga-Mylouthkia, 1976–1996. (Lemba Archaeological Project, Cyprus III.1). Studies in Mediterranean Archaeology 70:4. Paul Åströms Verlag: Sävedalen.

Sevketoglu, M. 2002
Akanthou-*Arkosyko* (Tatlısu-Çiftlikdüzü): the Anatolian connections in the 9th millennium BC. Pp. 98–106 in W. Waldren and J. Ensenyat (eds.) *World islands in Prehistory. International Insular Investigations. V. Deia International Conference of Prehistory.* British Archaeological Reports, International Series 1095: Oxford.

Sherratt, A. 1999
Cash-crops before cash: organic consumables and trade. Pp. 261–305 in C. Gosden and J. Hather (eds.) *The prehistory of food.* Routledge: London.

Simmons, A. 2001
The First Humans and Last Pygmy Hippopotami of Cyprus. Pp. 1–18 in Swiny 2001.

Simmons, A. and Associates. 1999
Faunal Extinction in an Island Society: Pygmy Hippopotamus Hunters of Cyprus. Plenum: New York.

Simmons, A. and K. O'Horo 2003
A Preliminary Note on the Chipped Stone Assemblage from Krittou Marouttou Ais Yiorkis, an Aceramic Neolithic site in Western Cyprus. *Neo-lithics* 1/03: 21–24.

Smith, B. 1995
The Emergence of Agriculture. Scientific American Library: New York.

Stanley Price, N. 1977
Khirokitia and the Initial Settlement of Cyprus. *Levant* 9: 66–89.

Stordeur, D. in press
De la vallée de l'Euphrate a Chypre? A la recherche d'indices de relations au Néolithique, in Guilaine and Le Brun 2003.

Swiny, S. (ed.) 2001
The Earliest Prehistory of Cyprus: From Colonization to Exploitation. Cyprus American Archaeological Research Institute Monograph Series 12. American Schools of Oriental Research: Boston.

Todd, I.A. 1987
Vasilikos Valley Project 6. Excavations at Kalavassos-Tenta 1. Studies in Mediterranean Archaeology 71:6. Åströms Förlag: Göteborg.

Vigne, J.-D., I. Carrère, J-F. Saliége, A. Person, H. Bocherens, J. Guilaine and F. Briois 2000.
Predomestic Cattle, Sheep, Goat and Pig During the Late 9th and the 8th Millennium cal. BC on Cyprus: Preliminary Results of Shillourokambos (Parekklisha, Limassol). Pp. 83–106 in H. Buitenhaus, M. Mashkour and F. Poplin, *Archaeozoology of the Near East IV, Proc. 4th Int. Symp. Archaeology of Southwestern Asia and Adjacent Areas.* Groningen: Archaeological Research and Consultancy.

Vita-Finzi, C. 1973
Palaeolithic Finds from Cyprus? *Proceedings of the Prehistoric Society* 39: 453–4.

von den Driesch, A. and J. Peters 2001
Früheste Haustierhaltung in der Südosttürkei. Pp. 113–119 in R. Boehmer. and J. Maran (eds.) *Lux Orientis. Archäologie zwischen Asien und Europa. Festschrift für Harald Hauptman zum 65. Geburstag.* Internationale Archäologie. Studia honoraria 12. Marie Leidorf GmbH: Rahden.

Watkins, T. 1973
Some Problems of the Neolithic and Chalcolithic Period in Cyprus. *Report of the Department of Antiquities, Cyprus:* 34–61.

Willcox, G. 2002
    Geographical variation in major cereal compo-
    nents and evidence for independent domestica-
    tion events in Western Asia, pp. 133–140 in R.
    Cappers and S. Bottema (eds.) *The Dawn of
    Farming in the Near East. Studies in the Near Eastern
    Production, Subsistence, and Environment* 6: 1999.
    Ex oriente: Berlin.
Zohary, D. and M. Hopf 1993
    Domestication of Plants in the Old World (2nd ed).
    Oxford: Clarendon Press.

Note on Cypriot site names

The names of archaeological sites in Cyprus con-
ventionally consist of two components: a village name
plus locality name. The latter is usually italicised.
When a site becomes well known this cumbersome
system is abbreviated to either the village or the locality name. Where locality name is used by itself, it may
remain in italics or be in regular font. Contributors'
preferences are retained here.

1

Bitter hippos of Cyprus: the island's first occupants and last endemic animals – setting the stage for colonization

Alan H. Simmons

Abstract

*Recent studies have challenged the long-held notion that Cyprus was not occupied prior to the island's Neolithic period, which itself was often regarded as an isolated and relatively uninteresting phenomenon. This research began with the interdisciplinary excavations at the controversial site of Akrotiri-*Aetokremnos, *which demonstrated that people had been in Cyprus far earlier than originally thought, at around 10,000 cal B.C. The site also strongly implicated humans in the extinction of the endemic Pleistocene pygmy hippopotamus. Subsequent research has documented a previously unknown, earlier, phase of the Aceramic Neolithic. This both shortens the chronological gap between* Aetokremnos *and the Neolithic, and shows direct material links with the Levantine mainland. This paper assesses the significance of* Aetokremnos *to both Cypriot and broader Near Eastern early Holocene prehistory.*

Introduction

Not too long ago, if one mentioned the Neolithic and Cyprus in the same breath, most archaeologists were underwhelmed. Conventional wisdom was that the Neolithic in Cyprus was nondescript and "unremarkable" (Held 1990: 21), if not downright boring, even though one of the largest Neolithic sites known in the Near East, Khirokitia, is located on the island. It was generally believed that the Cypriot Neolithic was a late development, founded by people from the mainland who imported a complete "Neolithic package" consisting of a sedentary village way of life and a small suite of domesticated plants and animals (as well as wild deer). Curiously, these Neolithic immigrants exhibited few material similarities to their points of origin (Le Brun *et al.* 1987). Many scholars, at least implicitly, believed that the Cypriot Neolithic had little to contribute to our broader understanding of the dynamic processes that are a hallmark of the period. Exciting new discoveries over the past 15 years, many discussed in this volume, have radically changed this perspective.

This new research has both expanded the duration of the Cypriot Neolithic and extended the chronological boundaries of the first human occupation of the island to pre-Neolithic times. It also suggests that these early visitors may have been responsible for accelerating the extinction of some of the unique endemic Pleistocene fauna of Cyprus. Additionally, these investigations have changed the way in which archaeologists working on the island regard the nature and interpretation of their data. This research has dramatically re-written our conception of human interactions in the eastern Mediterranean and has put Cyprus in the forefront of early Holocene Near Eastern archaeology. In this essay, I address some of these recent developments, focusing on the earliest evidence for human occupation of the island, as viewed from Akrotiri-*Aetokremnos*.

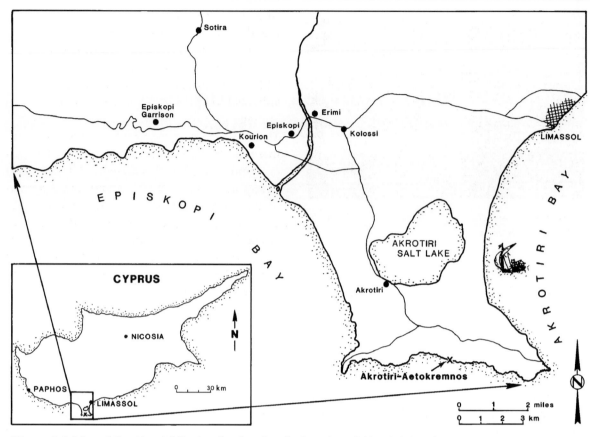

Figure 1.1 *Map of the Akrotiri Peninsula, showing the location of Akrotiri-*Aetokremnos

Akrotiri-*Aetokremnos* – research background

Sometimes unexpected findings come in small packages. This was certainly the case with Akrotiri-*Aetokremnos* (or "Vulture Cliff"), the controversial site that challenged conventional wisdom regarding the first humans in Cyprus. Although an outsider to Cyprus, I had the good fortune of being invited to excavate *Aetokremnos*, largely, I believe, because few archaeologists working in Cyprus at the time (the late 1980s and early 1990s) thought there was anything to the site. Stuart Swiny, former director of the Cyprus American Archaeological Research Institute (CAARI), however, was a persistent believer, and it was largely through his influence that I undertook the investigation of this intriguing site, the results of which have been thoroughly presented in Simmons (1999).

The importance of *Aetokremnos* revolves around two issues. The first is chronological and the second is the association of faunal and cul-tural materials. *Aetokremnos* is securely dated to the early tenth millennium cal BC. Until its excavation, there simply were no convincing sites documented in Cyprus that predated the Neolithic, believed to have begun around 6,500 BC with the Aceramic Neolithic Khirokita Culture (Le Brun *et al.* 1987; Stanley Price 1977; Todd 1987; Knapp, Held and Manning 1994). Thus *Aetokremnos* predated the (traditional) Aceramic Neolithic by over three thousand years. Recent work, however, summarized later in this paper and discussed in more detail elsewhere in this volume, has documented an earlier Aceramic phase at *ca.* 8,000 BC, thus shortening the gap between what we have termed the "Akrotiri Phase" and the earliest Neolithic on the island.

Not only is *Aetokremnos* the oldest site on the island, but, perhaps even more contentiously, it is associated with a huge assemblage of the extinct endemic Cypriot pygmy hippopotamus, *Phanourios minutus*. Such an association has never before been demonstrated, and we

Figure 1.2 *Photograph of* Aetokremnos, *showing cliff-side position (arrow)*

believe that humans were, in fact, instrumental in finalizing the extinction of these unique animals. It is thus with apologies to Lawrence Durrell's (1957) classic tale of intrigue in Cyprus that I draw the title of this essay, for the last Pleistocene creatures of the island undoubtedly would have been bitter indeed had they known the fate that awaited them at the hands of the ultimate predator.

Aetokremnos is a small and unimpressive collapsed rockshelter located on the southern coast of the island (Figure 1.1). It dramatically overlooks the Mediterranean Sea (Figure 1.2), and much of the locality has been lost to erosion. Initially discovered by amateurs associated with the Royal Air Force Western Sovereign Base Area, the surface indications of *Aetokremnos* were far from impressive, leading many to understandably question whether it even was an archaeological site.

The locality contained a surface scatter of hippopotamus bones, a layer of marine shell, and a few chipped stone artefacts. The likelihood of in situ deposits appeared slim, and there was no obvious connection between the bones and the artefacts. Numerous sites containing chipped stone artefacts occur in the area above the cliffs in which *Aetokremnos* is located, and could easily have washed down to the site, fortuitously mixing with a Pleistocene bone bed. Prior to our excavations, a radiocarbon determination on surface bone suggested a date of *ca.* 6,300 BC (uncalibrated), although two other determinations on bone indicated a more recent occupation. The earlier determination was intriguing, though,

since it suggested a contemporaneity with the island's Aceramic Neolithic occupation.

Despite the limited and questionable nature of the cultural materials at *Aetokremnos*, the possible association of cultural remains with animals thought to have become extinct before humans arrived on the island was tantalizing. Thus, the site piqued enough interest to warrant three seasons of investigations. Our excavations of approximately 50 square meters exposed nearly all that is left of *Aetokremnos*. Approximately one meter of vertical deposition is present, with four major strata occurring. Both Strata 2 and 4 contain artefacts, bones, and features, while Stratum 1 is a mixed context and Stratum 3 is a sterile zone. The majority of the artefacts are located in Stratum 2, while the majority of the hippopotamus remains occur in Stratum 4.

We recovered over a thousand chipped stone artefacts (Table 1.1), which are so far unique in Cyprus. They would not, however, be out of place in Epipalaeolithic or early Neolithic mainland assemblages. We note, however, that until

Class	N	%
Tools	128	12.5
Debitage:		
Core trimming elements	6	
Core tablets	1	
Primary flakes	13	
Secondary flakes	79	
Tertiary flakes	164	
Secondary blades	13	
Tertiary blades	65	
Bladelets	42	
Subtotal	383	37.5
Other Waste:		
Burin spalls	16	1.6
Microflakes		
(or "retouch flakes")	178	17.5
Cores	20	1.9
Debris (or "shatter")	296	29.0
Total	1,021	100.00

Table 1.1 *Summary of the chipped stone assemblage from* Aetokremnos

recently, detailed and systematic analyses of chipped stone artefacts in Cyprus have not been research priorities. This situation is changing, however, with comprehensive studies such as those carried out at *Aetokremnos* (Simmons 1999: 123–146) and by researchers such as Guilaine and colleagues (Guilaine *et al.* 1995; Guilaine and Briois 2001: 45–47) and McCartney (1999, 2001, this volume).

While the majority of the chipped stone occurs in Stratum 2, *ca.* 12% is located in Stratum 4, and there is absolutely no evidence of stratigraphic mixing. The materials are clearly of the same industry, with no discernable differences between strata. Although a wide range of raw material was used by the site's inhabitants, all was locally available on the island, and most was from Lefkara cherts. There is no obsidian (an imported material) in the assemblage. Overall, there is little patterning reflected in raw material selection. The wide range of materials present in the assemblage suggests an expedient technology in which easily available materials, as long as they were of sufficient quality, were used.

By far the most common type of platform was the simple, single platform, accounting for nearly 50 percent of both tools and debitage. Punctiform platforms also were common, attesting to the precise blade-like nature of much of the assemblage, and suggesting that percussion flaking was a common occurrence. Although flakes outnumber blades and bladelets (2.1:1), there is no denying the blade-like character of this assemblage, with the *Aetokremnos* blades being generally long and thin (average length = 44.2 mm, average width = 16.2 mm).

The core sample is small (N=20). Twenty-five percent of the cores are bladelet forms, while most of the remainder are varieties of flake cores. Although bladelets are common in the assemblage (11% of the debitage), they are not as abundant as these core figures suggest. It may be that some of the cores classified as bladelet forms actually represent extremely reduced, or exhausted cores. Of particular interest is the lack of naviform cores, which do occur (albeit in low numbers) in newly discovered Aceramic Neolithic sites (e.g., McCartney 1999; Guilaine and Briois 2001: 45–47).

Formal, retouched, tools comprise 12.5 percent of the *Aetokremnos* assemblage (Table 1.2). The tools are dominated by distinctive

Class and Type	N	%
Scrapers:		
Thumbnail	36	28.1
Side	7	5.5
End	3	2.3
Side/end	4	3.1
Scraper/plane	1	0.8
Scraper/knife	1	0.8
Burins	15	11.7
Burins on truncation	4	3.1
Burin on scraper	1	0.8
Backed pieces	2	1.6
Truncations	3	2.3
Unifacial knives	2	1.6
Pièce esquillée	1	0.8
Notches	3	2.3
Retouched blades	16	12.5
Retouched flakes	22	17.2
Microliths:		
Trapezoid	1	0.8
Truncation	2	1.6
Lunate	1	0.8
Retouched bladelet	2	1.6
Total	128	100.1

Table 1.2 *Tool typology for* Aetokremnos

"thumbnail scrapers," which form nearly 30 percent of the tools. Burins also are common in the *Aetokremnos* assemblage, as are other scraper forms. Together, retouched blades and flakes comprise over 25 percent of the tool assemblage. Perhaps most distinctive in this assemblage, apart from the thumbnail scrapers, is a low but consistent number of microlithic tools (nearly 5 percent of tools). Tools as a group were manufactured on a wide variety of debitage blanks, with 35.9% made on blades or bladelets, and 63.3% made on flakes. When compared with previously published reports on Cypriot chipped stone tools, the *Aetokremnos* tools have few counterparts, but comparisons with new detailed analyses of Aceramic Neolithic assemblages, such as those cited above, are certain to be interesting and may change this.

Vertebrates	NISP	%	MNI
pygmy hippopotami–*Phanourios*	218,459	98.3	505+
pygmy elephants–*Elephas*	229	0.1	3
deer–*Dama*	4	–	1–4
pigs–*Sus*	13	–	c. 4
genets–*Genetta*	2	–	1
mice–*Mus*	5	–	1
Birds	3,207	1.4	75+
Snakes–*Vipera/Natrix*	c. 245	0.1	14–40
tortoises–*Testudo*	25+	–	9–14
toads–*Bufo*	1	–	1
Fish	1	–	1
Total Vertebrates	222,190	99.9	–
Marine Invertebrates	73,365	–	21,576
Land Snails	90*	–	97
Total	295,645	–	–

Table 1.3 *Summary of faunal remains from* Aetokremnos*
*Excludes surface and Strata 1, 1/ 2, and 1–4, which are mixed strata.

In addition to chipped stone, numerous stone and shell beads were recovered, as were a small variety of ground implements. Eleven cultural features, most "casual hearths," also are documented. These occur in both Strata 2 and 4.

Of paramount importance, of course, was the huge faunal assemblage, consisting of over 215,000 bones, far more than usually occurs even at most paleontological sites on the island. Most (*ca.* 95%) is hippopotamus (Table 1.3), with a minimum of 505 individuals of all ages represented. At least three dwarf elephants occur, as do over 70 birds, primarily great bustard. A few other terrestrial animals also are present, as is a huge assemblage of over 70,000 marine invertebrates. The majority (88.1%) of the hippopotamus remains occurs in Stratum 4, while the bulk of the other fauna is in Stratum 2. Much of the bone is burned, and virtually none is articulated. To put the huge amount of fauna in perspective, while less than two percent of the hippopotamus bones occur in Stratum 2, this is still represented by 3,966 bones in this layer.

Finally, chronology is clearly of major significance. *Aetokremnos* is one of the best dated prehistoric sites on any of the Mediterranean islands. Thirty-one radiocarbon determinations provide a coherent set of absolute dates. With the three surface determinations and two others excluded as being outliers (see Wigand and Simmons [1999] for details), the calibrated average is cal BC 9,825. The range is 9,702–10,005 BC at a single standard deviation and 9,554 to 10,146 BC at two standard deviations. It is important to note that the time difference between Strata 2 and 4 is so small that it cannot be measured in radiocarbon years. We believe that the data indicate a relatively short-term occupation, perhaps of only a few hundred years, during the very early tenth millennium BC. Certainly the radiocarbon determinations alone provide compelling evidence that people and hippopotami co-existed. In this context, it is important to note that several (9 of 31) of the dates from *Aetokremnos* were obtained from hippopotamus bone. These dates make *Aetokremnos* the earliest site in Cyprus, and amongst the earliest on any Mediterranean island.

The context of *Aetokremnos*

In placing *Aetokremnos* in proper context, the site is unique from at least two perspectives. The first is its paleontological importance, and the second, far more important to readers of this volume, is archaeological. From the paleontological perspective, there are numerous fossil sites dating to the Pleistocene on several of the Mediterranean islands that contain endemic, island-adapted fauna, such as pygmy hippopotami and dwarf elephants and other unique animals (Reese1996b; Sondaar 1986). In Cyprus alone, there are over 30 such localities (Held 1992; Reese 1989, 1995; Swiny 1988). Even realizing this, however, the sheer abundance of bone at *Aetokremnos* makes the site stand out. With few exceptions, an association of these extinct animals with humans on any of the islands has only rarely been demonstrated. Indeed, the role that humans may or may not have played in the global extinctions of Pleistocene fauna is one of the most controversial issues in modern archaeology (Martin and Klein 1984).

It is the archaeological significance of *Aetokremnos*, especially as it pertains to extinction issues, that has stimulated the most interest in the site. Substantial archaeological and historical evidence, especially from the Pacific (Anderson 1991; Steadman 1995), demonstrates that humans have had immediate and long-lasting affects on islands, including, in many cases, the extinction of endemics. This is usually associated with comparatively late food-producing economies, and nearly always involves relatively small animals. When one attempts to extend human-induced extinction episodes back to the late Pleistocene or early Holocene, however, the evidence invoking direct predation by humans becomes much more equivocal. There essentially are two schools of thought in the debate–one proposes that human hunters were the prime cause of the extinctions, while the other minimizes the human role and looks, instead, to ecological factors (e.g., Diamond 1989; Grayson 1991; Martin and Klein 1984). Most researchers tend to favour the latter model.

While human induced impacts on the Mediterranean islands during antiquity have been especially harsh (Blondell and Aronson 1995; Blumler 1993; Patton 1996), there is little substantial evidence for the association of humans and Pleistocene fauna on the islands (Cherry 1992). Mallorca is one of the few examples where humans and such fauna have been associated in secure contexts at Neolithic sites (e.g., Burleigh and Clutton-Brock 1980; Waldren 1994). Claims for Late Pleistocene associations of extinct fauna with humans in Sardinia (e.g., Sondaar *et al.* 1991) are far less compelling. Thus *Aetokremnos* remains a very rare site.

Faunal issues aside, the antiquity of *Aetokremnos* is of considerable importance. For many years there have been claims for early (that is, pre-Neolithic) human occupation of many of the Mediterranean islands, including Cyprus (e.g., Adovasio *et al.* 1975; Stockton 1968; Vita-Finzi 1973). Cherry (1990, 1992), however, has convincingly demonstrated that there are few, if any, strong arguments for people being on most of the Mediterranean islands during the Late Pleistocene or Early Holocene. Given the claim that *Aetokremnos* exceeded the Khirokitia Culture by some three millennia, it is not surprising that the site had its sceptics. Let us now turn to a discussion of some of these issues.

The cultural status of materials from *Aetokremnos*

While few now argue with the empirical data from *Aetokremnos*, it is our interpretation of these data that has caused the most controversy. Perhaps the major problem for many of the site's sceptics relates to the validity of the association of the hippopotamus remains with the cultural data (e.g., Bunimovitz and Barkai 1996; Binford 2000; Reese 1996a; Simmons 1996). Few questioned that Level 2 was cultural, but some argued that Level 4, containing the majority of the faunal remains, was the result of a natural deposition of Pleistocene animals, and that any associated artefacts are merely fortuitous. We believe that the results of our analyses indicate that this is unequivocally not the case, or at least as unequivocally as anything can be in archaeology. In this context, it is useful to consider some specific issues that have been raised regarding the cultural nature of *Aetokremnos*. An expanded view of these arguments is presented in Simmons (1999: 283–336, 2001a, 2002).

To begin with, there is no question that the chipped stone artefacts are culturally manufactured, rather than representing "geofacts." Nor are they more recent "doukani flints." A detailed techno-typological analyses (Simmons 1999: 123–146) demonstrated that the chipped stone thus far has no counterparts in Cyprus, so one cannot make the argument that they are, for example, intrusive Neolithic materials. Furthermore, many of the artefacts are stratigraphically and directly associated with the hippopotamus remains. While some may question whether or not small tools such as those recovered from *Aetokremnos* could have been used in butchering animals such as hippopotami, there is abundant ethnographic evidence that small implements are indeed efficient butchery implements (e.g., Frison 1989; Haynes 1991).

The site's detailed and absolute chronology also unequivocally demonstrated that Levels 2 and 4 are, in radiocarbon years, indistinguishable. This indicates that the hippopotami were alive at the same time as the humans who occupied the site, a conclusion confirmed by several radiocarbon determinations on hippopotamus bone that are virtually the same as the dates from other materials.

A critical argument is, of course, stratigraphic. Mandel's detailed analysis (1999; Mandel and Simmons 1997) clearly demonstrates the stratigraphic integrity of the site, and shows absolutely no evidence for mixing by humans responsible for Level 2 cutting into Level 4, which conceivably could have accounted for the association of artefacts with the faunal materials. In addition, there is no geomorphic evidence for a sinkhole, water movement, or other natural displacements that could have resulted in the deposition of the bones. There also is a high amount of phosphorous in both Strata 2 and 4, indicating much organic activity. Finally, the "clean" nature of the shelter's floor, demonstrating no sediment accumulation, suggests that it was a prepared surface.

A contentious issue regarding the faunal assemblage from *Aetokremnos* is the apparent lack of cut-marks (Binford 2000; Olsen 1999). In an assemblage of over 500 hippopotami, it seems reasonable that butchery or cut marks should be present if humans were consuming these animals, and Olsen, who analyzed a sample of

the bones, remains unconvinced of the primary cultural association. We are, however, not as concerned, and can refute the issue that no cut-marks means no cultural association. There is an enormous, and contradictory, literature on the issue of cut-marks and other bone modifications in archaeological fauna (see Lyman [1994: 294–353] for a thorough summary, and Morlan [1984] for rigid criteria for recognizing artificial bone modifications). After a review of the literature, it is apparent that numerous arguments can explain either the lack or presence of cut-marks, and that context is of considerable importance.

A significant observation is that cut-marks often are relatively rare, even in many well-documented butchery assemblages. Soft tissues frequently shield bone from being marked (Shipman and Rose 1983: 86), and one might consider cut-marks on bone the signature of unskilled or inefficient butchers. There are ample ethnographic examples and experimental studies where it is apparent that cut-marks do not define butchery. Crader (1983: 135) has pointed out that the paucity of cut-marks is simply not a very reliable guide for understanding the degree of butchering of many carcasses. Frison (1989: 778) and Haynes (1988) comment extensively on the lack of cut-marks in modern elephant butchery experiments. During the intense African herd culling that Haynes summarizes, experienced culling crews did not, deliberately or accidentally, cut bones (Haynes 1991: 185). If steel tools often do not produce cut-marks, how likely is it that stone ones will?

A related issue involves cooking processes (cf. Marshall 1989: 17). Clearly, how an animal is cooked can relate to how it is butchered. If, for example, hippopotami were roasted whole at *Aetokremnos*, there may have been little need for butchering so invasive as to scar the bone, since the meat could have been pulled apart at articular joints with minimal cutting of tissue.

Another topic relating directly to the fauna is burning. About 29% of the bone at *Aetokremnos* is burned, much of it severely. It is doubtful that this degree and amount of burning could have a non-cultural origin. While some might argue that underlying bone could have been burned by overlying hearths, this is unlikely since even in such a scenario, the bone would not have been severely charred. In an experimental study, Stiner and colleagues point out that "...although bones were buried as deep as 15 cm below the coal bed, only those specimens in the first 5 cm were affected much by heat from the fire. Moreover, these shallowly buried bones were burned only to the point of carbonization..." (Stiner *et al.* 1995: 230). At *Aetokremnos*, Stratum 4 often exceeds 50 cm. in thickness, and burned bone occurs throughout the stratum, not only on the top of it. Furthermore, Stratum 2 frequently is separated from Stratum 4 by several cm of Stratum 3. The separation between the bottom of fire hearths in Stratum 2 and bone in Stratum 4 almost always exceeds 15 cm, and yet much of this bone is thoroughly burned. It is therefore exceedingly unlikely that the burning is the result of overlaying hearths. This could not have been caused by Level 2 fire hearths charring the underlying bone. Furthermore, not all the burned bone is even under the hearths.

Ultimately, the huge assemblage of bones at *Aetokremnos* is a taphonomic issue. To paraphrase Shipman (1979), "how did all those bones get there?" In addition to the issues mentioned above, we considered the possibility of a sinkhole, an accretional paleontological deposit of animals either accidentally falling off the cliffs above the site, or of sick animals going into the shelter to die. All three arguments seem very unlikely. As noted earlier, there is absolutely no geological evidence of a sinkhole or any geomorphic activity indicating that the bones were washed into the confines of the *Aetokremnos* shelter.

As for an accretional explanation involving animals falling off the cliffs, the lack of spreading vertically or horizontally on the cliffs argues against this. Furthermore, if they fell over the cliff, how did they get inside of the shelter? And, even if this occurred, why did they only accumulate in the *Aetokremnos* shelter?

As to the argument for a natural accumulation by sick animals, again, why would *Aetokremnos* be the only shelter used by ill hippopotami who had gone somewhere to die? It certainly is too small to hold over 500 hippopotami at once, and if it were a natural accumulation through time, why are virtually none of the over 200,000 bones articulated? Also arguing against the old, ill, and infirm scenario is the fact that 27% of the analyzed hippopotami

are under one year old (Reese and Roler 1999: 156–158). Finally, there are other fauna at the site, including many birds and shell, and these increase over time, suggesting that as the hippopotami were becoming scarcer, presumably due to overhunting, alternate economic resources were being used.

When all aspects of the site are examined, the most parsimonious explanation for the fauna is cultural. I might add that, while it is incumbent upon us to rigorously defend our argument, I suspect that if *Aetokremnos* were a mainland site and the bones were from, say, sheep rather than hippopotami, few would question the association. By examining all lines of evidence, we believe that the *Aetokremnos* shelter was used for protection and storage, and functioned as a processing site and bone cache; much of the bone may have been used for fuel. We have modelled that a small group of humans could have, within a relatively short period, eradicated remnant hippopotamus populations who may have already been suffering ecological stress due to climatic change.

The significance of Akrotiri-*Aetokremnos*

What then, ultimately, is the significance of *Aetokremnos*? The site remains controversial, and at least four major points are relevant. First, *Aetokremnos* firmly establishes a human occupation of Cyprus in the early 10th millennium B.C., making it one of the earliest occupied Mediterranean islands. While this occupation was likely short-lived, it was significant in that those responsible for *Aetokremnos* apparently subsisted primarily by hunting. There is no evidence to indicate that they had a Neolithic economy. This is important is dispelling some previously held notions that the Mediterranean islands were too impoverished to have supported hunter and gatherer populations beyond perhaps a few short visits (e.g., Cherry 1981: 58–59; Evans 1977: 4). Indeed, there is evidence suggesting that some islands may indeed have had Palaeolithic use, but the more plausible data for such occupations come from Aegean islands near the mainland (e.g., Broodbank 2000; Davis *et al.* 2001) rather than oceanic ones such as Cyprus. Overall, claims for pre-Neolithic occupations on most of the Mediterranean islands (summarized by Cherry [1990] and Simmons [1999: 14–27]) still do not stand up to critical scrutiny, as Cherry (1990, 1992) has clearly demonstrated. Thus *Aetokremnos* remains a rare example.

This begs the question as to the presence of other pre-Neolithic sites on Cyprus. What is missing, of course, are additional sites dating to the Akrotiri phase. Although there are numerous paleontological sites in Cyprus, none has a demonstrated association with cultural materials. Two do, however, have hints of this. The first is Xylophagou-*Spilia tis Englezou*, located on the southern coast (Reese 1995: 138–139). The evidence is flimsy, occurring in the form of charcoal mixed in with the hippopotamus remains, as well as a few pieces of chert. I have examined this site, and it seems an unlikely candidate for a cultural association, although this cannot be verified without proper excavation.

Far more intriguing are localities in northern Cyprus. Here, Akanthou-*Arkhangelos Mikhail*, a collapsed rockshelter, is located not far from the Aceramic Neolithic site of Akanthou-*Arkosyko*. Several chipped stone artefacts purportedly were associated with the hippopotamus site, but these apparently were lost (Reese 1995: 86–132). What is important is that the paleontological site and the nearby archaeological site seem to have little if any relationship. Thus far, recent excavations (Sevketoglu 2002) at the latter have not yielded any hippopotamus remains. Hence, to date *Aetokremnos* remains the sole representative of the Akrotiri Phase, although my feeling is that there must be other sites on the island that are similar to *Aetokremnos* even if none have yet been found. Indeed, some could be under water if they were oriented to coastal exploitations and became submerged with the rise of Holocene sea levels. This is certainly an issue for future investigations to deal with.

A second point of significance of *Aetokremnos* is that it has ramifications for how islands were colonized. Any pre-Neolithic voyagers to Cyprus had to possess a relatively efficient knowledge of seafaring and an appropriate technology. Certainly by the time of *Aetokremnos*' occupation, marine travel already was known in the Mediterranean (Perlès 1979, 2001: 36), so this issue is moot. But Cherry (1981, 1990) has made important distinctions between "occupation"

and "colonization," and certainly in the context of a permanent colonization episode, *Aetokremnos* is an unlikely candidate. The time frame between the prolonged occupation of the site, however, and the first evidence for more systematic colonization as represented by the early phases of the recently documented Cypro-PPNB (Peltenburg *et al.* 2001a, b) is less than 2000 years. Given the cultural dynamics of the Neolithic revolution, it is quite likely that the occupants of *Aetokremnos*, or their descendants, returned to their mainland points of origin and passed on knowledge about the island. This could have spurred interest in the more permanent colonization that we see during the Neolithic.

A third point is that *Aetokremnos* is one of the very few sites anywhere dating to the Pleistocene / Holocene boundary that shows a relationship between extinct mega-fauna (or "mini" mega-fauna in this case) and humans. Certainly we know that humans have rapidly induced extinctions on islands; as noted earlier, this is well documented in historic and late prehistoric contexts. What *Aetokremnos* does is project this back ten thousand years and thus it causes us to re-visit the role of humans in Late Pleistocene extinction episodes, as discussed earlier in this essay.

A final point of significance of *Aetokremnos* relates to archaeological epistemology, and is perhaps ultimately the most important contribution of the site (cf. Simmons 1991). For quite some time, many in Cyprus seem to have been believed that "archaeology equals architecture." Even for the Neolithic this was generally true, as exemplified by impressive sites such as Khirokitia and Kalavassos-*Tenta*. Claims for non-architectural sites or "artefact scatters," for the Neolithic or earlier, were easily dismissed due to poor reporting, questionable context, inadequate understanding of chipped stone, or incomplete comprehension of the formation processes resulting from hunter/gatherer activities, which often produce small, ephemeral sites. All this has been radically altered by the discovery of *Aetokremnos*, by detailed surveys (e.g., Rupp 1987) that record all sites located and not large ones with architecture, and, more recently, by the documentation of sites that are not "typical" Neolithic villages and that extend the chronological range of the Cypriot Aceramic Neolithic.

Expanding the Cypriot Neolithic

The Akrotiri Phase, represented by *Aetokremnos*, presented something of a chronological dilemma in that it was over 3,000 years earlier than the Khirokitia Culture. Who were these hippopotamus hunters, where did they come from, and were they ancestral to the Neolithic? My feeling is that they were disenchanted mainlanders who chose not to participate in the tumultuous changes that were occurring on the mainland during the initial stirrings of the Neolithic revolution. This was not a simple process, and it is likely that many people, for whatever reasons, chose not to become villagers. It is thus possible that those responsible for *Aetokremnos* may have been of a similar conservative nature, and simply chose to leave the Levant for uncharted territory. After all, Cyprus is an easy target from the mainland.

This brings to mind Avraham Ronen's (1995) intriguing, if unconventional, concept of "Asprots," who he feels represented the Khirokitia Culture. This is not the place to assess the "Asprots," but suffice it to say that those responsible for *Aetokremnos* could have been generalized Late Natufian or early (i.e. PPNA) Neolithic, people who arrived on an unoccupied island, found residual herds of an unique fauna, hunted them into extinction, and then left. But they did not forget Cyprus. And it is here where intriguing new research has both made *Aetokremnos* more plausible and added to the complexity of the Cypriot Neolithic.

Much of this new research is addressed in this volume, and it is not my intent to summarize it. There are, however, at least two major points of significance to address here. The first is chronological and the second is economic. The chronological issue is reflected by the exciting new discoveries at Kissonerga-*Mylouthkia* (Peltenburg *et al.* 2000, 2001a, b) and Parekklisha-*Shillourokambos* (Guilaine *et al.* 1995; Guilaine and Briois 2001; Vigne *et al.* 2000) that demonstrate an occupation dating to around 8,000 BC and that show direct artefactual links with the mainland Levantine PPNB. These sites, along with a component from Kalavassos-*Tenta* (Todd 2001) predate the aceramic Khirokitia Culture and form the basis of the "Cypro-PPNB" (Peltenburg *et al.* 2001b: 62–65). Equally significant is that both

Mylouthkia and *Shillourokambos*, while complex, are not traditional village localities.

The economic issue is just as intriguing, particularly regarding the beginning of cattle herding, and thus far is reflected at two sites. Prior to this research, cattle had been conspicuously absent from the Cypriot Neolithic larder, not making an appearance until the Bronze Age (Croft 1991). Now, however, cattle have been found at *Shillourokambos* (Vigne 2001; Vigne *et al.* 2000) and at *Ais Yiorkis*, a small upland locality a few kilometers east of Paphos. *Ais Yiorkis* also is of considerable interest, since available radiocarbon determinations suggest a late Cypro-PPNB occupation (Simmons 1998a,b, in press).

The presence of cattle has exciting implications. Initially, Ronen (1995) proposed that their absence during the Neolithic might have been due to ritual taboos, and the excavators at *Shillourokambos* seem to favour this interpretation (e.g., Vigne *et al.* 2000: 95). Both *Shillourokambos* and *Ais Yiorkis* appear to contain only limited amounts of cattle, and thus perhaps would support a symbolic interpretation. Certainly cattle did have ritual significance on the adjacent mainland (e.g., Mellaart 1998; but see Hodder and Matthews 1998 for alternative views). Since cattle have now been documented at two sites that appear to span the entire Aceramic Neolithic, however, their presence may be economic rather than ritual. We simply do not yet have enough information to make a strong conclusion one way or the other.

What does this new research mean to the Neolithic of Cyprus? First, we now know that Neolithic peoples arrived in Cyprus much earlier than suspected, thereby shortening the chronological gap between them and *Aetokremnos*. This raises the intriguing, but as of yet unverified, notion that those responsible for *Aetokremnos* may in fact have been ancestral to the Cypriot Neolithic. Secondly, this research is unfolding a story of an economically sophisticated Cypriot Neolithic adaptation. We have learned that not all early settlements were restricted to the coastal areas of Cyprus, nor were they all villages. Instead, diverse site types occur in a wide range of environments, including the uplands. Cattle have now been found at two non-typical village sites, indicating an economic dichotomy selecting against keeping them in villages. Perhaps they were moved around seasonally or with the availability of pastureland, and sites like *Ais Yiorkis* and *Shillourokambos* may represent specialized "ranching" occupations (Simmons 2001b). In short, the Cypriot Neolithic is far more complex than any of us originally thought, and certainly is not a watered-down version of the mainland.

Explaining the Neolithic Package: mainland connections

Since a theme of this volume is interaction between the mainland and Cyprus, and since I have worked extensively in both areas, I would like to conclude with some personal observations. We used to see very few similarities between the Aceramic (or Ceramic) Neolithic on the mainland and Cyprus. With the documentation of the Cypro-PPNB, however, there are distinct artefactual similarities, especially in terms of diagnostic chipped stone, particularly naviform core technology and projectile points. Presumably there also were cultural, and perhaps even ritual, similarities, and, as noted earlier, the ultimate reason for Neolithic peoples occupying Cyprus may have been one of social conservatism.

Given these new discoveries, it is logical to ask the question of where these early Cypriots came from. This is not a simple issue, and must be evaluated within the context of what was occurring in the wider Neolithic world at the time (cf. Bar-Yosef 2001). It may be erroneous at this early stage of research to try to pin-point an exact mainland source for the either the Akrotiri Phase or the Cypro-PPNB. My belief is that we simply do not yet have enough evidence to determine this.

The excavators of both *Shillourokambos* and *Mylouthkia* seem to favour a Syrian origin for the Cypro-PPNB, but the PPNB interaction sphere (cf. Bar-Yosef and Belfer-Cohen 1989) on the mainland is enormous and varied, and it probably would be a mistake to try to make subregional-specific connections. Certainly the southern Levant is an equally likely candidate, where a huge variety of Pre-Pottery Neolithic sites existed, ranging from substantial settlements such as Jericho (Kenyon 1957), to megasites like 'Ain Ghazal (Rollefson, Simmons, and Kafafi 1992; Simmons *et al.* 1988) or Wadi Shu'eib (Simmons *et al.* 2001), to much smaller, but incredibly elaborate settlements like Ghwair I (Simmons and Najjar 1998), and, finally, to Neolithic "hunters and gatherers" in many fringe areas (Bar-Yosef 2001). We also suspect that these Levantine PPNB peoples were capable of inducing tremendous ecological havoc (e.g, Köhler-Rollefson 1988; Köhler-Rollefson and Rollefson 1990; 1995; Rollefson 1997; Simmons *et al.* 1988), which may have provided an incentive to migrate to unoccupied regions, such as Cyprus.

There clearly was a lot going throughout the Near East during the early Neolithic, including a far greater degree of social complexity than had previously been suspected (cf. Kuijt 2000). It is entirely likely that continual and systematic contact with Cyprus was part of a pan-regional interaction sphere. Given the results of new investigations, it seems clear that Cyprus was a Neolithic "colony" far earlier and longer than initially believed, and that, at least during the Cypro-PPNB, close relationships were maintained with the Levantine mainland. By the Khirokitia Culture, however, many similarities had disappeared and the Neolithic developed a distinctive island-focused flavour. What happened? This is a question that should be put on the future research agenda. Certainly as more anthropologically-oriented studies are undertaken, the complexity of human interactions within the sensitive biogeographic constraints imposed by islands are being demonstrated. All of this new research, which must be evaluated within a broader, circum-Mediterranean perspective, adds to the increasingly elaborate trajectory of the Neolithic world. This make it a very exciting time to be doing Neolithic research, both on the mainland and in Cyprus, as the papers in this volume demonstrate.

References

Adovasio, J., G. Fry, J. Gunn, and R. Maslowski 1975
Prehistoric and Historic Settlement Patterns in Western Cyprus (With a Discussion of Cypriot Neolithic Stone Tool Technology). *World Archaeology* 6: 339–364.

Anderson, A. 1991
Prodigious Birds: Moas and Moa Hunting in Prehistoric New Zealand. Cambridge University Press: Cambridge.

Bar-Yosef, O. 2001
The World Around Cyprus: From Epi-Paleolithic Foragers to the Collapse of the PPNB Civilization. Pp. 129–164 in Swiny 2001.

Bar-Yosef, O. and A. Belfer-Cohen 1989
The Levantine "PPNB" Interaction Sphere. Pp. 59–72 in I. Hershkovitz. (ed.) *People and Culture in Change.* British Archaeological Reports, International Series, 508: Oxford.

Binford, L. 2000
Review of *Faunal Extinctions in an Island Society: Pygmy Hippopotamus Hunters of the Akrotiri Peninsula, Cyprus* by A. Simmons. *American Antiquity* 65: 771.

Blondel, J. and J. Aronson 1995
Biodiversity and Ecosystem Function in the Mediterranean Basin: Human and Non-Human Determinants. Pp. 43–120 in G. Davis and D. Richardson (eds.) *Mediterranean-Type Ecosystems: The Function of Biodiversity.* Springer-Verlag: Berlin.

Blumler, M. 1993
Successional Pattern and Landscape Sensitivity in the Mediterranean and Near East. Pp. 287–305 in D. Thomas and R. Allison (eds.) *Landscape Sensitivity.* John Wiley and Sons: New York.

Broodbank, C. 2000
An Island Archaeology of the Early Cyclades. Cambridge University Press.: Cambridge.

Bunimovitz, S. and R. Barkai 1996
Ancient Bones and Modern Myths: Ninth Millennium BC Hippopotamus Hunters at Akrotiri *Aetokremnos,* Cyprus? *Journal of Mediterranean Archaeology* 9: 85–96.

Burleigh, R., and J. Clutton-Brock 1980
The Survival of *Myotragus balearicus* (Bate, 1909) Into the Neolithic on Mallorca. *Journal of Archaeological Science* 7: 385–88.

Cherry, J. 1981
Pattern and Process in the Earliest Colonisation of the Mediterranean Islands. *Proceedings of the Prehistoric Society* 47: 41–68.

Cherry, J. 1990
The First Colonization of the Mediterranean Islands: A Review of Recent Research. *Journal of Mediterranean Archaeology* 3: 145–221.

Cherry, J. 1992
Paleolithic Sardinians? Some Questions of Evidence and Method. Pp. 29–39 in R. Tykot and T. Andrews (eds.) *Sardinia in the Mediterranean: A Footprint in the Sea.* Monographs in Mediterranean Archaeology 3. Sheffield Academic Press: Oxford.

Crader, D. 1983
Recent Single-Carcass Bone Scatters and the Problem of "Butchery" Sites in the Archaeological Record. Pp. 107–141 in J. Clutton-Brock and C. Grigson (eds.) *Animals and Archaeology: 1. Hunters and Their Prey.* British Archaeological Reports, International Series 163: Oxford.

Croft, P. 1991
Man and Beast in Chalcolithic Cyprus. *Bulletin of the American Schools of Oriental Research* 282/283: 63–79.

Diamond, J. 1989
Quaternary Megafaunal Extinctions: Variations on a Theme by Paganini. *Journal of Archaeological Science* 16:167–175.

Davis, J., I. Tzonou-Herbst and A. Wolpert 2001
Addendum: 1992–1999. Pp. 77–94 in T. Cullen (ed.) *Reviews of Aegean Prehistory.* Archaeological Institute of America: Boston.

Durrell, L. 1957
Bitter Lemons of Cyprus. Faber and Faber: London.

Evans, J. 1977
Island Archaeology in the Mediterranean: Problems and Opportunities. *World Archaeology* 9:12–26.

Frison, G. 1989
Experimental Use of Clovis Weaponry and Tools on African Elephants. *American Antiquity* 54: 766–784.

Grayson, D. 1991
Late Pleistocene Mammalian Extinctions in North America: Taxonomy, Chronology, and Explanations. *Journal of World Prehistory* 5:193–231.

Guilaine, J., F. Briois, J. Coularou, and I. Carrère 1995
L'Etablissement Néolithique de *Shillourokambos* (Parekklisha, Chypre). Premiers Résultats. *Report of the Department of Antiquities, Cyprus:* 11–32.

Guilaine, J. and F. Briois 2001
Parekklisha *Shillourokambos*: an Early Neolithic Site in Cyprus. Pp. 37–53 in Swiny 2001.

Haynes, G. 1988
Spiral Fractures, Cutmarks and Other Myths About Early Bone Assemblages. Pp. 145–151 in J. Wilig., C. Aikens and J. Fagan (eds.) *Early Human Occupation in Far Western North America: The Clovis-Archaic Interface.* Nevada State Museum, Anthropological Paper 21: Carson City.

Haynes, G. 1991
Mammoths, Mastodonts, and Elephants: Biology, Behavior, and the Fossil Record. Cambridge University Press: Cambridge

Held, S. 1990
Back to What Future? New Directions for Cypriot Early Prehistoric Research in the 1990s. *Report of the Department of Antiquities, Cyprus:* 1–43.

Held, S. 1992
Pleistocene Fauna and Holocene Humans: A Gazetteer of Paleontological and Early Archaeological Sites on Cyprus. Studies in Mediterranean Archaeology 95. Paul Åströms Förlag: Jonsered.

Hodder, I. and R. Matthews 1998
Çatalhöyük: the 1990s Seasons. Pp. 43–51 in R. Mathews (ed.) *Ancient Anatolia.* British Institute of Archaeology at Ankara. Oxbow Books: Oxford.

Kenyon, K. 1957
Digging Up Jericho. Benn: London.

Knapp, A. with S. Held and S. Manning 1994
The Prehistory of Cyprus: Problems and Prospects. *Journal of World Prehistory* 8: 377–453.

Köhler-Rollefson, I. 1988
The Aftermath of the Levantine Neolithic Revolution in Light of Ecologic and Ethnographic Evidence. *Paléorient* 14: 87–93.

Köhler-Rollefson, I. and G. Rollefson 1990
The Impact of Neolithic Subsistence Strategies on

the Environment: The Case of 'Ain Ghazal, Jordan. Pp. 3–14 in S. Bottema, G. Entjes-Nieborg and W. van Zeist (eds.) *Man's Role in the Shaping of the Eastern Mediterranean Landscape*. A.A. Balkema: Rotterdam.

Kuijt, I. (ed.) 2000
Life in Neolithic Farming Communities: Social Organization, Identity, and Differentiation. Kluwer Academic/Plenum Publishers: New York.

Le Brun, A., S. Cluzan S. Davis, J. Hansen and J. Renault-Miskovsky 1987
Le néolithique précéramique de Chypre. *L'Anthropologie* 91: 283–316.

Lyman, R. 1994
Vertebrate Taphonomy. Cambridge Manuals in Archaeology. Cambridge University Press: Cambridge.

Mandel, R. 1999
Stratigraphy and Sedimentology. Pp. 49–69 in Simmons 1999.

Mandel, R. and A. Simmons 1997
Geoarchaeology of the Akrotiri *Aetokremnos* Rockshelter, Southern Cyprus. *Geoarchaeology* 12: 567–605.

Marshall, L. 1989
Bone Modification and "the Laws of Burial." Pp. 7–24 in R. Bonnichsen and M. Sorg (eds.) *Bone Modification*. Center for the Study of the First Americans. University of Maine: Orono.

Martin, P. and R. Klein (eds.) 1984
Quaternary Extinctions: A Prehistoric Revolution. University of Arizona Press: Tucson.

McCartney, C. 1999
Opposed Platform Core Technology and the Cypriot Aceramic Neolithic. *Neolithics* 1: 7–10.

McCartney, C. 2001
The Chipped Stone Assemblage from *Tenta* (Cyprus), Cultural and Chronological Implications. Pp. 427–437 in I. Caneva, C. Lemorini, D. Zampetti and P. Biagi (eds.) *Beyond Tools. Redefining the PPN Lithic Assemblages of the Levant*. SENEPSE 9, ex oriente: Berlin.

Mellaart, J. 1998
Çatal Höyük: the 1960s Seasons. Pp. 35–41 in R. Matthews (ed.) *Ancient Anatolia*. British Institute of Archaeology at Ankara. Oxbow Books: Oxford.

Morlan, R. 1984
Toward the Definition of Criteria for the Recognition of Artificial Bone Alternations. *Quaternary Research* 22: 160–171.

Olsen, S. 1999
Investigation of the *Phanourios* Bones for Evidence of Cultural Modification. Pp. 230–237 in Simmons 1999.

Patton, M. 1996
Islands in Time: Island Sociogeography and Mediterranean Prehistory. Routledge: London and New York.

Peltenburg, E., S. Colledge, P. Croft, A. Jackson, C. McCartney and M. Murray 2000
Agro-Pastoralist Colonization of Cyprus in the 10th Millennium BP: Initial Assessments. *Antiquity* 74: 844–53.

Peltenburg, E., S. Colledge, P. Croft, A. Jackson, C. McCartney and M. Murray, M. 2001a
Neolithic Dispersals from the Levantine Corridor: A Mediterranean Perspective. *Levant* 33: 35–64.

Peltenburg, E., P. Croft, A. Jackson, C. McCartney, and M. Murray 2001b
Well-Established Colonists: Mylouthkia 1 and the Cypro-Pre-Pottery Neolithic B. Pp. 61–93 in Swiny 2001.

Perlès, C. 1979
Des Navigateurs Méditerranéens il y a 10,000 Ans. *La Recherche* 10: 82–83.

Perlès, C. 2001
The Early Neolithic in Greece. Cambridge University Press: Cambridge.

Reese, D. 1989
Tracking the Extinct Pygmy Hippopotamus of Cyprus. *Field Museum of Natural History Bulletin* 60: 22–29.

Reese, D. 1995
The Pleistocene Vertebrate Sites and Fauna of Cyprus. Geological Survey Department, Bulletin 9. Ministry of Agriculture, Natural Resources and Environment: Nicosia.

Reese, D. 1996a
Cypriot Pygmy Hippo Hunters No Myth. *Journal of Mediterranean Archaeology* 9: 107–112.

Reese, D. (ed.) 1996b
Pleistocene and Holocene Fauna of Crete and Its First Settlers. Monographs in World Archaeology 28. Prehistory Press: Madison.

Reese, D. and K. Roler 1999
Pygmy Hippopotamus. Pp. 156–161 in Simmons 1999.

Rollefson, G. 1997
The Neolithic Devolution: Ecological Impact and Cultural Compensation at 'Ain Ghazal, Jordan. Pp. 219–29 in J. Seger (ed.) *Retrieving the Past*. Cobb Institute of Archaeology: Mississippi.

Rollefson, G., A. Simmons and Z. Kafafi 1992
Neolithic Cultures at 'Ain Ghazal, Jordan. *Journal of Field Archaeology* 19: 443–470.

Ronen, A. 1995
Core, Periphery and Ideology in Aceramic Cyprus. *Quartär* 45–46: 178–206.

Rupp, D. (ed.) 1987
Western Cyprus: Connections–An Archaeological Symposium. Studies in Mediterranean Archaeology 77. Paul Åströms Förlag: Göteborg.

Sevketoglu, M. 2002
Akanthou-*Arkosyko* (Tatlısu-Çiftlikdüzü): the Anatolian Connections in the 9th Millennium BC. Pp. 98–106 in W. Waldren and J. Ensenyat (eds.) *World Islands in Prehistory–International Insular Investigations*. British Archaeological Reports, International Series 1095. Archaeopress: Oxford.

Shipman, P. 1979
What are All These Bones Doing Here? Confessions of a Taphonomist. Harvard Magazine Nov.–Dec.: 42–46.

Shipman, P. and J. Rose. 1983
Early Hominid Hunting, Butchering, and Carcass-Processing Behaviors: Approaches to the Fossil

Record. *Journal of Anthropological Archaeology* 2: 57–98.

Simmons, A. 1991
One Flew Over the Hippo's Nest: Extinct Pleistocene Fauna, Early Man, and Conservative Archaeology in Cyprus. Pp. 282–304 in G. Clark (ed.) *Perspectives on the Past.* University of Pennsylvania Press: Philadelphia.

Simmons, A. 1996
Whose Myth? Archaeological Data, Interpretations, and Implications for the Human Association with Extinct Pleistocene Fauna at Akrotiri *Aetokremnos. Journal of Mediterranean Archaeology* 9: 97–105.

Simmons, A. 1998a
Of Tiny Hippos, Large Cows, and Early Colonists in Cyprus. *Journal of Mediterranean Archaeology* 11: 232–241.

Simmons, A. 1998b
Test Excavations at Two Aceramic Neolithic Sites in the Uplands of Western Cyprus. *Report of the Department of Antiquities, Cyprus:* 1–17.

Simmons, A. and Associates 1999
Faunal Extinctions in an Island Society: Pygmy Hippopotamus Hunters of the Akrotiri Peninsula, Cyprus. Plenum/Kluwer Academic Press: New York.

Simmons, A. 2001a
The First Humans and Last Pygmy Hippopotami of Cyprus. Pp. 1–18 in Swiny 2001.

Simmons, A. 2001b
Villages Without Walls, Cows without Corrals. Paper Presented at the Neolithic of Cyprus Conference, Nicosia, May, 2001.

Simmons, A. 2002
The Role of Islands in Pushing the Pleistocene Extinction Envelope: The Strange Case of the Cypriot Pygmy Hippos. Pp. 406–414 in W. Waldren and J. Ensenyat (eds.) *World Islands in Prehistory–International Insular Investigations.* British Archaeological Reports, International Series 1095. Archaeopress: Oxford.

Simmons, A. in press
Preliminary Report of the 2002 Excavations at *Ais Yiorkis,* An Aceramic Neolithic Site in Western Cyprus. *Report of the Department of Antiquities, Cyprus.*

Simmons, A. and M. Najjar 1998
Al-Ghuwayr 1, A Pre-Pottery Neolithic Village in Wadi Faynan, Southern Jordan: A Preliminary Report of the 1996 and 1997/98 Seasons. *Annual of the Department of Antiquities of Jordan* 42: 91–101.

Simmons, A., G. Rollefson, I. Köhler-Rollefson, R. Mandel and Z. Kafafi 1988
'Ain Ghazal: A Major Neolithic Settlement in Central Jordan. *Science* 240: 35–39.

Simmons, A., G. Rollefson, Z. Kafafi, R. Mandel, M. Al-Najar, J. Cooper, I. Köhler-Rollefson and K. Roler Durand 2001
Wadi Shu'eib, a Large Neolithic Community in Central Jordan: Final Report of Test Investigations. *Bulletin of the American Schools of Oriental Research* 321: 1–39.

Sondaar, P. 1986
The Island Sweepstakes. *Natural History* 95: 50–57.

Sondaar, P., F. Martini, A. Ulzega and G. Hofmeijer 1991
L'homme Pléistocène en Sardaigne. *L'Anthropologie* 95: 181–200.

Stanley Price, N. 1977
Colonisation and Continuity in the Early Prehistory of Cyprus. *World Archaeology* 9: 27–41.

Steadman, D. 1995
Prehistoric Extinctions of Pacific Island Birds: Biodiversity Meets Zooarchaeology. *Science* 267: 1123–131.

Stiner, M., S. Kuhn, S. Weiner and O. Bar-Yosef 1995
Differential Burning, Recrystallization, and Fragmentation of Archaeological Bone. *Journal of Archaeological Science* 22: 223–237.

Stockton, E. 1968
Pre-Neolithic Remains at Kyrenia, Cyprus. *Report of the Department of Antiquities, Cyprus:* 16–19.

Swiny, S. 1988
The Pleistocene Fauna of Cyprus and Recent Discoveries on the Akrotiri Peninsula. *Report of the Department of Antiquities, Cyprus:* 1–14.

Swiny, S. (ed.) 2001
The Earliest Prehistory of Cyprus: From Colonization to Exploitation. Cyprus American Archaeological Research Institute Monograph Series 12. American Schools of Oriental Research: Boston.

Todd, I. 2001
Kalavasos *Tenta* Revisited. Pp. 95–107 in Swiny 2001.

Todd, I. (ed.) 1987
Vasilikos Valley Project 6: Excavations at Kalavasos-Tenta 1. Studies in Mediterranean Archaeology 71:6. Paul Åströms Förlag: Göteborg.

Vita-Finzi, C. 1973
Paleolithic Finds from Cyprus? *Proceedings of the Prehistoric Society* 39: 453–454.

Waldren, W. 1994
Survival and Extinction: Myotragus Balearicus, an Endemic Pleistocene Antelope from the Island of Mallorca. DAMARC 27, Donald Baden-Powell Quaternary Research Centre, Pitt Rivers Museum, University of Oxford: Oxford and Deìa Archaeological Museum and Research Centre: Deìa, Mallorca.

Wigand, P. and A. Simmons 1999
The Dating of Akrotiri *Aetokremnos.* Pp. 193–215 in Simmons 1999.

Vigne, J.-D. 2001
Large Mammals of Early Aceramic Neolithic Cyprus: Preliminary Results from Parekklisha *Shillourokambos.* Pp. 55–60 in Swiny 2001.

Vigne, J.-D., I. Carrére, J-F. Saliège, A. Person, H. Bocherens, J. Guilaine and F. Brios 2000
Predomestic Cattle, Sheep, Goat and Pig During the Late 9th and the 8th Millennium Cal. BC on Cyprus: Preliminary Results of *Shillourokambos* (Parekklisha, Limassol). Pp. 83–105 in M. Mashkour, A. Choyke, H. Buitenhuis and F. Poplin (eds.) *Archaeozoology of the Near East IVA,* ARC. Publicatie 32: Groningen.

2

Island colonization, insularity or mainstream?

Bill Finlayson

Abstract

This paper seeks to assess the relationship of Cyprus to the mainland in the early Neolithic, and the idea of insularity. This is achieved in part by an examination of the idea of island archaeology and by comparison with the nature of the early Neolithic on the mainland. The emphasis of the significance of the island context is considered to be more appropriate to the Pacific than the Mediterranean, while the early Neolithic of Cyprus is seen to reflect the diversity and adaptability of the mainland. Both observations suggest that Cyprus at this point in time was very much an active part of the wider PPNB cultural expansion.

Introduction

This paper was written in response to a brief from the conference organiser, to discuss the nature of island colonization, the use of islands, and the relationship between Cyprus and the mainland. The idea for the conference arose out of a number of current research issues, mostly concerning the significant discoveries made in Cyprus over the last few years (see Swiny 2001), but also a background of a rapidly changing data set from the adjacent mainland areas. In addition, there seemed to be an underlying suspicion that some scholars were approaching the evidence from Cyprus as though it was inevitably different, that the starting point of research should assume a distinctive island context. While the importance of local context and environment is clear, any assumption that being on an island makes a difference must be considered. Is an island really such a significantly greater step for colonization? The early Neolithic has many local variations on the mainland, that cannot be explained by insularity. Perhaps the evidence from Cyprus is important in other ways, ways that are of much greater significance to our understanding of the beginnings and spread of the Neolithic in general than simply to a local atypical trajectory.

The study of island colonization in the Mediterranean has a long history, but in recent terms a beginning can be found in Evans' 1973 article on islands as cultural laboratories. Since then there has been a roughly 10 year review, in 1981 and 1990 with Cherry and in 2000 with Broodbank's book on the Cyclades. One of the interesting features of Broodbank's excellent book is that it begins with a section on "island archaeology", but this rather surprisingly focuses on the Pacific. Surprising in a Cycladic context, less surprising in the context of both the quantity of recent work in the Pacific, and that island archaeology is a clearly defined entity in the Pacific. Island archaeology in the Mediterranean is a rather different thing. Indeed I will argue here that the need to think in insular terms is overstated and too often used as an explanation for cultural diversity.

The core of this volume is to consider the phenomenon of the early Neolithic and its appearance in Cyprus. Over the last few years there has been much excitement over the concept of an early aceramic Neolithic, with strong connections to the PPNB world on the mainland. Some of that excitement is misplaced, and people have been getting excited about the wrong things.

To give a few examples:

- Scholars have been excited about how early people arrived in Cyprus – yet we know that there is a much earlier site at Akrotiri (Simmons 1999, 2001). Equally importantly, we know that in a mainland context Cyprus is not particularly early – although certain aspects of the manifestation of the Neolithic appear precocious (Peltenburg *et al.* 2000).
- People have been excited by the technology they have inferred. Yet we still have no direct data on the maritime technology employed.
- And people have, as ever, been excited by the possibilities of studying the early Neolithic on an island laboratory. Yet this idea that was being promoted 30 years ago is singularly flawed, requiring a degree of isolation that was just clearly not the case.

This paper commences with a discussion of some of the broad issues of island colonization. This is then applied to the early Neolithic on Cyprus to assess which aspects are of real interest, and which have a bearing on mainstream mainland archaeology, not on an insular project that lies largely outwith the usual pattern of research.

Island Colonization

The first two issues relate to island colonization. These will be discussed first, returning to the issue of island laboratories later.

The first point to make, of course, is that there is nothing particularly remarkable about island colonization. We all know that Australia was colonised 40 to 60,000 years ago, which would have involved an open water crossing of about 65 km (*cf.* Gamble 1993). The arguments about precise dates are not important to the debate over Cyprus. It was a long way and a long time ago. There are of course arguments that Homo Erectus made the 25 km sea crossing to Flores in Indonesia 850,000 years ago (Morwood *et al.* 1999). There is some tentative evidence of Middle Palaeolithic island maritime activity in the Mediterranean, although mostly in areas that would not have been islands at that time. For current purposes all we need to know is that islands have been a normal human habitat for at least 40,000 years.

The second point is that to bring farm animals across doesn't necessarily require big boats. Combinations of carrying small infants and making larger animals swim have all been suggested in various situations. The technology of big boats is a red herring. As for the technology of small boats – we know that people used the sea and its resources in the Epi-Palaeolithic – we know that the obsidian in the Cyclades was used (by 8,000 years ago involving round trips of 300 km), and we know that Akrotiri was occupied, even if only for temporary visits. Estimates of distance to the northern Levant before current sea levels were attained range around 60 km (Simmons 1999), not a vast distance to travel.

Further to the west, Broodbank (1999) argues that following long-term exploration of the Aegean, farming spread to mainland Greece via the islands of the Aegean. The Aegean may have served as a maritime nursery, where coastal dwellers learnt their craft before becoming more adventurous. Boats and the sea go together and we should not be surprised that people on the surrounding mainland had them. A problem, of course, with the eastern Mediterranean is that there is no archipelago to practice around. What is more, arguments have been advanced that the eastern Mediterranean is resource poor, making marine foods a less important dietary element (Bar-Yosef and Meadow 1995). However, the rare fish remains from Hayonim Cave and El-Wad suggest that old archaeological recovery methods may be to blame for our lack of knowledge of the use of marine resources (Bar-Yosef and Meadow 1995). Now, of course, we are beginning to find out about coastal sites (Galili and Nir 1993; Galili *et al.* this volume).

Regardless of its economic importance, boat travel is often important, especially before domesticated draught, pack and riding animals became available. Rather than seeing boat travel as being difficult and involving major expeditions, we can regard it as the preferred, easy way of moving household and goods. Indeed, when calculations of distance and visibility of Cyprus are made, perhaps these should be based on coastal fishing, a good few kilometres from the mainland coast, rather than the best view from the Taurus. For basic calculations the distance in statute miles equals 1.224 times the square root of the height, in feet, above the surface (Encyclopaedia Britannica 2003). If, standing in your little boat, your eyes are 1.8 m above the waves, this would give you a horizon of 4.7 km. Should you choose to balance on the day's catch and thus raise your eyes to 2.5 m, this would give you a horizon just short of 5.6 km. However, this is the distance at which you could see another object at sea level. If you were on a Cypriot mountain at, shall we say, 1,900 m, your horizon would be about 154 km, so a fisherman could, theoretically, see the top of the mountain from nearly 154 km away. But only on a very clear day. On the other hand, the smoke from a forest fire would be very visible, even if island spotting techniques such as observing cloud banks and so on were not very far advanced in the largely island free Eastern Mediterranean. (As a side note, hippos eyes must be about 25 mm above sea level, giving them a horizon of only about 500 m – and that is from the top of a wave!)

This leads me to suggest that, rather than being surprised how early Cyprus was colonised, the more interesting question to pose is "why did it take people so long to colonise the Mediterranean islands?" Now there are several different parts to this question. The first involves the relationship between people and the sea. How do they view it and the islands within it? The second is what is it that colonization involves? Related to this is the issue of what sort of people colonised Cyprus. Here Peltenburg *et al.* (2000) make an important point. The novelty of the colonization of Cyprus is that it appears to have been the first island to have been colonised by *farmers*. Of interest here is that according to figures suggested by Broodbank (2000) by the date that the PPNB package was available, the minimum distance to Cyprus, 60 odd kilometres, is at the maximum distance for a journey. This is based on a combination of boat speeds of *ca.* 20 km a day and the difficulty of handling animals for longer than a two-day and one night trip.

People and the sea

It is important to remember that the sea is a different environment. It is one that has very different images depending on context. On Cyprus the most common one for modern visitors is the sea as a benign place for floating gently in. Yet the moment the difficulties of sea crossings start to be discussed then it becomes hostile, huge waves crash down on primitive craft, enforcing an isolation of islands. Most archaeologists are

not as familiar with the sea as coastal people would once have been. We tend to conceive of the sea in these stereotypical images.

The sea changes, and is a matter of perception – one moment friend another moment threat. It is also a matter of knowledge. If we know the seasons, the tides, the currents, our boat's capabilities, how to navigate, the sea becomes a different world. If we do not, we may not even be aware of when it is safe, when it is not. Different cultures react to the sea differently, and their reactions change over time. One of the fascinating aspects of Pacific archaeology is the history of seafaring. Despite the extended archipelago remaining the same, travel was not a constant. It has become commonplace knowledge that when western explorers reached the Pacific, many previous regular routes had become unused. The Tasmanians had turned their backs on the sea long before western explorers reached Tasmania.

Our current perception of islands in the Mediterranean seems a little unusual. Broodbank discusses "island archaeology" as a special field of study, beginning with Evans' article in 1973. The works he then cites as being important examples of island archaeology are all from the Pacific. The Pacific is not a good analogy for the Mediterranean. Nor can a single concept of island archaeology be applied to the Pacific and the Mediterranean. The Pacific environment is very different, indeed unique, as were the cultures that first explored and colonised it. In contrast, the early Neolithic in Cyprus is part of the mainstream: Cyprus is not isolated. Broodbank's term "extra-insular regions" (Broodbank 2000: 37), must surely be a somewhat tongue in cheek way to describe the mainland. He seeks to correct mainland-centric views of islands, but the island-centric view may not be any more helpful, at least during periods when contacts were good.

Colonization

Broodbank introduces his recent book with a series of questions: "Why do people go to islands? How do they choose to live after arrival?" and so on (2000: 3). There is in this, and in many other discussions of islands, an assumption that once people arrive, they stay. An important point for consideration is always that islands do not have to be colonised to be exploited – even relatively distant islands could be used for seasonal occupation. Isolation and insularity can be seasonal – with good summer links and no winter communication. This may reflect the nature of occupation in the Epi-Palaeolithic in Cyprus. Certainly there is no great weight of evidence indicating a permanent occupation, although of course a hunter-gatherer occupation may have been substantially restricted to the coast, now lost under sea level rise. Such temporary occupation is sometimes dismissed as indicating that there was no local population to mix with the new Neolithic population. However, we should be aware of the importance of prior exploration and familiarity with the sea. This may have made sure that Cyprus was not distant or exotic. Indeed, the early colonization by farmers may well indicate strong links to earlier maritime people, who knew the sea.

Bass (1998) and Bowdler (1995) have observed that variability in how islands are exploited suggests that the answer lies not in modelling, but in studying regional patterns. This pattern comes across very clearly in studies of the islands around Australia, which show great divergence in their history of occupation, which must to a great extent be the result of local historical context, rather than size, distance and environment.

Is it therefore a problem that Cyprus is colonised long before any of the other Mediterranean islands are? Cyprus lies next to the core areas of the early Neolithic, both to the east and to the north. One of the phenomena of the Pre-Pottery Neolithic B (PPNB) is that there appears to be a real take-off, an explosion of the PPNB interaction sphere. In that context the early colonization of Cyprus should be no surprise.

Island Laboratories

Rainbird (1999) has attempted a critique of the notion of island archaeology. His starting point is that not only do we treat islands as special places, but there is a long tradition in western literature that biases us against island people, as being isolated and suffering from this isolation. He attempts to do this by running through a series of texts from the 16th century with Thomas More's *Utopia*, Shakespeare's *The Tempest* in the 17th century, Defoe's *Robinson Crusoe* in the 18th century, Stevenson's *Kidnapped* and Hardy's *Well-Beloved* for the 19th century, and Golding's *Lord of the Flies*, Irvine's *Castaway*, and Theroux's *Happy Isles of Oceania* for the 20th century. Interestingly, his selection comprises mostly those that use the island setting deliberately to allow a literary laboratory-type experiment. The obvious exception is Stevenson, and here the character concerned rather than having a bad experience on an island has them on the mainland, on ship, in the sea, and back on the mainland again. The problem he has with islands is not realising that at first he is on a small tidal islet. Once this is solved and he escapes, although still on an island, albeit larger, he has few difficulties. Broodbank (1999) suggests some alternative views of islands in literature, including the island as paradise. Of course, one of the major exploring and colonising powers was Britain, itself an island. Being an island has often been raised as part of the British national mythology, even today with arguments about how European Britain is.

Even within chains of small islands, such as the Hebrides, work tends to be done in an island-centric manner (e.g. Mellars 1987). Even where studies were regional and looked at several islands – the land was the focus (Mithen 2000). More recent work has attempted to change this, by trying not to consider the islands as the object but to be concerned with larger landscapes (Hardy and Wickham-Jones 2003). The focus would become the seascape, research being conducted from the sea, on the edge of the sea, and looking across the sea. Rather than pick islands as units of study, a stretch of water was chosen, with its adjacent island and mainland coasts. This helped to make sense of site distribution, and completely removed the notion of insularity or isolation. Indeed, given the ease of boat travel as opposed to often difficult overland travel, the island often does not make sense as a territory for a single cultural, tribal, or family entity. The centre point of a settlement pattern could almost be seen as the sea. These seascapes are perhaps in Broodbank's terms islandscapes (Broodbank 2000). His term, described as an approach to island landscape and seascape, is not ideal. Unless the intention is to privilege islands, then the mainland component is as important. Indeed Broodbank states that, "In island archaeology, the identification of the island as the primary unit is simply an imposed view," (2000: 22) and he notes that adjacent coasts of rugged islands can be closer to each other than other coasts on the same island. Clearly the same can apply to mainland coasts. He raises this with reference to Rhodes, which often controlled mainland territory in "an economic symbiosis that more or less survived until the imposed boundaries of the 20th century AD" (2000: 23). Yet these boundaries are just the same as past boundaries. They reflect conscious decisions where to create insularity.

Isolation is, of course, not just a function of water, but also distance and visibility. Isolation and insularity are also cultural. Water can sometimes be a link and sometimes a barrier. Rainbird cites a Tongan anthropologist, Hau'ofa, as observing that the European concept of isolated dots in a vast ocean was entirely contradictory to the indigenous concept of islands as joined by a sea of islands (Rainbird 1999). Hau'ofa emphasised that the sea was an ordinary environment, for working and playing in. Islands are not cultural. Indeed, many scholars have emphasised that different cultures can exist on one island. Terrell *et al.* (1999) suggest, optimistically perhaps, that no archaeologist thinks that islands are isolated, they just often write as if they were.

Broodbank discusses contact between mainlanders and islanders in a framework where it is largely exotic, as perhaps it was when western explorers first began the detailed surveys in the Pacific. But he argues for an exoticism even in the "Mediterranean, where integration between islanders and mainlanders began in general much earlier, more tentatively and with less extreme technological distinctions," (2000: 9) despite what he sees as sustained contact from the start as perhaps being a feature of the Mediterranean. This is one of the reasons I do not believe Pacific archaeology is a good analogy for the Mediterranean, especially regarding issues of contact. Terrell *et al.* (1997) observe that even Pacific islands are rarely culturally isolated. Mediterranean islands are of course still less isolated. Indeed, arguably, the more an island becomes isolated, the less normal it becomes, and therefore the less suitable as a laboratory.

Evans (1973) noted that water can act as insulation, cutting off islands, or as a contact medium, linking them. Broodbank also notes that the degree of openness and closure "was to a large degree the decisions or customs of its islanders and those of people in the outside world" (2000: 19). This phenomenon is fairly typical. Returning briefly to the west of Europe, it has been argued that the earliest Mesolithic was almost exclusively marine – linking Ireland, the Hebrides and mainland Scotland across an Atlantic Mesolithic pond. At other times though the cultures of Ireland and Scotland clearly diverge – the sea, which was so important economically and as a means of communication, became a boundary. Perhaps something similar can be seen in Cyprus, which starts off as fairly standard PPNB, and appears to remain in contact with the mainland, until the Khirokitia culture which appears to increasingly go its own way. Even this does not necessitate loss of contact – indeed difference may be a deliberate expression of local identity within a wider cultural setting.

Peltenburg (this volume) has referred to the idea of "the materialisation of an island ideology" to explain divergence between the mainland and Cyprus, in particular in social organisation. He explains this in part by reference to the island being a new world where people were "bereft" of familiar social and environmental surroundings, and an assumption that mainland contacts were of low volume.

Mainstream mainland archaeology

Bar-Yosef has observed that as our evidence has improved we are getting better at the how and when of the beginnings of the Neolithic, but are still not really addressing the issue of why (Bar-Yosef 2001).

The PPNB appears as an explosive phenomenon on the mainland. This has often been seen as a quantum shift from the preceding PPNA, although as our evidence improves the shift does not appear so dramatic. Within the PPNB there are huge differences in site types and economies, we can identify a single but multifaceted phenomenon over a very large area. Differences in architecture, decoration, environmental location, and even economy are substantial, ranging from the burin Neolithic of the arid margins, with its apparent reliance on hunting, to the apparent ceremonial sites such as Göbekli Tepe (Schmidt 2001) and the large settlements such as 'Ain Ghazal (Rollefson *et al.* 1992). Whether the PPNB is described as a civilisation (Bar-Yosef 2001) is not important here. The significant fact is that Cyprus appears to be absolutely part of this mainstream. The enormous spread of the PPNB was not confined to the mainland, but made it to Cyprus, where the variations on the theme, adapted to the local environment, are within the wider spectrum of diversity. Although the appearance of some domesticated species is surprisingly early, the date of colonization (if that is what it was) is within a fairly normal run of the spread of the Neolithic. In this light, it is perhaps interesting to note that the early colonization of Crete appears to be chronologically in keeping with the spread of agriculture across mainland Anatolia. In other words, these islands are being colonised at the same date and rate as mainland counterpart areas.

Equally, that spread, which showed great diversity in its economic adaptation to local conditions, shows the same cultural robustness in Cyprus: a new variant economy is developed, in keeping with natural resources. It is absolutely characteristic of PPNB populations that, despite often being seen as the first true Neolithic, they did not impose a uniform farming economy wherever they went. That sort of model, which may be appropriate for some elements of the later spread of farming across mainland Europe, is not relevant here.

In many areas we are not sure how much this diverse response relates to adaptation by PPNB colonists, or to a natural variation as indigenous populations adopt PPNB elements and become part of the interaction sphere. In the south of Jordan we do not know whether the people from the site of Wadi Faynan 16, which is classically PPNA (Finlayson *et al.* 2000), transform themselves into the PPNB citizens of Ghuwayr 1, the classically PPNB site (Simmons and Najjar 2000). The dates overlap statistically and the sites occupy similar topographic positions a few hundred metres apart. It would appear clear that one site rapidly replaces the other. The question is: are the sites so different that the arrival of outsiders is required, or do the developments seen at the PPNA site lead rapidly to a PPNB type site with the arrival of new ideas?

The problem in Cyprus is different. There is a huge chronological gap in the evidence between Akrotiri and the Neolithic. New sites such as Shillourokambos (Guilaine and Briois 2001) and Mylouthkia 1 (Peltenburg *et al.* 2001) have narrowed the gap, but have not removed it. Arguments about permanence of residence, the loss of coastal sites due to sea level rise, and the relative invisibility of hunter-gatherer camps, can be cited as potential causes for this gap, but it remains. Perhaps at present all that can be said is that although it may be likely that the location of Cyprus was known to mainland populations, it is most probable that the Neolithic settlers arrived fresh from the mainland. Our lack of evidence of an already present population, or even the fact that the new fauna were introduced is not actually proof, it is the closeness of the package to the mainland that is most convincing.

The history of Cypriot prehistory shows very clearly the dangers of arguing from an absence of evidence. In 1977 Stanley Price argued that a very convincing case could be made for an initial colonization of Cyprus in the 6th millennium (Stanley Price 1977). At that time not only was there an absence of earlier sites: he thought he could make a convincing argument from both mainland and island positive evidence that the 6th millennium was the starting point. Yet we know that if initial occupation was focussed on the coast, it may have been lost following sea level rise, providing a taphonomic explanation for a scarcity of early sites.

Conclusion

Neolithic Cyprus appears to refute many classic ideas of "island archaeology". It is part of the mainland mainstream PPNB – as diverse as that interaction sphere is on the mainland. When it does become insular, it is as a cultural island, not as a result of greater physical insularity. There is no reason to suppose actual isolation. Insularity is a relative phenomenon (Braudel 1972) due to historical processes such as changes in shipping routes. The Khirokitia Neolithic divergence may be as much a process of the establishment of a local identity as indicating a surprising loss of contact with the mainland. Indeed, such cultural distancing may be the more obvious explanation of what is happening.

The real importance of Cyprus can be seen in such aspects as the evidence for early domestication of some species, and, perhaps more importantly that the Cypriot evidence lets us look at the causes of the beginnings of the Neolithic, in particular the social factors that appear to have driven both the inception of agriculture and its spread.

References

Bar-Yosef, O. 2001
   The World around Cyprus: from Epi-paleolithic foragers to the collapse of the PPNB civilisation. Pp. 129–164 in Swiny 2001.
Bar-Yosef, O. and Meadow, R.H. 1995
   The origins of agriculture in the Near East. Pp. 39–94 in T. D. Price and A.B. Gebauer (eds.) *Last Hunters, First Framers: New perspectives on the prehistoric transition to agriculture*. School of American Advanced Research Seminar Series, School of American Research Press: Santa Fe.
Bass, B. 1998
   Early Neolithic Offshore Accounts: Remote islands, Maritime Exploitation, and the Trans-Adriatic Cultural Network. *Journal of Mediterranean Archaeology* 11/2: 165–190.
Bowdler, S. 1995
   Offshore Islands and Maritime explorations in Australian prehistory. *Antiquity* 69: 945–958.
Braudel, F. 1972
   The Mediterranean and the Mediterranean World in the age of Philip II. London: Collins.
Broodbank, C. 1999
   The Insularity of Island Archaeologists: Comments on Rainbird's 'Islands out of time'. *Journal of Mediterranean Archaeology* 12/2: 235–239.
Broodbank, C. 2000
   An Island Archaeology of the Early Cyclades. Cambridge University Press: Cambridge.
Cherry, J.F. 1981
   Pattern and process in the earliest colonisation of the Mediterranean islands. *Proceedings of the Prehistoric Society* 47: 41–68.
Cherry, J.F. 1990
   The first colonization of the Mediterranean Islands: a review of recent research. *Journal of Mediterranean Archaeology* 3: 145–221.
Encyclopædia Britannica 2003
   "Horizon." Encyclopædia Britannica Premium Service. 17 Nov, 2003. http://www.britannica.com/eb/article?eu=41960.

Evans, J.D. 1973
   Islands as laboratories for the study of culture process. Pp. 517–520 in A.C. Renfrew (ed.) *The Explanation of Culture Change: Models in Prehistory*. Duckworth: London.
Finlayson, B., S. Mithen, D. Carruthers, A. Kennedy, A. Pirie, and R. Tipping 2000
   The Dana-Faynan-Ghuwayr Early Prehistory Project. *Levant* 32: 1–26.
Galili, E. and Y. Nir 1993
   The submerged pre-pottery Neolithic water well of Atlim-Yam, Northern Israel and its palaeoenvironmental implications. *The Holocene* 3(3): 265–70.
Gamble, C.S. 1993
   Timewalkers: the prehistory of global colonization. Alan Sutton: Stroud.
Guilaine, J. and F. Briois 2001
   Parekklisha Shillourokambos: An Early Neolithic site in Cyprus. Pp. 37–53 in Swiny 2001.
Hardy, K and C. R. Wickham-Jones 2003
   Scotland's First Settlers: an investigation into settlement, territoriality and mobility during the Mesolithic in the Inner Sound, Scotland. Pp. 369–384 in L. Larsson, H. Kindgren, A. Åkerlund, K. Knutsson and D. Loeffler (eds.) *Mesolithic on the Move*. Oxbow: Oxford.
McCartney, C. and E. Peltenburg 2000
   The Colonization of Cyprus: Questions of Origins and Isolation. *Neo-Lithics* 1/00: 8–11.
Mellars, P. 1987
   Excavations on Oronsay. Edinburgh University Press: Edinburgh.
Mithen, S. J. (ed.) 2000
   Hunter-gatherer landscape archaeology. McDonald Institute Monographs: Cambridge.
Morwood, M. J., F. Aziz, P. O'Sullivan, Nasruddin, D. R. Hobbs and A. Raza 1999
   Archaeological and palaeontological research in Central Flores, East Indonesia: Results of fieldwork 1997–8. *Antiquity* 73: 273–286.
Peltenburg, E., S. Colledge, P. Croft, A. Jackson, C. McCartney and M. A. Murray 2000
   Agro-Pastoralist Colonization of Cyprus in the 10th Millennium BP: Initial Assessments. *Antiquity* 74: 844–53.
Peltenburg, E., S. Colledge P. Croft, A. Jackson, C. McCartney and M. A. Murray 2001
   Well-established colonists: Mylouthkia 1 and the Cypro-Pre-Pottery Neolithic B. Pp. 61–93 in Swiny 2001.
Rainbird, P. 1999
   Islands out of time: Towards a critique of island archaeology. *Journal of Mediterranean Archaeology* 12/2: 216–234.
Rollefson, G. O., A. H. Simmons and Z. Kafafi 1992
   Neolithic Cultures at 'Ain Ghazal, Jordan, *Journal of Field Archaeology* 19: 443–70.
Schmidt, K. 2001
   Göbekli Tepe and the Early Neolithic Sites of the

Urfa Region. A synopsis of new results and current views. *Neo-Lithics* 1/01: 9–11.

Simmons, A. H. 1999
Faunal extinctions in an island society: pygmy hippopotamus hunters of the Akrotiri peninsula, Cyprus. Plenum: New York.

Simmons, A. H. 2001
The first humans and last pygmy hippopotami of Cyprus. Pp. 1–18 in Swiny 2001.

Simmons, A. H. and M. Najjar 2000
Preliminary Report of the 1999–2000 Excavation season at the pre-pottery Neolithic settlement of Ghwair I, southern Jordan. *Neo-Lithics* 1/00: 6–8.

Stanley Price, N.P. 1977
Colonization and Continuity in the early prehistory of Cyprus. *World Archaeology* 9: 27–41.

Stordeur, D. 2000
New Discoveries in Architecture and Symbolism at Jerf el Ahmar (Syria), 1997–1999. *Neo-Lithics* 1/00: 1–4.

Swiny S. (ed.) 2001
The Earliest Prehistory of Cyprus: from Colonization to Exploitation. Cyprus American Archaeological Research Institute, Monograph Series 2. American Schools of Oriental Research: Boston, MA.

Terrell, J. E., T. L. Hunt and C. Gosden 1999
The dimensions of social life in the Pacific: human diversity and the myth of the primitive isolate. *Current Anthropology* 38: 155–195.

3

Putting the colonization of Cyprus into context

Trevor Watkins

Abstract

There is a danger that we assume – as many did before – that the earliest sites that we know represent the colonization of the island. The purpose of the paper is to consider the question of the colonization of Cyprus but in a broader context than that of the recent archaeological discoveries on the island. Occurring in the final Pleistocene (if we include the Akrotiri site in the story) or the early Holocene, the colonization of Cyprus represents an early example of the expansion of modern humans to colonise the last remaining unpopulated lands, the previously uninhabited islands. The worldwide evidence is that this colonization was carried out by complex, sedentary or semi-sedentary hunter-gatherers as well as by simple farmers. Especially within southwest Asia, and particularly within the Levantine corridor, hunter-gatherers of the epi-palaeolithic period adopted new subsistence and settlement strategies. These hunter-gatherers are in principle candidates to be the first colonists of Cyprus as much as early farmers. Their strategy involved reliance on broad-spectrum hunting and harvests of seeds that imply storage, and the stored food supplies imply reduced mobility to the point of sedentary, year-round occupation of village sites. On the one hand, this new mode of hunter-gatherer life implies a different kind of relationship between human groups and the environment within which they acquired their subsistence. On the other hand, it also involves profound changes in the social group, both in its size, its social organization, and in the cognitive and psychological consequences for the individual. These societies were scarcely different in almost every way from the early farming societies. A hypothetical reconstruction is suggested in which the island was first colonised by complex hunter-gatherer groups at the end of the Pleistocene, who then maintained their network of exchanges and links with their mainland cousins until these were progressively eroded or abandoned in the seventh and sixth millennia BC.

The generally accepted account of the colonization of the Mediterranean islands (for example, Cherry 1981, 1990) is that in all cases it was carried out by groups of farmers, but elsewhere in the world groups of much earlier hunter-gatherers successfully colonised islands and island groups. Much closer to home, and much closer in time, in the closing centuries of the Pleistocene and the early millennia of the Holocene, the hunter-gatherer occupants of the Franchthi cave on the coast of the Argolid in Greece systematically used obsidian that they had obtained from the island of Melos, 150 km away in the Aegean (Perlès 1987). At very much the same time, the site of Akrotiri-*Aetokremnos* was being formed on the south coast of Cyprus itself (Simmons 1999). That there were sea-faring sailors about in the Mediterranean from at least the end of the Pleistocene is clear, and the vehicle for island colonization existed in practice, not just in theory.

Below the surface in some writing on the subject of the early Neolithic in Cyprus, there seems to be an implicit assumption that possession of domesticated plants and animals and established farming practices are a prerequisite for island colonization, but that is not so. In theory at least, we do not have to wait until cultivation and herding were established on the southwest Asian mainland (apparently in the late ninth and eighth millennia BC) before Cyprus could have been colonised. Colonization by hunter-gatherers would make Cyprus different from the other Mediterranean islands, but its situation adjacent to south and southeast Anatolia, Syria, Lebanon, Israel and Palestine places it adjacent to a dense cluster of semi-sedentary and sedentary hunter-gatherer communities in the final Pleistocene and earliest Holocene periods. In this context, we can recall that authorities such as Lewis Binford (1983) have argued that sedentism among hunter-gatherers is a response to 'packing', relatively high population densities. High population density could easily supply us with the motive for the colonization of new territories in the form of an uninhabited large island.

It is rather difficult to argue counter to a case that has not been made. It would require the construction of a straw man in order to set about refuting the argument for the colonization of Cyprus in the middle of the ninth millennium BC, because no-one has seriously put forward a reasoned case for it. The assumption of colonization at the time of the so-called "Cypro-EPPNB" seems to be based almost entirely on the parallels between Levantine mainland and Cypriot naviform core technology. Since the Cypriot sequence thereafter illustrates a steady divergence from mainland orthodoxy into insular difference, the point of maximum similarity (such as it is) is taken to be the time of colonization. The case for colonization in the mid-ninth millennium BC would certainly be less difficult to make than the case for colonization at the time of the Khirokitia phase, but it would still be the most difficult case to argue among several possible narratives. The problem with alternative scenarios that speak of earlier colonization and a longer history of occupation of the island is the lack of evidence. The absence of evidence, I should not need to remind readers familiar with archaeology, is not evidence of absence. The position taken in this paper is that the absence of evidence is a challenge to test the hypothesis of colonization in 'Cypro-EPPNB' times (mid-ninth millennium BC) against the existence of earlier phases of occupation on the island.

First, I should explain a little more about the human colonization processes world-wide, in order that we can view the colonization of Cyprus within a general context. Since much of the argument of this paper is concerned with establishing the possibility that the colonization of Cyprus may have been undertaken by hunter-gatherers, it will be helpful next to spend a little time in considering some of the characteristics and capabilities of complex hunter-gatherer societies. We may then try to apply some of these abstract and theoretical concepts to the hunter-gatherers of the Epi-palaeolithic period in southwest Asia, in order to make the point that there were societies capable of planning and executing the colonization of Cyprus at a date some millennia earlier than the newly discovered Neolithic settlements on the island. Finally, we need to bring these ideas back to the situation of Cyprus, in order to see what light they may shed on the island's colonization.

Colonization: modes and episodes

A ready starting-point for the consideration of human colonization over the long term and over the whole world is an essay by Colin Renfrew (1994) or the popular science book *Timewalkers* by Clive Gamble (1993). *Homo erectus* (or *Homo ergaster* as some would now prefer) had spread out of Africa into Eurasia by 1.8 million years ago. Most anthropologists and archaeologists now believe that *Homo sapiens* evolved in Africa and began to spread beyond that continent around 100,000 years ago (the dated burials of *Homo sapiens* at Qafzeh and es-Skuhl in Israel are chronologically critical), reaching Sahul (Papua New Guinea, Australia and Tasmania) as a single land-mass before 50,000 years ago, rather earlier than they spread into western Europe. The Americas were apparently reached rather later, around 13,000–15,000 years ago. The spread of Homo sapiens was more rapid and more extensive than the earlier human colonization of the Old World, but both represented the expansion of populations; nowhere was left empty when modern humans moved into new territories.

The spread of farmers out of the hearth-zones of farming therefore constitutes a rather different form of colonization. The expansion of *Homo sapiens* saw hunter-gatherers adapting to changing environments as they went. The direction of the primary movement (beyond NE Africa) was in general eastwards, an easier option than moving north across Eurasia, which would have involved much greater climatic variation and therefore much greater adaptability to different environmental zones. It has been argued recently that the expansion of *Homo sapiens* eastwards was made simpler because people had learned how to obtain coastal and marine resources, and could reduce the environmental variability of their expansionary journey by moving coastwise around the Indian Ocean and onwards into southeast Asia (Stringer 2000). The spread of farmers involved the carrying forward of cultivated crops and of domesticated animals.

The earliest known such hearth-zone of plant cultivation and animals herding was in southwest Asia, and the best-documented spread is across south-eastern and central Europe. Renfrew (1987, 1994) would tie to that spread of farming the expansion of Indo-European speaking farmers, matched by the spread of other linguistic groups out of southwest Asia in other directions. The general expansion of farmers at the expense of hunter-gatherers has reverberated on in other continents and in later millennia. For the sake of completeness, Renfrew's last form of colonization is that of 'élite dominance', in particular the spread of European peoples and powers in Africa, the Americas and Australia.

If we wished to argue that the new Cypriot sites represent the colonization phase, it would be sensible to relate the process to this third phase of colonization, the expansive spread of village-farming populations. But that need not be the case. Groups of modern humans successfully colonised the continental-scale island of Sahul (Papua New Guinea, Australia and Tasmania) between 50,000 and 60,000 years ago (Gamble 1993: 214–227), and the first island groups of the western Pacific (New Ireland and the Solomon Islands) were colonised before 30,000 years ago (Allen *et al.* 1988; Wickler and Spriggs 1988). Hunter-gatherer groups in southwest Asia might theoretically match what hunter-gatherer groups could achieve in other parts of the world. Especially in the last few millennia of the Epi-palaeolithic period[1], there were sophisticated and complex hunter-gatherer communities quite close to Cyprus, and it is therefore appropriate to turn now to the nature of complex hunter-gatherer societies, in order to make the point that complex hunter-gatherers are very similar in many ways to small-scale farming societies.

Recognising complex hunter gatherers

Most of us, certainly most archaeologists, have only an imaginary and intellectual acquaintance with the hunter-gatherer way of life. We have relied on anthropologists for our ideas, and I suspect that many of us retain outdated ideas in this regard. The standard image in modern times was established in the light of the publication of the book *Man the Hunter* (Lee and Devore 1968), and reinforced by Marshall Sahlins (1972). Classic hunter-gatherer bands were small (maximum 25–50), egalitarian, and mobile as well as fluid in composition. Mobile hunter-gatherer bands were described as living at low population densities, with a very modest sense of territoriality, accumulating very little material culture, and engaging in practically no storage of food. There were extraordinary contradictions within the essays contributed to *Man the Hunter*, but these began to be resolved only some years later (a good account of these matters is given by Kelly 1995: 14–37). Lewis Binford (1980, 1990) explored the four categories of hunter-gatherer settlement strategy that had been used by Murdock (1967) – fully nomadic, semi-nomadic, semi-sedentary and fully sedentary – and showed that mobility is related to environment. The most mobile hunter-gatherer societies in the ethnographic record are found in the most extreme conditions, in tropical forests and the Arctic. Between those environmental extremes, where availability of water sources is a (seasonally constraining factor), and where storing food against winter (in temperate forest zones) is a factor, more sedentary settlement strategies are found. Although Binford's reworking of Murdock's collected ethnographic data showed a spectrum, most people have retained the simple binary opposition between hunter-gatherers that Binford called foragers and those he called collectors. Binford's foragers exhibit high residential mobility. Collectors, on the other hand, tend towards semi-sedentism or sedentism, making few (if any moves of settlement during the year). They see to the obtaining of various resources, for example, hunted meat and raw materials for making chipped stone tools, by means of logistically organized foraging parties. Binford's collectors tend to live in larger groups, and their logistical strategies imply accumulation and organization, which in turn imply a degree of social complexity.

At very much the same time, Woodburn (1982) wrote a short article that identified either end of the hunter-gatherer spectrum in terms of the degree of immediate or delayed return involved. The classic, small, mobile hunter-gatherer band societies, he argued, were actively egalitarian and engaged deliberately in immediate return strategies. At the other extreme, delayed return strategies involved the up-front investment of labour and skill (for example, the construction and maintenance of boats or fish-traps and weirs), or labour expended on the accumulation of food supplies that were stored and consumed over a period. Alain Testart (1982) wrote of complex, sedentary hunter-gatherers, their involvement with food storage and the tendency towards hierarchical social organization. Hunter-gatherer societies that engage in food storage, he concluded are very similar to simple farming societies in terms of their social, settlement and economic characteristics.

We should not restrict our view of complex, sedentary hunter-gatherer societies to their settlement and subsistence strategies relative to the environments that they inhabit. There is important information concerning the cognitive and cultural differences of experience that sedentary hunter-gatherers encounter. Once again, it tends to relate complex, sedentary hunter-gatherers to sedentary farming-based societies, rather than the better-known mobile hunter-gatherer societies. The anthropologist Peter Wilson (1988: 4) points out that the sensory basis on which the operation of the primate social group and the mobile human band depend is sight as much as language, and he describes such a human society as the 'open society'. This is the social life for which evolution has fitted us through almost the whole of human evolution. The open society depends on people observing each other and paying frequent attention to what others in the group are doing. Wilson speaks of their ways of promoting open-ness – as Woodburn speaks of 'actively egalitarian' societies.

Wilson differentiates the 'open society' from the 'domesticated society': 'Domesticated people are those who live (and mostly work) in houses grouped together in hamlets, villages, and small towns as distinct from people of the past and the present who use only temporary dwellings or no dwellings at all (that is, Palaeolithic and contemporary hunter/ gatherers) and people who live in large cities and work in factories, offices, and so on' (Wilson 1988: 4). People in domesticated societies, whether farmers or hunter-gatherers, are sedentary, they typically build permanent houses, often investing considerable time, thought, effort and resources. The significant factor of living in a settlement of houses is cognitive in that the walls of the house act as a barrier to the attention and observation. The settlement is divided between public and open space and the private space within each house.

The domesticated society operates within a built environment that is permanent and artificial. And Wilson is at pains to illustrate how often the houses are used as frameworks of reference to ideas about themselves and their world. The house is much more than a shelter, for it embodies the social structure of the village community in households, it provides an analogue for larger structural ideas about the world, and is a concrete expression of thoughts and ideas about how their society functions within the wider world (Wilson 1988: 58). The permanent village of built houses is in marked contrast to the natural environment in which it is situated. Whereas the open society has 'focus', domestic society is concerned with 'boundedness' and boundaries. Dyson-Hudson and Smith (1978) likewise relate territoriality to the density of population, its degree of sedentariness, and the density of significant resources in the environment.

It is important to note that the authorities whose work I have been citing are anthropologists. Their data is ethnographic and their experience anthropological. For the most part, they are not knowledgeable or interested in the evolution of complex, sedentary hunter-gatherers in southwest Asia and their further development as farmers. Wilson in particular sets up the next step in our consideration of the nature of sedentary hunter-gatherer societies. I would suggest that the transition from classic, mobile hunter-gatherer bands of the Upper Palaeolithic to ever less mobile and more sedentary Epi-palaeolithic hunter-gatherer societies in southwest Asia represents the first experience of the novel conditions of the domestic society. That experience, I believe, provided the cognitive stimuli for making new ideas material, for constituting new concepts in concrete form – the house as a construct of the household, the village as a construct of the community, microcosms that formulate in symbolic terms the organization of the cosmos (Watkins 1990, 1992, and forthcoming, a, b and c).

Complex hunter-gatherers in southwest Asia

A lot of the pioneering and most interesting work on complex hunter-gatherer societies has been done on European hunter-gatherers of the final Palaeolithic and Mesolithic, but for our present purposes we should focus on the Epi-palaeolithic hunter-gatherer societies of southwest Asia, especially the east Mediterranean zone. The hunter-gatherers of the Upper Palaeolithic and Epi-palaeolithic of southwest Asia began to adopt new subsistence and settlement strategies from an early date. The distinctive feature of the subsistence strategies of our region is the adoption of heavy grinding and pounding implements. The information recovered from the early Epi-palaeolithic site of Ohalo II in the north of Israel (Kislev, Nadel and Carmi 1992; Nadel and Hershkovitz 1991; Nadel and Werker 1999) is particularly important. The unusual conditions of preservation (the site has been waterlogged for most of the time since its occupation, around 20,000 years ago) mean that we can see that some communities were already at least semi-sedentary, building huts and burying their dead within the settlement. Tens of thousands of seeds and fruits have been recovered from the site, revealing that more than one hundred plant species were in use. The people who lived at Ohalo II gathered acorns, wild emmer and barley together with a range of legumes and other plants. The diversity of plants shows that they were collecting foods across the full range of altitude, from below sea level up to more than 1,000 m above sea level, and across the full spectrum of ecological zones accessible from the site. Gazelle were hunted in numbers, and fish from the lake were also important. Other mammals that were exploited include fallow deer, fox and hare, and plenty of birds were taken, too. The seasons of occupation indicated by the plant remains extend through the spring, summer and autumn, and the evidence of the cementum growth in the gazelle teeth, together with the indications from the bird bones, suggest year-round occupation.

At Ohalo II, dating to the early stages of the Epi-palaeolithic in the heart of the Last Glacial Maximum period, we have evidence for the exploitation of a broad spectrum of plants and animals, the extensive use of storable plant foods, and the sedentary occupation of a settlement located at a place from which a variety of complementary ecological zones can be reached and exploited. The site of Neve David, situated in the mouth of a west facing valley in the Mount Carmel hills and dating to the middle Epi-palaeolithic, is a large, open village site (around 1,000 m²) where repeated seasonal occupation accumulated more than a metre of archaeological deposit (Kaufman 1989). It is classically situated at an eco-tone, where its inhabitants could access several complementary ecological zones from a single settlement. Ritualised burials occur within the settlement, pre-figuring what is better known form the late Epi-palaeolithic period in the southern Levant. Many of the characteristics of complex, semi-sedentary or sedentary hunter-gatherers that we associate with the relatively well-known Natufian culture (Bar-Yosef and Valla 1991) can be found much earlier in the Epi-palaeolithic period, thanks to recent discoveries. And the Epi-palaeolithic period, we now know, is a very long period, extending over some eight millennia. The developments – economic, social and cultural – of the Epi-palaeolithic period were very deep-seated;

Period	Approximate duration	Conventional terms
Period 0	14,000– 12,000 BC	Geometric Kebaran, Zarzian
Period 1	12,000–10,200 BC	Natufian, Zarzian
Period 2	10,200–8,800 BC	Proto-Neolithic, Khiamian, PPNA
Period 3	8,800–7,600 BC	Early–Middle PPNB
Period 4	7,600–6,900 BC	Late PPNB, Jarmo
Period 5	6,900–6,400 BC	Proto-Hassuna, Ubaid 0

Table 3.1 *Chronological scheme, based on that devised and used by members of the Maison de l'Orient at the University of Lyon (see Aurenche, Evin and Gasco 1987)*

they were by no means an invention of the final two millennia.

On the one hand, this new mode of hunter-gatherer life implies a different kind of relationship between human groups and the environment within which they acquired their subsistence (Watkins 1999). On the other hand, it also involves profound changes in the social group, both in its size, its social organization, its social relations and in the cognitive and psychological consequences for the individual. By the final Epi-palaeolithic period, there is evidence to indicate that groups were under pressure, and over the boundary between the Epi-palaeolithic and the early Neolithic periods there begin to appear major cultural changes, as well as the earliest evidence for morphological domestication of plants.

The long trend towards sedentism is marked by cognitive and cultural developments of just the kind that Wilson (1988) describes. It is best known in the late Epi-palaeolithic of the Levant, and the earliest Neolithic of a somewhat wider area, including the northern arc of the hilly flanks zone, at least as far as north Iraq. The extent to which our present knowledge is biased towards the late periods by the concentration of work on the Natufian sites must remain a speculation. That our previous understanding of the early Neolithic was geographically biased has been demonstrated by discoveries made in the late 1980s and 1990s during salvage archaeology in north Syria, southeast Turkey and northern Iraq. The contrast that Cauvin (1994, 2000) makes between the Natufian and the earliest Neolithic is perhaps over-dramatised. Many of the features that characterise the earliest

Neolithic can in fact be found in the preceding period. Cauvin's focus on the symbolic representation of what he argues are divinities tends to marginalize other aspects of symbolic material culture. From the final Epi-palaeolithic at least, we see a clear interest in the capacity of architecture to express ideas about and through the house (Watkins 1990, 1992). Increasingly, we are realising that communities have shaped their whole settlements, furnishing them with public spaces and elaborate communal buildings. Within the arena of the village, whether inside their houses or outside, in the public world, communities painted and modelled with plaster, buried their dead, retrieved skulls, engaged in rituals with plastered anthropomorphic and zoomorphic forms. In short, for the first time in human history they show us what is meant by 'meaningfully constituted material culture' (Hodder 1986). The houses, the villages, their territories and much of their material culture became a mode of signifying, constituting and memorialising beliefs and ideas.

One other feature of the lives of communities in the late Epi-palaeolithic and early Neolithic was their concern for networking. The new, sedentary village societies took care to maintain social and cultural links with each other, again using material culture, sharing tastes in microlithic tools, projectile points, exchanging Red Sea shells and Anatolian obsidian. At a different level, they also actively shared ideas about symbolic architecture, cult and ritual. While archaeologists have tended to concentrate their attention on the developed aceramic Neolithic of Periods 3 and 4 in the Levant (the PPNB, as a way of working chipped stone, because of its 'skull cult', as a dominant culture [Cauvin 2000], or as an interaction sphere [Bar-Yosef and Belfer-Cohen 1989]), many of the symbolic and ritual features can be traced in Period 2, the early aceramic Neolithic, and even in Period 1, the final Epi-palaeolithic period (see Table 3.1 for these periods). In recent years, new sites have been found and investigated that introduce a novel feature to the period, at least from Period 2 through to Period 4 or 5. Sites such as Nahal Hemar (Bar-Yosef 1985, Arensburg and Hershkovitz 1988), and now Kfar HaHoresh (Goring-Morris *et al.* 1998, Goring-Morris 2002), Göbekli (Schmidt 1998, 2001) and others in southeast Turkey show little or no sign of ordinary domestic architecture and residential occupation. Instead, they seem to be almost entirely concerned with symbolic representation in the form of architecture, sculpture, burial, use of human and animal body parts and ritual activities. If the settlements of the period had no similar signs of ritual activity and symbolic representation, they might be thought of as extramural cult sites that were the exclusive properties of particular village communities. Rather, these sites seem to be cult and ritual centres for local communities, which is what their excavators argue. Archaeologists have begun to be interested in how the novel, large, sedentary communities functioned as societies, but this new type of site would seem to illustrate the operation of inter-community networks that functioned in terms of shared beliefs, cults, rituals and iconography.

In short, from at least late in the Epi-palaeolithic period, people were, I believe, discovering the capacity for material culture to act as the fabric of networks of social relations of a new order. In other parts of the world, hunter-gatherer societies were crossing the sea to establish colonist communities in new, island territories more than 30,000 years ago. The complex hunter-gatherer societies of southwest Asia in the Epi-palaeolithic period, particularly the late Epi-palaeolithic, and even more particularly in the early Neolithic periods, were even better equipped socially, culturally and cognitively to undertake the colonization of the nearest Mediterranean island whose mountains were visible from the adjacent mainland.

The colonization of Cyprus

Until the recent discoveries, many archaeologists accepted the view of experts in Cypriot prehistoric archaeology that the Khirokitia phase of the Neolithic, in the seventh millennium BC (calibrated), was somehow the colonization of the island. The arguments against such a view (for example, Watkins 1973, 1980) required the assumption that there was at least one earlier and as yet undiscovered phase in the island's prehistory. We now know that phases earlier than the Khirokitia phase do indeed exist. The first lesson to learn from history, therefore, is that we should not jump to the conclusion that the new discoveries necessarily document the colonization of the island. If the recently discovered sites show that the previous, widely accepted account of Cypriot prehistory was based on defective evidence, there is no reason to think that our new state of knowledge is not also defective. It is at least premature and arguably it is also theoretically misguided to assume that 'Cypro-PPNB' colonists from the Levantine corridor stepped ashore on an uninhabited island at the time of the earliest presently known radiocarbon dates (e.g. Peltenburg *et al.* 2000, 2001: 37; Guilaine *et al.* 2000). The new evidence, especially the occupation sequences at Kalavasos-*Tenta* and Parekklisha-*Shillourokambos*, carries back the history of settlement at least to the later ninth millennium BC (calibrated). The earliest phases of occupation on these sites, plus the earlier of the dated shafts at Kissonerga-*Mylouthkia* (Peltenburg *et al.* 2000, 2001), constitute a *terminus ante quem*.

What this paper is attempting is to open up the possibility that the colonization of the island may have taken place considerably earlier than the earliest contexts referred to above. The main point to be made is that hunter-gatherer communities can on occasion colonize islands, and we should not assume that we must wait until plant and animal domestication has been established on the mainland for the colonization of Cyprus. The newly discovered sites in Cyprus, it may be argued, are not what one would expect of the first settlements of colonists. The size of the sites, for example, at Kissonerga-*Mylouthkia* and Akanthou in the northeast of the island implies substantial settlements with substantial populations.

I also urge that we do not apply the ambiguous term PPNB to Cypriot prehistory. It can mean a phase in the stratigraphy of Tell es-Sultan, ancient Jericho, a mode of forming and using cores and making chipped stone tools, an archaeological culture in the Childean sense, an interaction sphere, or the label for a period within the Neolithic. In my view, the newly coined term 'Cypro-PPNB' is even more dangerous in its ambiguity. For simplicity, let us use the neutral numbering of the Maison de l'Orient chronological scheme, as described by Aurenche, Evin, and Gasco (1987), and as used by Cauvin (1994, 2000). The relevant parts of the scheme are tabulated in Table 3. 1. In these terms, Akrotiri-*Aetokremnos* (Simmons 1999), situated chronologically at the boundary of the Pleistocene and the Holocene, belongs at the transition of Period 1 (the end of the Epi-palaeolithic) to Period 2 (the beginning of the Neolithic). The continuous occupation sequence on Cyprus is documented from the early part of Period 3, in the middle of the ninth millennium BC, to Period 5, in the early seventh millennium BC.

Whether or not there was occupation in Cyprus earlier than Period 3, the earliest dates that we have at present, in the first half of Period 3, stretch the notion of a colonization by groups of farmers close to breaking point. That, however, should not be a reason for asserting that what are at present the earliest dated archaeological contexts must represent the colonization. Aside from the cultivation and domestication of rye at the end of Period 1 at Abu Hureyra (Moore, Hillman and Legge 2000: 375–96), current expert opinion seems to be that the kind of intensive cultivation that leads to morphological domestication was becoming widely established during Period 3 (for example, Willcox 1998). In some parts of the Levant, morphologically wild cereal grains still form substantial amounts of crop assemblages into the later part of Period 3. Pre-domestication agriculture, a relatively non-intensive mode of cultivation and harvesting that seems not to induce genetic change in the population, was practised in Period 2 and possibly also in Period 1, although it is necessarily difficult to identify (Colledge 1998). Using correspondence analysis, a form of multi-variate analysis, Colledge has shown that the suite of species of wild or weed plants associated with

the food crops at Tell Mureybet shift and change between the last part of Period 1 through Period 2, representing changes in the modes of management and cultivation of the food plants on their way to morphological domestication. The Cypriot sites, however, are producing morphologically domesticated cereals (Willcox 2000; Peltenburg *et al.* 2001).

Willcox identifies early Period 3 sites in southeast Anatolia as marking the region where the suite of cereals in use most closely resembles the new material from Cyprus. By the end of Period 2 and the beginning of Period 3, sites on the northern-most stretch of the Euphrates in Syria (specifically Jerf el-Ahmar, dating to Period 2, and Dja'de, dating to the beginning of Period 3) were beginning to share some of these new cultivated cereals. Other lines of evidence have recently pointed to southeast Anatolia as the likely hearth-zone of the earliest domestication of wheat (Heun *et al.* 1997; Lev-Yadun *et al.* 2000). But the earliest accepted evidence for domesticated cereals scarcely antedates the Cypriot data. Similarly with the suite of animals, sheep, goat, pig, cattle and fallow deer, used by the inhabitants of Parekklisha-*Shillourokambos*. None of these species is believed to have been indigenous to Cyprus. Jean-Denis Vigne believes that the pig, sheep and cattle from the earliest phase of occupation were domesticated. Fallow deer have never been known to be domesticated, and we must suppose that the species was brought to the island with the idea of stocking it with a species for hunting. Vigne (2001) has observed that the age and sex pattern of the fallow deer killed by the inhabitants of Parekklisha-*Shillourokambos* resembles the distribution in nature, suggesting that the animals were hunted indiscriminately. And that, incidentally, implies that the species was well established when the *Shillourokambos* people were first hunting them. Daniel Helmer (pers. comm.) believes that there is evidence to indicate the presence of domesticated sheep, goat and cattle at early Period 3 sites in southeast Anatolia, but, again, at a date only a little earlier than the new dates from Cyprus.

The presence of domesticated cereals, lentil, pea and flax, and domesticated animals at sites in Cyprus close to the beginning of Period 3 is precocious. If we add in the possibility that the colonization phase was somewhat earlier than anything we have yet seen from the newly discovered sites, then we must ask where on the southwest Asian mainland were there domesticated plants and animals that could have served as stock for the island's first inhabitants. Because of the geographical gap between the Euphrates valley and the island of Cyprus, it is hard to think how to derive the suite of Cypriot domesticates from southeast Anatolia. An alternative hypothesis might be to derive the Cypriot stock from morphologically wild stock on the nearby Syrian and Turkish mainland, and to account for the domesticated morphology of the Cypriot species by reason of their removal to a new, isolated environment where they were intensively managed during the early stages of the establishment of the island's human population.

A hypothetical colonization model

What happens if we turn away from thinking that Cyprus was first colonized only at or a little before the middle of the ninth millennium BC, early in Period 3? What would an alternative hypothesis look like? A colonization earlier than Period 3 would necessarily imply that the colonists were not farmers and herders. However, as this paper has been at pains to point out, the sedentary and semi-sedentary, complex hunter-gatherers of the earlier Neolithic and the Epi-palaeolithic periods, were in many ways not very different from small-scale societies relying on farming. In addition, at least from the later Epi-palaeolithic period, these mainland hunter-gatherers were sophisticated in their exploitation and management of the environmental resources on which they depended. In particular, their exploitation of a range of plant species involved forms of cultivation that were all but indistinguishable from farming. If the beginnings of pre-domestication cultivation were easier to identify, we should not need to use genetically identifiable domestication as the criterion. That the inhabitants of Cyprus were capable of managing a wild species of animal is demonstrated by their introduction and exploitation of fallow deer. If they could manage fallow deer, might they not also have managed goats and sheep?

For economy of hypothesis, let us suppose that the island was first visited and then colonised by complex hunter-gatherer groups at the end of the Pleistocene. This would allow the curious and enigmatic site of Akrotiri-*Aetokremnos* (Simmons 1999) to play some role in the story. In the final millennium of the Pleistocene period, when the effects of the Younger Dryas phase were having their most severe impact on mainland sedentary hunter-gatherers, when communities such as Abu Hureyra were having to abandon their homes and find new locations for settlement (Moore and Hillman 1992; Moore, Hillman and Legge 2000), pressure would grow in the areas that were still capable of supporting such communities. If population was retreating as resources decreased, they would only add to population in the areas to which they retreated; if climatic deterioration was driving the retreat of woodland and plant-food resources, amounts of essential resources would be declining in the core areas of the Levant and the northern arc of the Fertile Crescent, too. Groups who had already been visiting Cyprus on seasonal hunting trips might then consider the option of colonising the island. Perhaps the indigenous meat supply of pygmy hippopotamus was already reduced, but intending colonists would be aware that they needed to stock the island with their preferred food crops, a suite of cereals and pulses. If not at the beginning of the colonization process, then soon after, they would need to bring in animal species. In consequence of their isolation and close management, and regardless of the degree to which they were cultivated or herded before they arrived, the plant and animal species that had been introduced would relatively rapidly develop the morphological traits of domestication.

Such complex, sedentary hunter-gatherer societies were accustomed to manipulating and managing resources in the environment, and they were also accustomed to maintaining extensive and effective networks of social and cultural exchange. Perhaps the established colonists were supplemented by further groups who crossed from the mainland to join them. Certainly, they continued to use their network links to obtain quantities of central Anatolian obsidian. Jean-Denis Vigne believes that the inhabitants of Parekklisha-*Shillourokambos* continued to supplement their animal stocks with further imports obtained from their mainland cousins. As part of their regular networking and exchanges, the Cypriot communities continued to develop their traditions of preparing cores and making chipped stone tools in step with developments within the PPNB chipped stone tradition of the Levantine mainland. As Carole McCartney makes clear in this volume, the earliest Cypriot assemblages presently known retain some traces of pre-PPNB traditions. As time went by, the Cypriot communities continued to adopt new tool-types and fashions in chipped stone working, in line with PPNB developments on the mainland.

The PPNB cultural phenomenon, some form of interaction sphere in all probability (Bar-Yosef and Belfer-Cohen 1989), gained in intensity through Period 4, involving societies over an ever extending area in more and more elaborate cultic, ritual and symbolic activities (the competitive emulation and symbolic entrainment of which Renfrew [1986] writes). For the communities on Cyprus, who had never been fully integrated in this extraordinary, intensive cultural phenomenon, the need for these links declined, and the growing cost of sustaining them seemed less worthwhile. Over time, participation in the expensive mainland interaction sphere was progressively eroded or abandoned.

The latter part of the above model uses information and the views of specialists. The former part of the model is entirely hypothetical. I would argue that the alternative hypothesis, that the newly discovered sites represent a stage of established colonization (omitting only the preliminary phase of visiting and exploration), is at least equally difficult to support from the available archaeological evidence. In order to sustain the hypothesis of an early Period 3 colonization, it would be necessary to resort to untestable explanatory devices in order to explain why the material culture in Cyprus is comparable to that on the Levantine mainland only in terms of the tradition of chipped stone working. The hypothesis proposed here is testable. It needs archaeological survey specifically targeted at locating aceramic sites, and one or two more archaeological accidents of the kind that have brought to light sites like Akrotiri-*Aetokremnos*, the shafts at Kissonerga-*Mylouthkia* or the settlement of Parekklisha-*Shillourokambos*. If, after another few

years, neither archaeological survey dedicated to the location of early prehistoric sites nor archaeological accident has brought to light sites earlier than Period 3, this hypothesis can be relegated to the status of a theoretical possibility with no basis in archaeological reality.

It is a fact of human nature that people tend to see what they have an expectation of seeing. People tend not to see things with which they are unfamiliar; things that are not already part of the vocabulary of their visual memory are easily missed. Archaeologists have now been shown new kinds of site, new and earlier archaeological cultures in Cyprus. There is every chance that these will be the catalyst for further discoveries, and already there is the beginning of a trend for yet more early prehistoric sites to be noted in Cyprus. Presumably archaeological surveyors have quickly learned that such sites exist to be found. Cyprus has for a long time been little more than an island curiosity, unconsidered by those working on the story of the Neolithic revolution unfolding on the Asian mainland. The recent early Neolithic discoveries in Cyprus have changed that: it is now clear that our knowledge of settlement, culture and the processes of transformation in this period are seriously deficient, both in Cyprus and on the mainland. These new discoveries and the potential that they indicate for further improvements in our understanding should attract more researchers into the field. And that may mean that we shall not have long to wait before further – and earlier – revelations are uncovered.

Notes

1   This is not the place to discuss the full extent, chronological and spatial, of increasingly complex hunter-gatherer societies. Although there were at least semi-sedentary societies in the upper Palaeolithic in some parts of central Europe, we should concentrate on the landmass closest to Cyprus and the end of the Palaeolithic period and the beginning of the Neolithic.

References

Allen, J., C. Gosden, R. Jones and J. White 1988
        Pleistocene dates for the human occupation of New Ireland, Melanesia. *Nature* 331: 701–709.
Arensburg, B. and I. Hershkovitz 1988
        Nahal Hemar cave: the Neolithic human remains. *Atiqot* 18: 50–58.

Aurenche O., J. Evin and J. Gasco 1987
Une séquence chronologique dans le Proche Orient de 12000 à 3700 BC et sa relation avec les données du radiocarbone. Pp 221–237 in O. Aurenche, M.-C. Cauvin and P. Sanlaville (eds.) *Chronologies du Proche-Orient*. British Archaeological Reports, International Series 379 (i–ii): Oxford

Bar-Yosef, O. 1985
A cave in the Desert : Nahal Hemar. The Israel Museum: Jerusalem.

Bar-Yosef, O. and A. Belfer-Cohen 1989
The Levantine 'PPNB' Interaction Sphere. Pp. 59–72 in I. Hershkovitz (ed.) *People and Culture in Change, Proceedings of the Second Symposium on Upper Paleolithic, Mesolithic and Neolithic Populations of Europe and the Mediterranean Basin*. British Archaeological Reports 508: Oxford.

O. Bar-Yosef and F. Valla (eds.) 1991
The Natufian Culture in the Levant. International Monographs in Prehistory. Archaeological Series 1: Ann Arbor, Michigan.

Binford L. R. 1980
Willow smoke and dogs' tails: hunter-gatherer settlement systems and archeological site information. *American Antiquity* 45: 4–20.

Binford, L. R. 1990
Mobility, housing and environment: a comparative study. *Journal of Anthropological Research* 46: 119–152.

Cauvin, J. 1994
Naissance des divinités, Naissance de l'agriculture: La Révolution des Symboles au Néolithique. CNRS Publications : Paris. Second, revised edition, 1997, published as:–

Cauvin, J. 2000
The Birth of the Gods and the Origins of Agriculture. Cambridge University Press: Cambridge.

Cherry, J. 1981
Pattern and processs in the earliest colonisation of the Mediterranean islands: a review of recent research. *Proceedings of the Prehistoric Society* 47: 41–68.

Cherry, J. 1990
The first colonisation of the Mediterranean islands: a review of recent research. *Journal of Mediterranean Archaeology* 3: 145–221.

Colledge, S. 1998
Identifying pre-domestic cultivation using multivariate analysis. Pp. 121–131 in Damania 1998.

Damania, A. B., J. Valkoun, G. Willcox and C. O. Qualset (eds.) 1998
The Origins of Agriculture and Crop Domestication. ICARDA: Aleppo.

Dyson-Hudson, R. and E. A. Smith 1978
Human territoriality: an ecological assessment *American Anthropologist* 80: 21–41.

Gamble, C. 1993
Timewalkers. Alan Sutton Publishing: Gloucester (hardback), Penguin Books: London (paperback).

Goring-Morris, N. 2002
The quick and the dead: the social context of Aceramic Neolithic mortuary practices as seen from Kfar HaHoresh. Pp. 103–136 in I. Kuijt (ed.) *Life in Neolithic Farming Communities Social Organization, Identity and Differentiation*. Kluwer Academic/Plenum Press: New York.

Goring-Morris N., R. Burns, A. Davidzon, V. Eshed, Y. Goren, I. Hershkovitz, S. Kangas & J. Kelecevic 1998
The 1997 Season of Excavations at the Mortuary Site of Kfar Hahoresh, Galilee Isreal. *Neo-lihtics* 3: 1–4.

Guilaine, J., F. Briois, J.-D. Vigne and I. Carrère 2000
Découverte d'un Néolithique précéramique ancien chypriote (fin 9e, début 8e millénaires cal. BC, apparenté au PPNB ancien/moyen du Levant nord. *Earth and Planetary Sciences* 300: 75–82.

Heun, M., R. Schäfer-Pregl, D. Klawan, R. Castagna, M. Accerbi, B. Borghi and F. Salamini 1997
Site of Einkorn Wheat Domestication Identified by DNA Fingerprinting. *Science* 278: 1312–1314.

Hodder, I. 1986
Reading the Past: current approaches to interpretation in archaeology. Cambridge University Press: Cambridge. (2nd revised edition, 1991).

Kaufman, D. 1989
Observations on the Geometric Kebaran: A View from Neve David. Pp. 275–286 in O. Bar-Yosef and B. Vandermeersch (eds.) *Investigations in South Levantine Prehistory*. British Archaeological Reports, International Series 497: Oxford.

Kelly, R. 1995
The Foraging Spectrum: Diversity in Hunter-Gatherer Lifeways. Smithsonian Institution Press: Washington.

Kislev, M. E., D. Nadel and I. Carmi 1992
Epi-palaeolithic (19,000 BP) cereal and fruit diet at Ohalo II, Sea of Galilee, Israel. *Review of Palaeobotany and Palynology* 71: 161–166.

Lee, R. and I. DeVore, I. (eds.) 1968
Man the Hunter. University of Chicago Press: Chicago.

Lev-Yadun, S., A. Gopher and S. Abbo 2000
The Cradle of Agriculture. *Science* 288: 1602–1603.

Moore, A. M. T. and G. C. Hillman 1992
The Pleistocene to Holocene transition and human economy in Southwest Asia: the impact of the Younger Dryas. *American Antiquity* 57: 482–494.

Moore, A. M. T., G. C. Hillman and A. Legge 2000
Village on the Euphrates. From Foraging to Farming at Abu Hureyra. Oxford University Press: New York and Oxford.

Murdock, G. 1967
The Ethnographic Atlas: A Summary. *Ethnology* 6/2.

Nadel, D. and I. Hershkovitz 1991
New subsistence data and human remains from the earliest Levantine Epipalaeolithic. *Current Anthropology* 32: 631–635.

Nadel, D. and E. Werker 1999
The oldest ever brush hut plant remains from Ohalo II, Jordan Valley, Israel (19000 BP). *Antiquity* 73: 755–764.

Peltenburg, E, S. Colledge, P. Croft, A. Jackson, C. McCartney and Mary Anne Murray 2000
Agro-pastoralist colonization of Cyprus in the 10th millennium BP: Initial Assessments. *Antiquity* 74: 844–853.

Peltenburg, E, S. Colledge, P. Croft, A. Jackson, C. McCartney and Mary Anne Murray 2001
Neolithic dispersals from the Levantine corridor: a Mediterranean perspective. *Levant* 33: 35–64.

Perlès, C. 1987
Les industries lithiques taillés de Franchthi (Argolide, Grèce I: Présentation générale et industries paléolithiques). University of Indiana Press: Bloomington.

Renfrew, C. 1986
Introduction: Peer Polity Interaction and Social Change. Pp. 1–18 in C. Renfrew and J. Cherry (eds.) *Peer Polity Interaction and Social Change.* Cambridge University Press: Cambridge.

Renfrew, C. 1987
Archaeology and Language: the puzzle of Indo-European origins. Jonathan Cape: London.

Renfrew, C. 1994
World Linguistic Diversity. *Scientific American* 270/1: 116–123.

Renfrew, C. 1998
Mind and Matter: Cognitive Archaeology and External Symbolic Storage. Pp. 1–6 in C. Renfrew and C. Scarre (eds.) *Cognition and Material Culture: the Archaeology of Symbolic Storage.* Cambridge University Press: Cambridge.

Sahlins, M. 1972
Stone Age Economics. Aldine: Chicago.

Schmidt, K. 1998
Frühneolitische Tempel. Ein Forschungs bericht zum präkeramischen Neolithikum Obermesopotamiens. *Mitteilungen der Deutschen Orientgesellschaft zu Berlin* 130: 17–49.

Schmidt, K. 2001
Göbekli Tepe, Southeastern Turkey: a preliminary report on the 1995–1999 excavations. *Paléorient* 26/1: 45–54.

Simmons, A. *et al.* 1999
Faunal Extinction in an Island Society: Pygmy Hippopotamus Hunters in Cyprus. Plenum: New York.

Stringer, C. 2000
Coasting out of Africa. *Nature* 405 (4 May 2000): 24–26.

Testart, A. 1982
The significance of food storage among hunter-gatherers: residence patterns, population densities and social inequalities. *Current Anthropology* 23: 523–537.

Vigne, J.-D. 2001

Paper given at a conference on the Cypriot Neolithic, organized by the French School of Archaeology in Athens and the Department of Antiquities, Cyprus, Nicosia, May 2001. See the WWW pages for Parekklisha-*Shillourokambos*, especially the page on herding and domestication, at http://www.france.diplomatie.fr/culture/culture_scientifique/archeologie/chypre/elevage

Watkins, T. 1973
Some problems of the Neolithic and Chalcolithic period in Cyprus. *Report of the Department of Antiquities, Cyprus:* 34–61.

Watkins, T. 1980
The aceramic Neolithic of Cyprus: economic status and cultural origins. *Journal of Mediterranean Anthropology and Archaeology* 1: 139–149.

Watkins, T. 1990
The origins of house and home. *World Archaeology* 21/3: 336–347.

Watkins, T. 1992
The beginning of the Neolithic: searching for meaning in material culture change. *Paléorient* 18/1: 63–75.

Watkins, T. 1999
The human environment. *Paléorient* 23/2: 263–270.

Watkins, T. in press, a
The Neolithic revolution and the emergence of humanity: a cognitive approach to the first comprehensive world-view. In J. Clarke (ed.) *The Transmission and Assimilation of Culture in the Near East.* British Academy Monograph.

Watkins, T. in press, b
Memes, memeplexes and the emergence of religion in the Neolithic. In Hans Georg K. Gebel, Bo Dahl Hermansen and Charlott Hoffmann Jensen (eds.) *Magic Practices and Ritual in the Near Eastern Neolithic,* Vol. 8, Studies of Production, Subsistence and Environment. Ex Oriente : Berlin.

Watkins, T. in press, c
Building houses, constructing worlds of meaning. *Paléorient* forthcoming.

Wickler, S. and M. Spriggs 1988
Pleistocene human occupation of the Solomon Islands, Melanesia. *Antiquity* 62: 703–706.

Willcox, G. 1998
Archaeobotanical evidence for the beginnings of agriculture in southwest Asia. Pp. 25–38 in Damania *et al.* 1998.

Willcox, G. 2000
Présence des céréales dans le Néolithique Précéramique de *Shillourokambos* à Chypre. *Paléorient* 26/1: 129–135.

Wilson, P. J. 1988
The Domestication of the Human Species. Yale University Press: New Haven.

Woodburn, J. 1982
Egalitarian societies. *Man* 17: 431–445.

4

The domestic status of the early Neolithic fauna of Cyprus: a view from the mainland

Liora Kolska Horwitz, Eitan Tchernov and Hitomi Hongo

Abstract

The early Neolithic fauna on Cyprus were introduced by the first human settlers. For many species, this event pre-dates their domestication on the mainland. In the absence of evidence for morphometric change in most Cypriot species, and the equivocal pattern of age, sex and skeletal element representation, it is concluded that these animals were wild rather than culturally managed or domesticated. Analogies from the historic and ethnographic literature document the release of wild animals on islands to serve as food sources ('ethnotramps'). It is also proposed that periodically, fresh stock was brought from the mainland to Cyprus and that at a later point in the Neolithic, this included domestic animal.

Introduction

The Pleistocene fauna of Cyprus, like that of the other Mediterranean Islands, lacked the progenitors of Old World herd animals (sheep, goat, cattle and pig), species which characterise the earliest Neolithic assemblages on the island (Guilaine *et al.* 1998a; 1998b; 2000; Vigne and Buitenhuis 1999; Vigne *et al.* 2000; Peltenburg *et al.* 2000, 2001a; 2001b). The endemic, non-flying Pleistocene fauna of Cyprus comprised a pygmy hippopotamus (*Phanourios minutes*) 2.5 feet high and less than 5 feet long; a pygmy elephant (*Elephas cypriotes*) which stood 3–4 feet high; an endemic species of genet (*Genetta cf. plesictoides*); two species of mice, possibly a shrew and reptiles (tortoise, snake) (Boekschoten and Sondaar 1972; Schwartz 1973; Reese 1989, 1996; 1999; Simmons 1999; 2001; Masseti 1998; Vigne 1999; Hadjisterkotis *et al.* 2000).

Although many of the Pleistocene taxa are thought to have colonized the island by swimming (Boekschoten and Sondaar 1972; Sondaar 1977; Vigne 1999), this concept does not hold for the Neolithic faunal package, whose main elements appear synchronously in several

sites and is linked with the arrival of the first settlers. There is no evidence for a land connection between the island and the mainland at this time. Moreover, the spectrum of immigrant fauna is selective and includes species that are unsuitable candidates for swimming or rafting over the long distance from the Anatolian or Levantine mainland to Cyprus (Davis 1989; Vigne 1999); at its nearest points there are 70 km between the northern-most tip of Cyprus at Cap Andreas to the southern coast of Turkey and 120 km between Cape Andreas and Latakiya, Syria (Karageorghis 1982). Furthermore, there is conclusive evidence from several other Mediterranean islands (Melos, Corsica and possibly Kythnos: Cherry 1990; Masseti 1998) that already in the 9th millennium BC hunter-gatherers had seafaring capabilities. Thus, it is generally accepted that the Neolithic taxa on Cyprus were intentionally transported from the mainland to the island by the first colonists (Poplin 1979; Davis 1984; Groves 1989; Cherry 1990; Schule 1993; Masseti 1998; Vigne 1999, 2001; Cucchi *et al.* 2002).

While the occurrence of animals outside their natural biogeographic range has been posited as indirect evidence of their domestic status (Zeuner 1963; Meadow 1989; Vigne *et al.* 1999), historic and ethnographic data shows that this is not necessarily the case, especially with regard to islands.

Analogies from other island fauna

There are several different ways in which animals may be introduced onto an island by people. The first, termed by Heinsohn (2001) *stowaways* or by Vigne (1999) 'facilitated immigrants', represents unintentional introductions of animals which were stowaways on seagoing vessels. These were usually small-sized animals, often commensals, such as rodents or reptiles, which live in or around human structures. They may be introduced accidentally through shipwrecks or landfalls. The introduction of the house mouse onto Cyprus falls into this category (Cucchi *et al.* 2002).

A second category represents *domesticates*, usually herd animals, that are intentionally or accidentally released on islands as sources of food or labour. An example of unintentional introduction are the pigs on Columbus's flagship the *Santa Maria*, which was wrecked off Haiti. The swine succeeded in swimming ashore, turned feral and became a major source of food during the 16th century on the island (Wing 1989). However, there are numerous examples of taxa such as sheep, goats, cattle, pigs, horses, rabbits and chickens, being intentionally introduced onto islands in the Indian, Atlantic and Pacific Oceans in order to provide fresh food for passing ships and/or food and labour for the colonies which were established on them (Holdgate and Wace 1971; Green 1974; Mueller-Dombois 1981; Reitz 1986; Atkinson 1989; Wing 1989; Ashmole and Ashmole 2000). In many cases animals escaped and turned feral.

Ferals are often described as reverting to the wild type in physical appearance and behaviour. A report on the goats of St. Helena written by Capt. Cavendish, commander of the first English ship to visit the island in 1588, states that although domestic goats had been introduced by the Spanish a mere 75 years earlier in 1513

> *There are on this island [St. Helena] thousands of goats, which the Spaniards call cabritos, which are very wild: you shall see one or two thousand of them together, and sometimes you may behold them going in a flock almost a mile long. Some of them are as big as an ass, with a mane like a horse and a beard hanging down to the very ground. They will climb up the cliffs which are so steep that a man would think it a thing impossible for any living thing to go there. We took and killed many of them for all their swiftness, for there be thousands of them upon the mountains* (Ashmole and Ashmole 2000: 136).

This quote emphasizes the wild-type appearance and behaviour of feral goats as well as the rapidity with which they reproduce in a predator-free environment. Croft (1991: 64) calculated that, following a single release of fallow deer on Cyprus, it would have taken this species only 150 years to colonize the entire island.

A third category of island introductions, and one which is the most relevant to the Cypriot case, is termed by Heinsohn (2001) *ethnotramps*. These represent captive wild animals that are economically and culturally favoured and carried around by people as food, pets, or for trade and ritual purposes. They are introduced onto islands either accidentally (escapees) or deliberately, i.e. animals released in order to provide food on an island, or what Heinsohn calls a 'game park' strategy. Perhaps the earliest evidence of an 'ethnotramp' is the Northern common cuscus (*Phalanger orientalis*), a marsupial which was introduced into New Ireland as early as 20,000 BP (Heinsohn 2001). Other examples given by him of Wallacian 'ethnotramps' include Javan Rusa deer (*Cervus timorensis*), a variety of cuscus (*Phalanger* sp.) and civet (*Viverricula* sp.) species, Indonesian wild pig (*Sus scrofa vittatus*), pademelons (*Thylogale* sp.) and cassowaries (*Casuarius* sp.). Examples from other regions include the central American red agouti (*Dasyprocta punctata*) which was introduced as a food source from the mainland to islands throughout the Lesser Antilles and as far west as the Virgin Islands (Morgan 1994), while the snow hare (*Lepus timidus*) was released in 1855 on the Faeroes islands for hunting (Bloch 1982). It is clear then that 'ethnotramps' vary enormously in the range of taxa used, their body size, behaviour, physiology, diet and ease of transportability.

Ethnotramps may also be passed from island to island. For example, Amerindians introduced a large rodent, *Isolobodon portoricensis*, which was endemic to the Caribbean island of Hispaniola, onto the Virgin Islands (Morgan and Woods 1986), while a cavy-like rodent called Desmarest's hutia (*Capromys pilorides*), was transported from Cuba to the island of Hispaniola to serve as a food source (Wing 1989).

An archaeological case study of 'ethnotramps' from the Jomon period, Japan

An excellent analogy to early Neolithic Cyprus, may be found in the Japanese archaeological record. Despite claims for the possible presence of 'domestic' pigs in the Jomon period, 12,000–300 BC, in Japan (e.g. Nishimoto 2001), it is generally accepted that there were no domestic pigs in this period. At this time, young pigs are often found in ritual contexts, which suggest that this taxon was treated differently from others such as deer, another common game animal of Jomon hunters (Kato 1980; Ono 1984). Remains of *Sus* are also frequently found in Jomon sites located on islands around mainland Japan, which are outside the natural biogeographic range of wild pigs, suggesting a special relationship with people (Kato 1980; Ono 1984).

On the large island of Hokkaido in northern Japan *Sus* remains are known from the late Jomon period (4,500 BP). On Izu islands, a series of islands scattered off Izu Peninsula south of Tokyo, remains of *Sus* are found from the middle of the early Jomon (6,000 BP) and continue throughout the Jomon period. Yamazaki (2001) showed that boar from Jomon sites in Hokkaido are generally larger than modern wild boar in central Japan. Boars found on Izu Islands are on the whole smaller (Yamazaki 2001).

The results of mitochondrial aDNA analysis of *Sus* remains from late Jomon (4–3,000 BP) and Epi-Jomon (2,300–1,300 BP) sites on the island of Hokkaido as well as from sites on the Izu islands, suggest that boar were brought there from Honshu Island, the main island of Japan (Ishiguro and Yamazaki 2001; Ishiguro pers.

com.). Although the minimum distance between northern Honshu and Hokkaido is less than 20 km, there is a break between the two islands in the biogeography of fauna and flora – Blakiston's Line. Among the Izu islands, the closest island is 20 km offshore from the Izu Peninsula. It is likely that *Sus* were transported to the islands together with other trade items. The question of whether Jomon hunters actually kept animals in their villages ('cultural management') or just transported wild boar they had captured to the islands, remains as yet an open issue. However, there is no evidence to indicate that these pigs were domestic.

The Cypriot record

Species representation

Based on the currently available data, it appears that the first animal introduced by humans into Cyprus may have been the pig (Vigne *et al.* 2000). At the site of Akrotiri, Reese (1999: Table 7–7) and Simmons (2001) report the presence of 9 pig bones in stratum 2 (upper and lower phases) as well as 5 bones in stratum 4B. There are also 4 contentious fallow deer bones which were recovered from stratum 1–2 (1 bone), stratum 2 (2 bones), and another single find from stratum 3. As noted by Reese (1996: 167 n. 1), the identification of these items as fallow deer is not accepted by two other researchers, F. Poplin and J.-D. Vigne (Vigne and Buitenhuis 1999), who have identified them as pig[1]. In the case of the suspected fallow deer remains, all finds were of 1st and 3rd phalanges while of the 14 pig bones identified, 9 were phalanges, 4 metapodials and 1 a tooth. This has led Reese (1996; 1999) to suggest that we may be dealing with remains of a skin and not a live animal. However, they may as easily represent food debris. The pig bones have not been directly dated, but absolute dates for the levels in which they were found gave an average calibrated date of 10,529 BP (Simmons 2001). If the data from the site of Akrotiri are accepted as being *in situ*, then this site represents the earliest human occupation on Cyprus. It then follows that the pig was the earliest introduced species to the island.

Archaeozoological reports are available for the sites of *Shillourokambos* and *Mylouthkia* whose

Period (BC)	Site	First appearance of Taxa
Pleistocene	Various sites	pygmy hippopotamus, pygmy elephant, genet, mouse
10th mil.	Akrotiri	pig
late 9th mil.	*Shillourokambos*	
	Early Phase A	sheep, goat, fallow deer, pig, cattle
	Mylouthkia IA	house mouse
mid 8th mil.	*Shillourokambos*	
	Early Phase B	dog, fox
late 8th mil.	*Shillourokambos*	
	Mid Phase B	cat

Table 4.1 *Table listing the first appearance of taxa in Cypriot sites*

earliest levels date to the early and mid-PPNB, 9,400–9,000 BP uncalibrated (Vigne and Buitenhuis 1999; Peltenburg *et al.* 2000; 2001a; 2001b; Vigne *et al.* 2000; Guilaine and Briois 2001; Vigne 2001; Cucchi *et al.* 2002). These data show that the main complex of Neolithic fauna was present on Cyprus some 1,000 years after the Akrotiri finds. In the earliest Neolithic occupation levels from the site of *Shillourokambos* (Early Phase A) a wide spectrum of new taxa is found comprising morphologically wild-type sheep, goat, cattle and Persian fallow deer. Remains of pig predominate (Vigne *et al.* 2000). The roughly contemporaneous Well 116 at the site of *Mylouthkia*, yielded remains of pig and goat as well as the first remains of domestic mouse (Peltenburg *et al.* 2000; 2001a; 2001b; Cucchi *et al.* 2002).

Cattle bones are found in three Cypriot sites – in the earliest levels at *Shillourokambos* (Vigne and Buitenhuis 1999; Vigne 2001; Vigne *et al.* 2000) and *Ais Yorkis* (Simmons 1998), both located in the southern part of Cyprus close to the coast, as well as in the site of Akanthou (*Tatlısu*) in northern Cyprus. This site is also located adjacent to the coast (Sevketoglu 2000). Thus cattle remains are only found in lowland sites and not in the mountains which would have been heavily wooded in the Neolithic period. It is the only species to disappear during the Aceramic Neolithic soon after its initial introduction. *Bos* is absent on Cyprus throughout the remaining Aceramic Neolithic and Chalcolithic and is re-introduced as a domestic species only in the Bronze Age (Croft 1991; 1996; Simmons 1998; Vigne *et al.* 2000).

Remains of the red fox and domestic dog first appear in *Shillourokambos* in the next phase (Early Phase B) dating to 9,000–8,500 BP uncalibrated. In the same site, but from a slightly later occupational phase, (Middle Phase B) dated to *ca.* 8500 BP uncalibrated, cat is added to the faunal repertoire (Guilaine *et al.* 2000; Vigne and Buitenhuis 1999; Vigne 2001; Vigne *et al.* 2000).

By the Late Phase at *Shillourokambos* (8,300–8,000 BP uncalibrated) and the equivalent deposits at *Mylouthkia*, all species which comprise the Cypriot Neolithic package are found on the island; sheep, goat, pig, cattle, fallow deer, cat, dog, fox and mouse.

A much more recent phase of faunal introductions accompanies the Bronze Age with the advent of equids, mustelids and domestic cattle (Croft 1991; 1996; Vigne 1999), while in the last 1000 years the presence of hare, rat, long-eared hedgehog and the spiny mouse has been documented (Vigne 1999).

As illustrated in Table 4.1, the timing of the faunal introductions onto Cyprus appears to have been staggered and attests to at least five separate introduction events. These colonization episodes document that contact between the mainland and island was maintained. Furthermore, in order to maintain viable herds as a source of meat, a constant influx of fresh stock from the mainland would have been required, at least in the initial period of colonization. If not, then the initial founder herds would have been rapidly decimated before they could reproduce themselves sufficiently to establish a viable herd. Using a computer simulation based on survivorship rates of modern, free-living Cretan goats, Ducos (2000) calculated the time required to establish a long-term caprine herd on a predator-free island like Cyprus. Given a founder herd of 10 animals, comprising an equal number of males and females, a fecundity rate of 0.9 and with a 70% immature male cull, at least 25 years would have been required to establish a viable herd which could have sustained itself while being culled at a rate of 50 animals per year, i.e. less than one animal per week. Whether the new animals were brought over intentionally to stock the island or represented leftover provisions from the sea journey is outside the scope of this paper. What is important is that in the long term, together with several agricultural crops, they facilitated the establishment and development of an insular culture on Cyprus.

A summary of the faunal census taken from Atkinson (1989) on the presence of fauna on islands in the Atlantic, Indian and Pacific Oceans is given in Table 4.2. Although this gazetteer does not take into account when the species were introduced, their relative abundance on the islands or if they still exist today, it does provide a general picture of which species were favoured by island colonizers. From this summary it is clear that of the domestic herd animals, pigs followed by goats were favoured for historic colonization of islands in the Indian and Pacific Oceans, while sheep and goats (equally) followed by pigs were favoured for introduction onto Atlantic Ocean islands (Table 4.2). Crabtree (1989) has cited several features which make pigs particularly amenable to being kept by primary colonists: they are omnivorous and recycle waste, have a high reproductive turnover, fast growth rate and provide a large quantity of high quality protein. It is not surprising then that the earliest evidence for an introduced species on Cyprus (in Akrotiri) is the pig (Reese 1996; 1999).

Simmons (1998) notes that wild cattle would have been behaviourally unsuited for the sea voyage to Cyprus, but gives no data to substantiate this claim. Cattle are relatively rare on all islands and were introduced onto only 23–30% of islands studied by Atkinson (1989). This may explain why cattle became extinct on Cyprus – not enough fresh stock was brought over from the mainland to replenish and maintain the founder herd. Deer are equally rare on islands

Oceans	Atlantic	Indian	Pacific
No. Islands	27	35	68
Species	%	%	%
Goat	48	43	40
Sheep	48	23	19
Pig	30	48	51
Cattle	30	23	23
Deer	11	23	15
Cat	74	57	43
Fox/Mongoose	7	11	15
Dog	30	28.5	44
Mouse	67	43	41

Table 4.2 *The occurrence of species on oceanic islands (frequencies of presence) (Data taken from Atkinson 1989: Appendix 70–75)*

(Table 4.2) while, of the non-food taxa, the house mouse and cat are the most frequently encountered (Table 4.2). Remains of cat and mouse are both found in the early occupation levels at *Mylouthkia* and *Shillourokambos*. Deer are one of the least common taxa introduced onto islands (Table 4.2), but on Cyprus fallow deer quickly dominated the archaeozoological record and continued to be the chief meat source in most sites until the late Chalcolithic (Legge 1982; Croft 1991; Flourentzos 1997; Vigne and Buitenhuis 1999; Peltenburg *et al.* 2000; 2001a; 2001b; Vigne *et al.* 2000; Vigne 2001).

Size, shape and demography

Based on the study of osteological remains, several diagnostic features have been used to determine the domestic status of an animal (e.g. Zeuner 1963; Meadow 1989; Vigne *et al.* 1999). These include reduction in body size and changes in body proportions, bone density and horn form which are associated with changing selective pressures and activity patterns under new environmental conditions (Zohary *et al.* 1998). In addition, there is a shift in the age and sex ratio of animals being culled, usually with a strong selection for immature males (Zeder and Hesse 2000).

In the early levels at *Shillourokambos* the goats and sheep are large and robust. Indeed, the

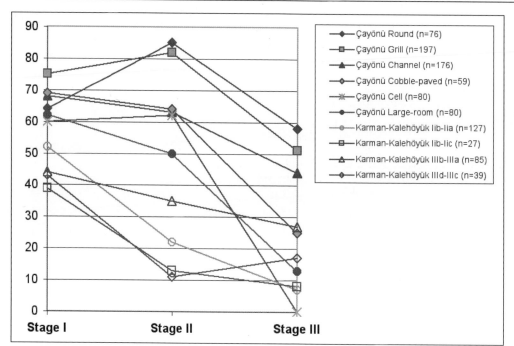

Figure 4.1
*Survivorship
curves for pig
based on
epiphyseal
fusion from
Çayönü and
Kaman-
Kalehöyük*

Legend:
- Çayönü Round (n=76)
- Çayönü Grill (n=197)
- Çayönü Channel (n=176)
- Çayönü Cobble-paved (n=59)
- Çayönü Cell (n=80)
- Çayönü Large-room (n=80)
- Karman-Kalehöyük IIb-IIa (n=127)
- Karman-Kalehöyük IIb-IIc (n=27)
- Karman-Kalehöyük IIIb-IIIa (n=85)
- Karman-Kalehöyük IIId-IIIc (n=39)

X-axis: Stage I, Stage II, Stage III

goats, sheep and fallow deer are the same size as those recovered from the later Aceramic site of Khirokitia as well as PPNB sites in the Near East (Davis 1984; 1989; 1994; Vigne *et al.* 2000; Vigne 2001). The goats from the Late Neolithic site of Vrysi (Legge 1982) are similarly large and of the same size as those from Khirokitia as well as the Aceramic Neolithic levels at Tell Abu Hureyra on the continent, indicating that no shift in size had occurred in this taxon for more than 3000 years. Similarly, horn morphology in both sheep and goats from *Shillourokambos* resembles that of wild animals (Vigne *et al.* 2000). For both sheep and goats there is evidence for selective culling focusing on young animals (aged on the basis of tooth wear as 1–2 years). There are few old animals in the sample and a bias for ewes. In contrast, for fallow deer, mainly adult animals are represented in Early Phase B at *Shillourokambos*. This changes in the later phase when mortality patterns are random and no clear trend is evident. The sex ratio for fallow deer in both phases at this site is 50:50. Based on the age and sex breakdowns it was concluded that the caprines represent managed animals while the fallow deer were hunted (Guilaine *et al.* 2000; Vigne 2001).

In contrast to the caprines and deer, pigs in the early Cypriot Neolithic sites are smaller than those from the Northern Levant, but correspond well with those of pigs from other Preceramic and Aceramic assemblages on Cyprus (Davis 1984; 1989; Vigne and Buitenhuis 1999). This, as well as the age profile which indicates selective culling of immature pigs, has led researchers (Vigne *et al.* 2000; Vigne 2001) to raise the possibility that they represent domestic animals. However, Ducos (2000) has shown that they are of similar size to pigs from some mid-PPNB southern Levantine sites. As such the size of the Cypriot pigs may be related to the size of animals in their population of origin or the selection of smaller animals for sea transport (Vigne *et al.* 2000) rather than to their being domestic. This later point should theoretically have affected all species equally, but this was not the case. The faster reproduction rate of pigs and hence shorter generation time could enable them to undergo rapid size change while the other herd animals remained unchanged.

Rosenberg *et al.* (1998) have claimed evidence for domestic pigs from as early as the late Natufian/early PPNA in the mainland site of Hallan Çemi (Turkey). These data are, however, contentious and are hotly disputed by archaeozoologists (e.g. Peters *et al.* 1999). The longest and best-documented record relating to the earliest stages of pig domestication in the Pre-Pottery Neolithic is found at the site of Çayönü located in the upper Tigris (Hongo and

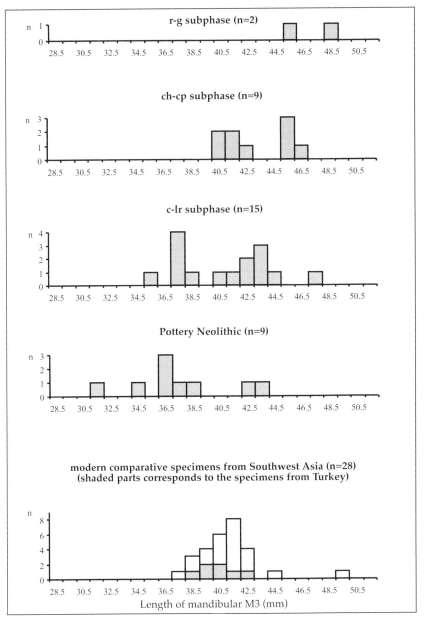

Figure 4.2 *Length of the M3 of Sus from Çayönü and recent comparative specimens (modified from Ervynck et al. 2002: Figure 13)*

Meadow 1998, 2000; Ervynck *et al.* 2002; Hongo *et al.* 2002). The sequence at Çayönü covers 3,000 years (10,200–7,500 BP uncalibrated), from the PPNA through to the Final PPNB and PN.

Epiphyseal fusion data shows that in the later phases at the site, fewer pigs survived into adulthood (Hongo and Meadow 1998; 2000; Hongo *et al.* 2002). This trend accelerates through time, especially in the mid-PPNB (Cobble-paved phase), Late PPNB (Cell phase) and Final PPNB (Large-room phase). As illustrated in Figure 4.1, during these phases of the PPNB, major kill-off took place between the subadult and adult stage (Hongo *et al.* 2002). Kill-off schedule of a fully

domestic population in the 2nd and 1st millennium BC from the site of Kaman-Kalehöyük in Central Anatolia, shows a very different slaughter pattern from that observed at Çayönü (Figure 4.1). At Çayönü, only in the later phases does the survival rate of pigs into adulthood more closely resemble that of a domestic population.

Size change of pigs at Çayönü was examined with reference to the length of the mandibular third molar (M3). These data suggest that smaller teeth appear in the later phases, although as illustrated in Figure 4.2, the majority of teeth still fall within the range of modern wild boar from the Near East.

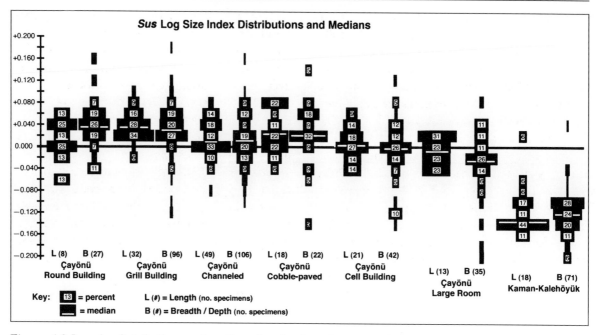

Figure 4.3 *Log size distributions and medians for pigs from Çayönü and Kaman-Kalehöyük*

The log size index distribution of post-cranial bone measurements shows a gradual change over time (Figure 4.3). Modern female wild pig from Turkey was used as the standard (see Hongo and Meadow 2000: Table 8 for standard measurements). There is a small, overall shift towards more gracile animals throughout the PPN. Although some smaller specimens exist as early as the Grill phase (9,200–9,100 BP; 8,300–8,100 cal BC), a small reduction in size, indicated by smaller median values, is observed only by the Late PPNB (Cell phase), and especially in the Final PPNB (Large-room phase). No major size diminution is observed in the Early PPNB, early mid-PPNB Channel Building phase (9,100–9,000 BP; 8,200–7,900 cal BC) which corresponds to the earliest phases at *Shillourokambos*. It is only in the Final PPNB, that the range of the size distribution becomes comparable to that of a domestic population, although most of the pigs are still larger than the domestic pigs from the site of Kaman-Kalehöyük. The shift in size is more visible in the breadth/depth measurements suggesting that animals were more gracile but not necessarily shorter.

The size index distributions as well as kill-off pattern in pigs from the later phases (Cell and Large-room phases) at Çayönü are comparable to

those from the site of Gürcütepe II, a roughly contemporaneous (Late–Final PPNB) site apparently with domestic pigs (Hauptmann 1999; Peters *et al.* 1999: Fig. 10; von den Driesch and Peters 1999). The changes through time observed at Çayönü are extremely subtle and cannot be readily considered as the results of domestication. Hongo and Meadow (1998) have tentatively suggested that while some pigs were being kept and reared within the community as early as 9,000 BP, most were managed in such a way that the breeding stock was not isolated from the wild population.

A parallel to the Çayönü situation may be found in an 8th century historical text from Japan which documents the 'loose' management of pigs. The text notes that pigs were brought to southwestern Japan in the early 5th century, though it is not clear in this document whether the pigs described were captured wild boar or domestic stock. In fact, in the ancient texts, the Japanese word 'boar' was often used to refer to both wild and domestic stock.

Upon request, land was given to the owner of the pigs and these animals were then released into the fields. Although a specialized pig-keeping caste managed the pigs and there was defined, private ownership of the pigs (Ikata 1945; Kamo 1976), it is unlikely that the pigs were penned and they were probably left to freely interbreed with wild boar who were abundant in the area. Referring to another 8th century text which documents the release of 40 pigs in the mountains, Ikata (1945: 480) suggests that "the domestic and wild pigs at that time were probably not so different from each other, and the domestic stock could readily return to the wild if they were released".

Pigs at Çayönü show a general trend towards smaller size and earlier slaughter schedule, which continues throughout the PPN. However, it is only in the Final PPNB that some of the Çayönü pigs show unequivocal characteristics of fully domestic animals. It is also apparent that active hunting of morphometrically wild boar continued at the site through the PPN. The Çayönü data then corroborate the wild status of pigs on the Near Eastern mainland in the early to early Mid-PPNB, a time span which is equivalent to the early occupation phases at *Shillourokambos* and *Mylouthkia*.

It may be concluded that in the initial Neolithic assemblages on Cyprus the animals conform in size and shape to the wild type, with the possible exception of pig. Vigne *et al.* (2000) suggest that this may be the result of the short amount of time which had elapsed since their arrival on the island and that more time was needed for size diminution to take place in these relatively slow reproducing species. However, if, as has been proposed (Guilaine *et al.* 2000; Vigne *et al.* 2000; Vigne 2001), these animals were already domestic or under some form of cultural management ('pre-domestication') on the mainland, some degree of morphometric change is expected to have occurred even before they arrived on Cyprus. Rates of morphometric change under modern methods of artificial selection are rapid, e.g. 30 years in cattle breeds (Hammond 1960). Although the pace of change may be slower in the absence of human intervention, such as in isolated founder populations experiencing new selective pressures, changes in body size and shape are still expected to occur quite rapidly and to be visible in the archaeological record where distinctions of less than 100 years are rarely perceived.

The absence of size reduction in the Cypriot fauna may also be related to the fact that at this time on the Near Eastern mainland, domestication of sheep and goat was in its infancy and had

perhaps not yet occurred for cattle or pig (Bar-Yosef and Meadow 1995; Peters *et al.* 1999; Hongo *et al.* 2002). The earliest evidence for domestic sheep is contemporaneous with or even slightly earlier than the Cypriot record, i.e. late PPNA/early PPNB, while goat may have been domesticated in the early PPNB. The earliest evidence for domestic cattle is later and dates to the mid-PPNB (Peters *et al.* 1999).

It should be noted that the onset of domestication in different species on the mainland was not synchronic, nor are the earliest domestic animals found together in the same assemblage, despite the fact that they inhabited the same region in the wild (Uerpmann 1987). Domestic animals are first found in inland sites located in the Euphrates Valley and Southeast Anatolia. As such, they are not situated in the same geographic region. Moreover, none of these sites is located on the Levantine or Cilician coasts, the areas closest to Cyprus.

The domestication of herd animals on the mainland appears to have been diachronically and geographically heterogeneous. It is extremely unlikely that the initial faunal package that arrived on Cyprus was comprised of animals from a variety of different Near Eastern regions as well as those of different status: wild (fallow deer), pre-domestic (sheep and goats and possibly cattle) and domestic (pig). Yet, on Cyprus we find this entire faunal package in the same sites from the very inception of the Neolithic occupation of the island.

With respect to the age and sex profiles, the Cypriot data are limited in scope as they are based on data from only one site, *Shillourokambos*. They may as easily be attributed to selective hunting, such as for tender meat, as to domestication, since caprines and pigs aged less than 2 years were specifically targeted. It may also reflect seasonal hunting with selection of the easier prey classes (fawns and ewes) since the adult male caprines were probably too agile to be caught/hunted and probably inhabited the higher elevations on the island.

Bodypart representation
The presence of all skeletal elements in an assemblage usually indicates on-site slaughter or access to complete carcasses. Currently, data on body parts for the Cypriot early Neolithic is

limited to *Shillourokambos* (Vigne *et al.* 2000). At this site there is evidence for bodypart selection in fallow deer with few axial skeletal elements represented for this species. This pattern was interpreted as representing animals which had been hunted in distant localities with only the meat-rich limb parts being brought back to the site. There were no other statistically significant differences between taxa in the representation of other skeletal elements. Sheep, goat and pig are represented by a more even distribution of bodyparts, which Vigne *et al.* (2000) have interpreted as evidence of on-site slaughter and hence support for the domestic status of these species. However, this pattern does not account for the presence in the assemblage of other skeletal elements of fallow deer which are even poorer in meat, such as the cranium (excluding the brain) or limb extremities (metapodia and phalanges), and their similar frequency to that found for pigs and caprines (Vigne *et al.* 2000). Size differences between prey animals determines which skeletal parts a hunter will leave at the kill site and which will be brought back to the living site (Lyman 1994). Given the considerable size differences between adult fallow deer and sheep, goat or pig, this factor offers an equally feasible explanation for the patterning found on Cyprus.

Conclusions

It is clear that the early Neolithic Cypriot fauna were introduced onto the island by people. However, their domestic status is questionable as:

1. The earliest introduced animals comprise species for which there is no evidence for their domestication on the mainland at this time (cattle and pig). It also includes species that were never domesticated (fallow deer, red fox). Indeed, fallow deer was the dominant meat animal in most Cypriot assemblages until the early Chalcolithic when domestic caprines replaced them (Croft 1991; Flourentzos 1997).
2. The colonising fauna arrived synchronously and are found in the same sites as a package. However, on the mainland these species are found together in the wild (northern Levant), but were not domesticated in the same geographic region, nor at the same time.
3. The Cypriot fauna are morphometrically indistinguishable from wild animals. The diminution observed in pig may be explained by factors other than domestication.
4. Their age and sex ratios as well as body part representation may as easily be interpreted as due to intentional selection during hunting and butchery as to domestication.

Archaeozoologists have argued (Guilaine *et al.* 2000; Vigne *et al.* 2000; 2001) that the Cypriot pigs were domestic animals while the caprines and cattle represent a state of pre-domestic husbandry where they remain unmodified morphologically but show signs of selective culling by age and sex as well as body part selection. Based on the faunal evidence explored in this paper, it is concluded that there is little unequivocal evidence for the domestic status of any of the Cypriot taxa at the time of their introduction to Cyprus. It is argued here, in much the same vein as by Ducos (2000), that although these animals were captured, transported on a seagoing vessel and then introduced into a new environment, they were brought to the island in a wild state. There are enough ethnographic, historical and archaeological sources to illustrate that this is not an isolated occurrence and that wild animals ('ethnotramps') have commonly been released onto islands in order to serve as a protein source. Perhaps these wild animals were initially intended as a stock of fresh food for the passage to Cyprus, but upon landfall they were either deliberately released to be exploited as a future food resource on an island which may have lacked animal resources, as has been suggested by Croft (1991) with regard to fallow deer, or else accidentally escaped.

It is further proposed here that multiple colonizing events of Cyprus took place during the Neolithic, because new species appear sequentially in the archaeozoological record of the island. There are also no indications for size change in sheep, goats or fallow deer until much later in the Cypriot record (Legge 1982; Davis 1984; 1989; 1994; Croft 1991; 1996). Multiple colonizing events/visits brought fresh stock to the island and ensured herd growth and survival as well as mediated against the fixing of new traits such as size diminution or changes in horn morphology in the slower reproducing species (sheep, goat, cattle). In contrast, pigs being faster reproducers, and possibly also the earliest colonizers, may have undergone some degree of size reduction despite the input of fresh stock. It should be noted that size reduction naturally occurs in medium and large sized mammals on islands due to changes in selective pressures (Sondaar 1977). Thus, the observed size reduction in pigs may be the outcome of natural processes and not necessarily domestication.

It is unlikely that the wild stock introduced to Cyprus underwent local, autochthonous domestication. This is substantiated by the disappearance of cattle which later re-appears on the island as a domestic form, introduced from the mainland. It is more feasible that the wild, founder-stock inter-bred with domestic animals which were brought from the mainland at a later date in order to replenish stock. The descendants of the first colonizing taxa are then the feral caprines found on many of the Mediterranean islands today (Masseti 1998; Kahila Bar-Gal *et al.* 2001), that have probably undergone extensive inbreeding with local domestic stock over time.

Notes

1   Due to the ongoing debate concerning the identity of the contentious 'fallow deer' bones, it seems most prudent at this stage to leave them out of this discussion. There is however no doubt as to the presence of pig in the site.

References

Ashmole, P. and M. Ashmole 2000
   St Helena and Ascension Island: A Natural History. Anthony Nelson: London.

Atkinson, I. 1989
   Introduced animals and extinctions. Pp. 54–75 in D. Western and M. C. Pearl (eds.) *Conservation for the Twenty-First Century.* Oxford University Press: Oxford.

Bar-Yosef, O. and R. Meadow 1995
   The origins of agriculture in the Near East. Pp. 39–111 in D. T. Price, and A. B. Gebauer (eds.) *Last Hunters, First Farmers: New Perspectives on the Prehistoric Transitions to Agriculture.* School of American Research Press: New Mexico.

Bloch, D. 1982
   Animal Life on the Faeroe Islands. Pp. 53–68 in G. K. Rutherford (ed.) *The Physical Environment of the Faeroe Islands.* Dr. W. Junk: The Hague.

Boekschoten, G. J. and P. Y. Sondaar 1972.
   On the fossil mammalia of Cyprus. *Proceedings of the Koninklijke Nederlandse Akademie van Wetenschappen–Amsterdam, Series B* 75 (4): 306–338.

Cherry, J. F. 1990
   The first colonization of the Mediterranean islands: a review of recent research. *Journal of Mediterranean Archaeology* 3(2): 145–221.

Crabtree, P. J. 1989
   Sheep, horses, swine and kine: A zooarchaeological perspective on the Anglo-Saxon settlement of England. *Journal of Field Archaeology* 16: 205–213.

Croft, P. 1991
   Man and beast in Chalcolithic Cyprus. *Bulletin of the American Schools of Oriental Research* 282/283: 63–79.

Croft, P. 1996
   Animal remains. Pp. 217–223 in D. Frankel and J. M. Webb (eds.) *Marki Alonia An Early and Middle Bronze Age Town in Cyprus. Excavations 1990–1994.* Studies in Mediterranean Archaeology 123:1. Paul Åströms Förlag: Jonsered.

Cucchi, T., J.-D. Vigne, J.-C. Auffray, P. Croft and E. Peltenburg 2002
   Introduction involontaire de la souris domestique (*Mus musculus domesticus*) à Chypre dès le Néolithique précéramique ancien (fin IXe et VIIIe millénaires av. J.-C.). *Compte Rendu du Palevolution* 1 : 235–241.

Davis, S. J. M. 1984
   Khirokitia and its mammal remains. A Neolithic Noah's ark. Pp. 147–162 in A. Le Brun (ed.) *Fouilles récentes à Khirokitia (Chypre) 1977–1981.* ADPF: Paris.

Davis, S. J. M. 1989
   Some more animal remains from the aceramic Neolithic of Cyprus. Pp. 189–221 in A. Le Brun (ed.) *Fouilles récentes à Khirokitia (Chypre) 1983–1986.* ADPF: Paris.

Davis, S. J. M. 1994
   Even more bones from Khirokitia: the 1988–1991 excavations. Pp. 305–333 in A. Le Brun (ed.) *Fouilles récentes à Khirokitia (Chypre) 1988–1991.* ADPF: Paris.

Ducos, P. 2000
   The introduction of animals by man in Cyprus: An alternative to the Noah's ark model. Pp. 74–82 in Mashkour *et al.* 2000.

Driesch, von den A. and J. Peters 1999
   Vorlaufiger bericht uber die archäozoologischen untersuchungen am Gürcütepe und am Göbekli bei Urfa, Türkei. *Istanbuler Mitteilungen* 49: 23–39.

Ervynck, A., K. Dobney, H. Hongo and R. H. Meadow 2002
   Born Free? New evidence for the status of *Sus scrofa* at Neolithic Çayönü Tepesi (Southeastern Anatolia, Turkey). *Paléorient* 27(2): 47–73.

Flourentzos, P. 1997

Excavations at the Neolithic site of Paralimni, A preliminary report. *Report of the Department of Antiquities, Cyprus:* 1–10.

Groves, C. P. 1989
Feral mammals of the Mediterranean islands: documents of early domestication. Pp. 46–58 in J. Clutton-Brock (ed.) *The Walking Larder: Patterns of Domestication, Pastoralism and Predation.* Unwin Hyman: London.

Guilaine, J. and F. Brios 2001
Parekklisha *Shillourokambos*: an early Neolithic site in Cyprus. Pp. 37–53 in Swiny 2001.

Guilaine, J., F. Briois, J. Coularou, P. Devèze, S. Philibert, J.-D. Vigne and I. Carrère 1998a
La site néolithique précéramique de *Shillourokambos* (Parekkisha, Chypre). *Bulletin de Correspondance Hellénique* 122 : 603–610.

Guilaine, J., F. Briois, J. Coularou, J-D. Vigne and I. Carrère 1998b
Les débuts du Néolithique à Chypre. *L`Archéologue* 33 : 35–40.

Guilaine, J., F. Briois, J.-D. Vigne and I. Carrère 2000
Découverte d'un Néolithique précéramique ancien chypriote (fin 9e, début 8e millénaires cal. BC), apparenté au PPNB ancien/moyen du Levant Nord. *Compte Rendu de l'Academie Scientifique de Paris. Earth and Planetary Sciences* 300: 75–82.

Green, R. H. 1974
Mammals. Pp. 367–396 in W.D. Williams (ed.) *Biogeography and Ecology in Tasmania.* Dr. W. Junk: The Hague.

Hadjisterkotis, E., B. Masala and D. S. Reese 2000
The origin and extinction of the large endemic Pleistocene mammals of Cyprus. *Biogeographia* 21: 593–606.

Hammond, J. 1960
Farm Animals. Their Breeding, Growth and Inheritance. 3rd edition. Edward Arnold: London.

Hauptmann, H. 1999
The Urfa region. Pp. 65–86 in M. Özdogan and N. Basgelen (eds.) *Neolithic in Turkey: The Cradle of Civilization.* Arkeoloji ve Sanat Yayınları: Istanbul.

Heinsohn, T. E. 2001
Human influence on vertebrate zoogeography: animal translocation and biological invasions across and to the east of Wallace's Line. Pp. 154–170 in I. Metcalfe, J. M. B. Smith, M. Morwood and I. Davidson (eds.) *Faunal and Floral Migrations and Evolution in SE Asia-Australasia.* A.A. Balkema Publishers: Lisse.

Holdgate, M. W. and N. M. Wace 1971
The influence of man on the floras and faunas of southern islands. Pp. 476–492 in T. R. Detwyler (ed.) *Man's Impact on Environment.* McGraw Hill: New York.

Hongo, H. and R. H. Meadow 1998
Pig exploitation at Neolithic Çayönü Tepesi (Southeastern Anatolia). Pp. 77–98 in S. M. Nelson (ed.) *Ancestors for the Pigs: Pigs in Prehistory.*

MASCA Research Papers in Science and Archaeology 15. University of Pennsylvania Museum: Philadelphia.

Hongo, H. and R. H. Meadow 2000
Faunal remains from Prepottery Neolithic levels at Çayönü, Southeastern Turkey: A preliminary report focusing on pigs (*Sus* sp.). Pp. 121–140 in Mashkour *et al.* 2000.

Hongo, H., R.H., Meadow B. Öksüz, B. and G. Ilgezdi 2002
The process of ungulate domestication in Prepottery Neolithic Çayönü, Southeastern Turkey. Pp. 153–165 in H. Buitenhuis, A. M. Choyke, M. Mashkour and A. H. Al-shiyab (eds.) *Archaeology of the Near East V.* ARC-Publicaties 62: Groningen.

Ikata, S. 1945
Nihon Kodai Kachiku-shi (History of Domestic Animals in Ancient Japan). Kawade-shobo: Tokyo (in Japanese).

Ishiguro, N. and K. Yamazaki 2001
Izu shoto oyobi Hokkaido shutsudo Jomon inoshishi ni tsuiteno DNA bunseki kekka (Results of DNA analysis of boar remains from Izu Islands and Hokkaido). Pp. 54–55 *Report of the Grant-in Aid Scientific Research (B) Basic Research of Boar in Islands during the Jomon Period.* (in Japanese).

Kahila Bar-Gal, G., P. Smith, E. Tchernov, C. Greenblatt, P. Ducos, A. Gardesein and L. K. Horwitz 2002
Genetic evidence for the origin of the Agrimi goat (*Capra aegagrus cretica*). *Journal of Zoology, London* 256: 369–377.

Kamo, G. 1976
Nihon Chikusan-shi (History of Stock Raising in Japan). Hosei University Press: Tokyo (in Japanese).

Kato, S. 1980
Jomon-jin no dobutu shiiku-tokuni inoshishi no mondai ni tsuite (Animal keeping by Jomon people especially on the issue of wild boar). *Rekishi Koron* 54: 45–50 (in Japanese).

Karageorghis, V. 1982
Cyprus. Thames and Hudson: London.

Legge, A. J. 1982
The vertebrate fauna. Pp. 76–81 in E. J. Peltenburg (ed.) *Vrysi A Subterranean Settlement in Cyprus.* Aris and Phillips: Warminister.

Lyman, R. Lee 1994
Vertebrate Taphonomy. Cambridge University Press: Cambridge.

Mashkour, M., A. M. Choyke, H. Buitenhuis and F. Poplin (eds.) 2000
Archaeozoology of the Near East IV. ARC-Publicaties 32: Groningen.

Masseti, M. 1998
Holocene endemic and anthropochorous wild mammals of the Mediterranean islands. *Anthropozoologica* 28: 3–20.

Meadow, R. H. 1989
Osteological evidence for the process of animal domestication. Pp. 80–90 in J. Clutton-Brock (ed.)

The Walking Larder: Patterns of Domestication, Pastoralism and Predation. Unwin Hyman: London.

Morgan, G. S. 1994
Mammals of the Cayman islands. Pp. 435–463 in M. A. Brunt and J. E. Davies (eds.) *The Cayman Islands: Natural History and Biogeography.* Kluwer Academic Publishers: The Netherlands.

Morgan, G. S. and C. A. Woods 1986
Extinction and the zoogeography of West Indian land mammals. *Biological Journal of the Linnean Society* 28: 167–203.

Mueller-Dombois, D. 1981
Some bioenvironmental conditions and the general design of IBP research in Hawai. Pp. 3–32 in D. Mueller-Dombois, K. W. Bridges and H. L. Carson (eds.) *Island Ecosystems. Biological Organization in Selected Hawaian Communities.* Hutchinson Ross: Pennsylvania.

Nishimoto, T. 2001
Jomon jidai no buta no mondai (On the problem of domestic pigs in the Jomon period). Pp. 43-44 *Annual Report of the Grant-in-Aid Scientific Research on Priority Areas (A1) " Interdisciplinary Studies on the Origins of Japanese Peoples and Cultures".* (in Japanese).

Ono, M. 1984
Jomon jidai no inoshishi shiyou mondai (On the problem of boar keeping during the Jomon period). Pp. 47–76 in Chihoushi Kenkyu Kyogikai (Local History Research Association) (eds.) *Kofu Bonchi: Sono Rekishi to Chiikise.* Yuzankaku: Tokyo.

Peltenburg, E., S. Colledge, P. Croft A. Jackson C. McCartney and M. A. Murray 2000
Agro-pastoralist colonization of Cyprus in the 10th millennium BP: initial assessments. *Antiquity* 74: 844–853.

Peltenburg, E., S. Colledge, P. Croft A. Jackson C. McCartney and M. A. Murray 2001a
Neolithic dispersals from the Levantine corridor: a Mediterranean perspective. *Levant* 33: 35–64.

Peltenburg, E., S. Colledge, P. Croft A. Jackson C. McCartney and M. A. Murray 2001b
Well-established colonists: *Mylouthkia* 1 and the Cypro-Pre-Pottery Neolithic B. Pp. 61–94 in Swiny 2001.

Peters, J., D. Helmer, A. von den Driesch and M. Saña Segui 1999
Early animal husbandry in the northern Levant. *Paléorient* 25 : 27–47.

Poplin, F. 1979
Origine du mouflon de Corse dans une nouvelle perspective paléontologique: par marronage. *Annals Genetique du Sel Animale* 11 : 133–143.

Reese, D. 1989
Tracking the extinct pygmy hippopotamus of Cyprus. *Field Museum of Natural History Bulletin* 60: 22–29.

Reese, D. 1996
Cypriot hippo hunters; no myth. *Journal of Mediterranean Archaeology* 9 (1): 107–112.

Reese, D. 1999
The faunal assemblages. Pp. 153–192 in A. H. Simmons (ed.) *Faunal Extinction in an Island Society: Pygmy Hippopotamus Hunters of Cyprus.* Kluwer Academic: New York.

Reitz, E. 1986
Cattle at Area 19, Puerto Real, Haiti. *Journal of Field Archaeolgy* 13: 317–328.

Rosenberg, M., R. Nesbitt, R. W. Redding and B. L. Peasnall 1998
Hallan Çemi, pig husbandry, and post-Pleistocene adaptations along the Taurus-Zagros arc (Turkey). *Paléorient* 24: 25–41.

Schule, W. 1993
Mammals, vegetation and the initial human settlement of the Mediterranean islands: a palaeoecological approach. *Journal of Biogeography* 20: 399–412.

Schwartz, J. H. 1973
The palaeozoology of Cyprus: a preliminary report on recent analysed sites. *World Archaeology* 5: 215–220.

Sevketoglu, M. 2000
Archaeological Field Survey of the Neolithic and Chalcolithic Settlement Sites in Kyrenia District, North Cyprus. British Archaeological Reports, International Series 834: Oxford.

Simmons, A. H. 1998
Of tiny hippos, large cows and early colonists in Cyprus. *Journal of Mediterranean Archaeology* 11: 232–241.

Simmons, A. H. 1999
Faunal Extinction in an Island Society: Pygmy Hippopotamus Hunters of Cyprus. Kluwer Academic: New York.

Simmons, A. H. 2001
The first humans and last pygmy hippopotami of Cyprus. Pp. 1–18 in Swiny 2001.

Sondaar, P. Y. 1977
Insularity and its effects on mammal evolution. Pp. 671–707 in K. Hecht, P. C. Goody and B. M. Hecht (eds.) *Major Patterns in Vertebrate Evolution.* Plenum: New York.

Swiny, S. (ed.) 2001
The Earliest Prehistory of Cyprus: From Colonization to Exploitation. Cyprus American Archaeological Research Institute Monograph Series 12. American Schools of Oriental Research: Boston.

Uerpmann, H.-P. 1987
The Ancient Distribution of Ungulate Mammals in the Middle East. Beihefte Tübinger Atlas Voderen Orients, Reihe A Naturwiss. No. 27. Dr. L. Reichert: Wiesbaden.

Vigne, J.-D. 1999
The large "true" Mediterranean islands as a model for the Holocene human impact on the European vertebrate fauna? Recent data and new reflections. Pp. 295–322 in N. Benecke (ed.) *The Holocene History of the European Vertebrate Fauna.* Verlag Marie Leidorf: Rahden.

Vigne, J.-D. 2001
    The large mammals of early Aceramic Neolithic Cyprus: Preliminary results from Parekklisha *Shillourokambos*. Pp. 55–60 in Swiny 2001.

Vigne, J.-D. and H. Buitenhuis 1999
    Les premiers pas de la domestication animale à l'ouest de l'euphrate: Chypre et l'Anatolie centrale. *Paléorient* 25 (2): 49–62.

Vigne J.-D., G. Dollfus and J. Peters 1999
    Editorial Note. The beginning of herding in the Near East: new data and new ideas. *Paléorient* 25 (2): 9–10.

Vigne, J.-D., I. Carrére, J-F. Saliége, A. Person, H. Bocherens, J. Guilaine and F. Briois 2000
    Predomestic cattle, sheep, goat and pig during the late 9th and 8th millennium cal BC on Cyprus: Preliminary results of *Shillourokambos* (Parekklisha, Limassol). Pp. 83–106 in Mashkour *et al.* 2000.

Wing, E. S. 1989
    Human exploitation of animal resources in the Caribbean. Pp. 137–152 in C. A. Woods (ed.) *Biogeography of The West Indies. Past, Present and Future.* Sandhill Crane Press: Florida.

Yamazaki, K. 2001
    Toshobu inoshishi to Honshu inoshishi no hikaku (Comparison between boar from the mainland and islands). Pp. 40–48 in *Report of the Grant-in-aid Scientific Research (B) Basic Research of Boar on Islands during the Jomon Period.* (in Japanese).

Zeder, M. A. and B. Hesse 2000
    The goats of Ganj Dareh: identification of the earliest directly dated domestic animals. *Science* 287: 2254–2257.

Zeuner, F. S. 1963
    A History of Domesticated Animals. Hutchinson: London.

Zohary, D., E. Tchernov and L. K. Horwitz 1998
    The role of unconscious selection in the domestication of sheep and goats. *Journal of Zoology, London* 245: 129–135.

5

Reappraisal of the archaeobotanical evidence for the emergence and dispersal of the 'founder crops'

Sue Colledge

Abstract

Archaeobotanical evidence for the emergence and dispersal of the founder crops was re-examined in the light of the recent finds of cereals in Cypro-Early Pre-Pottery Neolithic B levels at Kissonerga-Mylouthkia. Metrical analyses of the cereal grains suggested that they represented domestic glume wheat and hulled barley. The significance of these species on Cyprus at such an early date was assessed within the wider geographical context of the Levant, in particular with respect to the areas where, it has been proposed, the founder crop cereals originated. Closer scrutiny of the contextual associations of the samples in which domestic cereals were identified at Jericho (one of the three Pre-Pottery Neolithic A sites with records of domestic species) necessitated a reappraisal of the rates and directions of dispersal of the crops during the Early Pre-Pottery Neolithic B.

Introduction

Farming must of course have started in South West Asia. But in tracing its primary expansion thence, it must now be remembered that the first farmers were not necessarily also potters; the first peasant colonists to reach Europe may not have left a trail of potsherds to mark their tracks! And those tracks were not necessarily on land. Fishing communities along the Levant coasts could perfectly well have learned to supplement the produce of food-gathering by cultivating cereals and breeding stock. Such incipient food-producers, forced to colonise fresh territories might perfectly well have taken to their boats and paddled or sailed on the alluring waters of the Mediterranean to the next landfall – and then to the next (Childe 1973: 51–52).

Fluctuations in climate brought about significant alterations in the composition and distribution of the natural vegetation cover throughout the Levant during the Late Glacial stage in the Pleistocene (*ca.* 15,000–10,000 BP). The boundaries between the different phytogeographical regions would have shifted in accordance with temperature change and amount of rainfall. For example, the eastern and southern margins of the Mediterranean region would have become extended during the periods characterised by warmer and wetter conditions (Baruch and Bottema 1991; Willcox 1991: 120–121; Hillman in Moore *et al.* 2000: 76–84). At the time of the Late Glacial climatic optimum, coincidental with the Early Natufian (*ca.* 12,800/12,500–11,250 BP), an increase in the availability of plant resources in the vicinity of the settlements would have enabled more intensive exploitation of wild cereals (whose natural habitats are the park-woodland/forest-steppe of the Mediterranean phytogeographical region; Zohary and Hopf 2000: 35, 44, 65). During the Late Natufian (*ca.* 11,250–10,500 BP) the sudden deterioration of the climate after the onset of the Younger

Dryas (*ca.* 11,000–10,00 BP), when cold and dry conditions predominated, would have resulted in a significant diminution of those habitats favoured by the wild cereals. The necessity to maintain or increase yields of these plant foods, which had become less accessible, is thought to have been a strong enough incentive to have initiated some form of management (i.e. cultivation) of the wild stands, (Moore and Hillman 1992; Hillman in Moore *et al.* 2000: 376–378; Hillman *et al.* 2001). Harris (1989, 1990, 1996a, 1996b) suggests that these initial attempts at cultivation would have comprised only minimal human interference with the land and its resources. He describes a gradient of increasing energy input (an "evolutionary continuum of People-plant interaction") between the extremes of wild plant food procurement and crop-based agriculture, as the techniques for tending food plants and the land became more refined:

> Along it, the input of human energy per unit area of land exploited for plant foods increases, and so too does the modification of the 'natural' ecosystems, and their replacement by agro-ecosystems, which results from that energy input. The gradient of interaction extends from the (relatively) spatially diffuse activity of burning vegetation, through the more localized gathering, collecting, and protective tending of wild plant products, to the planting, sowing, weeding, harvesting, and storing of (undomesticated) crops, with associated irrigation and drainage, land clearance and tillage, eventually to crop domestication (Harris 1989: 18–19).

The first domestic cereal species would have evolved as a result of the use of harvesting and tending techniques that preferentially favoured the selection of plants with tough rachises (i.e. domestic-type rachises with spikelets that remain attached when the ears are ripe) over those with typically wild-type, brittle rachises (Hillman and Davies 1992: 124–132). Based on their results of experimental sowing and harvesting of wild wheats, Hillman and Davies calculated that the process of domestication would have been rapid, possibly taking between 20–200 years (*ibid.* 144).

Domestic crops appear in the archaeobotanical record during the Pre-Pottery Neolithic A in the Levant (*ca.* 10,200–9,500/9,300 BP) soon after, it has been suggested, the initial experiments at cultivation had taken place[1]. Zohary names eight founder crops of Neolithic agriculture (Zohary 1992: 82; 1996: 143–144). Three cereals: emmer wheat (*Triticum turgidum* subsp. *dicoccum*), barley (*Hordeum vulgare*), and einkorn wheat (*Triticum monococcum*), are included in the list, and the order in which they are cited here is, according to Zohary, the order of their importance as crops at the inception of agriculture. He states that the domestication of other plant species was concurrent with (or at "just a short time later" than) that of the cereals, and he names a further five taxa which played an important role in early agriculture. These are: lentil (*Lens culinaris*), pea (*Pisum sativum*), chickpea (*Cicer arietinum*), bitter vetch (*Vicia ervilia*) and flax (*Linum usitatissimum*). He notes also that these five species were less common (in terms of the numbers of finds) than the cereals on early agrarian sites. Zohary (1996, 1999) favours the theory of single, or at most very few, domestication events. He argues for this on the basis of the fact that: (i) patterns indicative of founder effects are present in the cultivated gene pool; (ii) of the many potential ancestors, only one wild progenitor has been identified for each domestic species; and (iii) of the many genes which could be responsible for the mutations which give rise to the morphological characteristics defining the domestic species (e.g. the tough rachis in cereals), the evidence is that the same gene in each taxon was involved throughout. In support of the theory, he states:

> Yet once the technology of crop cultivation was invented, and the domesticated forms of wheats, barley, pulses and flax first appeared, they probably spread over the Near Eastern arc in a manner similar to the way in which they later spread into Europe: not by additional domestications in each species but by diffusion of the already existing domesticates. In other words, soon after the first non-shattering and easily germinating cereals, pulses and flax appeared, their superior performance under cultivation became decisive, and there was no need for repeated domestication of the wild progenitors (Zohary 1996: 156).

Archaeobotanical evidence: problems of identifying the founder crops

For more than a hundred years there has been a certain degree of co-operation between the botanist and the archaeologist. Lignified and carbonised grain and wood found in archaeological excavations have been identified, and thus a certain aspect of dependency of man upon the plant world has been illuminated. …The realization that man and nature could not have been what they were without the profound influence of one upon the other is of quite recent date. This fundamental interdependency cannot be understood unless the remains of plants are synchronized with the proper cultural level (Helbaek 1960: 99).

Charting the evolution and spread of the founder crops based on archaeobotanical evidence has involved the examination and accurate identification of charred grains and chaff (or impressions in plaster/mudbrick) found in samples recovered from securely dated occupation levels at early Neolithic sites. The reported presence of taxa with correctly assigned domestic status at different localities and at different times has formed the basis of our knowledge about the distribution of the earliest cultivars and of their subsequent dispersion throughout the Levant, and beyond. Of the Pre-Pottery Neolithic A and Early Pre-Pottery Neolithic B sites (these being the cultural entities most critical in the investigation of the initial stages of crop-based agriculture), however, few have produced substantial quantities of well-preserved plant remains. The earlier the site the less well-preserved the plant material tends to be; the detrimental effects of the taphonomic processes, which lead to fragmentation and wear of external surfaces are superimposed on whatever distortions have been caused by the process of charring, all of which can obscure characteristics necessary to distinguish between different taxa. Added to which, there are inherent limitations imposed on our ability to identify cereals and other crops because correct species assignations can be based only on comparisons with specimens collected from modern populations, without the benefit of the knowledge of the full morphological range exhibited by equivalent ancient populations (Miller 1992;

Hillman *et al.* 1996: 197–198). So the problems faced by archaeobotanists who are, or who have been, responsible for identifying and ascribing domestic status to plant taxa should not be underestimated.

It is not surprising, therefore, that a great deal of research time has been devoted to the investigation of morphological characteristics of the critical elements of plant taxa that can be used to distinguish between species, and particularly between the wild progenitors and their domestic equivalents. With the advent of efficient recovery methods in the field (Hans Helbaek invented the technique of flotation in 1966; Helbaek 1966: 385), whereby large quantities of charred remains were separated from the mineral matrix of archaeological deposits, the problems associated with classifying specimens at an appropriate taxonomic level were exacerbated. This prompted increased effort on the part of archaeobotanists to resolve some of the more crucial identification dilemmas. For the past 30 years, Gordon Hillman has undertaken meticulous work that has led to the establishment of widely accepted definitions for recognising the differences between the seeds and chaff (etc.) of many closely related species. For example, his investigations of the charred plant remains from Epipalaeolithic levels at the site of Tell Abu Hureyra involved selecting and describing criteria that would facilitate identification of grains of wild einkorn, and wild and domestic rye (Hillman in Moore *et al.* 2000: 379–382). Unfortunately, however, much of Hillman's work remains unpublished or is reported only in summary form (see Hillman *et al.* 1996: 202–204; Hillman 2001: 34–36). Other archaeobotanists have also been at the forefront of investigative morphological studies with the aim of defining characteristics, which either when applied solely or in conjunction with others, could be used as the basis for identification (van Zeist 1970; Helbaek 1970; Körber-Grohne 1981; Jacomet 1987; Butler 1989; Hather 1993, to mention only a few). Different anatomical parts have been found to be more useful for different families or genera, for example, the chaff of cereals (components of the spikelet and rachis) has been found to possess more diagnostic features than the grains (Hillman *et al.* 1996; Hillman 2001: 29, 31; Kislev 1997: 226; Nesbitt and Samuel 1996: 55–58).

EDINBURGH UNIVERSITY LIBRARY
WITHDRAWN

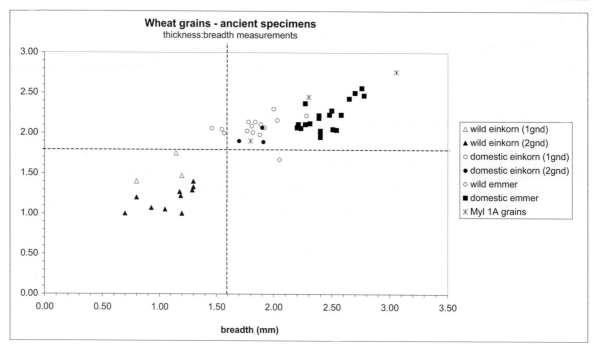

Figure 5.1 *Glume wheat measurements from the sites of: Erbaba (van Zeist et al. 1983); Çayönü (van Zeist et al. 1991–92); Wadi Jilat 7, Wadi Jilat 13, Iraq ed-Dubb, Dhuweila, Beidha, Wadi Fidan A/C (Colledge 2001); Tell Ramad, Tell Aswad, Tell Ghoraifé (van Zeist et al. 1982); Tell Mureybit (van Zeist et al. (1984a); Tell Ras Shamra (van Zeist et al. 1984b); Cape Andreas-Kastros (van Zeist 1981)*

Notes: in a majority of cases the mean breadth and thickness measurements of the grains (i.e. per sample) have been plotted; – dashed lines have been drawn on the plot to represent the minimum recorded breadth and thickness for the wheat grains from Kissonerga-Mylouthkia Period IA

However, in circumstances when only grains are preserved, or in contexts where there are few, poorly preserved chaff items, identifications have to be made on the basis of the former remains alone. Jones (1998) makes the point that in many instances finds of wheat grains have been relegated to the genus level (i.e. *Triticum* sp.) without further attempts to classify to the species level because of the perceived difficulties in taking this next step in the identification procedure. She suggests that this is tantamount to "throw[ing] out the baby with the bathwater", and whereby there is an inevitable loss of resolution for any interpretation (Jones 1998: 34). Her optimism in the potential to classify cereal grains into types, which when represented by large numbers can be "interpreted in terms of species names", is summed up as follows:

… it is not uncommon to find sites where a large proportion of the grains can be assigned

to one type or another. Indeed, the fact that grain from archaeological sites can so often be classified into these few types, whereas modern grain is so variable, may actually be providing us with useful information on the ancient gene pool (Jones 1998: 32).

The application of metrical analyses (i.e. measurements of the dimensions of taxa), together with the more subjective assessment of morphological criteria, has been found to be a more reliable method of substantiating identifications of cereal grains and chaff (see for example: Jacomet and Schlichtherle 1984; Kosina 1984; van Zeist *et al.* 1982, 1983, 1984 a, b, 1991–2). The potential for achieving a degree of consistency in categorisation consequently means that it should be possible to make intra- and inter-site comparisons of similarly named taxa. In archaeobotanical reports for early Pre-Pottery Neolithic sites, however, we are often faced with tantalising, but unverifiable, accounts of domestic species, largely because of the presentation of inadequate descriptions of the ancient specimens.

Evidence from the Kissonerga-*Mylouthkia* Cypro-Early Pre-Pottery Neolithic B archaeobotanical samples

With this in mind, it seemed appropriate to present the justification for the identifications made of the cereal taxa recovered from the Cypro-Early Pre-Pottery Neolithic B contexts (Period 1A) at Kissonerga-*Mylouthkia*. The charred plant remains from Period 1A were not exceptional either in terms of quantity or of the quality of preservation and, as such, conformed to the general trends for other early Pre-Pottery Neolithic sites in the Levant. A range of plant types was represented; Murray summaries the composition of the samples:

> *The samples are composed of a varying mixture of cereal grain and chaff, legumes, wild/weed seeds (especially wild grasses), fruit and oil plants, nuts, roots/tubers, and wood charcoal* (Murray 2003).

Of significance to this present debate was the presence in the samples of both whole and fragmentary glume wheat grains and hulled barley grains, and determination of their wild or domestic status was an obvious priority. As many as possible of the criteria, which previously have been used to differentiate between the grains of different cereal species, were examined. On the basis of subjective assessment of the gross morphological features alone it was suggested that the wheat grains in Period 1A were of domestic species, for the barley grains, however, it was not possible to assign either domestic or wild status (Peltenburg *et al.* 2001: 44–45). Metrical analyses were undertaken, therefore, in an attempt both to substantiate and also to suggest species (/type) identifications for the grains of the two cereal genera.

Figure 5.1 presents a scattergram diagram of thickness *versus* breadth for the wheat grains (10 whole grains/fragments) from Period 1A (length *versus* breadth comparisons were not appropriate

because of the fragmentary nature of some of the specimens). The measurements of the Kissonerga-*Mylouthkia* grains (i.e. mean values calculated per context) are plotted against those of *ca.* 1,500 identified specimens from 14 Neolithic sites in the Levant (see Figure 5.1 for references). Of note in this diagram is the fact that the wild einkorn-type grains form a distinct cluster and are separated from the grains of both domestic wheat species. These grains are apparently much narrower and thinner than the domestic forms. Similarly (but using measurements from one site only), it appears that wild emmer-type grains are much smaller than the grains of the domestic species. There is also a distinction between the grains of the two domestic species; on the basis of these comparisons of very limited data, it appears that the grains identified as emmer-types are broader than those identified as einkorn-types. Grains from Kissonerga-*Mylouthkia* Period 1A fall within the size limits defined here for domestic einkorn and domestic emmer-types. None is within the range of sizes occupied by the grains of the wild wheats. The metrical analyses thus seem to concur with the results of the more subjective morphological assessments and it is suggested (albeit tentatively), therefore, that domestic glume wheat grains were present in the Cypro-Early Pre-Pottery Neolithic B contexts at Kissonerga-*Mylouthkia*. Murray has also identified domestic glume wheat spikelet forks and glumes bases in the samples from Period 1A (Murray 2003); she comments, however, that "much of the [wheat] chaff was in poor condition". It is perhaps relevant to add that there is little evidence of wild wheat chaff on early Neolithic sites. Out of a total of *ca.* 40 recorded sites in the southwest Asia glume bases and spikelet forks were identified at only three: Çafer Höyük (de Moulins 1997), Jerf el Ahmar (Willcox and Fornite 1999) and Netiv Hagdud (Kislev 1997). With the exception of the finds from Netiv Hagdud, the numbers and frequency of occurrence of the chaff items in the samples from the other two sites are low (see Figure 5.2).

The barley grains from Period 1A (11 whole grains/fragments) were measured and compared with *ca.* 350 wild and domestic (hulled) barley grains recorded from 10 Neolithic sites in the Levant (see Figure 5.3 for references). Figure

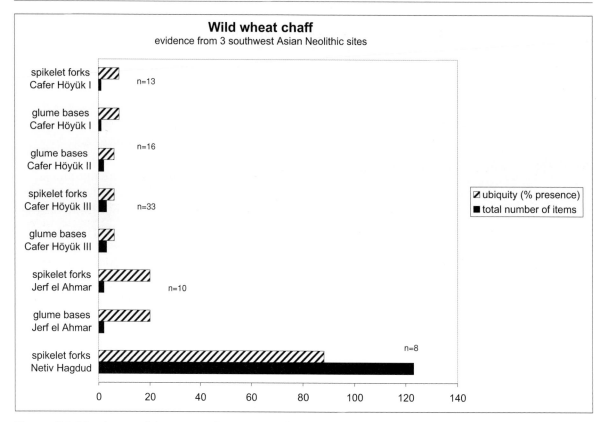

Figure 5.2 *Numbers and frequency of occurrence of wild wheat chaff items in samples from the sites of Cafer Höyük, Jerf el Ahmar and Netiv Hagdud (n = numbers of samples per phase/site). For references see p. 53*

5.3 presents a scattergram diagram of the thickness versus breadth measurements of these ancient specimens (the mean dimensions per context have been plotted for the Kissonerga-*Mylouthkia* specimens). The wild-type barley grains are distinct from those identified as domestic-type and there is minimal overlap either on the basis of breadth or thickness between the two. The Kissonerga-*Mylouthkia* grains from Period 1A clearly fall within the size range defined here as domestic barley. It is suggested (as tentatively as for the glume wheats), that domestic hulled barley was present in the Cypro-Early Pre-Pottery Neolithic B contexts. A small number of barley rachis internodes were found in the samples and these were also assigned to the domestic species (Murray 2003)

In summary, Murray has stated that the composition of the samples is typical of the waste fractions produced during the cleaning processes which take place after the cereals have been harvested and in preparation for their use: "[the samples] have the characteristics of fine

cleaning residues, i.e. high ratios of glume bases and weeds to grains and low numbers of grains per litre" (Murray 2003). It was concluded, therefore, that founder crop cereals were present in the earliest levels at Kissonerga-*Mylouthkia*, thus prompting questions relating to their appearance at such an early date on the island.

Whereas the wild progenitor of domestic barley (*Hordeum spontaneum*) is recorded in the *Flora of Cyprus* (Meikle 1985, 1834) and may, therefore, be a native species, the wild relatives of the other founder crop cereals (*Triticum boeoticum* and *Triticum dicoccoides*) are not. Murray (2003) notes also that wild einkorn and emmer were absent from the inventories of early botanical surveys carried out on the island (Holmboe 1914; Christodoulou 1959) and argues on this basis that there appears to be no indication that these were endemic species. She is careful to qualify her statements by saying that the absence of these taxa from the local flora does not preclude the possibility of their presence in antiquity, as the recent results from

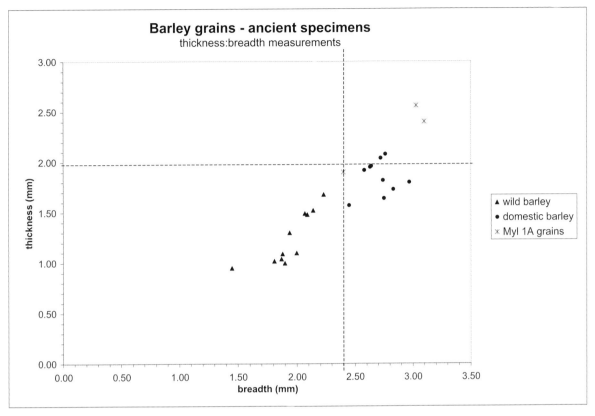

Figure 5.3 *Hulled barley measurements from the sites of: Çayönü (van Zeist et al. 1991–92); Wadi Jilat 7, Wadi Jilat 13, Iraq ed-Dubb, Dhuweila, Wadi Fidan A/C, Azraq 31 (Colledge 2001); Tell Ramad, Tell Aswad, (van Zeist et al. 1982); Tell Mureybit (van Zeist et al. 1984a)*

Notes: in a majority of cases the mean breadth and thickness measurements of the grains (i.e. per sample) have been plotted; dashed lines have been drawn on the plot to represent the minimum recorded breadth and thickness for the barley grains from Kissonerga-Mylouthkia Period IA

Parekklisha-*Shillourokambos* have demonstrated. Willcox identified wild barley (*Hordeum spontaneum*) and emmer wheat (for which he doesn't denote wild or domestic status) in Cypro-Early Pre-Pottery Neolithic B contexts at the site of Parekklisha-*Shillourokambos* (Willcox 2001).

On such limited botanical and archaeobotanical evidence it is difficult to assess the contribution of the local flora in the development of the subsistence economies of the early Pre-Pottery Neolithic settlements on Cyprus. For example, whether or not there was indigenous domestication of barley (the one founder crop cereal for which Zohary states there is clear genetic evidence of more than one domestication event: Zohary 1999) is a question that is perhaps unresolvable on the basis of present knowledge. The overwhelming body of evidence in the form of material culture, however,

is testimony of the likelihood of contact with the Levantine mainland during the Pre-Pottery Neolithic and of the transport of crops from sites there to the island (Peltenburg *et al.* 2000; 2001). The obvious questions that must then be asked are how, why and from where? Within the scope of this paper it is only the last of the three questions that can be addressed.

Evidence from the Levantine Pre-Pottery Neolithic A/ Early Pre-Pottery Neolithic B

It was considered pertinent to examine the archaeobotanical evidence from early sites on the Levantine mainland, in light of the fact that as Peltenburg has commented:

The Cypriot evidence fits uncomfortably with the widely held view that during the Early Pre-Pottery Neolithic B the new crops together with the techniques required to cultivate them successfully only spread to the north and east from the areas where the original 'domestication events' occurred (Peltenburg et al. 2001: 55).

In review articles collating archaeobotanical data from Pre-Pottery Neolithic sites, lists of species are, in many instances, apparently presented without critical evaluation of the provenance and date of the more significant finds (i.e. the domestic crops). It seemed timely, therefore, to 'revisit' these early sites, which have been fundamental to the establishment of models for the early development of crop-based agriculture, and to attempt to verify the contextual associations of the recorded plant taxa. It has been possible to do this as part of a research project initiated by Professor Stephen Shennan at the Institute of Archaeology, University College London that aims to re-examine primary data in source archaeological and archaeobotanical texts.[2] A comprehensive reappraisal of the evidence for the emergence and dispersal of the founder crops (as formulated under the auspices of the project) will be reported at a later date. It is appropriate, however, to present a reassessment of the provenance and dates of the plant remains from just one site, Jericho, because it serves to emphasise the necessity to substantiate the archaeobotanical evidence from the Levantine mainland before we can consider the Cypriot data within the broader geographical context.

There are records of domestic cereals from only three Pre-Pottery Neolithic A sites in the Levant: Iraq ed Dubb (Colledge 2001), Tell Aswad Ia (van Zeist and Bakker-Heeres 1982) and Jericho (Hopf 1983). The finds from these sites are, to varying degrees, controversial. The record of domestic einkorn from Jericho, for example, is thought by several authors to be worthy of closer scrutiny because of its presence at such an early date so far south of its supposed origin in southeastern Turkey (Zohary and Hopf 2000: 36, citing Heun et al. 1997). Hopf identified the crop from impressions in burnt plaster (2 whole spikelets and 1 fragment of an ear in profile with 2 spikelets; Hopf 1983: 605). She also

identified grains of domestic emmer in Pre-Pottery Neolithic A contexts, both in charred form and also from impressions (as impressions: 1 grain and 6 spikelets; *ibid.*: 605, 609). Hopf records two-row domestic barley as being more abundant and she identified grains in the charred remains and in the plaster impressions (as impressions: 23 grains, 1 fragment of an ear with 3 spikelets and 1 rachis internode; *ibid.*: 605, 609).[3] Two of the samples of charred remains (1020, 1019) were from trench D1, the southern arm of the larger cruciform trench to the west of the tell, and including the Pre-Pottery Neolithic A tower at its centre. They were both taken from stage VIII contexts of Kenyon's stratigraphic system (1020: VIIIA.xvia; 1019: VIIIA.xxii; Kenyon and Holland 1981: Plate 238), from which there are four ^{14}C dates that fit within the chronological brackets for the Early Pre-Pottery Neolithic B (Burleigh 1981: 501–504; 1983: 760–765; N.B. omitting the early laboratory dates which are considered to be unreliable: see Bar-Yosef and Kra 1994: 6; Bar-Yosef and Gopher 1997: 251).[4] The third sample in which Hopf identified domestic cereals (651) and the sample of plaster with impressions (172) were both from trench Tr1, the western arm of the larger cruciform trench, which is external to the town walls. Both were from stage X contexts of Kenyon's stratigraphic system (651: X.viiia; 172: X.viii; Kenyon and Holland 1981: Plate 236), approximately 2m above stage VIII but closely associated with a date of 9200 ± 70 BP for stage IX, and just below the Pre-Pottery Neolithic A/B boundary sealing the tower. The provenances of the archaeobotanical samples, therefore, are within levels defined culturally as Pre-Pottery Neolithic A (Bar-Yosef and Kra 1994: 6; Bar-Yosef and Gopher 1997: 251) but which would appear, however, to be contemporary in date with Early Pre-Pottery Neolithic B sites further to the north.

So, closer examination of the contextual association of the samples from just one of the Pre-Pottery Neolithic sites has resulted in the necessity to alter slightly the distribution maps of founder crops in the 10th millennium BP. The implications of this with respect to the models for their emergence and dispersal are no less significant. Certainly, the readjustment of dates for the earliest records of domestic species at Jericho reinforces theories of rapid spread during the

Early Pre-Pottery Neolithic B from their place of origin not only to the north and east (e.g. to the Jilat region of eastern Jordan) but also to the south and west (e.g. to sites on Cyprus). But only as further sites are excavated and as more archaeobotanical data become available will it be possible to locate exactly from where the early colonists, with their surpluses of grain, came.

Concluding remarks

In the light of Zohary's theories, a reappraisal of the archaeobotanical evidence for the origins of the founder crops was considered appropriate. Early finds of glume wheat and hulled barley at Kissonerga-*Mylouthkia*, which is beyond areas in which he has suggested the domestication events would have taken place, prompted this critical re-evaluation of the data. The measurements of thickness and breadth of the cereal grains from Period 1A at the site presented a more objective means of substantiating species classifications and also provided the basis for comparison with similarly named taxa from other Neolithic sites. Whereas the authenticity of identifications can rarely be verified and especially if there are inadequate descriptive records of the archaeological specimens, the provenance and dates of important finds can be reassessed with reference to source texts. For example, in the case of the domestic cereals found in Pre-Pottery Neolithic A levels at Jericho, after re-examination of the contextual associations of the samples from which they were taken, it was suggested that they were contemporary in date with the later Early Pre-Pottery Neolithic B, thus providing evidence to support the idea of the dispersal of the founder crops at this early stage, to the south and west (to Cyprus) of the areas in which, it has been proposed, they were domesticated.

Acknowledgements

I am extremely grateful to the Council for British Research in the Levant for financially supporting my participation at the conference. Dr James Conolly and Dr Ann Butler commented on the paper and I would like also to express my thanks to them.

Notes

1   Hillman has identified domestic rye grains in Epipalaeolithic levels at the site of Tell Abu Hureyra (Hillman *et al.* 2001), but as this species is not included in Zohary's list of founder crops these early finds have been omitted from the discussion.

2   The project, entitled 'The origin and spread of Neolithic plant economies in the Near East and Europe', is supported by a grant from the UK Arts and Humanities Research Board. Professor Stephen Shennan is the principal investigator, and Dr James Conolly (Institute of Archaeology, UCL) and Dr James Steele (Southampton University) are co-investigators.

3   Although archaeobotanical evidence based on impressions is considered by some to be less reliable than that based on charred remains, the preservation of such features as glume tips on the wheat spikelets (which are not usually extant in charred material) enables more accurate identification at the species level. Hopf, however, records a degree of uncertainty for her identifications made from the impressions.

4   The Early Pre-Pottery Neolithic B is a cultural entity which is well documented in the northern Levant, with dates of *ca.* 9,500/9,300–9,200 BP.

References

Baruch, U. and S. Bottema 1991
    Palynological evidence for climatic changes in the Levant *ca.* 17,000–9,000 B.P. Pp. 11–20 in O. Bar-Yosef and F. Valla (eds.) *The Natufian Culture in the Levant.* International Monographs in Prehistory, Archaeological Series 1: Ann Arbor, Michigan.

Bar-Yosef, O. and R. S. Kra 1994
    Dating eastern Mediterranean sequences: Introductory Remarks. Pp. 1–12 in O. Bar-Yosef and R. S. Kra (eds.) *Late Quaternary Chronology and Palaeoclimates of the Eastern Mediterranean. Radiocarbon.* The University of Arizona, Tuscon, and the Peabody Museum, Harvard University: Cambridge, USA.

Bar-Yosef, O. and A, Gopher 1997
    Chapter 10: Discussion. Pp. 247–266 in O. Bar-Yosef and A. Gopher (eds.) *An early Neolithic Village in the Jordan Valley.* American School of Prehistoric Research Bulletin 43. Harvard University, Peabody Museum of Archaeology and Ethnology: Cambridge, USA.

Burleigh, R 1981
    Appendix C: Radiocarbon dates. Pp. 501–504 in K. M. Kenyon and T. A. Holland (eds.) *Excavations at Jericho, Volume III, The Architecture and Stratigraphy of the Tell.* British School of Archaeology in Jerusalem: London.

Burleigh, R. 1983
Appendix D: Additional radio carbon dates for Jericho. Pp. 760–765 in K. M. Kenyon and T. A. Holland (eds.) *Excavations at Jericho, Volume V, The pottery phases of the Tell and other finds.* British School of Archaeology in Jerusalem: London.

Butler, A. 1989
Cryptic anatomical characters as evidence of early cultivation in the grain legumes (pulses). Pp. 390–407 in D. R. Harris and G. C. Hillman (eds.) *Foraging and Farming.* Unwin Hyman: London.

Childe, V. G. 1973
The Dawn of European Civilisation. 6th Edition (revised). Paladin: St Albans, Herts.

Christodoulou, D. 1959
The Evolution of Rural Land Use Patterns in Cyprus. Geographical Publications Limited: Bude.

Colledge, S. 2001
Plant exploitation on Epipalaeolithic and early Neolithic sites in the Levant. British Archaeological Reports, International Series, 986: Oxford.

de Moulins, D. 1997
Agricultural changes at Euphrates and Steppe sites in the mid 8th to the 6th millennium BC. British Archaeological Reports, International Series 683: Oxford.

Harris, D. R. 1989
An evolutionary continuum of people-plant interaction. Pp. 11–26 in D. R. Harris and G. C. Hillman (eds.) *Foraging and Farming.* Unwin Hyman: London.

Harris, D. R. 1990
Settling down and breaking ground: rethinking the Neolithic Revolution. Twaalfde Kroon-Voordracht. Stichting Nederlands Museum voor Anthropologie en Praehistorie: Amsterdam.

Harris, D. R. 1996a
Introduction: themes and concepts in the study of early agriculture. Pp. 1–9 in D.R. Harris (ed.) *The origins and spread of agriculture and pastoralism in Eurasia.* UCL Press: London.

Harris, D.R. 1996b
Domesticatory relationships of people, plants and animals. Pp. 437–463 in R. Ellen and K. Fukui (eds.) *Redefining nature: ecology, culture and domestication.* Berg: Oxford.

Hather, J. 1993
An archaeological guide to root and tuber identification. Volume 1, Europe and South West Asia. Monograph no. 28, Oxbow: Oxford.

Helbaek, H. 1960
The palaeoethnobotany of the Near East and Europe. Pp. 99–118 in R. J. Braidwood and B. Howe (eds.) *Prehistoric investigations in Iraqi Kurdistan.* Studies in Ancient Oriental Civilisation no. 31, Oriental Institute, University of Chicago. University of Chicago Press: Chicago.

Helbaek, H. 1966
Plant collecting, dry farming, and irrigation agriculture in prehistoric Deh Luran. Pp. 383–426 in F. Hole, K. V. Flannery and J. A. Neely (eds.) *Prehistory and human ecology of the Deh Luran plain.* Memoir of the Museum of Anthropology no 1. University of Michigan: Ann Arbor.

Helbaek, H. 1970
The plant husbandry of Hacilar. Pp. 189–244 in J. Mellaart, *Excavations at Hacilar 1.* Edinburgh University Press: Edinburgh.

Heun, M., R. Schäfer-Pregl, D. Klawan, R. Castagna, M. Accerbi, B. Borghi and F. Salamini 1997
Site of einkorn domestication identified by DNA fingerprinting. *Science* 278: 1312–1314.

Hillman, G. C. 2001
Archaeology, Percival and the problems of identifying wheat remains. Pp. 27–36 in P. D. S. Caligari and P. E. Brandham (eds.) Wheat Taxonomy: the legacy of John Percival. *The Linnean* (special issue no 3).

Hillman, G. C. and M. S. Davies, 1992
Domestication rate in wild wheats and barley under primitive cultivation: preliminary results and archaeological implications of field measurements of selection coefficient. Pp. 113–158 in P. Anderson-Gerfaud (ed.) *Préhistoire de l'agriculture: nouvelles approches expérimentales et ethnographiques.* Monographie du CRA 6, Éditions Centre Nationale Recherches Scientifiques: Paris.

Hillman, G. C., S. Mason, D. de Moulins and M. Nesbitt 1996
Identification of archaeological remains of wheat: the 1992 London Workshop. *Circaea* 12 (2): 195–209.

Hillman, G. C., R. Hedges, R., A. Moore, S. Colledge and P. Pettitt 2001
New evidence of Late Glacial cereal cultivation at Abu Hureyra on the Euphrates. *The Holocene* 11(4): 383–393.

Holmboe, J. 1914
Studies on the Vegetation of Cyprus. Bergens Museum Skrifter: A/S John Griegs Boktrykkeri.

Hopf, M. 1983
Appendix B: Jericho plant remains. Pp. 576–621 in K. M. Kenyon and T. A. Holland (eds.) *Excavations at Jericho, Volume 5, The pottery phases of the Tell and other finds.* British School of Archaeology in Jerusalem: London.

Jacomet, S. and H. Schichtherle 1984
Der kleine Pfahlbauweizen Oswald Heer's – Neue Untersuchungen zur Morphologie neolithischer Nacktweizen-Ähren. Pp. 153–176 in W. van Zeist and W. A. Casparie (eds.) *Plants and ancient man: studies in palaeoethnobotany.* Balkema: Rotterdam.

Jacomet, S. 1987
Prähistorische Getreidefunde: Eine Anleitung zur Bestimmung prähistorischer Gersten- und Weizen-Funde. Botanisches Institut der Universität, Abteilung Pflanzensystematik und Geobotanik: Basel.

Jones, G. 1998
Wheat Grain Identification – Why Bother? *Environmental Archaeology* 2: 29–34.

Kenyon, K. and T. A. Holland (eds.) 1981
    Excavations at Jericho, Volume III, The Architecture and Stratigraphy of the Tell. (plates) British School of Archaeology in Jerusalem: London.

Kislev, M. E. 1997
    Chapter 8: Early agriculture and paleoecology of Netiv Hagdud. Pp. 209–236 in O. Bar-Yosef and A. Gopher (eds.) *An early Neolithic Village in the Jordan Valley.* American School of Prehistoric Research Bulletin 43. Harvard University, Peabody Museum of Archaeology and Ethnology: Cambridge, USA.

Körber-Grohne, U. 1981
    Distinguishing prehistoric cereal grains of *Triticum* and *Secale* on the basis of their surface patterns using the scanning electron microscope. *Journal of Archaeological Science* 8: 197–204.

Kosina, R. 1984
    Morphology of the crease of wheat caryopses and its usability for the identification of some species: a numerical approach. Pp. 177–191 in W. van Zeist and W.A. Casparie (eds.) *Plants and ancient man: studies in palaeoethnobotany.* Balkema: Rotterdam.

Meikle, R. D. 1985
    Flora of Cyprus. Volume 2. The Bentham-Moxon Trust, Royal Botanic Gardens: Kew.

Miller, T. E. 1992
    A cautionary note on the use of morphological characters for recognising taxa in wheat (genus *Triticum*). Pp. 249–253 in P. Anderson-Gerfaud (ed.) *Préhistoire de l'agriculture: nouvelles approches expérimentales et ethnographiques.* Monographie du CRA 6, Éditions Centre Nationale Recherches Scientifiques: Paris.

Moore, A. M. T. and G. C. Hillman 1992
    The Pleistocene to Holocene transition and human economy in southwest Asia: The impact of the Younger Dryas. *American Antiquity* 57 (3): 482–494.

Moore, A. M. T., G. C. Hillman and A. J. Legge 2000
    Village on the Euphrates: from foraging to farming at Abu Hureyra. Oxford University Press: Madison, New York.

Murray, M.A. (2003)
    The Plant Remains. Pp. 59–71 in Peltenburg 2003.

Nesbitt, M. and D. Samuel 1996
    From staple crop to extinction? The archaeology and history of the hulled wheats. Pp. 41–100 in S. Padulosi, K. Hammer and J. Heller (eds.) *Hulled wheats. Proceedings of the First International Workshop on Hulled Wheats.* International Plant Genetic Resources Institute: Rome, Italy.

Peltenburg, E., S. Colledge, P. Croft, A. Jackson, C. McCartney and M. A. Murray 2000
    Agro–pastoralist colonization of Cyprus in the 10th millennium BP: initial assessments. *Antiquity* 74: 844–853.

Peltenburg, E., S. Colledge, P. Croft, A. Jackson, C. McCartney, and M. A. Murray 2001
    Neolithic dispersals from the Levantine Corridor: a Mediterranean perspective. *Levant* 33: 35–64.

Peltenburg, E. (ed.) 2003
    The Colonisation and Settlement of Cyprus. Investigations at Kissonerga-Mylouthkia, 1976–1996. Lemba Archaeological Project, Cyprus III.1. Studies in Mediterranean Archaeology 70:4. Åströms Förlag: Sävedalen.

van Zeist, W. 1970
    Prehistoric and early historic food plants in the Netherlands. *Palaeohistoria* 14: 41–173.

van Zeist, W. 1981
    Plant remains from Cape Andreas-Kastros (Cyprus). Appendix VI. Pp. 95–99 in A. Le Brun (ed.) *Un site néolithique précéramique en Chypre: Cap Andreas Kastros.* Recherche sur les grandes civilisations. Memoirs 5, Éditions ADPF: Paris.

van Zeist, W. and J. A. H. Bakker-Heeres 1982
    Archaeobotanical Studies in the Levant 1. Neolithic sites in the Damascus Basin: Aswad, Ghoraifé and Ramad. *Palaeohistoria* 24: 165–256.

van Zeist, W. and J. A. H. Bakker-Heeres 1984a
    Archaeobotanical Studies in the Levant 3. Late-Palaeolithic Mureybit. *Palaeohistoria* 26: 171–199.

van Zeist, W. and J. A. H. Bakker-Heeres 1984b
    Archaeobotanical Studies in the Levant 2. Neolithic and Halaf levels and Ras Shamra. *Palaeohistoria* 26: 151–170.

van Zeist, W. and Buitenhuis, H. 1983
    A palaeobotanical study of Neolithic Erbaba, Turkey. *Anatolica* 10: 47–89.

van Zeist, W. and G. J. de Roller 1991–92
    The plant husbandry of Aceramic Cayönü, SE Turkey. *Palaeohistoria* 33/34: 65–96.

van Zeist, W. and W. Waterbolk-van Rooijen 1985
    The palaeobotany of Tell Bouqras, eastern Syria. *Paléorient* 11 (2): 137–141.

Willcox, G. 1991
    Exploitation des espèces ligneuses au Proche-Orient: données anthracologiques. *Paléorient* 17 (2): 117–126.

Willcox, G. 2001
    Présence des céréales dans le Néolithique Précéramique de Shillourokambos à Chypre: Résultats de la campagne 1999. *Paléorient* 26: 129–135.

Willcox, G. and S. Fornite 1999
    Impressions of wild cereal chaff in pisé from 10th millennium uncal BP at Jerf el Ahmar and Mureybit: northern Syria. *Vegetation History and Archaeobotany* 8: 21–24.

Zohary, D. 1992
    Domestication of the Neolithic Near Eastern crop assemblage. Pp. 81–86 in P. Anderson-Gerfaud (ed.) *Préhistoire de l'agriculture: nouvelles approches expérimentales et ethnographiques.* Monographie du CRA 6, Éditions Centre Nationale Recherches Scientifiques: Paris.

Zohary, D. 1996
    The mode of domestication of the founder crops

of Southwest Asian agriculture. Pp. 142–158 in D. R. Harris (ed.) *The Origins and Spread of Agriculture and Pastoralism in Eurasia.* UCL Press Ltd.: London.

Zohary, D. 1999
Monophyletic vs. polyphyletic origin of the crops on which agriculture was founded in the Near East. *Genetic Resources and Crop Evolution* 46 (2): 133–142.

Zohary, D. and M. Hopf 2000
Domestication of Plants in the Old World. 3rd Edition, Oxford University Press: Oxford.

6

Abu Hureyra and the development of farming in western Asia: directions for future research

A. M. T. Moore

Abstract

Research at the early village of Abu Hureyra on the Euphrates River has demonstrated that agriculture began there ca. 13,000 cal BP. This confirms the primacy of western Asia as the region in which farming began earlier than anywhere else. Climatic fluctuations and, especially, the onset of the Younger Dryas, contributed importantly to the development of agriculture at the site. The transition to a mature farming way of life took place in a series of steps over several millennia. An ecological approach has proved most productive in elucidating the information recovered from Abu Hureyra. The inception of farming was, above all, about developing new ways of obtaining food. Future research needs to focus relentlessly on this fact, and should be directed towards recovering adequate samples of food remains from Epi-palaeolithic as well as Neolithic sites. Total recovery of economic evidence from sites under excavation should be the aim of all archaeologists concerned with the inception and development of agricultural societies in western Asia. The locations of sites and their environmental settings are also key elements in interpreting their economies. Application of the more refined data on climatic change that are now available is a critical element in advancing understanding. A landscape survey currently under way at Jericho illustrates several of these principles.

The inhabitants of the early village of Abu Hureyra on the Euphrates River in Syria were among the first people to develop agriculture anywhere in the world. The site thus stands as an important case study of the inception of agriculture, its causes, and the impact it had on contemporary society. The book that my colleagues and I recently published (Moore, Hillman and Legge 2000) was intended to be a comprehensive statement of the results of the research we have conducted there. The conference at Drousha in Cyprus on the Neolithic Revolution affords a timely opportunity to reflect on the outcome of the Abu Hureyra project, and to consider the research that should be undertaken in the future to advance our understanding of the development and spread of farming across western Asia and beyond. We may begin, then, by summarising the principal conclusions derived from the research at the site.

Abu Hureyra was settled *ca.* 11,500 BP uncalibrated or around *ca.* 13,500 calibrated BP (Stuiver *et al.* 1998) by hunters and gatherers whose descendants adopted farming. The first settlement was a village and its inhabitants were sedentary, supporting themselves year-round by foraging and hunting. Thus, sedentism preceded the development of farming by several centuries at Abu Hureyra. Agriculture began there *ca.* 11,000 BP or about 13,000 calibrated BP. Our research thus confirms the primacy of western Asia as the region in which the domestication of plants and animals and the development of a farming way of life occurred earlier than anywhere else in the world. The first domestic crop that the inhabitants cultivated was rye, an unanticipated discovery, followed rapidly by einkorn, other cereals, and lentils (Hillman *et al.* 2001). The inhabitants adopted farming as a way of keeping their community together at a time of abrupt environmental stress caused by the rapid onset of the Younger Dryas episode of cool, dry climate (Moore, Hillman and Legge 2000: 491).

Changes in the way of life of the inhabitants took place in a series of steps: first, the adoption of farming with continued foraging and hunting, next farming and herding with hunting and some residual foraging, then a mature Neolithic mixed farming economy. Once farming became the mainstay of the community, the population of the village grew manyfold leading to a huge increase in the size of the settlement, an impressive indication of the immediate consequences of the adoption of the new way of life. This was accompanied by important changes in social and community organization and the development of new crafts. The inhabitants, like their contemporaries elsewhere in the Levant and Anatolia, created a rich ideology of reverence for ancestors that found elaborate expression in rites of delayed burial of the dead and special treatment of skulls. Thus, the development of farming led to extraordinary and unprecedented cultural changes that were soon manifest across a broad reach of western Asia. The rich data from Abu Hureyra have enabled us to construct an integrated interpretation of the development of the community that inhabited the site such that we can see how the changing environment, the transformation in the economy, innovations in material culture, and social organization were all connected.

Research at Abu Hureyra:
the next steps

Village on the Euphrates presents our analyses and interpretations of the bulk of the material from Abu Hureyra. It offers our considered conclusions about the key questions that have arisen in the course of the research on the site, carried out over the last thirty years. Yet it cannot be the last word, for much remains to be done by us and by the next generation of researchers. The stratigraphic record of three of the excavated trenches remains to be published in detail, as do many of the artefacts from Abu Hureyra 2, the Neolithic village. The basic analyses of these aspects of the

research on the site were completed long ago, but it will require significant additional work to bring this material to publication.

The essential elements of the analysis of the organic material, both animal bones and plant remains, are explored in *Village on the Euphrates*, but much detailed work on this remarkable evidence should still be carried out. In particular, we intend to conduct additional studies of butchery and use of animal parts of both wild and domestic species. Meat was processed in different ways across the site, so there is considerable scope for further spatial studies of the distribution of bones. It is our intention to publish a complete archive of measurements of the animal bones, something that has not hitherto been presented from any contemporary site of significance. And more analysis needs to be done on the enormous bulk of plant remains from Abu Hureyra 2. Here much of the material consists of field weeds and other species associated with agricultural practices. The ecological characteristics of these plants during the early Holocene have scarcely been considered by archaeobotanists because of the lack of preserved remains. Thus, the botanical parameters of the early history of farming still need further detailed consideration. Many of the plants represented in the charred remains were used as medicines, hallucinogens, dyes, for cordage, and much else besides. These varied uses of plants by the ancient inhabitants of the site also need further study.

At every stage of the research we have had to determine chronological sequences with ever greater precision. The advent of accelerator radiocarbon (AMS) dating has enabled us to accomplish this aim, with remarkable results. In particular, we have been able to date directly specimens of the earliest domestic plants and animals (Hillman *et al.* 2001; Legge and Rowley-Conwy 1986). Yet, even at this advanced stage of research, we need to obtain more dates, for those other cereals such as einkorn that were cultivated very early at Abu Hureyra, and for a few of the stratigraphic sequences that remain to be dated in detail. Dating the minute charred fragments that represent the earliest remains of domestic plants continues to pose a challenge for the Oxford Laboratory with whom we have worked closely for many years (Hillman *et al.*

2001: 390), but we anticipate that in due course we shall be able to resolve the few remaining chronological issues as AMS dating continues to be refined.

Theoretical considerations

Much has been written over the years about the theoretical determinants of the inception of agriculture (among many recent contributions see: Cauvin 1994; Cowan and Watson 1992; Gebauer and Price 1992; Harris 1996; Smith 1995: 206–214), and we have also participated in that discussion (Moore, Hillman and Legge 2000: 14–17). The fundamental problem with many of the explanations that have been proposed is their remoteness from the archaeological evidence. And, especially, few of them have much to say about the context in which farming first developed, that is the settings of the key sites that date from before, during and after the transition.

In our research on Abu Hureyra we have found an ecological approach to be the most productive because of its emphasis on the relationships between the inhabitants of a site and the essential elements that sustained life in their surrounding environment. The notion of adaptation is still helpful here (Owen 1980: 170), although the relationship between the inhabitants of an early village and their surroundings was always more dynamic than this term implies.

The transition from foraging to farming was fundamentally a shift in economy from food getting to food raising, with all that this implies about the relationships of people with the plants and animals from which they derived their sustenance. It follows that theoretical approaches should focus on the basic changes that took place in the economy. And let us never forget that food is at the centre of our considerations. Thus, discussions that have little to say about food, its nature, its multiple sources, and the means of processing it are unlikely to provide helpful insights into how and why people developed farming.

The change in economy from foraging to farming had an immediate impact on social and community organization and, in ways not yet well understood, influenced emerging new systems of belief. These developments in society

and ideology have only recently begun to receive the concentrated study that they require (Aurenche and Kozlowski 1999; Byrd 1994; Fortin and Aurenche 1998). They are being taken very seriously in the renewed excavations currently underway at Çatal Hüyük (Hodder 1996: 3, 360–362). In the years ahead much more attention needs to be given to analyzing the considerable amount of relevant evidence that has already been accumulated, using appropriate models to help structure the data. Such studies transcend the investigation of a single site and so would form excellent material for research by the next generation of doctoral students who rarely have opportunities to initiate excavations of their own.

Yet it remains the case that ecological approaches which have given due consideration to environmental factors have yielded the most productive explanations of how and in what circumstances people developed agriculture. They have helped determine the contexts in which agriculture was developed by early farming societies and so have enriched our understanding not only of how the economic transformation came about but also of the accompanying social and ideological changes. Scholars who have attempted to analyse these matters through the reverse process of reasoning have failed to provide satisfactory explanations for the beginning of agriculture (Cauvin 1994: 87–101). It follows that research conducted from an ecological perspective is likely to continue to provide valuable insights in the future.

Nature of the evidence

If the transition from foraging to farming was above all a change in economy, in the basic day to day matter of obtaining enough to eat, then it follows that direct evidence for food must be an essential element in research. In most investigations of sites in western Asia this evidence consists of animal bones and charred seeds with other carbonized plant remains. Today, if the recovery techniques are sufficiently refined and the soil conditions favourable then other organic materials, phytoliths, soft plant tissue of roots and tubers, coprolites, minute bones, rodent teeth, and even fishscales, may be retrieved. And the relatively new technique of micromorphology promises to yield valuable additional information about food processing activities (see, for example, Matthews *et al.* 1996 and references therein). The greatest possible variety of direct evidence of food use can be most helpful in reconstructing prehistoric diet. Yet serious analysis requires enormous samples, especially of bones and charred seeds. At Abu Hureyra we recovered over two metric tons of animal bones and 500 litres of plant remains. Even these samples, vastly larger than those obtained from any other terminal Pleistocene – early Holocene village site, have scarcely been sufficient to enable us to answer the key questions we have posed concerning the adoption of farming. Those who excavate early sites that pertain to the transition from foraging to farming need to engage in systematic recovery of the largest possible samples of animal bones and plant remains if they are to contribute usefully to greater understanding. Today, that effectively means total processing of all excavated soil through water sieving and other techniques.

Some discussions of late foragers and early farmers in western Asia have invoked indirect evidence from artefacts, for example the presence or absence of sickle blades on a site or the possible uses of grinding stones to process cereals and other foodstuffs (Henry 1989: 36–38, 196). Such evidence from artefacts is always equivocal because the tools could have been used for a variety of purposes. Certainly, they are insufficient to infer food processing practices with any precision, let alone something as fundamental as the inception of farming. Even the most painstaking microwear analyses can provide only limited evidence of plant processing activities, as Anderson reminds us (1992: 206–207), although such studies can add useful corroborative information.

The research at Abu Hureyra has advanced in step with developments in chronometric, especially radiocarbon, dating. The first dates from the site were obtained by the British Museum using the conventional radiocarbon method on large samples of charcoal. The advent of accelerator (AMS) dating provided us with the means to address chronological problems that had hitherto been beyond our reach (Moore

1992). It also enabled us for the first time to date individual seeds of plants and bones of animals directly and so to establish precisely and unequivocally the date of the earliest use of domesticates at Abu Hureyra. Because AMS dating allowed us to date such small samples, we avoided the problems that arise from trying to date such events indirectly from dates on charcoal samples from associated deposits. The success of this approach at Abu Hureyra should encourage others to apply it elsewhere. For it is now clear that only AMS direct dating of individual bones and seeds from domestic species can establish the process of the development of farming with precision. It follows that the most useful results will be obtained from systematic dating of samples from long occupation sequences that transcend a single cultural or economic phase.

Environmental matters

The last decade of research has revealed just how rapid and multiple were the climatic fluctuations that marked the transition from Pleistocene to Holocene. In addition to the regular cycles of climate change at 1,000–1,500, 100 and 10–12 year intervals (Bond *et al.* 1997; Perry and Hsu 2000, Taylor *et al.* 1993), there were unique events, the impact of which created worldwide effects; of these the millennium-long Younger Dryas episode was the most significant for this discussion. We have learned that such major climatic shifts could occur in just a few years. It now appears that the onset of the Younger Dryas, for example, took about a decade as did its ending, far less than the span of a human lifetime (Mayewski *et al.* 1993; Severinghaus *et al.* 1998). These major shifts had an immediate impact on annual and perennial plants, then in turn on the humans, ruminants and other species that depended on such plants for sustenance. Archaeological evidence has tended to blur the sharpness of the impact on humans of these environmental fluctuations, mainly because the data are so imperfect, often representing a palimpsest of activities carried out over generations, and collected with less than full commitment to total recovery. Consequently, it is only recently that we have begun to appreciate that the archaeological record, if examined with enough care, might indicate that the human response to such climate-induced fluctuations in vegetation, soils and other resources was also rapid and, on occasion, of lasting effect.

Another factor that calls for much more detailed research than it has received hitherto is the environmental setting of early villages. Clearly, the inhabitants of these sites, whether foragers or farmers, depended largely on resources available in the vicinity for their subsistence. But the needs of foragers were different from those of farmers. The former needed the greatest possible variety of micro-habitats within a short walk of the site while the latter required fertile, well-watered arable soils to sustain agriculture. This is the main reason why the sites of late Epi-palaeolithic foragers and early Neolithic farmers are rarely found in the same place. Much can be learned about the potential economy of a given site from an examination of its setting even before it has been excavated. Serious study of the environs of a site that has yielded significant amounts of economic evidence can reveal a great deal about the way in which its inhabitants exploited the surrounding landscape. This approach was pioneered by the British Academy Major Research Project on the Early History of Agriculture led by Eric Higgs of the University of Cambridge but has been neglected since. Our work at Abu Hureyra has demonstrated just how much can be learned from research conducted in much greater depth than Higgs and his colleagues were able to do. By relating the activities on a site revealed by archaeology to their natural setting, vastly more can be ascertained about the nature of foraging and farming around the time of the transition to agriculture.

At Abu Hureyra we have learned that the economic and other changes which accompanied the development of a farming way of life took place in a series of abrupt adjustments followed by periods of consolidation (Moore, Hillman and Legge 2000: 509). We were able to determine this because the sequence of occupation was sufficiently long, at least 4,500 radiocarbon years or 5,600 years in real time, to cover several episodes of major economic change, including the shift from foraging to farming.

Such sequences are extraordinarily rare, and most of our evidence comes from sites of short duration that represent but one or at most two episodes along the multi-step progression from foraging to a mixed farming economy. It follows that much more is to be gained from examining sites of long duration that enable the archaeologist to contrast one economic episode with another. Furthermore, more will be learned when such sites are located in contrasting environments because it is unlikely that the transition from foraging to farming took precisely the same path in the different regions of western Asia with their variations in climate, topography and vegetation. But experience tells us that such sites will always be few in number.

Jericho, a case study

It is with such considerations in mind that we have begun a landscape survey around Jericho (Moore 2000), itself one of those rare multi-period sites where agriculture apparently began very early. Jericho was first inhabited towards the close of the Pleistocene, probably by a community of hunters and gatherers. Later, it is likely that the economy of the village changed as farming was adopted there, with spectacular results. The inhabitants expanded the size of their village, surrounded it with a series of walls and constructed the famous tower as well as other impressive remains. The site continued to be inhabited, with interruptions, down to the first millennium BC and the surrounding area has supported habitation and various human activities almost continuously to the present. Such a long sequence is unique, yet why people settled Jericho in the first place and how they sustained themselves over so many years remain elusive questions. For the locality is anything but attractive for settlement, particularly when compared with adjacent regions to the west, north and east: an arid salt desert at the bottom of the Rift Valley with few natural resources.

With this in mind we have begun to reconstruct what the landscape would be like today without human interference and how it may have changed since the site was first occupied. The project is still in its early stages, but a word on methods and results is in order here. We have based our research on a combination of up-to-the-minute satellite imagery studies and fieldwork of a more traditional nature, including studies of vegetation, topography and geomorphology. These have already produced preliminary insights that have given us an initial sense of what some of the factors might have been that conditioned settlement in the Jericho area. The region is one of extraordinary topographic contrasts as one passes from the heights of the Judean Hills in the west, down to the valley floor and then up to the hills around Salt in the east. The Judean Hills are slashed by deep wadis that have evidently acted as conduits for rain-bearing winds from the west. Our botanists, Andrew Fairbairn and Amanda Kennedy of University College, London have found that these have pushed some of the moister vegetation zones farther east than the standard vegetation maps would suggest, to within walking distance of Jericho. Thus, there is reason to suppose that in the past a much greater range of vegetation would have been accessible to the inhabitants of Jericho than its present barren environs would indicate. The question of what vegetation might have been of interest to late Pleistocene foragers and early farmers is further complicated by the fact that African plants penetrate up the Rift Valley as far as Jericho and so are found beside other genera of a more familiar western Asian aspect.

Earlier investigators understood quite well that there were multiple sources of water in the form of valley-edge springs up and down the Rift Valley from Jericho (Conder and Kitchener 1883: 221–229; Tristram 1865: 200, 238), something that is far from obvious today because so many of them have been pumped dry in recent years. Explanations for the existence of Jericho have tended to emphasise the location of the site beside ʿAin es-Sultan, Elisha's spring (Dorrell 1978: 11; Kenyon 1981: 1). But the question should really be put another way: why was Jericho located there in preference to one of the other springs in the region which might also have provided water for an early settled community? Finally, the location of the site on an ancient shoreline of Lake Lisan raises significant questions about the relation of this Pleistocene lake to human settlement of the region (Neev

and Emery 1995: 93; Niemi 1997: 230). It seems to us that the timing of the shrinking of the lake during the Late Glacial and the initial settlement of Jericho are likely to have been closely linked. Only further geomorphological investigations can elucidate this relationship.

Broader considerations

People across western Asia participated in the transition from foraging to farming, though at somewhat different times and in circumstances that varied from one region to another. Yet it is exceedingly difficult to understand the context in which farming developed in each region because we know so little about the way of life of Epi-palaeolithic hunters and gatherers. The emphasis of much research over the last thirty years has been to develop ever finer distinctions in material culture based mainly on flint assemblages, as Edwards, Macumber and Head have remarked (1996: 123–126; see for example Henry 1989, chapters 5, 6; Goring-Morris 1987), with much less attention being given to site function and economy. We know something about the distribution of late Epi-palaeolithic sites, at least in parts of the Levant, and also the variations among them in size and material contents (Bar-Yosef and Valla 1991; Goring-Morris 1987). But there have been few studies of the locations of sites and their relationship to their contemporary environments. And although animal bones have been recovered from many sites, plant remains have not. In consequence, we know all too little about what people ate, let alone how they obtained their sustenance and the variations in their diet from season to season. It is little wonder, then, that our theories of agricultural development remain at such a distance from archaeological fact. A major task ahead must be to excavate Epi-palaeolithic sites where there is a reasonable prospect of recovering organic evidence, using techniques that will ensure complete recovery of such material. This needs to be combined with detailed ecological studies that will relate the activities of the ancient inhabitants of such sites to their environment. Recent work at Wadi Hammeh 27 and Ohalo II (Edwards *et al.* 1988; Kislev, Nadel and Carmi 1992) indicates that the potential for such studies is there, but much more remains to be done if we are significantly to enlarge our understanding of the antecedents of the development of farming.

A further need is simply to expand our knowledge of the Epi-palaeolithic across western Asia. Neolithic sites have been found in a variety of locations over much of the region but all too often those sites that represent the final stages of a foraging way of life have simply not been identified. So, for example, we still know little about the Epi-palaeolithic of Syria, although a few sites have been excavated in specific localities, among them the Middle Euphrates and the Anti-Lebanon Mountains. And the Epi-palaeolithic of Anatolia remains largely unexamined. The recent surveys and excavations of early sites in connection with the resumption of work at Çatal Hüyük promise to add to our understanding (Baird 1996; Watkins 1996), but it seems, nonetheless, that Epi-palaeolithic sites remain elusive in the Konya Basin as elsewhere in Anatolia (Esin 1999: 17). Furthermore, Anatolia is so huge that insights gained from work in one locality will need to be greatly amplified through research in other regions. A good example of what can be learned from hitherto unexplored areas may be seen in the series of excavations conducted by Rosenberg at Hallan Çemi and other sites in the Tigris drainage in south-east Anatolia (Rosenberg 1994; Rosenberg *et al.* 1998). Here Rosenberg has been able to demonstrate that a late Pleistocene group inhabited a settlement year round prior to the development of farming. Their successors seem to have adopted agriculture relatively early.

Climatic fluctuations and, in particular, the sharp onset of the Younger Dryas were major factors in precipitating the development of farming across western Asia. Yet the earliest stages of agricultural development remain little known as few sites dating from this period have been located and excavated. Accordingly, we do not understand in any detail the circumstances in which people adopted farming as the new way of life began to spread. These are likely to have varied from one locality to another simply because of the differences in climate and topography across western Asia as well as in the nature of prior Epi-palaeolithic modes of life. The most difficult episode to elucidate is that of the transition itself, for the reasons adduced

above, namely the different resource requirements of foragers and farmers and thus the locations of their sites.

As the farming economy took hold and foraging diminished in importance, populations grew and sites expanded in size. For this reason Neolithic sites of the ninth millennium BP (uncalibrated) are relatively abundant and many of them have been excavated, especially in the Levant. Consequently, we know more about the material culture of this phase and some details of the economy of these sites. But in the ninth and on into the eighth millennium farming began to spread far beyond western Asia, to Crete, Greece and south-eastern Europe, North Africa, and eastward into central Asia. This process took a new wave of colonists to Cyprus even earlier, in the late tenth millennium BP as we now know (Guilaine 2000: 140). Sites documenting the various phases of the spread of farming have been known for some time, even if the process remains somewhat obscure, despite several bold attempts to model it (Ammerman and Cavalli-Sforza 1984: 67–71; Cavalli-Sforza, Menozzi and Piazza 1994: 253–254; Renfrew 1989: 265). We need to prepare fresh synthetic studies of the evidence from sites already identified and excavated and to apply models of human and economic dispersal with some rigor if we are to advance our understanding of this crucial episode of agricultural dispersal.

The later stages of the Neolithic and the ensuing Chalcolithic period were among the first episodes of village life to be examined systematically by archaeologists, beginning early in the last century. Because interested archaeologists have concentrated over the last forty years on examining the development of farming, however, these periods have not received the intense scrutiny they deserve. There are some excellent exceptions, of which the work by Akkermans, Huot, Roaf and their colleagues are good examples (Akkermans 1990; Huot 1989; Roaf 1989), but the fact remains that we still do not know very much about the nature and organization of the subsistence economy and social arrangements of late Neolithic and Chalcolithic sites This is all the more regrettable because it was during these periods that the crucial changes took place in economy, society and the nature of settlements that brought about the formation of the first towns, with all that this implies for future cultural developments across western Asia. This must be the focus of serious attention by archaeologists in the years ahead.

Final thoughts

We have made significant progress over the last thirty years towards understanding the setting of the Neolithic Revolution and how it came about in western Asia. Sustained archaeological research in core regions has established detailed archaeological sequences from the Epi-palaeolithic to the Chalcolithic, while investigations in other areas have yielded outline cultural frameworks, at least. And we now have a reasonably good idea of the chronology of the successive cultural stages based on radiocarbon dating. New environmental information, much of it obtained in the last few years, has established a very different context for the transition from foraging to farming than was imagined only a couple of decades ago. If the actual processes of agricultural inception and spread are still too thinly documented, we may hope that much more information will be forthcoming once systematic methods of recovery are universally applied. I would add that the time is long past in which this could be considered an optional addition to the normal process of excavation. The research at Abu Hureyra has provided a clear understanding of how and why agriculture developed at that site, so that we now have a much stronger set of explanations for the process there than we did before. But this all needs substantial validation and testing elsewhere. It is time to renew our investigation of the inception and spread of farming, and of its longer-term consequences, with new models in mind and with a determination to develop that detailed understanding of this fundamental transformation in human existence that has shaped our own world.

References

Akkermans, P. M. M. G. 1990
   Villages in the Steppe. Universiteit van Amsterdam: Amsterdam.

Ammerman, A. J. and L. L Cavalli-Sforza 1984
   The Neolithic Transition and the Genetics of Populations in Europe. Princeton University Press: Princeton.

Anderson, P. C. 1992
   Experimental cultivation, harvest and threshing of wild cereals and their relevance for interpreting the use of Epipalaeolithic and Neolithic artifacts. Pp. 179–209 in P. C. Anderson (ed.) *Préhistoire de l'agriculture.* CNRS Editions: Paris.

Aurenche, O. and S. K. Kozlowski 1999
   La naissance du néolithique au proche orient. Editions Errance: Paris.

Baird, D. 1996
   The Konya Plain survey: aims and methods. Pp. 41–46 in Hodder 1996.

Bar-Yosef, O. and F. R. Valla (eds.) 1991
   The Natufian Culture in the Levant. International Monographs in Prehistory: Ann Arbor.

Bond, G., W. Showers, M. Cheseby, R. Lotti, P. Almasi, P. deMenocal, P. Priore, H. Cullen, I. Hajdas and G. Bonani 1997
   A pervasive millennial-scale cycle in North Atlantic Holocene and Glacial climates. *Science* 278: 1257–1266.

Byrd, B. F. 1994
   Public and private, domestic and corporate: the emergence of the Southwest Asian village. *American Antiquity* 59 : 639–666.

Cauvin, J. 1994
   Naissance des divinités. Naissance de l'agriculture. CNRS Éditions: Paris.

Cavalli-Sforza, L. L., P. Menozzi. and A. Piazza 1994
   The History and Geography of Human Genes. Princeton University Press: Princeton.

Conder, C. R. and H. H. Kitchener 1883
   The Survey of Western Palestine III. Palestine Exploration Fund: London.

Cowan, C. W. and P. J. Watson 1992
   The Origins of Agriculture. Smithsonian Institution Press: Washington D.C.

Dorrell, P. 1978
   The uniqueness of Jericho. Pp. 11–18 in R. Moorey and P. Parr (eds.) *Archaeology in the Levant.* Aris and Phillips: Warminster.

Edwards, P. C., S. J. Bourke, S. M. Colledge, J. Head and P. G. Macumber 1988
   Late Pleistocene prehistory in the Wadi al-Hammeh, Jordan Valley. Pp. 525–565 in A. N. Garrard and H. G. Gebel (eds.) *The Prehistory of Jordan.* British Archaeological Reports, International Series, 396: Oxford.

Edwards, P. C., P. G. Macumber and M. J. Head 1996
   The Early Epipalaeolithic of Wadi el-Hammeh. *Levant* 28: 115–130.

Esin, U. 1999
   The Neolithic in Turkey: a general review. Pp. 13–23 in M. Özdogan and N. Basgelen (eds.) *Neolithic in Turkey.* Arkeoloji ve Sanat Yayinlari: Istanbul.

Fortin, M. and O. Aurenche 1998
   Espace naturel, espace habité en Syrie du nord (10e –

2e *millénaires av. J-C).* Bulletin of the Canadian Society for Mesopotamian Studies 33/Travaux de la Maison de l'Orient 28.

Gebauer, A. B. and T. D. Price (eds.) 1992
Transitions to Agriculture in Prehistory. Monographs in World Archaeology 4. Prehistory Press: Madison.

Goring-Morris, A. N. 1987
At the Edge. British Archaeological Reports, International Series, 361 (i): Oxford.

Guilaine, J. 2000.
Tête sculptée dans le néolithique pré-céramique de *Shillourokambos* (Parekklisha, Chypre). *Paléorient* 26/1: 137–142.

Harris, D. R. 1996
The Origins and Spread of Agriculture and Pastoralism in Eurasia. UCL Press: London.

Henry, D. O. 1989
From Foraging to Agriculture. University of Pennsylvania Press: Philadelphia.

Hillman, G., R. Hedges, A. Moore, S. Colledge and P. Pettitt 2001
New evidence of Lateglacial cereal cultivation at Abu Hureyra on the Euphrates. *The Holocene* 11: 383–393.

Hodder, I (ed) 1996
On the Surface: Çatalhöyük 1993-95. McDonald Institute for Archaeological Research/British Institute for Archaeology at Ankara: Cambridge.

Huot, J.-L. 1989
'Ubaidian village of lower Mesopotamia. Permanence and evolution from 'Ubaid 0 to 'Ubaid 4 as seen from Tell el'Oueili. Pp. 18–42 in E. H. Henrickson and I. Thuesen (eds.) *Upon this Foundation.* Museum Tusculanum Press: Copenhagen.

Kenyon, K. M 1981
Excavations at Jericho III. British School of Archaeology in Jerusalem: London.

Kislev, M.E., D. Nadel, and I. Carmi 1992
Epipalaeolithic (19,000 BP) cereal and fruit diet at Ohalo II, Sea of Galilee, Israel. *Review of Palaeobotany and Palynology* 73: 161–166.

Legge, A. J. and P. A. Rowley-Conwy 1986
New radiocarbon dates for early sheep at Tell Abu Hureyra. Pp. 23–35 in J. A. J. Gowlett and R. E. M. Hedges (eds.) *Archaeological Results from Accelerator Dating.* Oxford University Committee for Archaeology: Oxford.

Matthews, W., C. French, T. Lawrence and D. Cutler 1996
Multiple surfaces: the micromorphology. Pp. 301–342 in Hodder 1996.

Mayewski, P. A., L. D. Meeker, S. Whitlow, M. S. Twickler, M. C. Morrison, R. B. Alley, P. Bloomfield and K. Taylor 1993
The atmosphere during the Younger Dryas. *Science* 261: 195–197.

Moore, A. M. T. 1992
The impact of accelerator dating at the early village of Abu Hureyra on the Euphrates.

Radiocarbon 34, 3: 850–858.

Moore, A. M. T. 2000
The Jericho Project. *Newsletter of the British School of Archaeology in Jerusalem* 2, 1.

Moore, A. M. T., G. C. Hillman and A. J. Legge 2000
Village on the Euphrates. Oxford University Press: New York.

Neev, D., and K. O. Emery 1995
The Destruction of Sodom, Gomorrah, and Jericho. Oxford University Press: New York.

Niemi, T. N. 1997
Fluctuations of Late Pleistocene Lake Lisan in the Dead Sea Rift. Pp. 226–236 in T. N. Niemi, Z. Ben-Avraham and J. R. Gat (eds.) *The Dead Sea.* Oxford University Press: New York.

Owen, D. F. 1980
What is Ecology? Oxford University Press: Oxford.

Perry, C. A. and K. J. Hsu 2000
Geophysical, archaeological and historical evidence support a solar-output model for climate change. *Nature* 97: 23, 12433–12438.

Renfrew, C. 1989
Archaeology and Language. Penguin: London.

Roaf, M. 1989
'Ubaid social organization and social activities as seen from Tell Madhhur. Pp. 91–146 in E. H. Henrickson and I. Thuesen (eds.) *Upon this Foundation.* Museum Tusculanum Press: Copenhagen.

Rosenberg, M. 1994
Hallan Çemi Tepesi: some further observations concerning stratigraphy and material culture. *Anatolica* 20: 121–140.

Rosenberg, M., R. Nesbitt, R. W. Redding and B. L. Peasnall 1998
Hallan Çemi, pig husbandry, and post-Pleistocene adaptations along the Taurus-Zagros arc (Turkey). *Paléorient* 24/1: 25–41.

Severinghaus, J. P., T. Sowers, E. J. Brook, R. B. Alley and M. L. Bender 1998.
Timing of abrupt climate change at the end of the Younger Dryas interval from thermally fractionated gases in polar ice. *Nature* 391: 141–146.

Smith, B. D. 1995
The Emergence of Agriculture. Scientific American Library: New York.

Stuiver, M., P. J. Reimer, E. Bard, J. W. Beck, G. S. Burr, K. A. Hughen, B. Kromer, G. McCormac, J. van der Plicht and M. Spurk 1998
INTCAL98 radiocarbon age calibration, 24,000–0 cal BP. *Radiocarbon* 40: 1041–1083.

Taylor, K.C., G. W. Lamorey, G. A. Doyle, R. B. Alley, P.M. Grootes, P. A. Mayewski, J. W. C. White and L. K. Barlow 1993
The 'flickering switch' of late Pleistocene climate change. *Nature* 361: 432–436.

Tristram, H. B. 1865
The Land of Israel. S.P.C.K.: London

Watkins, T. 1996
Excavations at Pınarbası: the early stages. Pp. 47–57 in Hodder 1996.

7

Social space in early sedentary communities of Southwest Asia and Cyprus

Edgar Peltenburg

"a house as little as can accommodate you and land as much as you can see".
(Traditional Cypriot saying)

Abstract

The change from curvilinear to rectilinear architecture in the early Neolithic of Southwest Asia is a well-known phenomenon with many socio-economic implications. Now that it is becoming increasingly clear that inhabitants of Cyprus were in close contact with the mainland from at least the late 9th millennium calibrated BC, the persistence of the curvilinear tradition on the island long after the emergence and elaboration of the rectilinear mode on the continent stands out as a particularly strong anomaly within general Near Eastern architectural developments. This paper explores reasons for the dichotomy in the use of social space. The first part makes a case for strong links between distinctive house types in the Mediterranean Levant/North Mesopotamia and Cyprus. The substantive second part argues that an island ideology of co-operative endeavour acted as a check on the establishment of the kind of unegalitarian behaviour which led to privatisation of domestic space on the mainland. Stresses within this ideology, it is suggested, contributed to the eventual abandonment of Khirokitia. The divergent trajectories of early Neolithic spatial organization in Cyprus and the mainland shed light on the nature of social transformations that accompanied the adoption of farming.

The expansion of nascent farming lifestyles in and after the Early Holocene, ones that accompanied major population growth, is widely regarded as an irrevocable turning point in human development (e.g. Bar-Yosef 1998, 2000; Bar-Yosef and Meadows 1995; Harris 1996, 1998). In addition to occasional autonomous breakthroughs, this was primarily accomplished by two mechanisms: migration of farmers into new territory and the adoption of selected farming practices by hunter-gatherers. Differentiation between the two is often difficult to detect in the archaeological record, yet it is critical since it constitutes formative junctures that shaped the subsequent course of history. The island of Cyprus presents a more clear cut case of colonization by early farmers than is available on the western Asiatic mainland where many of the initial stages of staple production took place (*cf.* Bar-Yosef and Meadows 1995; Byrd 1992; Cauvin 2000). While we cannot rule out the possibility that pre-existing insular complex foragers adopted agriculture (Watkins, this volume), there is as yet no evidence for this process and some against it. For example, foragers are unlikely to have stayed on an island with such circumscribed subsistence resources. According to Simmons (this volume), the shellfish and bird-eating visitors to Akrotiri eventually abandoned Cyprus. Also, the earliest known

Stage	Dates BP	Dates cal BC	Colonization phases
Akrotiri	10,665*	9703*	**Exploration:** ephemeral forager/hunter visitors
?	10,500–?	9500–?	**Colonization?** first settlers
Cypro-EPPNB	?–9100	?–8100	**Colonization:** early agro-pastoral settlers
Cypro-MPPNB	9100–8500	8100–7500	**Consolidation:** contact with mainland
Cypro-LPPNB	8500–8000	7500–7000	**Expansion:** less external contact
Khirokitian	8000–6500	7000/6500–5800/5500	**Florescence** of Aceramic Neolithic

* average of large series of dates (Simmons et al. 1999)

Table 7.1 *Phases of early human utilisation and settlement of the island of Cyprus*

colonists possessed a mainland culture and an economy that shows little modification to suit a distinct ideology of putative indigenous hunter-gatherers (Peltenburg *et al.* 2001, 2003).

Using the example of Cyprus, this paper explores a particular instance of long term development of a successful early farming migrant community. To do so, I shall focus on house form, the house being a principle context of *habitus* that reflexively structures and is structured by individuals operating within evolving social systems (e.g. Parker Pearson and Richards 1994). It has long been regarded as an essential expression of cultural identity and social relations in archaeology (Childe 1929). I will also focus on 'public' architecture. I wish particularly to evaluate the divergent paths of architectural evolution in Cyprus and the Levantine mainland, not so much in their formal typologies, but in terms of the active role in which house 'blueprints' operated in the reproduction and transformation of early sedentary societies. Before assessing these trajectories, we need to look at certain buildings in the PPN of Syro-Mesopotamia and their congeners in Cyprus.

The following points are assumed:
- communities engaged in farming began to appear in certain areas of Southwest Asia during the PPNA (Bar-Yosef 2000; Moore *et al.* 2000);
- we are dealing with an island that was first successfully colonised at least by the EPPNB from mainland donor areas *ca.* 101 km to the east and *ca.* 69 km to the north (Peltenburg *et al.* 2000, 2001; Guilaine *et al.* 2000);

- Table 7.1 represents the chronology and likely human colonization phases of Cyprus. "Cypro-PPNB" is regarded as a chronological, not a Childean cultural entity. It refers to an era that witnessed close interactions and developments between populations living primarily in the Levant, and certainly not one that demands that everyone resided in rectilinear houses, with or without plaster floors.

Dwelling and public structures

Two recent sets of archaeological discoveries provide an opportunity to evaluate social organisation associated with early curvilinear architectural schemes in Southwest Asia and Cyprus. For our purposes, their significance needs to be considered against the background of recent understanding of Cypriot prehistory.

A major feature of the Khirokitian is the well-known, heavy-walled circular dwelling that epitomizes the building tradition of the type-site, Khirokitia. Its late date in relation to mainland parallels has long perplexed unilineal evolutionists who were constrained to account for it by referring to the generalised island stereotypes of isolation and archaism. Before the advent of radiocarbon dating, it was compared to the circular structures of the Halafian, also misleadingly called *tholoi* (Dikaios 1953: 333). It has since been demonstrated that the Cypriot *tholoi* probably had flat roofs (Le Brun 1989: 28–31). With C[14] dates, the Cypriot examples were shown to be too early to be derived from the Halaf, but they were still much later than

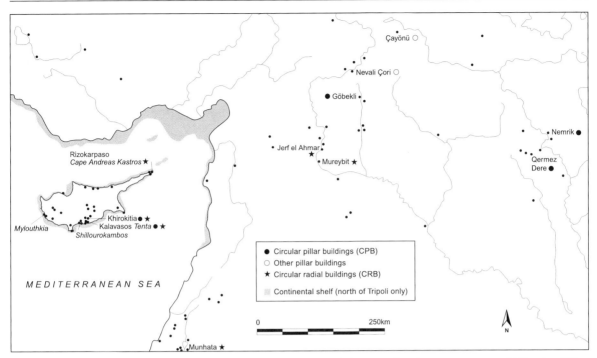

Figure 7.1 *Map of early sedentary sites in Southwest Asia and Cyprus showing occurrences of Circular Pillar Buildings and Circular Radial Buildings, and the likely maximum extent of the Mediterranean palaeocoastline north of Tripoli*

their other hypothetical precursors of the Natufian and PPNA in the southern Levant (Mellaart 1975: 131; Dikaios 1962: 193, 194). In any case, there are so many differences of detail that analogies beyond the simple circular plan do not bear close scrutiny. Then, during the 1970s–80s, significant variants within the Cypriot tradition were found on other aceramic sites, at Kalavasos-*Tenta* (*Tenta*) and Cape Andreas-*Kastros* (Cape Andreas) (Todd 1987; Le Brun 1981a). The Khirokitia type-site orthodoxy was broken, but investigation of regional, functional and chronological disparities within the island, and relations abroad, were stillborn.

Turning to recent discoveries, we now have more compelling parallels for the classic Cypriot aceramic dwelling forms on sites from Jerf el Ahmar to Nemrik in Upper Mesopotamia (Figure 7.1). They belong to the 10th–8th millennium calibrated BC (see below). Second is the discovery during the 1990s of pre-Khirokitian Cypriot sites that, at last, provide evidence for occupation on the island which largely fills the chronological gap between the mainland and Khirokitian building forms (Guilaine *et al.* 2000; Peltenburg *et al.* 2000). Consideration of these

insular discoveries, moreover, has led to the re-dating of the *Tenta* Period 2 settlement to the Cypro-LPPNB (Peltenburg *et al.* 2001). This is important because, for the first time, we have details of a coherent settlement plan that precedes the Khirokitian. Period 2 has several building levels at the crown of the site, so the re-dating significantly narrows the lacuna that existed between new continental discoveries and the classic Cypriot aceramic small circular building form. It was probably established on the island by the later 9th millennium calibrated BC. Evidence for its early development is forthcoming from timber structures at *Mylouthkia* and *Tenta* (Peltenburg *et al.* 2003: 8–9; Todd 1987: Figure 37a) and in stone from *Shillourokambos* (Guilaine *et al.* 1995: 18, Figure 6, Plate I.1; Guilaine and Briois 2001: 44). The sub-square pre-Khirokitian building plans that also co-existed on the island, the result of different adaptive strategies, functional variation or the mixed origin of the builders, are not considered here (*cf.* Sevketoglu 2002: 103).

Within this widespread circular building tradition are a host of minor variations, but two of the most distinctive classes may be singled out:

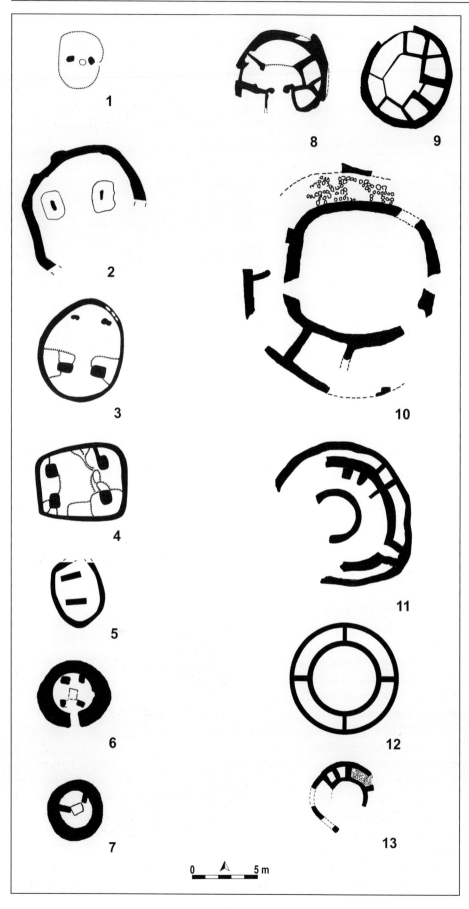

Figure 7.2
Circular Pillar Buildings (1-7) and Circular Radial Buildings (8-13). Plans to scale. 4. shows sub-rectilinear version, 7. use of attached piers

1 *Qermez Dere;*
2 *Göbekli;*
3, 4 *Nemrik;*
5, 11 *Kalavasos-Tenta;*
6, 7, 12 *Khirokitia;*
8 *Mureybet;*
9 *Jerf el Ahmar;*
10 *Munhata;*
13 *Cape Andreas-Kastros.*

(1, 3, 4, 8 *after Aurenche and Kozlowski 1999: Figure 7-1. 6, 7-2.2,5, 7-3.4; 2 after Beile-Bohn* et al. *1998: 48, Figure 20; 5; 11 after Todd 1987: Figure 20; 6, 7; 12 after Le Brun 1984: Figures 15. 2, 24. 2, 32.1a; 9 after Stordeur* et al. *2000; 10 after Perrot 1964: 326, Figure 2; 13 after Le Brun 1981: Figure 2. 578)*

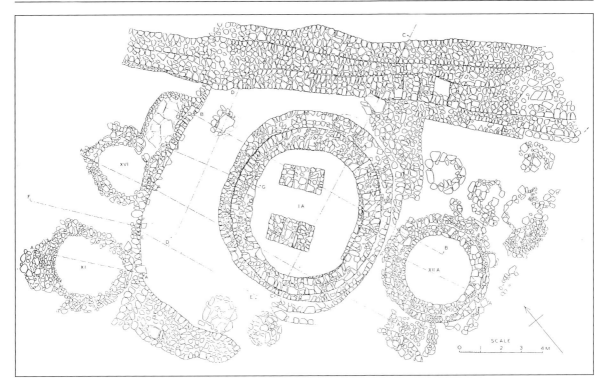

Figure 7.3 *Tholos 1A compound at Khirokitia (Dikaios 1953: Plate 3)*

the circular pillar building (CPB) and the circular radial building (CRB).

The Circular Pillar Building (CPB) in
N. Mesopotamia/SE Anatolia and in Cyprus

The small circular building with stone and mud brick walls, and internal, disproportionately large rectilinear pillars, is a major class of Cypriot aceramic Neolithic architecture (Figures 7.2. 5–7; 7.3). It is one of the monocellular circular building types that occur throughout the large exposures of Khirokitia and at *Tenta*. Free-standing pillars, or piers as they are called at *Tenta*, are the most distinguishing features of this class. They occur frequently at *Tenta* and less so at Khirokitia where partition piers extending inwards from the walls (Figure 7.2.7) are more common (Todd 1987: Figure 57; Dikaios 1953; Le Brun 1994). The two may be structurally related, although they divide space differently. Dikaios (1953), Le Brun (1981a, b) and Todd (1987) describe varieties and positions. Pillars occupy such a large amount of the restricted floor space (e.g. *ca.* 35% in Khirokitia Tholos 1A: Figure 7.3) that it is assumed they are necessary supports for heavy roofs or lofts. While this might be a

cumbersome possibility, plastered tops and the stepped pillar at Khirokitia, which was weakest where it needs weight-bearing strength, shows that free-standing, non–structural pillars also existed (Figure 7.4). At Khirokitia, pillars are sometimes recessed (Figure 7.3). Many retain traces of a plaster coating, and in one instance at

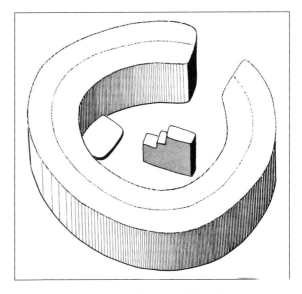

Figure 7.4 *Stepped pillar from Khirokitia: isometric drawing reconstruction (Le Brun 1994: 60, Figure 18)*

Figure 7.5 *Pillar 2 in the 'Schangenpfeilergebäude' at Göbekli (Schmidt 1999: Plate 6)*

than the earliest definite examples in Cyprus, at *Tenta*. Pillars were also used for some time within the rectilinear architectural format that came to prevail. Two to four pillars are common, they are sometimes linked (Nemrik), they have rectilinear plans and they are large in relation to internal space. These formal similarities with the Cypriot examples are striking, especially when one considers that such massive supports are not really necessary for small buildings where appropriate roofing timber was available. At Nemrik, compacted marl pillars succeeded wooden posts. Since here too buildings remain quite small, this is unlikely to be due to scarcity of timber in upper Mesopotamia.

The Nemrik evolution from post to pillar prompts Kozlowski and Kempisty (1989/90) to take a functionalist view of the use of pillars. Other evidence, however, indicates a symbolic rather than exclusively structural role. At Qermez Dere, where the stone slab cores served as armatures for the *tauf* modelled surfaces, perhaps anthropomorphic in shape, they are more stelae than pillars (Watkins 1989–90; *cf.* Stordeur *et al.* 2000: 40, Figure 7.11 for contemporary zoomorphic stelae). We should not stress the distinction between functional and symbolic amongst what was probably a variety of pillar-like features. Examples like the rectilinear monoliths of Göbekli prominently displayed modelled decoration (Figure 7.5) Much of this is representative, as at *Tenta*. One repeated motif, the recumbent animal with forepaws extended (Figure 7.6B), even bears a similarity to the figure with uplifted arms on the *Tenta* pillar and on a stone bowl from Khirokitia (Figure 7.6 A, C). At Göbekli and Nevali Çori, the pillars are far grander than warranted by function alone.

So, as in Cyprus, the CPB comprised a strong architectural tradition in Upper Mesopotamia. In both regions, the CPBs have relatively massive rectilinear pillars placed inside circular units where they considerably reduce already exiguous floor space. We have also seen that the pillars are far more massive than warranted by the dictates of practicality. Indeed, they could be regarded as functionally redundant in Cyprus where many CPBs are no more than easily spanned huts (e.g. 1.4–4 m diam. at *Tenta*, with one large one at 4.9 m.). The recurrence of such impractical components suggests links between

Tenta the pillar was decorated with two figures in red paint (Figure 7.6A). Internal installations on the little remaining floor space include platforms, hearths, pits and basins. Sub-floor burials were found at Khirokitia, but there were few at *Tenta*.

Circular buildings with similarly distinctive pillars are now known within the varied spectrum of building plans in N. Mesopotamia from the 10th millennium calibrated BC (Figure 7.2. 1–4). The latest may occur at Nemrik (Kozlowski and Kempisty 1989–90), but they are still earlier

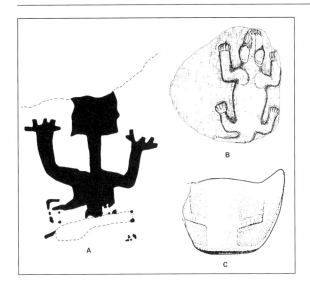

Figure 7.6 *Figures with uplifted 'arms' A. Painting on pillar in Structure 11 at Kalavassos-Tenta (Todd 1987: Figure 39); B. High relief Göbekli sculpture of animal with extended forepaws (Beile-Bohn et al. 1998: 69, Figure 32); C. Relief figure on side of stone bowl from Khirokitia (Le Brun 1989: 173, Figure 52. 9)*

the two regional expressions rather than independent invention by assumed complex hunter-gatherers on the island. Given its chronological precedence and diversity in Upper Mesopotamia, the CPB in Cyprus was probably derived from the east, together with many other aspects of material culture (e.g. Peltenburg *et al.* 2003: 95; Stordeur 2003). The extra labour required to construct these imposing features, especially the stone monoliths at Göbekli and elsewhere, and the stunning repertoire of motifs on their shafts and capitals, implies that pillars were not merely functional. Their transmission to and persistence in Cyprus were connected with symbolism as much as spatial behaviour and function. Construction, decoration and use thus played an active role in the reproduction of a conserved ideology. This ideology may have varied although recurrent associations with the dead suggest links with the ancestors (Schirmer 1989/90). Pillar buildings contain many skulls at Çayönü (below floor) and Qermez Dere (in fill); and inhumations at Khirokitia and Nemrik.

There are three contingent factors that bear on the proposition that the CPB architectural traditions were related and not independent: chronology, longevity and geography.

To argue that the ancestry of the Cypriot CPB is to be found in western Asia does not overcome the problem of a chronological gap between latest mainland and first Cypriot occurrences. At Nemrik the CPB may have continued as late as the early 8th millennium calibrated BC, and in Cyprus the earliest definite occurrences are in the later 8th. Other connections, however, are closest with the upper Euphrates area where currently the latest examples are in the EPPNB, so this hiatus remains a problem, probably one of archaeological recovery.

With respect to longevity, archaeologists have frequently asked why the roundhouse (*cf.* CPB) in Cyprus persisted well after its demise on the continent (e.g. Stordeur 2003). This is part of the wider issue of divergent social behaviour discussed below, but it should be stated here that other evidence exists to demonstrate marked material culture continuity on the island. Successful colonists seem to have retained many aspects of their earlier mainland lives. They include ground stone tool types, representational art forms and media, a growing array of incised stones and certain chipped stone types (McCartney, this volume). Some elements may continue into the mainland PPNB, but many are typical of the PPNA or earlier (Stordeur 2003). The retention of outsized pillars, therefore, conforms to an attested island trait. As symbolic structures, they were vitally important to the cognized world inhabited by the settlers.

Last is the obvious absence of CPBs in the adjacent mainland zone (Figure 7.1). While colonists probably came from several homelands, since marine transgression affected a large area, the Syro-Cilician region was probably the springboard for many maritime ventures to Cyprus. In particular, SSE Anatolia was the most likely departure point for obsidian exported to the island, home of the translocated fallow deer and, uniquely, of the package of founder crops in the Cypro-EPPNB. Two general features support such a derivation: a multiplicity of similarities with northern mainland cultures rather than isolated adaptations, and the argument that migrants require sound knowledge of their destination and navigational skills needed to travel to the island (Peltenburg *et al.* 2001). Such knowledge was most obviously available in the maritime nursery area of adjacent coastlands.

The earliest architectural evidence we have from that region, however, at Late PPNB Ras Shamra VC, is rectilinear (de Contenson 1992: Figures 9–13). It suggests that western Syria generally moved apace with the mainland trend towards the adoption of multi-roomed rectilinear buildings, and that PPNA-EPPNB sites with CPBs await discovery. One alternative, namely that some communities there or in SE Anatolia continued to live in CPBs into the M–LPPNB (as at Nemrik?) and then emigrated to Cyprus, is possible, but less likely. Even more unlikely, given the evidence for year-round activities at Cypriot sites, is the possibility that mobile groups used rectangular buildings on the mainland for one time of year, and circular on Cyprus for another, like the Navajo *ramadas* and *hogans* (Kent 1990: 134, Figure 9. 2).

Significant implications flow from the argument that the CPB tradition was established on the island during the colonization phases (Table 7.1). First, migrants presumably brought it with them before it ceased on the western mainland, and at the moment that seems to be before *ca.* 8500–8000 calibrated BC. This means that colonists probably arrived earlier than we have evidence for at present and that one day we may recover a Cypro-PPNA or a post-Akrotiri variant. Second, archaeologists have long believed that accelerated demic diffusion and colonization were the result of farming. Unless there were special environmental reasons (Peltenburg *et al.* 2001), this reconstruction implies that both farming and expansionary pressure already existed in the PPNA. Major movements are believed to have taken place later, in the MPPNB, when sites like Abu Hureyra supposedly reached impressive sizes, so our argument indicates that, in addition to budding-off, there were other mechanisms in a much longer process of dispersal (*cf.* Cauvin 2000: 137–220; Moore *et al.* 2000: 520). Last are questions about domestication. If these pioneers possessed the complete suite of plant domesticates that they had later, at the end of the Cypro-EPPNB, then the domestication of some will be earlier than currently believed (Colledge, this volume). If not, then the permanent settlement of the island took place as domestic strains were coming on stream, innovations that were rapidly appropriated by the new islanders. Also, the trans-location

to and probable management in Cyprus of 'wild' cattle, pig (?), caprids and deer discloses the existence of close animal controls before full domestication is evident in morphological and age profile terms.

The Circular Radial Building (CRB) in the Levant

This diverse class comprises circular structures of more varied sizes than the CPB, with a relatively spacious, installation-free, central circular or sub-circular space and radial, non-communicating cells at the periphery. In Aurenche's terminology, it equates with round pluricelluar buildings (Aurenche 1981: 188). The cells may be within or beyond the main wall of the structure, but in both cases they are integral parts of the structures, arranged radially, like the pens for livestock in the EBA Vounous enclosure model (Peltenburg 1994). They are usually smaller than the central core, sometimes considerably so. On the mainland, CRBs occur at Mureybet III, Jerf el Ahmar and Munhata 3; in Cyprus at Cape Andreas, Khirokitia and *Tenta* (Figure 7.2. 8–13).

Muryebet Str. 47 is well-built with central court and, against the interior of the main wall, a large platform and six cells. It is considered an important structure that yielded many objects, including figurines. One cell contained a cache of bird bones, another an oven. That the type had a special role is clear from the position, subterranean construction, contents and relative size of Jerf el Ahmar structure EA 30 (Stordeur *et al.* 2000). Its internal plan is virtually the same as Mureybet Str. 24. Located at the centre of a group of smaller, above ground, sub–rectilinear structures facing the CRB, it must have been a focal point for this part of the community. In its central area lay a spread–eagled, headless body covered by debris from its destruction. Stordeur suggests EA 30 was probably a communal, multifunctional building, used for storage, meetings and rituals. She compares its role to a N. American pueblo *kiva*. It contained high quality, utilitarian items and at least one cell had the appearance of a silo. Another CRB, EA 7, was found on the east tell (Stordeur and Abbès 2002: 568, Figure 2). All three Euphratean examples belong to the Late Mureybetian of the PPNA.

The last mainland example, at Munhata, is much later, well within the PPNB, a date which signals the continuation of architectural variability in the mainland PPNB (see Aurenche 1981: Table 22). Reports of postholes within the central 10 m diameter paved area of the large complex suggest that it was at least partially roofed (Perrot 1964: 327). Peripheral, external cells are up to 3 m wide and 6 m long. Some had raised floors and may have been for hard wear since they were cobbled. Externalised cells like these also occur on Cyprus.

At Cape Andreas there is a group of miniature versions of the Munhata CRB type (Le Brun 1981a: Figures 2–8). Their central areas are up to 4 m in diameter, sometimes carefully paved and normally installation free. As at Munhata, a single encircling row of cells or annexes radiate from the external walls, some sturdily paved. The restored plan of another Cypriot example, S. 111 at Khirokitia, is much more regular (Figure 7.2.12). Its diameter is *ca.* 9.2 m, its central court *ca.* 4.8 m. No floor was found. Located in the West Sector of the site at the end of a sequence of CPBs, it is the only example reported from Khirokitia (but *cf.* Str. 96). Le Brun (1984: 65–67) proposed that *Tenta* S. 14 (Figure 7.2.11) also belonged to this class and that the Cypriot examples were all terminal Khirokitian, so appreciably later than the Munhata CRB. However, the uniformly earlier, pre-Khirokitian dates associated with the *Tenta* example demonstrates that the CRB was a recurrent functional type and not an exclusively late design that resolved the constraints of the internally segmented small circular buildings (*cf.* Le Brun 1984: 65–7, Figure 32).

The CRB co-existed with the CPB at *Tenta*. Complex S. 14 has three concentric walls (max external diam: 12.32 m) comprising a central court with external diam 4.2 m, and two sets of much smaller, internal peripheral cells bounded by 'buttresses' or cross walls (Todd 1987: 43). There are no internal features in the core and only a pendant and picrolite fragments were recovered (Todd 1987: 85). The complex arrangement is a unique variant within the CRB tradition, but the concept of internal peripheral cells and its obvious centrality at the summit of a hillock surrounded by small CPBs, demonstrate strong spatial and conceptual affinities with the Jerf el Ahmar layout (see Peltenburg *et al.* 2001: 41, Figure 4). S. 14 was the last of three large circular structures on the summit. We do not know if predecessors had radial cells, but their

importance is indicated by their even greater size, central location and, in one case, red-painted floor (S. 17: Todd 1987: 86).

The chronological gap between mainland occurrences and insular examples is less than in the case of the CPB because of the existence of the Munhata CRB. However, the paucity of known mainland CRBs and internal continuity on the island make it difficult to argue that Cypriot examples represent renewed influence from the east. It may be more prudent to observe that the CRBs at *Tenta* and the other sites were clearly part of a curvilinear tradition which can be traced back to the Cypro-EPPNB when many aspects of colonists' mainland origins are evident. The CRB, therefore, may be one more instance of continuity, and in this case we can see from Munhata that Cyprus was not alone in retaining and conservatively developing earlier traditions. Individual communities undoubtedly had their own reasons for building designs, ones that may cut across our concepts of culture areas and unilineal evolution. In Cyprus however, it remains the case that the curvilinear tradition stands out as a particularly strong anomaly within general Near Eastern architectural developments.

Island and mainland: continuity and change

The contrast between domestic architecture on the mainland and Cyprus during the 8th – 6th millennium calibrated BC is striking given the ubiquity (outside the arid zone) of the emergence of new social systems that underpinned the development of multi-roomed rectangular architecture in the east (e.g. Flannery 1972; Byrd 1994) and evidence for contact between the two regions (Peltenburg *et al.* 2001, 2003; Stordeur 2003). Whether or not the circular buildings described above belong to a common cultural tradition, divergences in the development of the use of space by these early food producers merit closer scrutiny. Two issues are explored here. First, inter-cultural spatial contrasts are evaluated as a means to understand the social dynamics of groups that may have descended from common ancestral traditions. Second, and following from the first, is the proposal that the disappearance of the Khirokitian, a vexed problem in Cypriot pre-history, may be due to group-oriented society's inability to cope with problems of scalar stress and the growth of household autonomy.

Social space and social organisation

It is a truism that architecture is at least partly socio-economic statement (e.g. Parker Pearson and Richards 1994). In a stimulating paper Flan-nery (1972; see also 2002) robustly attempted to correlate spatial developments in the Neolithic of the Near East with changes in social structure by using ethnographic analogies. He argued that circular houses were indicative of more tempo-rary residence, of nomadic or semi-nomadic groups, a view that is still common (e.g. Henry 2003: 12), and, above all, of a more sharing, com-munal lifestyle, especially with respect to food production and consumption. He equated such early sites on the Asiatic mainland with com-pound systems in Africa in which buildings were occupied by one or two people, and risk and storage were communally shared. These polygy-nous extended systems inhibited intensification of production at the individual or family level, and they were only overcome when private pro-duction and consumption gradually came to pre-dominate. A key element of his argument is the decline of communal granaries in favour of household storage, that is, of obligatory sharing in favour of the independence of sub-groups. The appearance of more spacious rectilinear houses in the PPNB was felt to indicate the establish-ment of nuclear families. Their design reflects and confers potentials for expansion of house-holds. Space is more readily segmented and rooms can more easily be added for the purposes of storage of intensified production and for housing members of the domestic mode of pro-duction. These arguments, of course, have wider ramifications insofar as the privatisation of pro-duction by family units was a major driving force for the rise of hereditary inequalities in society.

Flannery's reconstruction has more recently been implicitly criticised, for example by Bogucki (1999: 193–4), who proposes 'proto-households' as instigators of agriculture, and explicitly by Byrd (2000) and Banning (2002) who contend that nuclear families resided in domestic structures from the Natufian through the PPNB. Byrd deploys several arguments. Two main ones are that households likely became the basic social unit with sedentism and agricultural production and that Naroll's mean of 10 m² floor area per individual is too generous. Acceptance of Naroll's formula would suggest that nuclear family residences appear in the southern Levant primarily in the PPNB, in line with Flannery's model. Using ethnographic hunter-gatherer data, Byrd (2000: 82, 83) suggests that mean floor area per individual was less, thus allowing for the existence of nuclear families in the earlier circular as well as later elaborated rectilinear dwellings. Substantial change occurred in the southern PPNB when increases in size and inter-nal segmentation are interpreted as evidence for increased nuclear household autonomy. This is accompanied by the appearance of non-residen-tial, public structures which are regarded as venues for the resolution of inter-communal ten-sions (Byrd 1994; Adler and Wilshusen 1990). There was significant inter and intra-regional variation. In the north, at sites like PPNA Jerf el Ahmar, the observed changes may have hap-pened earlier (Stordeur *et al.* 2000).

There are enormous difficulties in identifying archaeological correlates for extended family households, nuclear households, groups consist-ing of multiple households like Kuijt's Houses and other systems (e.g. Kuijt 2000b; Blanton 1997; Netting *et al.* 1984; Wilk and Rathje 1982; Brück and Goodman 1999). The outlines of possible early sedentary and food producing types of com-munity organisation and changes in them are becoming clearer in the southern Levant (Flan-nery 1972; Byrd 1994; Bar-Yosef 1995; Kuijt 2000a; Kuijt and Goring-Morris 2002), less well known in the north (*cf.* Cauvin 2000; Stordeur *et al.* 2000; Schirmer 1989–90; Schmidt 1998, 1999) and hardly at all in Cyprus. Given the meagreness of the Cypriot evidence, a broad brush, tentative approach may be most appropriate at this stage. Two general assumptions are made here: first, from the onset of sedentism and during the process of neolithization, when in many societies surplus production became increasingly possible, a com-munal, sharing ethos contended with the claims of incipient sub-groups such as nuclear family households to hoard foodstuffs and accumulate wealth, and second, this lengthy dynamic is generally reflected in the contrast between simple, standardised use of space in the built

Figure 7.7 *Reconstruction of the* Tenta *village (Todd 1998: 33, Figure 15. Drawn by John Brogan)*

environment with a more heterogeneous organization (*cf.* Kent's [1990] architectural segmentation). In evaluating the Cypriot evidence it would be most useful to focus on domestic structures, storage and integrating facilities since building types and storage are sensitive indicators of early social organisation and change.

The Cypro-LPPNB *Tenta* settlement plan consists of small, mainly unsegmented (save for pillars) CPBs arranged contiguously, without divisions, around a principal building, CRB structure 14 (Figure 7.7). The average internal area is 6.51 m², well below Naroll's formula per individual and low for hunter-gatherers (Byrd 2000: 84, Figure 2). It was *ca.* 10 m² if we add hypothesized lofts (Todd 1987: 31), but that too is more consistent with individual rather than nuclear family occupancy. The general plan is reminiscent of some of Flannery's more spacious ethnographic compounds with similarly small, homogenous structures around a main hut (Flannery 1972: 32, Figure 1).

At the later site of Khirokitia, where population density might have led to socio-economic complexity and the privatisation of storage (Flannery 2002: 44), residential architecture comprises essentially the same monocellular structures as at *Tenta*, with similar small sizes (Level IIIb = average of 4.55 m² per structure: Le Brun *et al.* 1984: 70) and restricted internal arrangements. Their more massive appearance is due to the use of much thicker walls, a local response to erosion on the site's steep slopes. Dikaios, however, identified three exceptions to the prevailing undivided spatial organisation. Each of his three complexes was walled off from the rest of the settlement, thus creating sharply divided private space suitable for storage. Inside the complex was a main structure (with burials) and one or two smaller ones for domestic or workshop purposes (Figure 7.3; Dikaios 1953: 39, 148, 158, Figures 75, 84). Le Brun (1984: 63–4, Figures 8–10) postulates the existence of other houses comprised of groups of structures without yard walls, and he also alludes to the existence of much larger, extended families with a multiplicity of domestic spaces. As he admits, there are few arguments to support these discrete spatial divisions within the community (Le Brun 2002: 25), but Dikaios' examples are enough to show the existence of a few physically demarcated complexes that may be equated with nuclear family households. Analysis of installations and the sub-floor mortuary record from current excavations should eventually elucidate domestic building occupancy and functions more clearly.

Other sites like Cape Andreas and Petra tou Limniti contain even less evidence for differential use of social space. Thus, the limited settlement record in Cyprus indicates the dominance of collectivities with a sharing, egalitarian ethos. Only Khirokitia evinces limited signs of emergent sub-groups.

Storage arrangements are pivotal indicators of communal claim to acquired food (*cf.* central storage) or the privatisation of produce (in-house storage). Buildings are monocellular with little space for on-floor storage. Only one structure at *Tenta*, S. 34, and one at Khirokitia, Str. 99, have been proposed as granaries (Todd 1987: 102; Le Brun 1984: 63, Plate 8.4/5). Being relatively small and shallow, pits at all sites are unsuitable as silos (Dikaios 1953: 205–211; Le Brun 1981a: 23; Todd 1987: 50). Of course, there may have been ad hoc use of abandoned dwellings as granaries, but there is little evidence to support the claim. In this context, it is worth noting that Dikaios (1953: 209) estimated that 31% of structures in his excavations at Khirokitia had no hearths, and Todd (1987: 49) reports that there were only three definite intramural ones at *Tenta*. The more common extramural fireplaces suggest that much cooking occurred in public outside buildings, so the absence of an internal hearth does not necessarily mean that the building was a granary. Hypothesized mezzanines in CPBs and other structures, similar to that depicted in the Jericho house model (Garstang 1936: Plate 40b), could also have been used for storage, as in the case of sendes (lofts) in the vernacular architecture of Cyprus (Christodoulou 1959). If this were the case, however, one would have expected more grain samples from Cypro-PPNB and Khirokitian buildings with hearths. Given that animals were penned outside the crowded, enclosed settlements, granaries might have been outside too. From this brief analysis, it is clear that storage venues are difficult to isolate in the Cypriot Neolithic. One facility worth considering is the CRB.

Socially integrative, non-domestic structures seem to proliferate in PPNA–B sedentary communities in Upper Mesopotamia and in the PPNB in the southern Levant. Three or four of these "special function buildings" (in some cases CRBs) were excavcated at Çayönü, others at Nevali Çori, Jerf el Ahmar, Göbekli and Beidha, for example (Byrd 1994; Schirmer 1989/90; Schmidt 1998; Stordeur *et al.* 2000). Such elaborate facilities may have served a multiplicity of purposes (Adler and Wilshusen 1990) and no doubt different societies emphasized different communal strategies in negotiating novel situations. Not all associated communities were large (e.g. Jerf el Ahmar), hence they may not all manifest the need for hierarchical institutions to mediate tensions within expanding early sedentary populations. Cauvin (2000: 120), for example, highlights the problem of correlating these precocious structures with institutionalised inequalities in society. He prefers to interpret them as corporate expressions and regards them as collective architecture for occasional gatherings in which the village participated, an interpretation that suits the layout and other evidence from *Tenta*.

These public structures appear at a time when cereal crops become increasingly important, and with them new imperatives for bulk storage of harvested crop and seed corn. It is suggested above that one function of the Jerf el Ahmar and Tell Mureybet public structures may have been for storage. Where there is little evidence for storage facilities in associated buildings, it may be that communities held stocks in common at certain times in the agricultural cycle in such structures. Who the controlling body was is a moot point, but the absence of obvious inequalities in burials and other aspects of behaviour suggest the existence of acephalous segmentary societies in which leaders could not hold hereditary office (*cf.* Kuijt 2000b). Turning to the CRBs at sites like Cape Andreas and *Tenta*, they occur in settlements of small homogenous structures. Thus, group-oriented society with civic leadership for the construction of village boundary walls and the CRB at *Tenta* seems to have prevailed in Cyprus, with some evidence for family households at Khirokitia (below). In contrast, the southern Levantine data presents a correlation between the appearance of public structures and emphasis on more articulated residences that are equated with growing independence of families (Byrd 1994).

We need to broaden the contextual, and especially the ecological, analysis if we seek to account for the tenacious retention of these Cypriot collectivities when compared to the mainland where sub-groups and perhaps autonomous households are much more evident. With the recovery of a lengthy pre-Khirokitian sequence, it is becoming possible to deal tentatively with cultural evolution in which particular systems were historically constituted. In outline, colonists arrived with specific PPNA traditions, and with managed subsistence stocks (Colledge and Horwitz *et al.*, this volume). Heavily reliant on these introductions, settlers had to make exceptional investments in their success, whereas mainlanders, with a greater variety of resources at their disposal and more easily replenished stocks, could adopt a variety of subsistence strategies. This emphasis on tried and tested 'artificial' subsistence patterns on the island was successful, since the same translocated crops and animals (except cattle) continue through the Khirokitian. In contrast to the situation of resource abundance on the mainland, risk management for subsistence resources and humans in the new, circumscribed environment of an island may have emphasized co-operation and suppressed the growth of individual or sub-group interests. Historical contingency, therefore, outweighed the general dynamic towards privatization of storage seen in many parts of the mainland.

Yet, there are only 25–35 sites of this long, *ca.* 3000 year, period known on the island (Figure 7.1 and Held 1992). Actual numbers were certainly higher, but restricted surface scatters of chipped stone, consistent with only a few buildings, if such existed at all, is likely to be representative. With such a low density population, there was little competition for productive resources. Thus, conflict for territories and the need for institutions to regulate access to resources or to integrate larger populations were virtually non-existent. In the absence of signs of conflict, the village walls at *Tenta* and Khirokitia are probably boundary markers rather than evidence of conflict. Nor was competition forthcoming from being a member of an archipelago with resource complementarity, as in the Aegean (Broodbank 2000). Persistent

indications of a low population run counter to the arguments that increased population always results from sedentism and the adoption of farming. Depressed numbers may be due to particular health problems like thalassaemia (Le Mort 2003; Peltenburg *et al.* 1998: 88–9, 104, 119–20), but whatever the reasons, the contrast with some regions of the mainland is instructive.

There we see larger and, sometimes, more closely spaced communities where competition for territories and high population densities generated the emergence of marked social differences. Inequalities grew in areas of resource abundance, and elaborate non-domestic buildings were erected in settlements like Nevali Çori, Çayönü and Göbekli. It is not only sedentism and agriculture *per se* which ineluctably led to changes in social organisation, but also competition and emulation between groups with varied access to resources and knowledge. Once a vying dynamic was established, peer polity interaction may be a better model to tackle the question of the growth of novel forms of social organisation at these times.

According to this view of the island's early prehistory, it was the limited influx of migrants, inhibitors of population expansion, restricted ecosystem and lack of inter-group competition that promoted continuity of the communal system. A key factor may lie in the size of sites. For Flannery (2002), larger population aggregates led to increased individual ownership. The limited Cypriot evidence at our disposal suggests that, with the exception of Khirokitia, sites remained small. These conditions of stability in the face of profound mainland changes should not be understood as the result of a closed system and isolation, although there may have been long term weakening of ties with related continental communities. Occurrences of obsidian and carnelian, and the adoption of mainland chipped stone types and production techniques, demonstrate that transmaritime exchanges lasted throughout the Cypro–PPNB and Khirokitian (Briois *et al.* 1997; Dikaios 1953; McCartney, this volume). But these were low volume exchanges. They did not entail social re-organization such as might follow from the need for surplus production for trade purposes, perhaps instigated by prestige-hungry elites. Uniformity of buildings and paucity of exotic goods in

Khirokitian burials indicate application of checks on the emergence of sustained individualising behaviour. Similarly, the restricted nature of long-distance interaction after the Cypro-MPPNB also implies that islanders in general were probably unaware of the socio-economic gulf that separated them from developments elsewhere. In these circumstances, there was no need for them to accentuate their differences from 'the other'. It would be misplaced to think of island continuity as a rejectionist movement, a conscious disavowal of what had become increasingly alien mainland social systems. There does not seem to have been enough interaction for this to be an instance of Hodder's proposition that the degree of material culture differences between groups depends on the degree of social and economic stress between them (Hodder 1985). Rejection or ignorance of other mainland innovations like pottery may also be due to the limited nature of contacts, the usefulness of island products (wood containers/baskets) and a desire to express collective identity through goods, that is the materialization of an island ideology.

This ideology was no doubt forged over a prolonged period, but ultimately it may have referred to the initial shock of colonization, a process of altering space and time (*cf.* Gosden 1994). In establishing a successful existence in a new world largely bereft of the older social and environmental surroundings, settlers confronted perceived instability by retaining traditions like the CPB that harked back to earlier times. In other words, there was a deliberate creation amongst bounded societies of a dynamic of stability in the face of what for some, at least, must have been a precarious experiment. With only low volume subsequent maritime contacts, the ascendancy of the co-operative system in Cyprus was maintained because it was advantageous to do so, because there were insufficient incentives for change, and because of the reinforcing effects of a distinct evolutionary trajectory, as seen, for example, in the proliferation of stone vessel manufacture.

Communal mode tension and transition: the case of Khirokitia

The extinction of the Khirokitian may now be contextualised within the nature of early Cypriot society as outlined above. After *ca.* 5500 calibrated BC, this culture disappears from the archaeological record of Cyprus, and there is a lengthy gap of about a millennium for evidence of any occupation on the island (Held 1992 underestimates the length). When the settlement record resumes in the Late Neolithic, it is strikingly different from the Khirokitian. To date, natural causes have been adduced for this profound transformation or even for a possible abandonment of the island. Dikaios (1953) pointed to increasing mortality rates at Khirokitia, but more recent excavations have not confirmed such a pattern (Le Mort 2003). Held prefers to attribute the breakdown to dry conditions at the start of the Posglacial Climatic Optimum, leading to adaptive strategies such as fission and deer hunting (in Knapp *et al.* 1994: 408). While it is premature to try to establish the priority of causes in this debate, an essential goal of archaeological discourse, emphasis here is placed on social factors.

As we have seen, most aceramic settlements were small, and they possessed an egalitarian organization. *Tenta* is only *ca.* 0.2 ha. The same ethos prevailed at Khirokitia, but with a relatively large population aggregate, estimated at 300 – 600 inhabitants (Le Brun 1984: 71), the site is atypical of Neolithic Cyprus. In spite of extensive excavations since 1936, it lacks evidence for status differences amongst the habitation's large, non–domestic structures, save for enclosure walls of the type that recur at *Tenta*. Le Brun (1994: 139–142) mentions a few discrete open areas between some buildings as places for the conduct of public ceremony and decision-making, the equivalent of Adler and Wilshusen's (1990) bounded spaces. Their distribution and small size points to fragmentation rather than cohesion and he is only able to postulate the existence of 'subtle' regulatory mechanisms. Spatial organisation at the site of *Tenta* (Figure 7.7), and Neolithic people's choice of prominent landmarks for their settlements, suggest that pertinent structures may be located at or near the crown of the site (*cf.* Peltenburg 2003: 101). That aside, the overall character of the settlement is one of a proliferation of small circular huts and rarity of discernible independent clusters (above). The very existence of the latter, however, suggests that the prevailing egalitarian basis of

Cypriot Neolithic society was under pressure at Khirokitia. Greater social differences are also evident in the burial record of the site, one in which there are more grave goods than at other sites like *Tenta* and *Shillourokambos*.

Long regarded as the height of aceramic Cypriot achievement, this unusually large community does not seem to have widely developed the multi-roomed residential units we have seen on the mainland, consistent with increased household autonomy and storage. We also still have no evidence for public facilities to cope with increased scalar stress inherent in such a large community. In other words, its size exceeded the socio-economic basis of traditional Neolithic society on the island. Problems of scheduling resources, for example, must have arisen since, while the settlement was situated in territory that could easily sustain a small group, the location was in a topographically fragmented landscape, less than ideal to meet the subsistence requirements of a substantial, nucleated population. This is clear from diachronic faunal data. Towards the end of its existence, Khirokitians experienced subsistence stress since deer statistics declined appreciably then and unusually high numbers of ovicaprids indicate a more laborious means of production (Davis 1994). Lacking evidence for new political structures, it could only be a matter of time before the stresses came to a head within the polity. Normally, we might expect this to be restricted to community fission, but so unusual was Khirokitia, with important inter-regional links (carnelian, obsidian), that it may have operated as a central place. When it broke up, the effects were felt island-wide.

The ensuing millennium or so is a "Dark Age" in Cypriot prehistory. A possible insight into the nature of the transformation that took place concerns the role of CRBs. Returning to Khirokitia, there are hints that a shift in lifestyle occurred in the final aceramic occupation. There, on top of a long history of CPBs and other small circular structures, a CRB was installed, the first attested example at Khirokitia (Str. 111: Figure 7.2.12). We have argued that this type of building may have served as a communal storehouse and other public functions. At Cape Andreas, it is significant that flimsy CRBs were largely empty and that work areas, finds and installations were concentrated outside. Spatial behaviour there is

consistent with the use of CRBs as storage facilities and occasional shelters for groups favouring an extra–mural existence. In other words, Cape Andreas suggests populations that, apart from CRBs, left ephemeral traces of occupation and activity foci.

If this reconstruction is applied to the unprecedented establishment of Str. 111 at Khirokitia, the late transformation implies that some inhabitants began to adopt different settlement strategies before finally deserting the site, and that the island was not abandoned. Subsequently, they eschewed large–scale, heavily built–up environments in preference for less archaeologically visible home bases, as at Dhali-Agridhi, a camp which potentially extends into the "Dark Age" (Lehavy 1989). If the high levels of deer at Late Neolithic Sotira (Ducos 1965) are representative, society may have concentrated on deer exploitation. In brief, it may have adopted a more mobile lifestyle. Unlike the otherwise analogous settlement pattern developments in the southern Levant where large sites like 'Ain Ghazel shrank markedly in size during the PPNC–PN, to be replaced by simpler communities with altered economic strategies (and the resurgence of circular buildings in the Yarmukian, and in the north the pre-Halaf), deteriorating climatic conditions do not seem to have played a role in this profound insular transformation (*cf.* Simmons 2000).

In sum, once it had attained its exceptional size without introducing the necessary organisational adjustments to deal with antipathies between the private and the transparently reciprocal social systems, Khirokitia became an unstable aberration. Far from being the standard for early Neolithic Cyprus, it was exceptional. Its demise entailed far-reaching effects that spelt the end of built-up settlements with circular plans for dwellings and other units, a tradition whose roots may be traced to the colonists who probably arrived on the island before *Mylouthkia* 1A and *Shillourokambos* Early Phase A.

Summary

In this paper I have tentatively essayed a model of divergent paths of social organisation amongst early farming communities brought about by emigration in the 9thww millennium calibrated BC from Southwest Asia to Cyprus. Crudely stated, the model is partly based on the simplified correlation of monocellular huts in the built environment with a generalised sharing regime, and larger, articulated dwellings and a more heterogeneous use of space with the accentuation of private storage. It was postulated that the circular pillar building (CPB) and circular radial building (CRB) forms in Cyprus were derived from N. Syria/SE Anatolia, and that this building tradition was brought by migrants in the frontier phase of colonization from Syro-Cilicia to Cyprus during the PPNA/EPPNB.

Whether or not the postulated connection is confirmed, the ensuing divergence of social development in the two regions is clear. A more egalitarian system persisted in Cyprus in spite of contacts with profoundly altered mainland societies because it functioned as a context for stability, an ideology that was regarded as essential for people who had colonised a physically separate world, who relied on an intensively managed and recently 'domesticated' staples subsistence base and who had no native major alternative subsistence resources. Its persistence was also due to several other factors, chiefly the absence of competition between farming groups and between these and others such as hunter-gatherers. This model can be tested against other sources of archaeological evidence for social space when they become available.

The distinctive Cypriot trajectory highlights the regional character of the neolithization process, and it has general implications for an understanding of the Neolithic transformation in Southwest Asia. For example, the long-term paucity of Neolithic sites on the island demonstrates that the adoption of farming did not necessarily lead to population increase. The question that remains to be resolved is whether this was due to particular characteristics of islands, even though Cyprus is a large one, or simply another regionally adaptive feature. A corollary of demographic increase is often held to be migratory expansion, but in this case Cyprus is unlikely to have been the platform for Neolithic dispersals westwards into the Mediterranean. Yet another implication of the contrasting trajectories concerns the idea that agriculture and sedentism *per se* led to the growth of greater

socio-political complexity of the kind seen during the mainland PPNA–B. The Cypro-PPNB and Khirokitian show that other dynamics must be considered, in particular, competition between groups, concentrated centres of population and diversity of lifestyles.

Within the island, this analysis of spatial organisation suggests that there is a need to reappraise the nucleated settlement of Khirokitia as a community that ultimately consisted of a maladjusted polity, ill-suited to deal with the stresses manifested by the emergence of more autonomous households amongst a communally organised society. The disappearance of the Khirokitian is unlikely to have resulted in the abandonment of the island. Spatial behaviour rather points to a change in the nature of sedentism, one that led to less archaeological visibility.

Acknowledgements

I am grateful to Diane Bolger, Andrew McCarthy, Philip Karsgaard and anonymous reviewers for their valued comments and insights. They won't agree with all that's written here, but I have tried to incorporate their improvements, and remain responsible for the rest. My warmest thanks also to A. Le Brun, K. Schmidt and I. A. Todd for permission to reproduce figures; and to D. Stordeur for allowing me to quote from her forthcoming publication. Drawings by L. Crewe (Figure. 7.1) and A. Jackson (Figures. 7.2, 3).

References

Adler, M. and Wilshusen R. 1990
   Large-scale integrative facilities in tribal societies: cross-cultural and southwestern US examples. *World Archaeology* 22 : 133–44.
Aurenche, O. 1981
   La maison orientale. L'architecture du Proche Orient Ancien des origines au milieu du quatrième millénaire. P. Geuthner: Paris.
Aurenche, O. and S. Kozlowski 1999
   La naissance du néolithique au proche-orient. Paris: Errance
Banning, E. 2002
   Spatial and architectural aspects of neolithization. Pp. 307–312 in A. Hausleiter, S. Kerner and B. Müller-Neuhof (eds.) *Material Culture and Mental Spheres. Rezeption archäologischer Denkrichtungen*

in der Vorderasiatischen Altertumskunde. Interna-tionales Syposium für Hans J. NISSEN, Berlin, 23.-24. Juni 2000. Alter Orient und Altes Testament 293. Ugarit-Verlag: Münster.

Bar-Yosef, O. 1995
Earliest food producers – Pre Pottery Neolithic (8000–5500). Pp 190–201 in T. Levy, *The Archaeolo-gy of Society in the Holy Land.* Leicester University Press: London.

Bar-Yosef, O. 1998
Agricultural Origins: Caught Between Hypothe-ses and a Lack of Hard Evidence. *The Review of Archaeology* 19: 58–64.

Bar-Yosef, O. 2000
The impact of radiocarbon dating on Old World Archaeology: past achievements and future prospects. *Radiocarbon* 42: 23–35.

Bar-Yosef, O. and A. Belfer-Cohen 1989
The Levantine 'PPNB' Interaction Sphere. Pp. 59–72 in I. Hershkovitz, *People and Culture in Change. Proceedings of the Second Symposium on Upper Paleolithic, Mesolithic and Neolithic Popula-tions of Europe and the Mediterranean Basin.* British Archaeological Reports, International Series 508: Oxford.

Bar-Yosef, O. and R. Meadows 1995
The Origins of Agriculture in the Near East. Pp. 39–94 in T. Douglas Price and A. Gebauer, *Last Hunters, First Farmers: New Perspectives on the Pre-historic Transition to Agriculture.* School of Ameri-can Research Press: Sante Fe.

Beile-Bohn, M., C. Gerber, M. Morsch and K. Schmidt 1998
Neolithische Forschungen in Obermesopotamien. Gürcütepe und Göbekli Tepe. *Isanbuler Mitteilun-gen.* 48: 5–78.

Blanton, R. 1997
Houses and Households: A Comparative Study. Plenum: New York.

Boguchi, P. 1999
The Origins of Human Society. Blackwell: Oxford.

Briois, F., B. Gratuze and J. Guilaine 1997
Obsidiennes du site Néolithique Précéramique de Shillourokambos (Chypre). *Paléorient* 23: 95–112.

Broodbank, C. 2000
An Island Archaeology of the Early Cyclades. Cam-bridge University Press: Cambridge.

Brück, J. and M. Goodman 1999
Making places in the prehistoric world: themes in set-tlement archaeology. UCL Press: London.

Byrd, B. 1992
The Dispersal of Food Production Across the Levant. Pp. 49–61 in A. Gebauer and T. Douglas Price, *Transitions to Agriculture in Prehistory.* Monographs in World Archaeology 4. Prehistory Press: Madison, Wisconsin.

Byrd, B. 1994
Public and private, domestic and corporate: the emergence of the Southwest Asian Village. *Amer-ican Antiquity* 59: 639–66.

Byrd, B. 2000
Households in Transition. Neolithic Social Orga-nization within Southwest Asia. Pp. 63–98 in Kuijt 2000a.

Cauvin, J. 2000
The Birth of the Gods and the Origin of Agriculture. Cambridge University Press: Cambridge.

Childe, V. G. 1929
The Danube in Prehistory. Oxford University Press: Oxford.

Christodoulou, D. 1959
The evolution of the rural land use pattern in Cyprus. Geographical Publications Ltd: Bude.

Davis, S. 1994
Even More Bones from Khirokitia: the 1988–1991 Excavations. Pp 305–313 in Le Brun 1994.

de Contensen, H. 1992
Préhistoire de Ras Shamra: Les Sondages Strati-graphiques de 1955 à 1976. Éditions Recherche sur les Civilisations : Paris.

Dikaios, P. 1953
Khirokitia. Oxford University Press: Oxford.

Dikaios, P. 1962
The Stone Age. Swedish Cyprus Expedition IV.1A: 1–204. The Swedish Cyprus Expedition: Lund.

Ducos, P. 1965
Le daim a Chypre aux epoques préhistoriques. *Report of the Department of Antiquities, Cyprus:* 1–8.

Flannery, K. 1972
The origins of the village as a settlement type in Mesoamerica and the Near East: a comparative study. Pp. 25–53 in P. Ucko, R. Tringham and G. Dimbleby (eds.) *Man, settlement and urbanism.* Duckworth: London.

Garstang, J. 1936
Jericho: City and Necropolis. *Liverpool Annals of Archaeology and Anthropology* 23: 67–76.

Gosden, C. 1994
Social Being and Time. Blackwell: Oxford.

Guilaine, J., F. Briois, J. Coularou and I. Carrère 1995
L'Etablissement néolithique de *Shillourokambos* (Parekklisha, Chypre). Premiers résultats. *Report of the Department of Antiquities, Cyprus:* 11–32.

Guilaine, J., F. Briois, J.-D. Vigne and I. Carrère 2000
Découverte d'un Néolithique précéramique ancien chypriote (fin 9e, début 8e millénaires cal. BC), apparenté au PPNB ancien/moyen du Levant nord. *Earth and Planetary Sciences* 300: 75–82.

Guilaine, J. and F. Briois 2001
Parekklisha *Shillourokambos.* An Early Neolithic Site in Cyprus. Pp. 37–53 in S. Swiny (ed.) *The Ear-liest Prehistory of Cyprus: From Colonization to Exploitation.* Cyprus American Archaeological Research Institute Monograph Series 12. Ameri-can Schools of Oriental Research: Boston.

Guilaine J. and A. Le Brun (eds.) 2003
Le Néolithique de Chypre. Actes du colloque interna-tional organisé par le département des antiquités de Chypre et l'Ecole française d'Athènes, Nicosie 17-19

mai 2001. Bulletin de Correspondance Hellénique Suppl. 43.

Harris, D. 1996
The origins and spread of agriculture and pastoralism: an overview. Pp. 552–573 in D. Harris (ed.) *The Origins and Spread of Agriculture and Pastoralism in Eurasia.* UCL Press Ltd: London.

Harris, D. 1998
The Origins of Agriculture in Southwest Asia. *The Review of Archaeology* 9: 5–11.

Held, S. 1992
Colonization and Extinction on Early Prehistoric Cyprus. Pp 104–64 in P. Åström (ed.) *Acta Cyprus: Acts of an International Congress on Cypriote Archaeology Held in Göteborg on 22-24 August 1991.* Studies in Mediterranean Archaeology Pocketbook 114.2. Paul Åströms Förlag: Jonsered.

Henry, D., C. Cordova, J. White, R. Dean, J. Beaver, H. Ekstrom, S. Kadowki, J. McCorriston, A. Nowell and L. Scott-Cummings 2003
The Early Neolithic Site of Ayn Abu Nukhayla, Southern Jordan. *Bulletin of the American Schools of Oriental Research* 330: 1–20.

Hodder, I. 1985
Symbols in action. Cambridge University Press: Cambridge.

Kent, S. 1990
A cross-cultural study of segmentation, architecture, and the use of space. Pp. 127–32 in S. Kent (ed.) *Domestic Architecture and the Use of Space.* Cambridge University Press: Cambridge.

Knapp, A. with S. Held and S. Manning 1994
The Prehistory of Cyprus: Problems and Prospects. *Journal of World Prehistory* 8: 377–453.

Kozlowski S. and A. Kempisty 1989–90
Architecture of the pre-pottery neolithic settlement in Nemrik, Iraq. *World Archaeology* 21: 348–362.

Kuijt. I. ed. 2000a
Life in Neolithic Farming Communities. Social Organization, Identity, and Differentiation. London.

Kuijt, I. 2000b
Keeping the Peace: Ritual, Skull Caching, and Community Integration in the Levantine Neolithic. Pp. 137–62 in Kuijt 2000a. Kluwer Academic/ Plenum Publishers: London.

Kuijt, I. and N. Goring-Morris 2002
Foraging, Farming, and Social Complexity in the Pre-Pottery Neolithic of the Southern Levant: A Review and Synthesis. *Journal of World Prehistory* 16: 361-439.

Le Brun, A. 1981a
Un site néolithique précéramique en Chypre: Cap Andreas-Kastros. Recherche sur les grandes civilisations. Mémoire no 5 . APDF: Paris.

Le Brun, A. 1981b
Remarques sur l'utilisation de l'espace á Khirokitia et au Cap Andreas-*Kastros* (Chypre). Pp. 457–66 in *Préhistoire du Levant. Chronologie et organisation de l'espace depuis les origines jusqu'au*

VIe millénaire. Éditions du Centre National de la Recherche Scientifique: Paris.

Le Brun, A. 1984
Fouilles Récentes à Khirokitia (Chypre) 1977-1981. APDF : Paris.

Le Brun, A. 1989
Fouilles Récentes à Khirokitia (Chypre) 1983-1986. APDF : Paris.

Le Brun, A. 1994
Fouilles Récentes à Khirokitia (Chypre) 1988-1991. APDF : Paris.

Le Brun, A. 1997
Khirokitia. A Neolithic Site. Bank of Cyprus Cultural Foundation: Nicosia.

Le Brun, A. 2002
Neolithic Society in Cyprus: A Tentative Analysis. Pp. 21–31 in D. Bolger and N. Serwint (eds.), *Engendering Aphrodite: Women and Society in Ancient Cyprus.* Cyprus American Archaeological Research Institute Monograph 3. American Schools of Oriental Research: Boston.

Lehavy, Y. 1989
Dhali-Agridhi: The Neolithic by the River. Pp. 203–243 in L. Stager and A. Walker (eds.) *American Expedition to Idalion, Cyprus 1973-1980 (Oriental Institute Communication 24).* Chicago University Press: Chicago.

Le Mort, F. 2003
Les sépultures de Khirokitia, in Guilaine and Le Brun 2003.

Mellaart, J. 1975
The Neolithic of the Near East. Thames and Hudson: London.

Moore, A., G. Hillman and A. Legge 2000
Village on the Euphrates. From Foraging to Farming at Abu Hureyra. Oxford University Press: Oxford.

Netting, R., R. Wilk and E. Arnould 1984
Households: Comparative and Historical Studies of the Domestic Group. University of California Press: Berkeley.

Parker Pearson, M. and C. Richards (eds.) 1994
Architecture and Order. Approaches to Social Space. Routledge: London.

Peltenburg, E. 1994
Constructing authority: the Vounous enclosure model. *Opuscula Atheniensia* 20 : 157–162.

Peltenburg, E., *et al.* 1998
Lemba Archaeological Project (Cyprus) II.1A. Excavations at Kissonerga-Mosphilia, 1979-1992. Studies in Mediterranean Archaeology 70:2. Paul Åströms Förlag: Jonsered.

Peltenburg, E., S. Colledge, P. Croft, A. Jackson, C. McCartney and Mary Anne Murray 2000
Agro-pastoralist colonization of Cyprus in the 10th millennium BP: initial assessments. *Antiquity* 74: 844–53.

Peltenburg, E., S. Colledge, P. Croft, A. Jackson, C. McCartney and M. Murray 2001
Neolithic Dispersals from the Levantine Corridor: a Mediterranean Perspective. *Levant* 33: 35–64.

Peltenburg, E., *et al.* 2003
  The Colonisation and Settlement of Cyprus. Investigations at Kissonerga-Mylouthkia, *1976-1996. (Lemba Archaeological Project, Cyprus III.1).* Studies in Mediterranean Archaeology 70:4. Paul Åströms Förlag: Sävedalen.

Perrot, J. 1964
  Les premières campagnes á Munhata (1962–1963). *Syria* 41: 323–45.

Schirmer, W. 1989–90
  Some aspects of building at the 'aceramic neolithic' settlement of Çayönü Tepesi. *World Archaeology* 21: 363–87.

Schmidt, K. 1998
  Steir, Fuchs und Kranish. Der Göbekli Tepe bei Sanlıurfa und die Bilderwelt des obermesopotamischen Frühneolithikums. *Nürnberger Blätter zur Archäologie* 14: 155–70.

Schmidt, K. 1999
  Frühe Tier- und Menschenbilder vom Göbekli Tepe - Kampagnen 1995–1998. Eine komenteirter Katalog der Grossplastik und der Reliefs. *Isanbuler Mitteilugen* 49: 5–21.

Sevketoglu, M. 2002
  Akanthou-Arkosyko (Tatlısu-Çiftlikdüzü): the Anatolian connections in the 9th millennium BC. Pp. 98–106 in W. Waldren and J. Ensenyat (eds.) *World islands in Prehistory. International Insular Investigations. V. Deia International Conference of Prehistory.* British Archaeological Reports, International Series 1095. Oxford.

Simmons, A. 2000

Villages on the Edge: Regional Settlement Change and the End of the Levantines Pre-Pottery Neolithic. Pp. 211–30 in Kuijt 2000a.

Simmons, A. and Associates. 1999
  Faunal Extinction in an Island Society: Pygmy Hippopotamus Hunters of Cyprus. Plenum: New York.

Stordeur, D. 2003
  De la vallée de l'Euphrate a Chypre? A la recherche d'indices de relations au Néolithique, in Guilaine and Le Brun 2002.

Stordeur, D., M. Brenet, G. Der Aprahamian and J.-C. Roux 2000
  Les Bâtiments communautaires de Jerf el Ahmar et Mureybet horizon PPNA (Syrie). *Paléorient* 26 : 29–44.

Stordeur, D. and F. Abbès 2003
  Du PPNA au PPNB: mise en lumière d'une phase de transition á Jerf el Ahmar (Syrie). *Bulletin de la Société préhistorique Française* 99: 563-595.

Todd, I. 1987
  Vasilikos Valley Project 6. Excavations at Kalavassos-Tenta 1. Studies in Mediterranean Archaeology 71:6. Paul Åströms Förlag: Göteborg.

Todd, I. A. 1998
  Kalavasos-Tenta. Bank of Cyprus Cultural Foundation: Nicosia.

Watkins, T. 1989–90
  The origins of house and home? *World Archaeology* 21: 336–47.

Wilk, R. and W. Rathje (eds.) 1982
  Archaeology of the Household: Building a Prehistory of Domestic Life. American Behavioral Scientist 25.

8

The emergence of the Mediterranean Fishing Village in the Levant and the anomaly of Neolithic Cyprus

Ehud Galili, Avi Gopher, Baruch Rosen
and Liora Kolska Horwitz

Abstract

The economy of the traditional Mediterranean Fishing Village (MFV) is defined as one based on both agro-pastoral and marine exploitation. This subsistence base first developed on the Levantine coast in the Pre-Pottery Neolithic C period (the end of the 9th and first half of the 8th millennium BP uncalibrated), as documented at the site of Atlit-Yam, Israel. Likewise, on Cyprus, an integrated terrestrial-marine economy appears only some 1000 years after the initial establishment of settlements on the island. The absence of large-scale fishing in the earliest sites on the island is paradoxical as to reach Cyprus requires well developed maritime skills, characteristic of fishing communities. In addition, on Cyprus, excavated water-wells pre-date the earliest ones documented on the mainland and the possibility that this technology could have been first developed on the island is discussed. The possible causes for the late appearance of the MFV on both the Levantine coast and Cyprus are also discussed. One of the explanations offered is that in both cases, fishing was a low preference mode of production, to which Neolithic communities turned only once the quantity and/or quality of terrestrial resources were reduced or impaired.

Introduction

Intensive research has been invested in studying the exploitation of terrestrial resources (faunal and floral) during the transition from hunting and gathering to food production in the Neolithic of the Near East (Bar-Yosef and Belfer Cohen 1989; Lev-Yadun *et al.* 2000; Zohary 1996; Bar-Yosef and Meadow 1995). The utilization of marine resources, however, has not been widely discussed, probably because of the lack of data. Thus, the role of the exploitation of marine resources in the Neolithic Revolution still needs to be clarified. Issues yet to be studied are where and when marine components combined with other agro-pastoral elements, how this combined agro-pastoral-marine subsistence system crystallized,

and the timing and manner in which it spread throughout the Mediterranean region.

It is suggested that a Traditional Mediterranean Village (MFV) should reflect features associated with permanent, sedentary settlements such as dwellings, storage facilities, production facilities and ritual activities (e.g. burials). The subsistence system practiced in the MFV should include exploitation of domestic plants and animals, that is, most of the terrestrial elements of production that appear in Butzer's (1996) definition as elaborated below. In addition there should be indications of intensive and permanent exploitation of a wide range of marine resources (Galili *et al.* 2002).

In this study we will discuss the origin of the MFV on the Levantine littoral and its

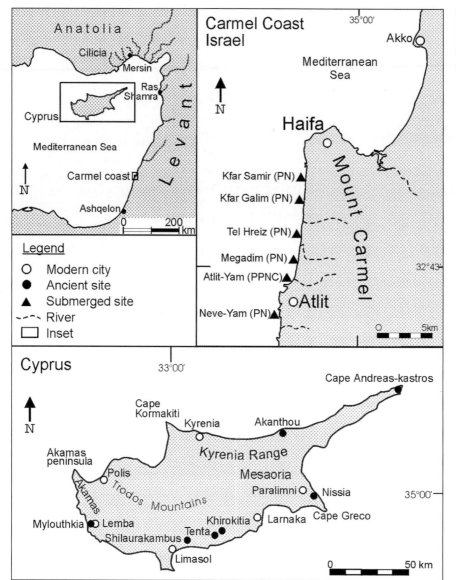

Figure 8.1
*Location map of the sites
mentioned in the text
(Drawing S. Ben-Yehuda)*

connection to the Pre-Pottery Neolithic (PPN) colonization of Cyprus. This study is based mainly on new archaeological discoveries on the mainland and the adjacent island.

The submerged archaeological evidence from the Israeli coast

Because of the flat topography of the continental shelf of the South East Levantine coasts, and a global rise in sea level of about 30–50 m since the beginning of the Holocene (van Andel and Lianos 1983; Bard *et al.* 1996), many coastal Neolithic sites in this region were submerged. Some are close to shore and others are found at a considerable

distance offshore. A number of sites are currently exposed and have undergone erosion and destruction by the sea, while others that may still be covered by sediments are protected.

Recent sand quarrying and the erection of marine and coastal constructions along the Israeli coast, have resulted in the rapid erosion of unconsolidated sediment on the sea bottom. As a consequence, several Neolithic settlements dating to the 9th to 7th millennium BP (uncalibrated) were exposed on the sea-bed along the Carmel coast. The sites (Figure 8.1) include a Pre-Pottery Neolithic C (PPNC) settlement called Atlit-Yam (AY), and five Pottery-Neolithic (PN) settlements belonging mainly to the Wadi Rabah culture (Figure 8.2).

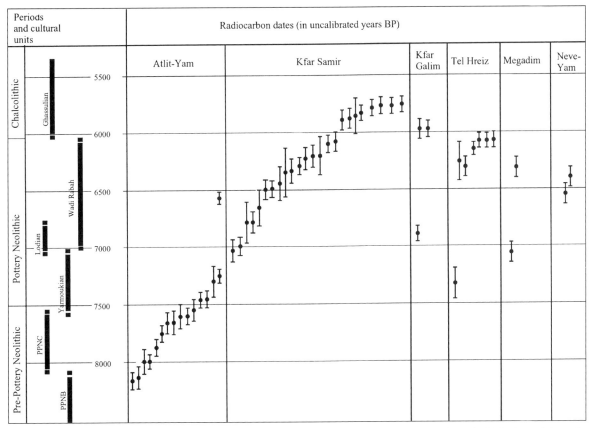

Figure 8.2 *Cultural entities in the Southern Levant (after Gopher and Gophna 1993) and* [14]*C dating of the submerged sites off the Carmel Coast (drawing S. Ben-Yehuda)*

The PPNC site of Atlit-Yam

The site of Atlit-Yam (Figure 8.1) is situated some 200–400 metres off shore, at a depth of 8–12 m and extends over an area of *ca.* 40,000 m². Radiocarbon dates for the site (Figure 8.2) give a range of 8180–7300 yr BP (uncalibrated) (Galili *et al.* 1993; Galili, Sharvit and Shifroni 1999). The architectural finds consist of stone-built water-wells (Galili and Nir 1993; Galili and Sharvit 1998), foundations of rectangular structures, a series of long unconnected walls, ritual installations and stone-paved areas (Galili *et al.* 1993). In addition, 65 human skeletons were discovered in both primary and secondary burials. In at least four of the male individuals, an inner ear pathology – auditory exostosis – caused by diving in cold water, was observed (Hershkovitz and Galili 1990, 1991; Hershkovitz *et al.* 1991; Eshed pers. comm. 2001).

Faunal remains included bones of wild and domestic sheep/goat, pig, cattle and dog, as well as more than 6000 bones of marine fish. Most of them belong to *Balistes carolinensis*, the grey triggerfish, a few to Serranidae, Sparidae, Sciaenidae, Mugillidae and other families (Galili *et al.* 1993; Zohar *et al.* 1994, 2001). Artefacts made of stone, bone, wood and flint (such as fishing net sinkers, hooks, knives) that may be associated with fishing activities, were also recovered, as well as large quantities of botanical remains, including seeds of domesticated wheat, barley, lentil and flax (Galili *et al.* 1993; Kislev *et al.* 1996). The archaeological material indicates that the economy of the site was complex and based on the combined utilization of terrestrial and marine resources involving plant cultivation, livestock husbandry, hunting, gathering and fishing (Galili *et al.* 2002; Galili *et al.* in press).

Pottery Neolithic sites

The five PN sites; Kfar Samir, Kfar Galim, Tel Hreiz, Megadim and Neve Yam (Figure 8.1), which were submerged at depths of 0.5–5 m, were dated to 7100–6300 BP (uncalibrated) (Figure 8.2). The finds from these sites, include water wells constructed of alternating layers of tree branches and stones, as well as pit-installations some lined with undressed stones, others dug into the clay sediment. The pits contained waste of olive oil extraction including thousands of crushed olive-pits (Galili and Weinstein-Evron 1985; Galili *et al.* 1989,1997). Bones of domestic animals and fish were also found (Horwitz *et al.* 2002) as well as artefacts made of stone, wood, and flint. The ceramic assemblage included a variety of vessels for cooking and storage. At Neve-Yam, a cemetery comprising stone-built graves that contained six human skeletons was recovered. It represents one of the earliest known organized cemeteries located apart from the dwelling area of the site (Galili *et al.* 1998). The economy of the PN settlements was based mainly on terrestrial resources, cultivation and herding. The exploitation of marine resources continued but appears to have been on a smaller scale than in the previous PPNC (Horwitz *et al.* 2002).

The non-submerged archaeological evidence from the Levant

The Final PPN site of Ashqelon Marina in Israel's southern coastal plain is situated on a 15–20 m high beach cliff at a distance of about 100 m from the present-day coastline (Perrot and Gopher 1996). It yielded round and oval dwelling pits, silos and shallow basins, numerous sickle blades, a few arrowheads, axes and other tools. The fauna included bones of wild animals, domesticated sheep and cattle and goats whose domestic status is unclear. In addition, a few fish bones were recovered. It is not clear whether the site was a typical MFV, or else a seasonal station for agriculturalists, pastoralists, fishermen and traders from inland settlements (Galili *et al.* 2002).

The late PN site of Ras Shamra lies about 1500 m from the present-day coastline. The domestic assemblage of layer VC consisted of lentil, emmer wheat, pea and linseed, goat, sheep, pig and cattle. Remnants of tuna and shark, as well as tools associated with fishing, demonstrate fishing techniques that would have facilitated the procurement of large pelagic fish (Galili *et al.* 2002). It is possible that Ras Shamra represents a parent site whose marine fishing satellite is presently submerged, or perhaps a site with extensive trade links to the coast.

The Late PN Cilician site of Mersin-Yumuktepe lies close to the source area of cultigens and domestic animals, and as such is of special interest (Caneva 1999). As no complete structures or installations were found, it is impossible to assess the nature of the occupation. The botanical and faunal remains indicate a mixed subsistence economy including domestic sheep, goat, cattle and pig. Six species of fish have been identified as well as five species of molluscs. Although the site lies close to the sea today, it is unclear how far inland it was situated from the Neolithic coastline (Galili *et al.* 2002).

The emergence of the Mediterranean-Levantine fishing village

The traditional Mediterranean subsistence system has been defined by Butzer (1996) as based on the cultivation of cereals (wheat and barley), fruit trees (olives, grapes, almonds and figs), vegetable gardening, husbandry of sheep and goats (for meat, milk and wool) and the maintenance of cattle for traction.

As illustrated by the data from the submerged sites along the Carmel coast, the combined agro-pastoral-marine subsistence system, the so-called 'Mediterranean fishing village,' first appeared on the Levantine coasts at the end of the 9th millennium BP (uncalibrated). The site of Atlit-Yam contains most of the components of the Mediterranean subsistence system as defined by Butzer. In addition, the archaeological material from the site points to the intensive utilization of marine resources. To date, this site is possibly the earliest example of a MFV in the Levant, which combined agro-pastoral components with marine elements.

Prior to the PPNC, there is evidence for only limited fishing and exploitation of marine resources by local hunting and gathering communities (e.g. Lernau and Lernau 1994; Schick 1993). Moreover, there is no evidence for a combined economy based on domestic plants and animals together with intensive use of marine resources in sedentary sites (Galili *et al.* 2002). Once it was established in the PPNC, this combined agro-pastoral-marine subsistence system spread relatively rapidly throughout the eastern basin of the Mediterranean, and then westward along the coasts of Europe.

The reason for the emergence of the earliest fishing villages on the Levantine coast and not elsewhere along the Mediterranean, is probably related to the fact that they are close to the core area of plant and animal domestication. Why had this development taken place over a thousand years after the first agro-pastoral sedentary settlements in the Near East? A model proposed by Rollefson and others (Rollefson *et al.* 1992; Rollefson and Kohler-Rollefson 1999; Bar-Yosef and Belfer-Cohen 1989) ascribes the collapse of the late PPNB socio-economic system to environmental degradation caused by the intensive exploitation of natural resources around permanent settlements (deforestation, over-grazing). In an attempt to cope with this crisis, new economic strategies evolved during the subsequent PPNC. These new strategies involved nomadic pastoralism and dry farming that enabled the penetration into marginal semi-arid and arid areas (Horwitz *et al.* 1999; Martin 1999). In the Mediterranean climatic zones, fully agro-pastoral societies turned for the first time to the wide-scale exploitation of marine and coastal resources. The latter represents the beginning of the MFV in the Levant.

It is possible that agro-pastoralists turned to fishing when the benefits from other economic options declined. Moreover, the arduous and dangerous nature of fishing, may have made this a low-priority mode of subsistence when alternative forms were available. Thus, only in a period of crisis, fishing offers an alternative and/or supplementary protein source to terrestrial resources. Hyden *et al.* (1987) note that a subsistence base that combines terrestrial and marine resources offers a more stable economy being less vulnerable to fluctuations in resource availability.

It cannot be totally discounted that Neolithic fishing villages, earlier than Atlit-Yam, existed along the Levantine littoral and are presently covered by the sea or have been destroyed through marine erosion. However, this possibility is unlikely, as none have been discovered to date despite intensive land and underwater surveys.

Some new Neolithic discoveries on Cyprus

An interesting chapter in the archaeology of the Eastern Mediterranean is the colonization of Cyprus (Cherry 1990; Le Brun *et al.*1987; Le Brun 1987; Todd 1982; Watkins 1996). It has been suggested (Peltenburg *et al.* 2000, 2001a, b) that economic pressure on the mainland, combined with pre-existing nautical know-how, facilitated the early colonization of the island during the early PPN. Excavations carried out in Cyprus in recent years have revealed *in-situ* archaeological layers in PPN sites located in the southwest, western and northern coastal regions of the island, dating to the early 10th millennium BP.

Mylouthkia

This multi-component site is located on the southwest coast of the island, *ca.* 100 m from the water line, and 20 m. above sea level. Excavations revealed PPN water wells, one dated to 9400–9050 BP and the other dated to 8250–7950 BP (uncalibrated) (Peltenburg *et al.* 2000, 2001a, b). In the oldest well infant bones were found. Traces of rodents, amphibians and reptiles were also recovered. The other well contained 22 whole skeletons of sheep, as well as bones of goats, pigs (probably domesticated), deer and small animals. In addition, scattered human bones, including an artificially deformed skull were recovered. Plant remains include domestic einkorn, emmer wheat and hulled barley and wild and/or domesticated forms of lentil, pea, vetch, olive, fig and grape (Peltenburg *et al.* 2000, 2001a, b). No trace of permanent occupation, such as built dwellings and/or other structures have so far been discovered in association with the wells. Evidence for exploitation of marine resources include thousands of limpet shells, fish bones in a very bad state of preservation, and a single artefact made of a pig tusk, which was identified as a fishhook.

Shillourokambos

The site is located northeast of Limassol, about 5 km from the coast. Two phases of occupation were identified: early to middle PPNB (9400–9000 BP) and mid PPNB (9000–8600 BP; uncalibrated) (Guilaine *et al.* 1998a, b, 2000). Architectural remains include post holes, curvilinear structures, paved areas, raised stone platforms constructed of stone and ash and deep shafts identified as water wells. Multiple human burials, in which the skulls were separated and concentrated together, were recovered in a cave that was adjacent to one of the well shafts.

The fauna of the early phase included pigs which were possibly already domesticated, sheep and goats (possibly wild), cattle in the early stages of domestication and some fallow deer. Several scores of fish bones were recovered, but it is not known as yet from which phase. The bones belong to large groupers and rays (Desse, per comm. 2001). Plant remains included domestic barley and wild wheat.

Tenta

The site of *Tenta* is located between Larnaca and Limassol about 5 km. north of the coast. The site includes PPN and PN occupational phases. The early layers were dated to 9400–9000 BP (uncalibrated) (Todd 1982, 1989, 1998). These layers are represented solely by post-holes that did not form any clear architectural plan. Human burials from this period were also discovered. From the later phase of the PPN, round brick and stone buildings and traces of a wall surrounding the site were found. The layers from the early stages contain numerous fallow deer bones and sea-shells (Todd 1982, 1998, 2001).

Akanthou-Arkosyko (Tatlısu)

This site is located today adjacent to the northern coast and has recently been identified as representing an Aceramic Neolithic deposit (Sevketoglu 2000: 75–82). Peltenburg *et al.* (2001) ascribe part of it to the early/mid- PPNB. Cattle and fallow deer remains have been found at the site, and with the exception of 14 shells, no indications for marine adaptation have been reported to date (Sevketoglu 2000: 77). It is possible that in the PPN this site was located at some distance inland.

Discussion

Due to the proximity of Cyprus to the Levantine mainland, the presence of a marine barrier and the early dates for the settlement of the island, Cyprus offers a laboratory for investigating the evolution of the Mediterranean mode of subsistence.

The new data summarized above shows that Cyprus was already colonized in the 10th millennium BP (uncalibrated) and that the early colonizers brought with them several domestic plant and animal species (Vigne *et al.* 2000; Peltenburg *et al.* 2000, 2001b; Guilaine *et al.* 2000). This episode coincides with the first appearance of only some of the domesticates on the mainland. The mainland settlements with the suitable elements of both agriculture and domestic animals which could have served as the base from which Cyprus was settled are all situated inland about 100–200 km from the coast (Peltenburg *et al.* 2000; Zohary 1996: 143; Lev-Yadun *et al.* 2000). According to Peltenburg *et al.* (2000), no coastal settlements that could have been the point of origin for such an early colonization event have as yet been identified on the shores of the Levant or southern Anatolia. They also argue that neither the wave advance model used to account for the spread of farming in Europe (Ammerman and Cavalli-Sforza 1984), nor its modification, leap-frog dispersal (Van Andel and Runnels 1995) fit the facts presently known about the colonization of Cyprus. They suggest that the settlers of Cyprus could not have originated inland as inland populations would have lacked seafaring abilities and would have been unaware of the agricultural potentials of the island and could not have targeted it for colonization. Peltenburg *et al.* (2000) propose that the earliest colonizers of Cyprus must have come from the coast of Syria or Cilicia and were indigenous PPN coastal agro-pastoralists habituated to seafaring. They recognized the presence of Cyprus and its agricultural potential and may have settled the island as an outcome of a regional crisis due to a possible environmental change. It is proposed here that the available archaeological data indicates that the Cypriot Neolithic record is somehow anomalous. The "Neolithic Anomaly of Cyprus" is composed of four main parameters:

A. The possible appearance of an agro-pastoral society on the island, earlier than on the mainland coasts.

B. The early colonists on the island appear to have mainly exploited terrestrial resources and relied less on marine resources, despite their proximity to the coast. Thus, the true MFV, as we know it from the PPNC site off Atlit-Yam on the Israeli littoral, appears relatively late on the island, only at the beginning of the 8th millennium BP (uncalibrated). This is surprising because in order to reach the island in the first place, nautical skills were required.

C. The construction of water wells on the island antedates the earliest known mainland wells by over a 1000 years.

D. The early colonists of the island brought from the mainland and managed fallow deer–a wild animal which was not domesticated or managed in this manner elsewhere (Ronen 1995). They also brought with them pig, goat, sheep and cattle, at a time when these animals may not yet have been fully domesticated on the mainland (Horwitz *et al.*, Chapter 4 this volume).

Based on the archaeological material available to date from the Levantine coast and Mediterranean islands, the following explanations for the "Anomaly of Neolithic Cyprus" may be offered. The early and mid-PPN sites discovered to date in Cyprus were basically communities engaged in agriculture, with a limited, if any, investment in domestic animals and a low level of involvement in the exploitation of marine resources. The settlements were established by new immigrants from the mainland (Fertile Crescent region) that were attracted by the unpopulated and pristine environmental conditions. There is no doubt that significant navigational skills, as well as an acquaintance with the sea and knowledge of the target, were needed in order to transfer people, animals and goods to Cyprus. The presence of PPN farmers on the island suggests that sea-going people, possibly local hunter-gatherers who utilized marine resources and lived on the shores of the Levant, aided these people. These coastal populations, who possessed the necessary navigation skills may have served as "ferry-men" who transported Neolithic populations living in the hinterland of the Levant to Cyprus. One should emphasize that there is no evidence for sedentary agro-pastoral PPN sites on the coasts of the Levant and South Anatolia according to our present knowledge (Peltenburg *et al.* 2000, 2001).

The relative paucity of evidence for intensive fishing in the early Cypriot sites may be explained by the fact that the early colonists of Cyprus had only limited knowledge of fishing. Terrestrial resources probably supplied their needs and enabled a sufficient level of subsistence. Evidence for an intensive reliance on both marine and terrestrial resources comes only from later coastal sites on the island dated to the end of the Aceramic Neolithic such as Cape Andreas-Kastros, and Khirokitia (Le Brun 1987), as well as Ceramic Neolithic sites such as Paralimni-Nissia (Flourentzos 1997).

An alternative suggestion is that the new settlers had the necessary skills for navigation and maritime exploitation. However, since fishing is considered arduous and risky, they preferred to focus on the exploitation of the highly productive land. Only later, probably following a reduction in the productivity of terrestrial resources, competition or socio-economic developments, they turned to marine resources. This model may explain the appearance of the intensive marine exploitation on the island only 1000 years after it was first colonized by agriculturists.

A similar pattern of economic development (a "lag-time" in the integration of marine elements in the economy) is observed in the Levant (see above). It should be noted that on the Aeolian Islands (north of Sicily) and on Sardinia, the first Neolithic settlers relied mainly on agriculture. Fishing communities appeared only later (Castagnino Berrlinghieri 2002; 2000–2001).

Another possible explanation for the absence of fishing villages in early/mid PPNB Cyprus and the coast of the Levant, is that such sites have not yet been discovered. Such sites may be covered by sediments, submerged or eroded.

Water wells

The above-suggested scenarios may explain the late appearance of fishing villages on Cyprus, but they do not account for the early appearance of water wells. The earliest water wells discovered so far on the adjacent mainland are dated to the end of the 9th millennium BP (uncalibrated) (Galili and Nir 1993; Galili and Sharvit 1998). Judging by the relatively advanced technology used in the construction of the water wells at Atlit Yam it seems that these wells may have been preceded by an earlier technological stage (Galili *et al.* in press). Features of this advanced technology (as discovered at Atlit-Yam) include the construction of a stone built well-head, stone-built walls and excavated well-bottom that penetrates the bedrock. Widespread surveys and excavations of PPN sites in the Levant have not thus far revealed pre-PPNC water wells. This is hard to explain since a deep shaft used as a water well has a better chance of surviving the ravages of time than shallow structures, which are susceptible to erosion and post-depositional processes. Two explanations can be offered.

The first is that water wells were invented on the mainland in places where a high water aquifer existed in the sub-soil. The high aquifer facilitated the development of a permanent water source through excavation. This know-how was transported from the mainland to Cyprus by the first PPN colonists and facilitated the year-round occupation of the island. The mainland PPNB wells have as yet not been discovered either due to the thick overburden of sediment covering them at present, or because they have collapsed or been totally eroded.

An intriguing possible alternative is that wells were first invented on Cyprus due to the crucial need for water. Most of the rivers on the island are not perennial, thus, water must often have been the primary limiting factor for year-round human habitation. Geological and geomorphological conditions on Cypriot coasts (Nir 1993; Simmons 1999) may have enabled the early inhabitants to easily locate subterranean water sources. In the coastal regions of Paralimni, (East Mesaoria), a high water aquifer enables relatively easy access to subterranean water and even today farmers in this area obtain their water supplies from shallow wells. On the north coast of the Pentadaktylos Range (Keryneia Range), perennial streams existed until recently (Simmons 1999). Perennial streams may also have existed in the southwest coasts of the island. Although many rivers are currently dry, water can be located even at the end of the summer by observing concentrations of hydrophilic plants near outlets. Therefore, in this northern coastal region water could have been

Figure 8.3 *Active water spring in the coastal cliffs near the* Mylouthkia *water wells. Black arrow points to the location of the Neolithic wells, a white arrow points to the spring (picture taken August 2001)*

located relatively easy (Sevketoglu 2000: 44). A similar situation was observed on the West Coast of the Akamas Peninsula and to its north in the Polis region. Near Shillourokambos, modern plantations are still irrigated by water from shallow wells. In the Lemba region, coastal erosion and/or tectonic uplifting created coastal cliffs in which water-bearing rock formations are exposed. Active springs were recently observed on the seaside aspect of these coastal cliffs *ca.* 150 m from the Mylouthkia wells (Figure 8.3).

Based on the Mylouthkia wells, Peltenburg *et al.* (2001) suggested that water-divining skills were used to locate deep subterranean water streams. This conclusion was reached due to the discovery of small watercourses at the bottom of the wells. Arriving at these watercourses from the surface requires great precision. Judging by the available archaeological data from the Mylouthkia wells and by observations on the coastal cliffs of the Lemba region, an alternative to the "water-divining" theory is offered. A water-bearing formation (aquifer) situated on top of a positive confining bed aquiclude, which is tilted seaward, may have existed in the region. Thus, sub-surface runoff may have flowed at the bottom of the havara formation (into which the wells are dug), on top of the confining bed. It would have been easy to locate such subterranean runoff by surveying the adjacent coastal cliffs, where bedrock and the water-bearing formation were exposed. Thus, the small watercourses at the bottom of the Mylouthkia wells could have been a post-well formation. Such channels could have been created by water flow, which eroded the soft havara formation after the excavation of the well or even have been dug by the PPN well-diggers. Under these circumstances, it seems that water-divining was unnecessary for detecting water sources in the region. We may summarize this section by the unconventional suggestion that it is possible that well digging was first developed on the island of Cyprus during the PPN. This know-how could have been transferred to the mainland later, or independently developed on the mainland.

Conclusions

The first permanent coastal agricultural settlements in which exploitation of marine resources are a major component of the subsistence system (MVFs) first appear on the Levantine coasts towards the end of the 9th millennium BP (uncalibrated). This postdates the first permanent agro-pastoral settlements on the Levantine mainland by over 1000 years. The reason for this is perhaps that fishing was arduous and risky, and thus a less favoured subsistence form when other resources were available.

The findings from Cyprus indicate that major components of the Mediterranean agricultural system (domesticated plants and possibly domesticated animals) arrived on the island from the Levantine hinterland and passed through the Levantine coasts over 1000 years prior to the appearance of the MFVs on these coasts.

People brought animals to the island for consumption, possibly even before they were fully domesticated on the mainland (Horwitz *et al.* Chapter 4 this volume). It seems that the early settlers selected a whole range of animals for transportation that were amenable for management and hunting.

Finds from Cyprus indicate that the people who arrived on the island were involved at first in agriculture, animal husbandry, and hunting. They incorporated marine resources into their subsistence system on a wide scale only over 1000 years after their arrival, perhaps due to a reduction in the productivity of the island. This mode of human behaviour is applicable to other Mediterranean islands such as Sardinia and the Aeolian islands.

It is possible that well-digging was first developed during the early PPNB on the island of Cyprus due to the crucial need for permanent, reliable sources of drinking water, facilitated by the hydrological conditions in the island's coastal areas, which facilitated year-round occupation.

References

Ammerman, A.J. and L.L. Cavalli-Sforza 1971
    Measuring the rate of spread of early farming in Europe. *Man* 6: 674–688.
Bar-Yosef, O. and A. Belfer-Cohen 1989
    The Levantine `PPNB` International Sphere. Pp. 59–72 in I. Hershkovitz (ed.) *People and Culture in Change, Proceedings of the 2nd Symposium on Upper Paleolithic, Mesolithic and Neolithic Populations of Europe and the Mediterranean Basin.* British Archaeological Reports 508: Oxford.
Bar-Yosef, O. and R. Meadow 1995
    The Origins of agriculture in the Near East. Pp. 39–111 in D.T. Price and A.B. Gebauer (eds.) *Last Hunters, First Farmers: New Perspectives on the Prehistoric Transitions to Agriculture.* School of American Research Press: Santa Fe, New Mexico.
Bard, E., B. Hamelin, M. Arnold, L. Montaggioni, G. Cabioch, G. Faure and F. Rougerie 1996
    Deglacial sea-level record from Tahiti corals and the timing of global meltwater discharge. *Nature* 382: 241–244.
Broecker, W.S. 1994
    Massive iceberg discharges as triggers for global climate changes. *Nature* 372: 421–424.
Butzer, K.W. 1996
    Ecology in the Long View: Settlement Histories, Agrosystemic Strategies, and Ecological Performance. *Journal of Field Archaeology* 23: 141–150.
Caneva, I. 1999
    Early farmers on the Cilician coast: Yumuktepe in the seventh millennium BC. Pp. 105-114 in M. Özdogan (ed.) *Neolithic Turkey.* Arkeoloji ve sanat Yayinlari: Istanbul.
Castagnino Berlinghieri, E.F. 2000–2001
    The Aeolian Islands, Crossroads of the Mediterranean Maritime Routes of the South Tyrrhenian. Phd Thesis (Unpublished) University of Bristol, UK.
Castagnino Berlinghieri, E.F. 2002
    Attività umana e assetto costiero nella Protostoria eoliana: nuovi risultati di ricerca. Pp. 23-35 in *Proceedings of the Convegno Internazionale "Strumenti per la Protezione e la Valorizzazione del Patrimonio Culturale Marino nel Mediterraneo",* Università di Milano Bicocca, Università di Palermo e Regione Siciliana, (Palermo- Siracusa 2001), Casa editrice Giuffrè: Milano.
Cherry, J.F. 1990
    The First Colonization of the Mediterranean

Islands: A Review of Recent Research. *Journal of Mediterranean Archaeology* 3: 145–221.

Flourentzos, P. 1997
Excavations at the Neolithic site of Paralimni. A preliminary report. *Report of the Department of Antiquities, Cyprus:* 1–10.

Galili, E. and M. Weinstein-Evron 1985
Prehistory and Paleoenvironment of Submerged Sites along the Carmel Coast of Israel. *Paléorient* 11: 37–52.

Galili, E. and Y. Nir 1993
The submerged Pre-Pottery Neolithic water well of Atlit Yam northern Israel, and its paleoenvironmental implications. *The Holocene* 3: 265–270.

Galili, E. and J. Sharvit 1998
Submerged Neolithic water wells from the Carmel coast of Israel. Pp. 31–44 in H. Koschik (ed.), *Landschaftsverband Rheinland, Rheinisches Amt für Bodenkmalpflege Brunnen der Jungsteinzeit, Internationales Symposium Erkenlenz*, October 1997. Habelt: Bonn.

Galili, E., J. Sharvit and A. Shifrony 1999
Atlit-Yam Excavations 1993–4. Hadashot Arkheologiyot *Excavations and Surveys in Israel* 109: 30–31.

Galili, E., M. Weinstein-Evron, and D. Zohary 1989
Appearance of olives in submerged Neolithic sites along the Carmel coast. *Journal of the Israel Prehistoric Society* 22: 95.

Galili, E., M. Weinstein-Evron, I. Hershkovitz, A. Gopher, M. Kislev, O. Lernau, L. K. Horwitz and H. Lernau 1993
Atlit Yam: A prehistoric site on the sea floor of the Israeli coast. *Journal of Field Archaeology* 20: 133–140.

Galili, E., D. J. Stanley, J. Sharvit and M. Weinstein-Evron 1997
Evidence for earliest olive production in submerged settlements off the Carmel coast. *Journal of Archaeological Science* 24: 1141–1150.

Galili, E., J. Sharvit, and A. Shifrony 1998
Neve Yam–Underwater Survey. *Excavations and surveys in Israel* 18: 35–36.

Galili, E., O. Lernau, and I. Zohar in press
Fishing and Marine Adaptation at Atlit-Yam, a Submerged Neolithic Village off the Carmel Coast Israel. *Atiqot.*

Galili, E., R. Rosen, A. Gopher and L. Horwitz 2002.
The Emergence and Dispersion of the Eastern Mediterranean Fishing Village: Evidence from Submerged Neolithic Settlements off the Carmel Coast, Israel. *Journal of Mediterranean Archaeology* 15.2: 167–198.

Gopher, A. and R. Gophna 1993
Cultures of the Eighth and Seventh Millennia BP in the Southern Levant: A Review for the 1990s. *Journal of World Prehistory* 7: 297–353.

Guilaine, J., F. Briois, J. Coularou, J.-D. Vigne and I. Carrère 1998a
Les débuts du Néolithique à Chypre. *L'Archéologue* 33 : 35–40.

Guilaine, J., F. Briois,.J. Coularou, P. Devèze, S. Philibert, J.-D. Vigne and I. Carrère 1998b
La site néolithique précéramique de *Shillourokambos* (Parekklisha, Chypre). *Bulletin de Correspondance Hellénique* 122: 603–10.

Guilaine, J., F. Briois, J.-D. Vigne and I. Carrère 2000
Découverte d'un Néolithique précéramique ancien chypriote (fin 9e, début 8e millénaires cal. BC), apparenté au PPNB ancien/moyen du Levant nord. *Comptes rendus de l'Academie Scientifique de Paris, Sciences de la Terre et des Planetes* 330 : 75–82.

Hayden, B., B. Chisholm and H. P. Schwartz 1987
Fishing and Foraging, Marine Resources in the Upper Paleolithic of France. Pp. 279–291 in O. Soffer (ed.) *Pleistocene Old World: Regional Perspectives.* New York: Plenum Press.

Hershkovitz, I. and E. Galili 1990
8000- year- old human remains on the sea floor near Atlit, Israel. *Journal of Human Evolution* 5: 319–358.

Hershkovitz, I. and E. Galili 1991
The morphological significance of the Homo I skeleton from the PPNB submerged site at Atlit Yam Israel. *Bulletin et Memoires de la Societé d'Anthropologie de Paris. N.s.* 3 : 83–96.

Hershkovitz, I., E. Galili and B. Ring 1991
Des Squelettes Humains 8000 ans Sous la Mer: Indications sur la vie sociale et economiques des habitants de la Cote Sud du Levant la period Néolithique Précéramique. *L`Anthropologie* 95: 639–650.

Horwitz, L.K., E. Galili, J. Sharvit and O. Lernau 2002
Fauna from Five Submerged Pottery Neolithic sites off the Carmel Coast. *Journal of Israel Prehistoric Society* 32: 147–174.

Horwitz, L. K., E. Tchernov, P. Ducos, C. Becker, A. Von Den Driesch, L. Martin and A. Garrard 1999
Animal Domestication in the Southern Levant. *Paléorient* 25(2): 63–80.

Kislev, M., A. Hartman and E. Galili 1996
Evidence from Atlit Yam for a colder climate during the PPNC period. *Proceedings of the Annual Meeting of the Israel Prehistoric Society.* Pp. 14 (Hebrew).

Le Brun, A. 1987
Chronologie relative et chronologie absolue dans le Néolithique Chyriote. Pp. 525–548 in O. Aurenche, J. Evin and P. Hours (eds.) *Chronologies in the Near East.* British Archaeological Reports, International Series 379. Archaeopress: Oxford.

Le Brun, A., S. Cluzan, S.J.M. Davis, J. Hansen and J. Renault-Miskovsky 1987
Le néolithique précéramique de Chypre. *L'Anthropologie* 91 : 283–316.

Lernau, O. and H. Lernau 1994
The Fish Remains. Pp. 111–124 in M. Lechevallier and A. Ronen (eds.) Le Site de Hatoula en Judee Occidentale, Israel. *Hatoula, Memoires et Travaux du Centre de Recherche Francais de Jerusalem, 8.*

Lev-Yadun, S., A. Gopher and S. Abbo 2000
    The Cradle of Agriculture. *Science* 288: 1602–1603.

Martin, L. 1999
    Mammal Remains from the Eastern Jordanian Neolithic, and the Nature of Caprine Herding in the Steppe. *Paléorient* 25(2): 87–104.

Nir, Y. 1993
    The Coast of Cyprus. *(Mimeograph) Report of the Geological Survey of Israel.* Geological Survey Department Ministry of Agriculture, Natural Resources and Environment Cyprus.

Peltenburg, E., S. College, P. Croft, A. Jackson, C. McCartney, and M. Murray 2000
    Agro-pastoralist colonization of Cyprus in the 10th millennium BP: initial assessments. *Antiquity* 74: 844–853.

Peltenburg, E., S. College, P. Croft, A. Jackson, C. McCartney and M. Murray 2001a
    Neolithic dispersals from the Levantine corridor: a Mediterranean perspective. *Levant* 32: 35–64.

Peltenburg, E., P. Croft, A. Jackson, C. McCartney and M.A. Murray 2001b
    Well established Colonists: Mylouthkia I and the Cypro-Pre-Pottery Neolithic B. Pp. 61–93 in S. Swiny (ed.) *The Earliest Prehistory of Cyprus: From Colonization to Exploitation.* Cyprus American Archaeological Research Institute Monograph Series 12. American Schools of Oriental Research: Boston.

Perrot, J. and A. Gopher 1996
    A late Neolithic site near Ashkelon. *Israel Exploration Journal* 46: 145-66.

Rollefson, G., A. Simmons and Z. Kafafi 1992
    Neolithic Cultures at `Ain Ghazal, Jordan. *Journal of Field Archaeology* 19: 443–470.

Rollefson, G.O. and I. Kohler-Rollefson 1999
    The Collapse of the Early Neolithic Settlements in the Southern Levant. Pp. 73–89 in I. Hershkovitz (ed.) *People and Culture in Change, Proceedings of the 2nd Symposium on Upper Paleolithic, Mesolithic and Neolithic Populations of Europe and the Mediterranean Basin*, British Archaeological Reports, International Series, 508: Oxford.

Ronen, A. 1995
    Periphery and Ideology in Aceramic Cyprus. *Quartär* 45: 177–206.

Schick, T. 1993
    Kebara Cave. Pp. 852–855 in E. Stern, A. Lewinson-Gilboa and J. Aviram (eds.) *The New Encyclopedia of Archaeological Excavations in the Holy Land*, The Israel Exploration Society: Jerusalem.

Simmons, A.H. (ed.) 1999
    Faunal Extinction in an Island Society. Pygmy Hippopotamus Hunters of Cyprus. Plenum: New York.

Todd, I. A. 1982
    Radiocarbon dates for Kalavassos-Tenta and Kalavassoa-Ayious. *Report of the Department of Antiquities, Cyprus:* 8–11.

Todd, I. A. 1989
    Early Prehistoric Society: A view from the Vasilikos Valley. Pp. 2–13 in E. Peltenburg (ed.) *Early Society in Cyprus*. Edinburgh University Press: Edinburgh.

Todd, I.A. 1998
    Kalavasos-Tenta. The Bank of Cyprus Cultural Foundation: Nicosia.

Sevketoglu, M. 2000
    Archaeological Field Survey of the Neolithic and Chalcolithic Settlement sites in Kyrenia District, North Cyprus. British Archaeological Reports, International Series, 834. Archaeopress: Oxford.

Van Andel, T.H. and N. Lianos 1983
    Prehistoric and historic shorelines of the southern Argolid peninsula: a subbottom profile study. *International Journal of Nautical Archaeology and Underwater Exploration* 12: 303–324.

Van Andel, T. and C. Runnels 1995
    The Earliest Farmers in Europe. *Antiquity* 69: 481–500.

Vigne, J.-D., I. Carrére, J.-F. Saliège, A. Person, H. Bocherens, J. Guilaine and F. Brios 2000
    Predomestic Cattle, Sheep, Goat and Pig During the Late 9th and the 8th Millennium Cal. BC on Cyprus: Preliminary Results of Shillourokambos (Parekklisha, Limassol). Pp. 83–105 in M. Mashkour, A. Choyke, H. Buitenhuis and F. Poplin (eds.) *Archaeozoology of the Near East IVA*, ARC. Publicatie 32: Groningen.

Watkins, T. 1996
    Excavations at Pınarbası: the Early Stages. Pp. 47–57 in I. Hodder (ed.) *On the surface: Çatalhöyük 1993-95.* British Institute of Archaeology at Ankara Monograph 22. Oxbow: Oxford

Zohar, I., T. Dayan, E. Spanier, E. Galili and O. Lernau 1994
    Exploitation of grey triggerfish (Balistes carolinesis) by the prehistoric inhabitants of Atlit Yam, Israel: A preliminary report. Pp. 231–270 in W. van Neer (ed.) *Proceedings of the 7th meeting of the ICAZ Fish Remains Working Group.* Annales de Musée Royal de l'Afrique Centrale. Sciences Zoologiques no. 274. Tervuren.

Zohar, I., T. Dayan, E. Galili and E. Spanier 2001
    Fish Processing During the Early Holocene: A Taphonomic Case Study from Coasts, Israel. *Journal of Archaeological Science* 28: 1041–1053.

Zohary, D. 1996
    The Mode of domestication of the founder crops of Southwest Asian agriculture. Pp. 142–158 in D. Harris (ed.) *The Origins and Spread of Agriculture and Pastoralism in Eurasia.* UCL Press: London.

9

Cypriot Neolithic chipped stone industries and the progress of regionalization

Carole McCartney

Abstract

Until recently we were still looking to define the Cypriot Aceramic Neolithic as a local variant akin to the 'PPNC' or 'increasingly regional' PN cultures of the Levant. Fresh evidence from Cyprus, however, has increased the depth of the Cypriot Aceramic Neolithic some 2000 years, showing clear parallels that define the island part of the widespread PPNB 'inter-action sphere'. At the same time, development in the research of late Epi-Palaeolithic and Neolithic Cultures on the mainland has shown that the concept of increasing regionalization is no longer appropriate. Instead, the progress of the Neolithic should be viewed as phenomena of shifting regional affinities that came about when various cultural elements spread by the process of diffusion. Such elements can be traced in details of the chaînes opératoires *and final tool forms of the chipped stone industries documented on the island. In focusing on such elements, we may begin to see lines of continuity that suggest the possibility of a longer antiquity for the development of the Cypriot Aceramic. Although exhibiting its own unique identity, it was part of developments of the eastern Mediterranean mainland from the late Epi-Palaeolithic.*

Regionalization

The Aceramic Neolithic period of Cyprus was formerly held to be 'original' and unrelated to the PPN culture in the Levant (Le Brun 1989). Aceramic Cyprus appeared to fit more comfortably with the diversity of local cultures documented at the start of the Pottery Neolithic or as part of the increasing regionalization said to define the end of the PPNB period (Kozlowski and Gebel 1994: 600). Although it has always been compared to the PPNB of the Levant, research on Cyprus, especially as documented at the type-site of Khirokitia, emphasized the differences from the PPNB uniformity (cf. Le Brun 1989). This site, dated to *ca.* 6,000 BC uncalibrated (from *ca.* 8,000 BP/7,000 calibrated BC), is synchronous with the end of the PPNB period and the beginning of the Pottery Neolithic on the Levantine mainland, thus setting the stage for interpretations of contrast. With circular stone architecture, a 'poorly developed' chipped stone industry, burials retaining skulls, a highly developed ground stone vessel industry and figurines focused on males rather than females, Cyprus appeared to have little in common with PPN developments in the Levant.

Recent evidence from Cyprus has increased the depth of the Aceramic period some 2000 years. It now possesses the low levels of similarity necessary to be assigned to the 'large scale phenomena' of the PPNB interaction sphere (Gopher 1994a: 389). Numerous material culture parallels and ^{14}C dates from the recently excavated sites Kissonerga-*Mylouthkia* (hereafter *Mylouthkia*) and Parekklisha-*Shillourokambos* (hereafter *Shillourokambos*) place the beginning of the Cypriot Aceramic Neolithic *ca.* 9,200 BP or *ca.* 8,200 calibrated BC (Figure 9.1). New evidence provided by the analysis of the chipped stone assemblage from

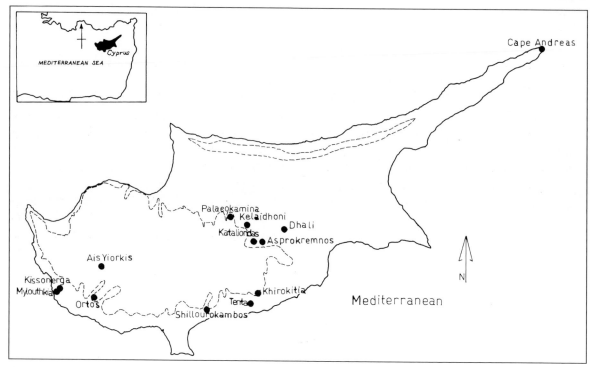

Figure 9.1 *Map of Cyprus with sites mentioned in the text*

Kalavasos-*Tenta* (hereafter *Tenta*) confirms previously known early dates belonging to *Tenta* period 5 and re-dates the bulk of the *Tenta* occupation to *ca.* 8,500–8,000 BP (*ca.* 7,500–7,000 calibrated BC) (Todd 1987, in press; McCartney in press, see below). Parallels in the chipped stone industries, iconography and economy of Aceramic Cyprus with those of the Levantine PPNB are now clearly evident (see Peltenburg *et al.* 2000; 2001a, b and references therein).

At the same time, the development in Neolithic research throughout the Near East in recent decades has demonstrated an increasing variety of site types, variability in material culture including architecture, mortuary tradition, iconography, ritual and economy, which has begun to challenge previously rigid concepts of things 'Neolithic', (e.g. Goring-Morris *et al.* 1995). Attributes of the Khirokitian culture previously held to distinguish the Cypriot Aceramic such as round structures or male figurines have been shown to have precedents in these new data from Anatolia and the Levant.

Research on the earlier Epi-Palaeolithic and PPNA periods has demonstrated considerable local variability alongside broader continuities through time. Many of the lithic indicators once

thought to define the PPNB were initiated in the PPNA, while all PPNA type fossils (sickle blades, perforators, heavy tools, projectiles) are said to originate in the Natufian (Bar-Yosef 1996: 208; Belfer-Cohen and Goring-Morris 1996: 217–219). The recognition of numerous regional facies, has demonstrated considerable local variability from at least the beginning of the Neolithic period, with developments by the LPPNB having evolved on the basis of different local backgrounds (Gebel and Kozlowski 1996: 460). In Anatolia, for example, the early Neolithic/PPNA emerges out of various late Epi-Palaeolithic traditions with possible origins for the north-eastern region from the Zagros, to the south-east in the Natufian, while the Öküzini culture of the southern coast appears to have influenced the central region (Gebel and Kozlowski 1996; M. Özdogan 1999: 227–228). Considerable continuity of these varied influences is evident in the early Neolithic/PPNA, and subsequently they appear in later PPNB assemblages that retain microlithic and/or geometric elements, alongside pressure flaking and bidirectional core techniques, and a range of point types. In the Northern Levant, the PPNA Khiamian shows a blade industry retaining

Natufian geometrics, which disappear by the subsequent Murebetian when the first naviform cores and short tanged points appear to herald the EPPNB (M.-C. Cauvin 1994: 279–288). In the Southern Levant facies, the Sultanian also emerges out of the Natufian through the Khiamian showing particular traits, including the Beit Ta'amir knives, Hagdud tuncations, and numerous bifacial chipped axes and adzes (Bar-Yosef 1996: 209; Belfer-Cohen and Goring-Morris 1996: 223). The PPNA has been described as more diverse than the preceding late Epi-Palaeolithic period, spreading farther to the north (Mureybet III) and east (Qermez Dere), while exhibiting several localized variants (Gebel and Kozlowski 1996: 459). The picture is one of variability in the Eastern Mediterranean (eastern wing of the Fertile Crescent or the 'Levant') by *ca*. 9,600 BP (9,000 calibrated BC). Unified by the presence of Khiam points, the PPNA interaction sphere extended from the Sinai to the Jebel Sinjar (Kozlowski 1994: 143–145; Bar-Yosef 1996: 210; Gebel and Kozlowski 1996: 454; Gopher 1996b: 451). The distribution of obsidian from central Anatolia demonstrates the existence of more wide ranging contacts across the East Mediterranean mainland already by the PPNA.

Geometrics, namely triangles, some quadrilaterals and numerous lunates, as well as other microliths are said to define the Natufian lithic industry (Belfer-Cohen and Goring-Morris 1996: 223). The subsequent development of PPNA industries shows the use of large single platform cores, long sickle blades, a few remnant lunates (which decline rapidly, or disappear, by the end of the period), and the development of polished stone axes and adzes (M.-C. Cauvin 1994: 279; Belfer-Cohen and Goring-Morris 1996: 217; 1996b: 451). It is significant that the use of bidirectional cores first appears in the PPNA as a secondary strategy to the dominant unidirectional methods. Lithic industries of the PPNB complete the trend towards the macro-lithic being heavily blade based and characterized by the widespread use of the naviform blade core method, long tanged arrowheads, long blade 'sickles' and other long blade tools (Quintero and Wilke 1995; Kozlowski 1999).

The concept of *increasing* regionalization *ca*. 8,000 BP (*ca*. 7,000 calibrated BC), therefore, no longer seems appropriate to describe trends of

that period. The 'progress' is not one of increasing regionalization, since regional variability always existed, but of shifting regional affinities as various cultural elements spread by the process of diffusion of ideas, sometimes by direct colonization. For example, during the PPNA in Southeastern Anatolia, sites like Hallan Çemi show closer affinity to the Zagros region, while the advent of the PPNB shows a shift in ties to the Northern Levant, as attested at sites like Çayönü and Nevali Çori (Özdogan and Balkan-Atli 1994: 205–206). A northward direction of influence noted for the Khiam point in the PPNA saw a shift to a north-south direction with the Helwan point from Mureybet at the start of the PPNB (Gopher 1989: 91: Bar-Yosef 1996: 210). Other areas of regional interaction between the Levantine and Mesopotamian extremes have been suggested for the Khabur region of the Euphrates (Hole 1996). Areas lying beyond the Levantine 'corridor', that have as yet not produced sites dated to these periods, have been assumed to be beyond the reach of these Neolithic processes of diffusion skipped over in the 'budding-off' of emigrant groups (Bar-Yosef 1996: 211). New evidence from Cyprus dating to *ca*. 8,200 calibrated BC, however, requires that we re-evaluate concepts that once excluded such areas as Cyprus from consideration of these developments. Regionalism does not only belong to the end of the Neolithic, it is part of all phases of the Neolithic. It can be charted on margins like the island of Cyprus where the mixing of chronologically and culturally specific traits appear to require the definition of a zone of regional interaction in the area of the north-east Mediterranean coast (cf. Peltenburg *et al*. 2001a: 54–60; Finlayson this volume). It is against this background of continuity and regional variability, elements which suggest the possibility of multiple interactions between the mainland and Cyprus, that we must evaluate the evidence of the Cypriot Aceramic.

Elements of continuity and transformation

The study of the process of lithics diffusion typically focuses on the *chaînes opératoires*, the particular learned 'ways of doing,' that demonstrate intention and represent the reproduction of social practice. The presence and persistence of diagnostic *chaînes opératoires* away from their region of origin has become accepted as evidence for the direct diffusion of ideas and at times populations (Lemonnier 1993: 3–5; Graves-Brown 1995: 13; Bar-Yosef 1996: 208). Chronological discussions of the development of Cypriot Aceramic Neolithic industries according to specific *chaînes opératoires* has been outlined elsewhere (McCartney 1999, in press; Guilaine *et al.* 2000; Peltenburg *et al.* 2001a, b). The present discussion will focus, instead, on specific diagnostic elements (both technical and formal) within the *chaînes opératoires* and the resulting sets of tools, that appear to indicate similarities or patterns of diffusion between Cyprus and the East Mediterranean mainland. Given that Cypriot assemblages do not correspond exactly to any single known mainland example, we need to view such elements as trends accumulated through a long process of assimilation from possibly wide-ranging 'parent' traditions. The practice of selecting elements of material culture takes place only in the context of social practice, whereby it is reproduced and transformed (Jones 1997: 120–126). This focus allows us to appreciate the active choices made by Cypriot knappers to bring about the transformation of the technical system through time.

The desire to find social 'meaning' in material culture has given rise to the analysis of technical systems and technical knowledge, media through which material culture is transformed. The technical system is defined at any given moment by: 1) existing artefacts, operational sequences, the physical relationships between techniques, and 2) socially translated technical knowledge, which provides the context of meaning (Lemonnier 1993: 12, 13). Because every technical system is continually evolving and subject to a mixture of conservatism and change, it is the process of 'translation' or selection from various possible technical solutions on the basis of social meaning that we ultimately aim to unravel. In other words, "to deal with technical choice is to deal with the conditions of change and continuity in material culture," (Lemonnier 1993: 21–24). Material culture, because it represents a 'transformation of behaviour,' is part of social negotiation with objects

becoming actively manipulated, acting as symbols in social relations (Schofield 1995b: 4–6; Jones 1997: 115). The use of objects as symbols leads to geographically and chronologically discrete styles, spread by a culture expanding out of its homeland area or in extending alliances through trade, allowing societies to accommodate distant relatives. The selection or continuity of finished forms, for example, arrowheads, outlines boundaries of such interaction at a given point in time. Such traits are a product of similar 'enculturative milieu,' but not necessarily maps of ethnic groups (Bar-Yosef 1996: 211, 212; Gamble 1995: 23; Jones 1997: 115, 122, 123).

Technical solutions require considerable technical knowledge in order to be mechanically viable. They must be compatible with the existing technical system, provide solutions (or appropriate forms) that fit with social tradition and meet the expectations of the society that uses them. For change to occur, there also needs to be some social or technical requirement needing change (Lemonnier 1993: 3–12; Gamble 1995: 13; Graves-Brown 1995: 10–13). Models of technological analysis, therefore, require that we ask three questions of the artefact material; 1) what kinds of features show choices, 2) what physical and social properties underlie technical choices, 3) are these choices merely arbitrary, constraining the evolution and transformation of the technical system and the society (Lemonnier 1993: 9). The second deals with both physical properties and social properties, not a simple function versus style dichotomy, while the third aspect deals with the realm of possibilities. Analysis of the tools alone could, for example, hide cases of arbitrary formal similarity. In the physical world, properties, procedures and materials limit the number of possibilities for achieving a specific technology, but the process of cultural translation restricts the selection of the correct answer for any given context. In other words, the social selection of a technology is determined for reasons other than technical efficiency. Technically redundant elements can, therefore, be retained where they have cultural significance such as conveying status or identity.

When trying to distinguish among various technical or formal possibilities, it is necessary to concentrate on 'invariant' properties required in the practical sense of tool function, as well as properties of design or form, which allow us to trace social practice and historical context. For example, formless edges, corners or surfaces, which 'remain static' are embedded in the knapping process even though our perception of resulting form changes (Graves-Brown 1995: 12, 13). The present preliminary analysis will look at elements of technology and form, or socially constructed design, in an attempt to identify indicators of 'tradition' for the purposes of understanding diffusion processes to Cyprus. Since all artefacts deploy design, they represent social/historical constructs. We are looking, therefore, at the 'material results of traditions of practice' (Graves-Brown 1995: 13). In this sense, the design concept of a tool is more important than its raw material or function (*ibid.*, 14; Lemonnier 1993: 14). Elements introduced into a technological system must be compatible and consistent with existing elements (in other words be of the same technological level) and be understood in light of existing knowledge, fitting physically within existing practices of how elements can be combined, and in what order. Once accepted, an element becomes part of the system's continuing adaptation (Lemonnier 1993: 12–14).

In isolating such properties, we attempt to approach an understanding of social 'meaning,' culture identity and tradition, where we may begin to understand the process of diffusion. We are required to focus on active participation or interaction, rather than passive generalizations like 'isolation' or 'loss of skill' that have been used to define Cypriot Neolithic chipped stone in the past. 'Regionalism is only partly constrained by physical barriers, and partly by ideas and practices embedded in the symbolic system' (Lemonnier 1993: 2–3). For too long chipped stone materials from Cypriot Aceramic sites have been defined on the basis of deficiencies, while assuming that these 'omissions' or differences from mainland PPNB industries represent a simple one to one presence/absence equation between artefacts and human contact. Such inferences fail to evaluate possible social relations between the chipped stone technology and transformations of meaning in terms of the social groups involved. On the basis of the elements to be discussed the following points will be considered:

1) How many waves/episodes of contact with Cyprus were there through time and from what possible geographic points of origin?
2) What elements within the Cypriot Aceramic Neolithic industries indicate a 'heritage' of these waves of diffusion?
3) To what degree does the evolution of Cypriot industries represents the translation of such inherited elements into a uniquely Cypriot statement of social meaning and identity?

The Cypriot evidence

Chronology of industries

Lying outside the Levantine corridor on the western margin of the PPNB interaction sphere, recent evidence of the Cypriot Aceramic Neolithic has been divided into three phases broadly corresponding to the E/MPPNB, LPPNB and Final PPNB phases on the mainland. The industries belonging to these phases, early, middle and late Cypriot Aceramic (or Cypro-PPNB) have been discussed in detail elsewhere (Peltenburg *et al.* 2001a, b; McCartney in press). Specific technological and typological features exhibiting elements of inherited tradition belonging to three excavated assemblages (*Mylouthkia*, *Tenta* and *Shillourokambos*) and three surface collected sites (Ayia Vavara-*Asprokremnos*, Politico-*Kelaïdhoni*, and Agrokipia-*Palaeokamina*, hereafter *Asprokremnos*, *Kelaïdhoni* and *Palaeokamina* respectively) form the basis of the present discussion (Todd 1987; McCartney 1998a; Guilaine *et al.* 2000; Given and Knapp in press; Peltenburg *et al.* 2001a, b; 2003). On the basis of the three excavated assemblages; *Mylouthkia*, *Tenta*, and *Shillourokambos*, the three surface collections from *Asprokremnos*, *Kelaïdhoni*, and *Palaeokaminia* can be assigned to the early and middle phases of the Cypriot Aceramic Neolithic (Table 9.1). Having been defined on the basis of the type-site of Khirokitia, the industry belonging to the late phase of the Cypriot Aceramic (or Khirokitian) is known from numerous assemblages across the island; Cape Andreas-*Kastros*, Dhali-*Agridhi*, Kataliondas-*Kourvellos*, Kholetria-*Ortos*, Kissonerga-*Mosphilia*, Kritou-*Ayias tis Yeorkis* (hereafter Cape Andreas, Dhali, Kataliondas, *Ortos*, Kissonerga

Date	Phasing	Mainland Period	Cypriot Assemblage
10,600–? BP 10,000 cal BC	'Akrotiri'	Late Natufian	Aetokremnos
??	??	PPNA	??
9,200–8,500 BP 8,200–7,500 cal BC	Early Cypriot Aceramic (Cypro-EPPNB/MPPNB)	EPPNB/MPPNB	*Mylouthkia* 1A *Tenta* Period 5 *Shillourokambos* A/B *Kelaïdhoni*
8,500–8,000 BP 7,500–7,000 cal BC	Middle Cypriot Aceramic (Cypro-LPPNB)	LPPNB	*Mylouthkia* 1B *Tenta* Periods 4–2 *Shillourokambos* Middle *Asprokremnos* *Paleokamina*
8,000 – 6,500 BP 7,000–5,500 cal BC	Late Cypriot Aceramic (Khirokitian)	Final PPNB/PPNC	*Tenta* Period 1 Khirokitia *Ayias Yeorkis* *Mosphilia* 1A Cape Andreas *Ortos* Dhali *Kataliondas*

Table 9.1 *Chronological phasing for Cypriot Aceramic Neolithic assemblages (dates and Cypro-PPNB phasing based on Peltenburg* et al. *2000).*

and *Ayias Yeorkis*) and *Tenta* to name a few (Stekelis 1953; Watkins 1979; Lehavy 1980; Le Brun *et al.* 1981; 1984; Simmons 1996; 1998; McCartney 1998b).

As a crucial part of the following discussion, it should be noted that the bulk of the *Tenta* assemblage (periods 4–2) has been re-dated to the middle Cypriot Aceramic on the basis of the chipped stone and analysis of the ¹⁴C dates in relation to context (McCartney in press; Todd in press). This reappraisal of the chronology in light of the lithic assemblage will be detailed in the forthcoming report on the chipped stone industries of the site (Hordynsky and McCartney forthcoming). In brief, the presence of well stratified dates belonging to the end of the middle Cypriot Aceramic phase from within the structure 14 complex and structures 34 and 58 of period 2 marks the end of a sequence (periods

4–2) of stratified occupation on the Top of the Site (see Todd 1987). The range of sixth millennium BC uncalibrated dates (from *ca.* 7,600 BP) primarily from the Lower South Slopes can be demonstrated to overlie structures belonging to periods 4–2 or belong to external or derived contexts. Technically and typologically the materials belonging to the Lower South Slope structures are directly parallel to materials belonging to periods 4–2 from the Top of the Site, and belong to the same industry.

Elements of the Cypriot chipped stone industries

It should be noted from the start, that comparative materials from numerous sites throughout the Levant and Anatolia are considered for discussion purposes without any assumption of direct demic diffusion from any singular parent culture. Similarly, the terms 'PPNA' and 'PPNB' are used in the broadest sense as chronological periods and extensive spheres of interaction between numerous 'ethnic' groups. The discussion of technical and formal design elements is made to highlight potential type fossils of the diffusion process that demonstrate the active and non-unilinear record of colonization; in other words, a socially determined record of active selection and continuity of lithic tradition.

Various traditions are readily apparent in the core technology belonging to early Cypriot Aceramic assemblages including: bidirectional naviform-related (*sensu lato*), classic naviform (*sensu strictu*), single platform and change of orientation methods used for blade production. Smaller single platform cores sometimes made on flakes were used for bladelet or small blade production, while discoidal and irregular cores were used for the manufacture of flakes. This variety of methods exhibits elements derived from the PPNB tradition, but also elements showing continuity with preceding late Epi-Paleolithic/Natufian and PPNA *chaînes opératoires*.

Elements of continuity

The use of unidirectional cores during the Cypriot Aceramic demonstrates continuity with late Epi-Palaeolithic/PPNA traditions on the mainland. Single platform cores were prominent during the Natufian through the PPNA, becoming a secondary focus of blade production by the PPNB. During the early PPNA, Khiamian, there was a continued use of small exhausted cores typical of the final Natufian, while by the later PPNA Sultanian of the southern Levant, larger unidirectional blade cores became the norm (Bar-Yosef 1996: 209; Belfer-Cohen and Goring-Morris 1996: 222, 223). This pattern is repeated in Cyprus. The earliest known core technology on the island shows the dominant use of heavily reduced bladelet cores for the production of short blades and bladelets at Akrotiri-*Aetokremnos* (hereafter *Aetokremnos*) (Simmons 2000: 12). The presence of crested pieces suggests the use of a ventral crest on some cores. In addition to bladelets, the blades produced were small on average in comparison to those of the succeeding Cypriot Aceramic, while the majority of the tools were produced on flakes (*ibid.*). By the Aceramic period, single platform core reduction follows a number of distinct *chaînes opératoires*.

At *Shillourokambos* (ancient phases A/B) bladelets or small blades were removed from large burin-like flakes as well as small single platform cores that were linked specifically with the production of bladelets for the manufacture of glossed crescents, (Guilaine *et al.* 2000: 79; see below). Similarly, at *Tenta* burin-like cores-on-flakes as well as small unidirectional bladelet cores are present (from period 5) and they are linked to the manufacture of crescent glossed segments and unretouched glossed bladelets. This use of small and/or heavily exhausted bladelet or small blade cores appears to be derived from the late Natufian or early PPNA use of such cores for the production of geometrics including crescent shaped glossed tools. Also at *Tenta*, larger single platform cores as well as change-of-orientation cores were also used in blade production recalling the dominant later PPNA tradition. At *Tenta* and *Asprokremnos* a limited number of single platform blade cores (and corresponding core trimming elements) exhibit dorsal crested or transverse preparations reminiscent of core preparation methods seen at PPNB sites such as Cafer Höyük (Calley 1985: 90; Hole 1996: 7; McCartney 1998a: Figures 1. 1, 2).

The manufacture of flakes, dominant in the Natufian and PPNA as at *Aetokremnos*, continues into the PPNB, running parallel with the use of blade methods (Belfer-Cohen 1994: 97; Simmons 2000: 12). Similarly, in spite of the dominant use of blade blanks in tool manufacture, 'ad-hoc' flake production is present in all of the Cypriot Aceramic Neolithic assemblages, based on discoidal or a variety of more irregular core forms (McCartney 1998a: 87; Guilaine *et al.* 2000: 79; Peltenburg *et al.* 2003). It is notable that a dichotomy between formal blade and *ad hoc* flake *chaînes opératoires* is often noted as a characteristic of PPNB assemblages in the Levant where it reveals a general continuity with earlier traditions (e.g. Goring-Morris *et al.* 1995: 95).

Use of the naviform method (*sensu strictu*) for blade production clearly demonstrates the diffusion of a tradition typically attributed to the PPNB, but developed first at Mureybet, where it appeared by the end of the PPNA Murebetian (III) (M.-C. Cauvin 1994: 281; Schmidt 1996: 366). In the N. Levant, naviform cores (*sensu strictu*) were used for the production of 'preferential' blades employed in the manufacture of arrowheads (Abbès 1994; M.-C. Cauvin 1994: 288). This classic naviform method was transferred to the island *ca.* 9,200 BP as shown at *Shillourokambos* ancient phase A. The preferential blades used for arrowhead manufacture during phases A and B at *Shillourokambos* indicate a close link between this site and the tradition of the Northern Levant (Guilaine *et al.* 2000: 79, 81; Briois *et al.* 1997: 97). Elsewhere, at *Mylouthkia* 1A, *Tenta* period 5, *Kelaïdhoni*, *Palaeokamina* and *Asprokremnos*, the use of a bidirectional naviform-related (*sensu lato*) blade core technology is indicated. High indices of bidirectional dorsal scars on blade blanks and tools, core trimming elements (including primary crested blades and upsalon blades), as well as bi-directional cores in these assemblages provide ample evidence of this core technology (McCartney 1998a: 87; 1999; Peltenburg *et al.* 2003). At *Shillourokambos*, butt type distributions belonging to the ancient phase (A/B) demonstrate high proportions of punctiform and/or filliform butt types, an element confirming the use of the naviform method (*sensu strictu*) (Guilaine *et al.* 2000: 79). The paucity of detailed platform preparation evidence or refittable reduction sequences require the use of a general bidirectional label at *Mylouthkia* 1A and for the surface collected sites. At *Tenta* period 5, however, bidirectional cores made on cobbles or thick tablets showing no dorsal core preparation confirms the use of a bidirectional method (*sensu lato*) like that seen in PPNA/EPPNB assemblages in Southeastern Anatolia preceding the introduction of naviform cores (*sensu strictu*) by the M/LPPNB (e.g. Cauvin *et al.* 1999: 97; A. Özdogan 1999: 52). The Cypriot pattern of bidirectional core technology (*sensu lato*) may in some cases, therefore, be similarly reminiscent of the earlier PPNA/EPPNB tradition seen outside the Northern Levant.

Transformation of core technology

From *ca.* 8,500 BP in the middle phase at *Shillourokambos*, Guilaine *et al.* (2000: 80) record a change in the bidirectional core technology. The transformation was marked by changes in raw material selection (see below), and an end to intensive platform preparation resulting in a loss of skill and an end to the production of preferential blades. This shift in core technology, along with a decline in arrowhead production and the disappearance of cattle, has been interpreted at *Shillourokambos* as indicative of the cessation of contacts between Cyprus and the Levantine mainland (Guilaine *et al.* 2000: 80, 81). A similar pattern of change in terms of the core technology at *Mylouthkia* 1B appears to support the technical shifts recorded at *Shillourokambos*. At *Tenta*, however, during period 4 there was a brief increase in the amount of butt edge preparation possibly related to the former peak in naviform (*sensu strictu*) core reduction seen elsewhere. The same two methods of opposed platform core reduction (prepared and unprepared) documented in period 5 were used subsequently. The dominant method in which no preparation was given to the dorsal surface of the core, typically relied on the tabular form of the preferred raw material to provide core form, a feature recorded at sites on the mainland (cf. Baird 1994: 531; Gebel 1996: 268; McCartney 1998c: 68). Crest preparations were made to set the platforms and objective core face while the presence of other kinds of core trimming elements shows continuity of the core shaping and maintenance practices corresponding to stages of the naviform method (*sensu strictu*). A smaller number of bidirectional cores in the assemblage demonstrates remnant dorsal crests or transverse preparations on the dorsal surface of the core comparable to naviform core form (*sensu strictu*). From period 4 to period 1 (Khirokitian) there was a gradual decline in the use of opposed platform core technology, but such cores continued to be utilized selectively for the production of blades throughout (McCartney in press). The picture is one of general continuity rather than change in the bidirectional core technology between periods 4–1 at *Tenta*. This continuity may, as suggested above, indicate the perpetuation of a PPNA heritage, but the moderate increase in platform preparation, greater percentage of bi-directional cores and lithic caches belonging to period 4 suggest a brief experiment with at least elements of the naviform method (*sensu strictu*).

Problems with a model of isolation based on evidence provided by a single site are also found in the continuity of both arrowheads and cattle elsewhere on the island after 8,500 BP (Peltenburg *et al.* 2001a: 53, see below). An alternative interpretation of the changes in the bidirectional *chaîne opératoire* at *Mylouthkia* and

Shillourokambos sees the various elements as technologically consistent with and corresponding to the alternatives in core technology and raw material already available. This much had been documented by the technical system at *Tenta* (cf. Lemonnier 1993: 5–7). The correspondence of all of the main elements of change in bidirectional core technology (raw material, platform preparation and blade character) at the same technological level demonstrates appropriate technical responses to the desired tool types. The stimulus for these changes, therefore, needs to be sought in the realms of social meaning, since the only constraint to change is the presence of the particular material resource and the intellectual means to exploit it (Lemonnier 1993: 12). It is important to recognize the invariant properties that survived the shift in technology, namely, a continued demand for long, flat, parallel-sided blades, though no longer the fine delicate blades of the naviform method (*sensu strictu*). This demand for flat straight-sided blades (used for cutting plants or skin, sometimes showing gloss) originated in the Natufian (Anderson and Valla 1996: 349). The production of 'specialized' naviform blades at large LPPNB settlements like Ain Ghazal and Basta, relied on a large population base and the 'commercial' demand generated and permitted by that large population base (Quintero and Wilke 1995; Quintero 1996; Gebel 1996). As well as a significant product demand, this 'specialization' was based on a potential for producing goods beyond basic subsistence requirements. Without these criteria, craft specialization would collapse as it did in the subsequent PPNC/PN (Gebel 1996: 262). In the middle phase of the Cypriot Aceramic (or Cypro-LPPNB) we find simplification rather than the intensification, with the continuity of small scale farming settlements rather than the large agglomerations more typical of the LPPNB Levant (Peltenburg *et al.* 2001a: 53; see also Peltenburg this volume). In Cyprus, a different local tradition based on the continuity of a generalized bidirectional core technology (exhibiting parallel shaping and maintenance practices, but without significant butt preparation) characterizes a socially motivated choice not to continue the investment necessary for naviform core technology (*sensu strictu*) by *ca.* 8,500 BP. A similar, though somewhat later shift

from naviform cores (*sensu strictu*) towards unidirectional and/or change-of-orientation core reduction, has been documented by the increasingly flake-based Final PPNB/PPNC and subsequent Late Neolithic industries of the Near East (e.g. Gopher 1994b: 564; Quintero and Wilke 1995: 19, 20).

Raw material selection

The prominent use of high quality 'translucent' chert (the finest quality type of Lefkara chert) distinguishes the early Cypriot Aceramic (Cypro-E/MPPNB). 'Translucent' chert was dominant at *Mylouthkia* Period 1A, *Shillourokambos* Ancient phase A/B as well as in the three surface collected assemblages from *Kelaïdhoni*, *Palaeokaminia* and *Asprokremnos* (Guilaine *et al.* 2000: 78-79; McCartney in press; Xenophontos pers. comm.). This high quality raw material was already exploited *ca.* 10,600 BP at *Aetokremnos* among other raw materials (predominantly Lefkara chert varieties) for the production of flakes, blades and bladelets without specific raw material selection (Simmons 2000: 12). During the Aceramic, in contrast, 'translucent' chert was selectively utilized for long blade production from bidirectional including naviform (*sensu strictu*) cores indicating a 'pre-conditioned knowledge' associated with the naviform tradition of the PPNB Levant (Bar-Yosef 1996: 212; Quintero 1996: 235). 'Translucent' chert at *Tenta* 5 represented a little more than a quarter of the total raw material distribution. Rather than dominating blade production, this material was selected for the manufacture of small blades or bladelets used for glossed tools, for well made discoidal cores for flakes, as well as being utilized for a number of bidirectional blade cores. In contrast, flake production from elsewhere during the early Aceramic phase was relegated to poor quality materials using '*ad hoc*' reduction methods.

Shifts in the core technology from *ca.* 8,500 BP in the middle Aceramic were associated with changes in raw material utilization. Moderate Lefkara cherts with their numerous limestone inclusions and brittle characters are not suitable to the production of durable fine blade blanks. Shifts in the bidirectional core technology outlined above, particularly changes in butt configuration from the punctiform/filiform types of the classic naviform method to broad plain and facetted types of the bidirectional method (*sensu lato*), enabled more robust and durable blades to be produced, making moderate Lefkara cherts viable for long blade production. This transformation of raw material selection, like that of the core technology was compatible with the range of possibilities offered by the Cypriot landscape and the technological tradition available at the time (cf. Lemonnier 1993: 12). By the middle Cypriot Aceramic a change to the dominant use of moderate quality cherts is evident at *Mylouthkia* (1B) and *Shillourokambos* (middle/recent phases), while at *Tenta* a different local tradition shows the continued use of locally abundant moderate chert already from period 5. The selection to utilize materials immediately available near the site at *Tenta* from *ca.* 9,200 BP more closely resembles the *Aetokremnos* pattern and like the reliance on a generalized bidirectional blade core method appears closer to the PPNA tradition on the mainland. At *Tenta*, as elsewhere, a trend toward more moderate quality cherts is marked by an increase in the use of granular dense Lefkara translucent by the late Aceramic (Khirokitian) period 1 (McCartney in press).

Because the classic naviform core technology required very high quality chert, changes in raw material selection in Cyprus *ca.* 8,500 BP (like other shifts in the bidirectional core technology) correspond to a retreat from the kind of high status, easily pressure retouched long blades afforded by the best quality chert and naviform cores (*sensu strictu*) (cf. Quintero 1996: 235, 240). An alternative hypothesis focusing on the raw material and technical changes of *ca.* 8,000 BP in the Levant associates changes of economy, notably a decline in hunting and therefore residential mobility, with corresponding changes in access to lithic resources embedded in the hunting round (Molist and Ferrier 1996: 440, 441). The latter has been partly supported by Guilaine *et al.* (2000: 80–81) based on changes in the economy at *Shillourokambos* noted above. 'Translucent' cherts, however, are readily available in the Cypriot landscape. Their presence indicates that shifts in raw material utilization *ca.* 8,500 BP represent deliberate choice, rather than limitations in access (particularly when we have no reason for inferring territorial limits to material access). Instead, the use of moderate

raw materials appears to direct the simplification of the bidirectional core technology, with the primary focus being the continued production of flat parallel-sided long blades. The latter, even if more 'robust,' were suited to the tool demands of small-scale farming settlements that characterized the Cypriot Aceramic period. These farmers may have become less interested in exchange networks based on prestige items like fine blades and arrowheads, yet the basic tradition of blade making using bidirectional cores survives throughout the Pre-Pottery Neolithic on Cyprus as on the mainland. Perhaps, lacking the economic or social incentive of the intensified LPPNB market as on the mainland allowed for changes that permitted the technological system on the island to 'return' in effect to a 'PPNA state.'

Obsidian is the only exotic raw material used in Aceramic Cyprus. Present in all phases, comparatively high percentages of this material were recovered from early Aceramic assemblages. At *Mylouthkia* 1A obsidian represents 12% of the total sample, and at *Shillourokambos* some 2% of the total sample is documented by a larger number of individual pieces (Briois *et al.* 1997). While this peak in number of artefacts may demonstrate a more active participation in obsidian exchange networks in the early phase of the Aceramic, the continued presence of this material implies that the apparent 'decline' in obsidian trade contact is something of a 'red herring.' Indeed the *ca.* 300 pieces (nearly all bladelets) from *Shillourokambos* could have arrived on the island in one small bag. The continued presence of obsidian, particularly in the form of a fine pressure retouch point tang from Khirokitia, demonstrates the increasing 'prestige' status of this exotic material type in Cyprus as on the Levantine mainland during the LPPNB (Christou 1994: 664). According to Gamble (1995: 23, 24) the 'scale of the raw material transfers is equivalent to the level of social complexity.' Changes in the selection of raw material and the decrease in the amount of imported obsidian on Cyprus appear more readily understood in terms of the level of social complexity rather than being defined in terms of cultural 'isolation.' While it seems likely that groups from the middle phase of the Cypriot Aceramic were marginalized in terms of the exchange networks of

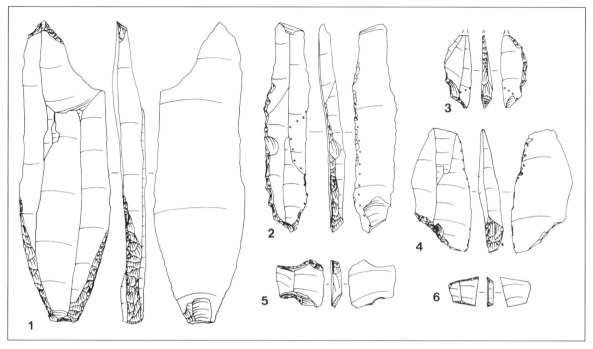

Figure 9.2 *Kalavasos*-Tenta *chipped stone. 1) 'tanged blade'; 2) backed and truncated glossed blade; 3) glossed crescent; 4) truncated glossed blade; 5) and 6) double truncations*

obsidian and arrowheads, this economic independence does not translate directly into an 'isolated' social identity. Cyprus was notably less marginalized from the obsidian trade network than some sites on the eastern margin of the interaction sphere, such as LPPNB Dhuweila where obsidian was entirely absent (Betts 1998). Instead, we appear to have in Cyprus a significant degree of regional autonomy, and an enduring identification with symbolic elements of identity originating in traditions on the mainland (see also below).

Tanged pieces

Arrowhead types belonging to the Cypriot Aceramic and morphological parallels on the mainland have been discussed in detail elsewhere (Peltenburg *et al.* 2001a: 51, 2002; McCartney in press, and references therein). In terms of the present discussion of traits, it is important to note their variety. Arrowhead or broken tang samples belonging to each of the assemblages are at present unique, and demonstrate wide-ranging chronological and geographical parallels in Levant and Southeast Anatolia. Elements of retouch character and location on arrowheads from early Cypriot Aceramic assemblages

demonstrate parallels in the manufacture of arrowheads from E/MPPNB throughout the East Mediterranean mainland. Importantly, as if predicting the lower priority given to the exchange of arrowheads, Byblos points do not precede naviform (*sensu strictu*) core technology (seen for example at MPPNB Çayönü), but arrive in Cyprus as part of the complete cha ne opératoire *ca.* 9,200 BP (Caneva *et al.* 1994: 254–259; A. Özdogan 1999 : 47, 52; Guilaine *et al.* 2000 : 79; Peltenburg *et al.* 2001a: 51). From *Tenta* two microlithic tanged points belonging to a secure period 5 context are at present unique in terms of the *chaînes opératoires* employed, belonging to the bladelet *chaînes opératoires* of the glossed tools (Figure 9.2). These diminutive points, therefore, belong to a different tradition than the long blade points from Myloutkia 1A, *Shillourokambos* (A/B) or *Kelaïdhoni*.

Arrowhead tangs, including Byblos examples from *Tenta* periods 4–2, three pressure retouched tangs from Kissonerga and the pressure flaked obsidian tang from Khirokitia, demonstrate that arrowheads (though always rare) continued in use through the middle and late phases of the Cypriot Aceramic. Importantly, a number of these later examples exhibit covering pressure retouch an element of retouch technology indicative of the later parts of the PPNB on the mainland. They are unlikely to have occurred independent of continued contact with the mainland traditions. The Kissonerga pressure retouched pieces, in particular, represent significant continuity of skill, especially when the relatively poor quality of the chert is considered.

Despite being a major index fossils of the PPNB, the rarity of arrowheads on the island of Cyprus appears to be another 'red herring' if we remember the rarity of other index fossils such as glossed blades (or 'sickles') from desert areas of the mainland (Bar Yosef 1996: 208; Betts 1998: 113). Indeed, Hole (1996: 7) has suggested that arrowheads represent 'artefacts of the open steppe.' While their rarity may indicate a low networking frequency, the arrowhead tangs found in Cypriot assemblages are likely to have had highly charged symbolic roles in Aceramic Cyprus as status items and/or markers of ethnic identity as suggested for such artefacts from Levant. Since it is the 'finished forms,' that delineate the boundaries of an interaction sphere, the rare Cypriot arrowhead no doubt carried special meaning on the island (cf. Bar Yosef 1996: 212). It seems unlikely that their role can be accounted for solely by hunting, especially in light of the continued tradition of hunting deer long after the disappearance of tanged points from the island. From a purely functional point of view, it is probable that different methods of hunting or forms of herding were employed from the earliest phase of the Aceramic since projectiles never figure highly in tool counts.

A transformation of the arrowhead form is documented by the 'tanged blades' belonging to middle and late phase Cypriot Aceramic chipped stone industries. This new tool form shows the 'borrowing' of earlier arrowhead features (Lemonnier 1993: 21). 'Tanged blades' defined by Stekelis (1953: 411) for the Khirokitia assemblage are widely recognized as one of the diagnostic features of assemblages dated to the Late Cypriot Aceramic (Khirokitian) phase, for example at *Ortos* (Simmons 1996: 35, 36). Examples of these tools have also been recovered from *Tenta* and *Asprokremnos* (McCartney 1998a: 88; in press; Peltenburg *et al.* 2001a: 53). They appear at *Tenta* during the period 4 sample at the beginning of the middle Aceramic phase corresponding to the transformations in raw material use

and core technology documented above. The *Asprokremnos* example is relatively unique since it was made on an elongated flake of high quality 'translucent' chert. A greater proportion of the tool sample in this assemblage was made on the Lefkara basal variety (McCartney 1998a: 87). Typically on 'robust' blades struck from both bidirectional and unidirectional cores, the 'tanged blades' exhibit abrupt bilateral, and at times, semi-bifacial basal retouch. The distal end may be pointed by abrupt direct retouch or left unretouched. The links, particularly between pre-existing elements of tang configuration and the long blade blank type borrowed from earlier PPNB arrowhead features, appear obvious in spite of changes in retouch character and robustness of the blade blank. These innovations were chosen in accordance with established technical features and logically belong to existing social strategies of meaning used to perpetuate group identity and/or individual status (Lemonnier 1995: 17, 18; Jones 1997: 115).

Rather than functioning as projectiles, Cypriot 'tanged blades' could be interpreted as long tanged knives or 'daggers' like examples seen in assemblages such as Nevali Çori or Nahal Oren from the E/MPPNB. These tools exhibit a projectile morphology and knife related use-wear (Bar-Yosef and Alon 1988: 9, 10, Figures 6–8; Schmidt 1996: 366, Figure 5, 369). Like the glossed Beit Ta'amir knives of the southern Levantine PPNA, they appear to have played a partly symbolic role, as demonstrations of 'achievement' of knapping craft related to the bidirectional core tradition across the Mediterranean (Bar-Yosef and Alon 1988: 10; Noy 1996). At *Tenta*, 'tanged blades' are relatively rare (some 40 definite with up to 64 examples including probable broken artefacts), and were recovered from all areas of the site. Bifacial edge damage located typically on the medial to distal lateral edges of these tools suggests a function related to cutting, while use-wear analysis of *Tenta* examples indicates a distinct use in comparison to backed or other 'knife-like' tools (Hordynsky and McCartney in press). It is possible that these 'tanged' tools may have been used in a 'ceremonial' or 'symbolic' capacity (like the arrowheads) or as special status 'knives' distributed perhaps one per household. At present there is no evidence like the single context distribution of 'unusual' pressure retouched points in the 'ritual' building at Nevali Çori (Schmidt 1996: 370–375).

Glossed pieces

Glossed tools from the six Cypriot Aceramic assemblages discussed in this paper demonstrate regional variability across the island and provide considerable evidence of selected trait or 'element' transmission through time. *Mylouthkia* 1A shows finely denticulated glossed blades, which though broken parallel the tradition of long glossed blade prevalent in the E/MPPNB Levant and Southeast Anatolia (Gopher 1996a: 156; Quintero, Wilke and Waines 1997: 281). In contrast to the above, a second tradition using blades and especially bladelets for the manufacture of geometric glossed crescents, some of which exhibit oblique gloss, is documented in the early and middle Cypriot Aceramic phases at *Tenta*, early *Shillourokambos* as well as surface collected *Kelaïdhoni* (Guilaine 2000: 79; McCartney in press). Unretouched glossed bladelets and finely denticulated glossed blades (like those from *Mylouthkia*) as well as backed and/or truncated blades or segments comprise the high degree of variability of glossed tools from *Tenta*. The use of crescents (as well as unretouched glossed bladelets) represents a marked difference in the use of unidirectional small blade or bladelet *chaînes opératoires* showing continuity of a late Natufian tradition in contrast to long blade *chaînes opératoires* belonging to PPN traditions.

On the basis of chronological proximity, it was suggested earlier that Cypriot glossed crescents may correspond to the continued tradition of using geometrics in south-eastern and central Anatolia during the PPNB (Peltenburg *et al.* 2001a: 52; McCartney in press). It is interesting that assemblages fitting this description such as Asiliki Höyük dated to *ca.* 8,700 BP also exhibit pointed blades, backed blades and/or truncated blades typical of the Cypriot Aceramic particularly from the middle phase (or Cypro-LPPNB) onwards (Balkan-Atli 1994: 215).

While historically more distant, it may be more accurate to consider the glossed crescent tools from Cyprus in light of the lunate tradition diagnostic of the Natufian of the Levant. Lunates belonging to the Late Natufian are ubiquitous and diagnostic of a phase of Natufian 'influence,'

that had encompassed the southern Levant reaching as far north as the Euphrates at Mureybet by *ca.* 10,300 BP, and including coastal sites in the region of the Anti-Lebanon (Copeland 1991; Bar-Yosef 1998: Figure 3). The presence of at least one lunate, in addition to other microliths from the assemblage at *Aetokremnos* on the island of Cyprus, helps to mark the site as part of this wider Mediterranean phenomena (Bar-Yosef 1998: 145–147; Simmons 2000: 12). Lunates continued in use into the subsequent PPNA cultures of the Levant, declining significantly by *ca.* 9,400 BP in the Sultanian of the Southern Levant, having already disappeared by the Murebetian *ca.* 10,000 BP in the Northern Levant when glossed tools became increasingly longer (M.-C. Cauvin 1994: 281–288; Belfer-Cohen and Goring-Morris 1996: 223). Late Natufian and final Natufian lunates are typically small *ca.* 15–18 mm and <15 mm respectively with PPNA lunates basically in the same size range 10–23 mm in length (Belfer-Cohen 1994: 91–96). In comparison, the Cypriot Aceramic crescents, ranging from *ca.* 30–50 mm in length, are relatively large, but comparable to larger examples from Hayonim or the Anatolian examples noted above (Balkan-Atli 1994: Figure 2; Anderson and Valla 1996: Table 6). Specific retouch elements link the Cypriot glossed segment tradition closer to that of the Natufian/PPNA Levant, namely, the use of both bipolar and a crude helwan like retouch in creating the convex backing on some tools. Helwan lunates are said to be absent from the Late and Final Natufian, except on large sites with a previous helwan tradition or surviving in small numbers as, for example, on the eastern margin of the Levant in the Black Desert of Transjordan (Belfer-Cohen and Goring-Morris 1996: 219; Betts 1998: 19). Instead, Final Natufian lunates, particularly in the north, frequently used bipolar retouch on lunates and triangular varients (Belfer-Cohen and Goring-Morris 1996: 222). Bipolar retouch is present in the *Tenta* assemblage from the early Cypriot Aceramic (period 5) sample on backed blades and continues through to the end of the site's occupation on both the crescent shaped glossed tools as well as backed blades. A similar retouch pattern was also noted on backed blades belonging to the middle Aceramic phase (1B) at *Mylouthkia* (Peltenburg *et al.* 2003).

Prevalent in the Mediterranean zone, glossed tools in the *Tenta* assemblage represent a mixture of type resembling PPNA assemblages of the southern Levant, which including lunates, sickles and Beith Ta'amir knives (Belfer-Cohen 1994: 96; Belfer-Cohen and Goring-Morris 1996: 223). A number of truncated examples from *Tenta* period 4 demonstrate morphological parallels to examples from PPNA Mureybet III (Figure 9.2; M.-C. Cauvin 1994: 284, Figures 3. 1–3). Cypriot Aceramic glossed tools, therefore, demonstrate enormous continuity with crescents showing the retention of a 'Natufian short sickle' along side long sickle blades sometimes truncated from the PPNA and finely denticulated examples characteristic of the PPNB tradition. By the end of the middle Aceramic phase as illustrated by *Tenta* period 2 larger 'robust' blade segment examples became more prevalent. This characteristic shift in glossed tool character shows corresponding adjustments in tool type to the trend away from 'translucent' chert and changes in core technology discussed earlier. These more 'robust' glossed crescents from middle Aceramic *Tenta* find contemporary parallels at Levantine sites like Halula and Assouad demonstrating a parallel evolution with glossed tools of the LPPNB Levant (M.-C. Cauvin 1983; Molist and Ferrier 1996: 439, Figures 1, 9, 10).

The Cypriot Aceramic tradition of glossed crescents, ultimately has its origin in the late Epi-Palaeolithic traditions seen throughout the Near East. The continuity of lunates in the PPNA of the Levant, and both geometrics and microliths in Anatolia and the Zagros demonstrate significant continuity of tradition between the 'end' of hunter-gather and 'beginning' farming traditions of the Near East (cf. Belfer-Cohen and Goring-Morris 1996). The presence of crescents and other microliths in early Aceramic Cyprus could reflect a persistent tradition from *ca.* 10,600 BP and/or influxes from a heterogeneous tradition on the northeastern coastal zone of the Mediterranean coast (cf. Peltenburg *et al.* 2001a: 58). Like the survival of late Epi-Palaeolithic and PPNA core technologies noted above, patterns of glossed tools in Cyprus demonstrate considerable continuity of tradition on the island reflecting Natufian/PPNA trends mixed with PPNB traits.

Other Geometrics

In addition to the crescents described above, a number of artefacts recovered from *Tenta*, *Kelaïdhoni* and *Palaeokamina* may be classed as geometrics and/or microliths. On the basis of this current distribution (also including *Aetokremnos* see below, and the *Shillourokambos* crescents) a local regional variant of the Cypriot Aceramic may be defined for the central part of the island (McCartney in press). The microliths include a small number of tools made on bladelets exhibiting fine abrupt unilateral or bilateral retouch, with an odd variety of geometric pieces, including a crude backed triangle (possibly a lunate variant), the crescents discussed above and a number of double truncations (Belfer-Cohen and Goring-Morris 1996: 219). Such pieces appear at *Tenta* period 5 and the sample from *Kelaïdhoni*. They continue to be found sporadically in the subsequent middle Cypriot Aceramic phase belonging to *Tenta* periods 4–2 as well as *Palaeokamina*. The majority of the bi-trucated pieces belong to the middle Cypriot Aceramic phase (*Tenta* periods 4–2) and especially *Palaeokamina* where a significant number of such tools were recovered. While a few of these double truncated tools were made on small flakes, blade and occasionally bladelet segments were more typically selected. It is notable that the double truncations from both *Tenta* and *Palaeokamina* were selectively produced from the high quality red-brown 'translucent' chert, while the dorsal scar patterns on these pieces demonstrated the use of both the bidirectional and unidirectional core technologies.

These double truncations have been discussed elsewhere (McCartney in press) as 'trapezes' and suggested to demonstrate a possible link with Anatolia. In PPNA Northeastern Anatolia continuity with the Zagros tradition is shown by the presence of geometrics and other microliths, while in Southeastern Anatolia microliths continued in use in PPNB assemblages (Hole 1996: 7; Cauvin *et al.* 1999: 90–97). In the Zagros geometric tools, triangles, trapezes, rectangles or lunates, and other microliths were prevalent in the tool repertoire through the Neolithic (M'lefatian and Nemrickian: Kozlowski 1994: 145; Hole 1995). During the PPNA and EPPNB in Eastern Anatolia, this tradition encouraged the production of geometrics and microliths at sites like Hallan

Çemi and Cafer Höyük before Levantine influences of the Taurus facies of the PPNB replaced this eastern tradition (Koslowski 1994: 148; Gebel and Kozlowski 1996: 460; Cauvin *et al.* 1999: 90–97). Continuity of microliths including geometrics at Neolithic Asikli Höyük represents a parallel continuity attributed to a local Epi-Palaeolithic Öküzini tradition (Balkan-Atli 1994: 221; Kozlowski 1994: 145).

Alternatively, while lunates were always dominant, quadrilaterals with oblique truncations notably trapezes and rectangles formed part of Late and Final Natufian assemblages, declining rapidly in the PPNA to disappear by the PPNB (Belfer-Cohen and Goring-Morris 1996: 223). While chronologically more distant, it seems equally possible on the basis of current evidence, that the Cypriot Aceramic tradition of double truncations and other geometrics represents the selective continuity of this Levantine Epi-Palaeolithic trait seen on the island first at *Aetokremnos* (Simmons 2000: 12). Some double truncated segments from Aceramic Neolithic Cyprus appear to more accurately reflect the hagdud truncation belonging to the PPNA tradition of the Southern Levant, though the total absence of Khiam points (found together with hagdud truncations in all published cases) and other PPNA type fossils is striking (Belfer-Cohen 1994: 93; Nadel 1994; Gopher 1996b: 447–450). Hagdud truncations, typically made on bladelet or narrow blade segments characteristically show straight or concave transverse truncations at one or both ends. In contrast, trapezes belonging to the Anatolian/Zagros tradition show truncations that are typically steeply oblique. Hagdud truncations said to be geographically limited in distribution to the Southern Levant, contrast the more ubiquitous Khiam point. The presence of gilgal truncations at Qemerz Dere and the long distant contacts which existed to permit Central Anatolian obsidian to reach PPNA sites in the Southern Levant, however, demonstrates the wider contacts of the PPNA interaction sphere (Betts 1994: 196; Bar-Yosef 1996: 210). Importantly, one of the few Natufian/PPNA sites located near the Mediterranean coast is that of Nachirini cave in the Anti-Lebanon, which shows hagdud or 'nachcharini' bitruncated rectangles, providing the closest geographic parallel with the island of

Cyprus (Copeland 1991: 31). These tools are known from only two sites dated to the EPPNB, namely Jilat and Mujahiyia in the southern Levant having disappeared elsewhere by that date (Gopher 1996a: 156). It is possible that the Cypriot double truncations, like the 'trapezes' of the Zagros and Anatolia, may have functioned as arrowheads or barbs (much like the transverse arrowhead that became popular during the Late Neolithic in the Levant), since they disappear in mainland assemblages with the appearance of arrowheads (Nadel 1994: 414; Hole 1995: 4). Here again the presence (though rare) of both geometrics and arrowheads in Cypriot Aceramic assemblages demonstrates a unique mixing of traditions and continuity of traits from various periods and regional influences as documented on the mainland.

Conclusions

Active choice

In our search for an explanation of the diffusion of culture traits to areas such as the island of Cyprus, we must view material culture is an active agent in the maintenance of complex social relations, reflecting the transformation of tradition and therefore identity (Lemonnier 1993). The role of technological/typological continuity (in other words 'heritage') versus the transformation of the technical system demonstrates markers of social identity that may be regionally bounded. Traits characteristic of one region appearing in another suggest patterns of diffusion that are not necessarily uni-directional. "The acquisition of new classes of elements places groups in new relations to one another," because material culture symbolizes the relationships between people and things (Schofield 1995b: 4, 5). Material culture can demonstrate similar 'enculturative milieu' without necessarily presenting 'maps of ethnic groups' (in other words they are enculturative 'interaction-spheres'; Jones 1997, 122, 123; Bar-Yosef 1996; 1998). The presence or absence of single economic commodities such as obsidian or arrowheads cannot be taken as direct functional equivalents for cultural isolation, when social choice and motivation have not been considered. It is the strategic manipulation of material culture that represents the foci of

Epi-Paleolithic/PPNA *'Heritage' traits*	*'PPNB' traits*	*'Evolved Cypriot' traits [?]*
single plat blade cores		
bladelet cores		
bidirectional core tech. tech	naviform core tech	simplified naviform-related core
microlithic tools		
	blade dominance	
high quality chert		moderate quality Lefkara chert
	obsidian pressure bladelets	
	Byblos points	tanged blades
	Ovular points	
	Amug points	
glossed crescents/lunates	glossed blades	mixed glossed tool tradition
glossed bladelets	truncated glossed segments	
truncated glossed blades		
bipolar retouch	pressure retouch	
'helwan'-like retouch		
'hagdud' truncs/trapezes		
backed bladelets		

Table 9.2 *Summary of 'elements' in Cypriot Aceramic chipped stone assemblages*

interaction rather than of relative social isolation or geographical distance (Jones 1997: 115). The presence of tanged arrowheads and naviform core technology (*sensu strictu*) and the absence of Khiam points in Cypriot Aceramic assemblages clearly demonstrates membership in the PPNB inter-action sphere. Membership in this sphere, however, does not preclude additional points of origin, which are required to explain the bladelet core technology, bidirectional core technology (*sensu lato*), crescents, and double truncations. The origins of such elements of the chipped stone technical system provide an outline of the traditions culminating in the Cypriot Aceramic identity, an identity that developed as an integral part of the East Mediterranean mainland, rather than geographically separate sphere.

Elements of Tradition

Elements of the core technology clearly define the possible mechanical solutions, while elements demonstrated by tool design show not only functional expectations, but display a socially determined mixture of conservatism and change. 'No society lives in total isolation, the possibility of borrowing always exists, thus every social system consists of a mixture of conservatism and change' (Lemonnier 1993: 22).

The continuity of specific elements (and therefore continuity of tradition) arises from the need to give 'meaning' to material culture. The 'meaning' as defined by Cypriot Aceramic assemblages is marked not only by features recording PPNB traits, but numerous features demonstrating a 'heritage' of the Epi-paleolithic/PPNA traditions (Table 9.2). If we accept that arrowheads were imbued with 'meaning' beyond their practical function for hunting, namely, a symbolism of group identity used by forager groups to maintain long distance exchange networks (cf. Bar-Yosef 1996: 210), then the continuity of arrowheads (though rare) or the long 'tanged blade' element invented by the middle Cypriot Aceramic suggests that similar symbolism was retained on the island. Cypriot 'tanged blades', appearing precisely with changes in raw material selection and core technology, demonstrate an appropriate technological solution required for 'ideological' stability. Despite the transformations in the technological system that mark the distinctiveness of the Cypriot identity, these 'tanged blades' mark clear links with the PPNB hunting 'heritage.'

Glossed crescent segments, other geometrics and microliths and the bladelet core technology used to produce them similarly illustrate a 'heritage' that can be extended back to the Natufian developing though the PPNA. The tradition of using long blades shows an element typical of E/MPPNB Levant with origins in the traditions of the PPNA. Accordingly, unidirectional and bidirectional (*sensu lato*) core technologies correspond to PPNA mainland traditions, while naviform (*sensu strictu*) core reduction marks the arrival of PPNB tradition by *ca.* 9,200 BP. Simplification in the bidirectional core technology *ca.* 8,500 BP suggests a 'return' to the PPNA tradition following an 'experiment' with the naviform method. The latter, though technically superior, did not permit the utilization of the ubiquitous moderate cherts nor was this expensive technology sustainable for the small scale farming economy of Aceramic Cyprus. Aceramic assemblages in Cyprus also demonstrate different degrees to which these Epi-palaeolithic/PPNA traditions were present on the island, suggesting different 'parent cultures' and/or different degrees of conservatism versus a willingness to change. In general, the Cypriot Aceramic chipped stone assemblages currently available imply considerable continuity considering their diversity and the mixture of traditions represented.

Regional trends

On the basis of currently available evidence from Cyprus we may summarize with the following points:

1) The island was first visited *ca.* 10, 600 BP during the Late Natufian at Akrotiri-*Aetokremnos*.
2) Exclusively hunting groups could not have permanently inhabited Cyprus if they had to rely on the indigenous fauna.
3) The island could not have been colonized in the Natufian or PPNA and then become isolated due to the number of PPNB elements present in the chipped stone assemblages.
4) An active role for Cyprus as part of mainland Neolithic developments is required by the inter-play of points 1 –3, and the hybrid nature of the Aceramic chipped stone industries. This interaction may point to an as yet undetected northeastern Mediterranean Epi-Palaeolithic/Neolithic cultural milieu.

The summary points suggest distinct Epipaleolithic/PPNA and PPNB waves of contact on the island, while pointing to multiple influences. The variety of elements and assemblages discussed above suggests a slow process of acculturation rather than an abrupt colonization of a barren landscape at any single date. Differences between the various Cypriot Aceramic assemblages and the lack of specific items like Khiam points implies that no single 'pure' Natufian or PPNA group could lie at the foundation of the Cypriot Aceramic. Instead, the diversity of these assemblages shows the existence of a rich cultural background from which elements were selected. This hybrid nature of the Cypriot Aceramic assemblages suggests the possibility of discovering of hybrid 'parent' groups in currently poorly studied areas of the northeastern Mediterranean coastal region (cf. Peltenburg *et al.* 2001a). Diversity and continuity in the lithic evidence also imply the membership of the island within this mainland sphere at a level of interaction commensurate with the level of social complexity evident at Cypriot Aceramic sites. It seems likely, therefore, that the model of EPPNB reproduction of mainland culture on the island during the early Aceramic with a single transformation in the middle Aceramic phase represents an oversimplification. A more dynamic interpretation of change is needed in which the Cypriot Aceramic is viewed in terms of the selection of culturally meaningful elements showing a more regionally distinct but active participant marking the western fringe of the Levantine interaction sphere.

References

Abbès, F. 1994
Techniques de débitage et gestion de silex sur le Moyen-Euphrate (Syrie) au PPNA final et au PPNB ancien. Pp. 299–312 in Gebel and Kozlowski 1994.

Anderson, P. and F. Valla 1996
'Glossed Tools' from Hayonim Terrace: Black Choice and Functional Tendencies. Pp. 341–362 in Kozlowski and Gebel 1996.

Baird, D. 1994
Chipped Stone Production Technology from the Azraq Project Neolithic Sites. Pp. 525–541 in Gebel and Kozlowski 1994.

Balkan-Atli, N. 1994
The Typological Characteristics of the Asikli Höyük Chipped Stone Industry. Pp. 209–221 in Gebel and Kozlowski 1994.

Bar-Yosef, O. 1996
Late Pleistocene Lithic Traditions in the Near East and Their Expression in Early Neolithic Assemblages. Pp. 207–216 in Kozlowski and Gebel 1996.

Bar-Yosef, O. 1998
On the Nature of Transitions: the Middle to Upper Paleolithic and the Neolithic Revolution. *Cambridge Archaeological Journal* 8:2: 141–163.

Bar-Yosef, O. and D. Alon 1988
Nahal Hemar Cave: The Excavations. *'Antiqot* 18: 1–18.

Bar-Yosef, O. and F. R. Valla 1991
The Natufian Culture in the Levant. International Monographs in Prehistory, Archaeological Series 1: Ann Arbor.

Betts, A. 1994
Qermez Dere: The Chipped Stone Assemblage. Pp. 189–203 in Gebel and Kozlowski 1994.

Betts, A. (ed.)1998
The Harra and the Hamad: Excavations and Surveys in Eastern Jordan, vol. 1. Sheffield Archaeological Monographs, 9. Sheffield Academic Press: Sheffield.

Belfer-Cohen, A. 1994
The Lithic Continuity in the Jordan Valley: Natufian into the PPNA. Pp. 91–100 in Gebel and Kozlowski 1994.

Belfer-Cohen, A. and N. Goring-Morris 1996
The Late Epipalaeolithic as the Precursor of the Neolithic: the Lithic Evidence. Pp. 217–225 in Kozlowski and Gebel 1996.

Briois, F., B. Gratuze and J. Guilaine 1997
Obsidiennes du Site Néolithique Précéramique de *Shillourokambos* (Chypre). *Paléorient* 23/1: 95–112.

Calley, S. 1985
Les Nucléus en Obsidienne du Néolithique de Cafer Höyük (Turquie): Étude Préliminaire sur les Techniques de Taille. Pp. 87–105 in J. Cauvin (ed.) *Cahiers de l'Euphrate, 4.* Èditions Recherche sur les civilisations: Paris.

Caneva, I., A. Conti, C. Lemorini and D. Zampetti 1994
The Lithic Production at Çayönü: A Preliminary Overview of the Aceramic Sequence. Pp. 253–266. in Gebel and Kozlowski 1994.

Cauvin, J., O. Aurenche, M.-C. Cauvin and N. Balkan-Atli 1999
The Pre-Pottery Site of Cafer Höyük. Pp. 87–103. in Özdogan and Basgelen 1999.

Cauvin, M.-C. 1983
Les Faucilles Préhistoriques du Proche-Orient Données Morphologiques et Fonctionnelles. *Paléorient* 9/1: 63–79.

Cauvin, M.-C. 1994
Synthèse sur les industries lithiques Néolithique Précéramique en Syrie (Synthesis contribution.) Pp. 279–297 in Gebel and Kozlowski 1994.

Christou, D 1994
Chroniques des fouilles et découvertes archéologiques à Chypre en 1993. *Bulletin de Correspondance Hellénique* 118: 647–693.

Copeland, L. 1991
Natufian sites in Lebanon. Pp. 27–42 in Bar-Yosef and Valla 1991.

Gamble, C. 1995
Lithics and social evolution. Pp. 19–26 in Schofield 1995a.

Gebel, H. G. 1996
Chipped Lithics in the Basta Craft System. Pp. 261-270 in Kozlowski and Gebel 1996.

Gebel, H. G. and S. K. Kozlowski 1994
Neolithic Chipped Stone Industries of the Fertile Crescent. Studies in Early Near Eastern Production, Subsistence, and Environment 1. Ex Oriente: Berlin.

Gebel, H. G. and S. K. Kozlowski 1996
Remarks on Taxonomy and Related Questions of Neolithic Chipped Stone Industries of the Fertile Crescent, as related to Their Contemporaries in the Adjacent Regions. Pp. 453–460 in Kozlowski and Gebel 1996.

Given, M. and A. B. Knapp 2003
The Sydney Cyprus Survey Project: Social Approaches to Regional Archaeological Survey. Monumenta Archaeologica. The Cotsen Institute of Archaeology, University of California: Los Angeles.

Gopher, A. 1989
Diffusion Process in the Pre-Pottery Neolithic Levant: The Case of the Helwan Point. Pp. 91–105 in I. Hershkovitz (ed.) *People and culture in change.* British Archaeological Reports, International Series, 508: Oxford.

Gopher, A. 1994a
Southern-Central Levant PPN Cultural Sequences: Time-Space Systematic Through Typological and Stylistic Approaches. (Synthesis Contribution). Pp. 387–392 in Gebel and Kozlowski 1994.

Gopher, A. 1994b
Pottery Neolithic 6th/5th Millennia B.C. Industries of the Southern Levant. Pp. 563–566 in Gebel and Kozlowski 1994.

Gopher, A. 1996a
   What Happened to the Early PPNB? Pp. 151–158 in Kozlowski and Gebel 1996.

Gopher, A. 1996b
   A Preliminary Report on the Flints from 'Ain Darat, a PPNA Site in the Judean Desert. Pp. 443–452 in Kozloswki and Gebel 1996.

Goring-Morris, A.N., Y. Goren, L. K. Horwitz, I. Hershkovitz, R. Leberman, J. Sarel and D. Bar-Yosef 1995
   The 1992 Season of Excavations at the Pre-Pottery Neolithic B Settlement of Kfar Hahoresh. *Journal of The Israel Prehistoric Society* 26: 74–121.

Guilaine, J., F. Briois, J.-D. Vinge and I. Carrère 2000
   Découverte d'un Néolithique précéramique ancien chypriote (fin 9e, début 8e millénaires cal. BC), apparenté au PPNB ancien/moyen du Levant nord. *Earth and Planetary Sciences* 330: 75–82.

Graves-Brown, P. M. 1995
   Stone tools, dead sheep, saws and urinals: a journey through art and skill. Pp. 9–17 in A. J. Schofield 1995a.

Hordynsky, L. and C. McCartney forthcoming
   The Tenta Chipped Stone, in I.A. Todd (ed.) *Vasilikos Valley Project 7: Excavations at Kalavasos-Tenta vol 2*. Studies in Mediterranean Archaeology 71.7. Paul Åströms Förlag: Sävedalen.

Hole, F. 1995
   Report on the Microliths Sub-Group. *Neolithics* 1/95: 4–5.

Hole, F. 1996
   A Syrian Bridge Between the Levant and the Zagros? Pp. 5–14 in Kozlowski and Gebel 1996.

Jones, S. 1997
   Ethnicity and Material Culture: Towards a theoretical basis for the interpretation of ethnicity in archaeology. Pp. 106–127 in S. Jones (ed.) *The Archaeology of Ethnicity: Constructing Identities in the Past and Present*. Routledge: London.

Kozlowski, S. K. 1994
   Chipped Neolithic Industries at the Eastern Wing of the Fertile Crescent (Synthesis Contribution). Pp. 143–171 in Gebel and Kozlowski 1994.

Kozlowski, S. K. 1999
   The Big Arrowhead Industries (BAI) in the Near East. *Neo-Lithics* 2/99: 8–10.

Kozlowski, S. K. and H. G. Gebel 1994.
   Editor's Concluding Remarks on Chipped Lithics Techno-Taxa and Interaction Spheres Throughout the 9th to 6th Millennium B.C. Pp. 596–601. in Gebel and Kozlowski 1994

Kozlowski, S.K. and H. G.Gebel 1996
   Neolithic Chipped Stone Industries of the Fertile Crescent, and Their Contemporaries in Adjacent Regions. Studies in Early Near Eastern Production, Subsistence, and Environment 3. Ex Oriente: Berlin.

Le Brun, A. 1981
   Un site Néolithique Précéramique en Chypre: Cap Andreas-Kastros, APDF: Paris.

Le Brun, A. 1984
   Fouilles Récentes à Khirokitia (Chypre) 1977–1981. APDF: Paris.

Le Brun, A. 1989
   Le Néolithique de Chypre et sa relation avec le PPNB du Levant. *Paléorient* 15/1: 161–167.

Lehavy, Y. 1980
   Excavations at Dhali-Agridhi: 1972, 1974, 1976, Dhali-Agridhi: The Neolithic by the River. Pp. 204–243 in L. Stager and A. Walker (eds.) *American Expedition to Idalion, Cyprus 1973–1980*, Oriental Institute Communications 24: Chicago.

Lemonnier, P. 1993
   Introduction. Pp. 1–35 in P. Lemonnier (ed.) *Technological Choices: Transformation in Material Cultures Since the Neolithic*. Routledge: London.

McCartney, C. 1998a
   Preliminary Report on the Chipped Stone Assemblage from the Aceramic Neolithic Site of Ayia Varvara-*Asprokremnos*. *Levant* 30: 85–90.

McCartney, C. 1998b
   Chipped Stone Report. Pp 249–293, in E. Peltenburg (ed.) *Lemba Archaeological Project, Cyprus, Excavations at Kissonerga*-Mosphilia, *vol. II.1B*, University of Edinburgh, Occasional Paper 19: Edinburgh.

McCartney, C. 1998c
   Lithic Technology. Pp. 59–93 in Betts 1998.

McCartney, C. 1999
   Opposed Platform Core Technology and the Cypriot Aceramic Neolithic. *Neo-Lithics* 1/99: 7–10.

McCartney, C. 2003
   The *Mylouthkia* and *Tenta* Chipped Stone Assemblages and Their Interpretation within a redefined Cypriot Aceramic Neolithic. In J. Guilaine and A. Le Brun (eds.) 2003. *Le Néolithique de Chypre. Actes du colloque international organisé par le département des antiquités de Chypre et l'Ecole française d'Athènes, Nicosie 17-19 mai 2001 (Bulletin de Correspondance Hellénique* Suppl. 43).

Molist, M. and A. Ferrier 1996
   Industries Lithiques pendant la période 8000–7500 B.P. à Tell Halula dans le cadre d'Euphrate moyen Syrien. Pp. 431–442 in Kozlowski and Gebel 1996.

Nadel, D. 1994
   New Symmetry of Early Neolithic Tools: Arrowheads and Truncated Elements. Pp. 407–421 in Gebel and Kozlowski 1994.

Noy, T. 1996
   Long Sickle Blades. A Case of Cultural Change in the PPN in the Southern Levant. Questions and Remarks. Pp. 377–383 in Kozlowski and Gebel 1996.

Özdogan, A. 1999
   Çayönü. Pp. 35–63 in Özdogan and Basgelen 1999.

Özdogan, M. 1999
   Concluding Remarks. Pp. 225–236 in Özdogan and Basgelen 1999.

Özdogan, M. and N. Balkan-Atli 1994
South-East Anatolian Chipped Stome Sequence (Approach for a Synthesis). Pp. in Gebel and Kozlowski 1994.

Özdogan, M. and N. Basgelen 1999
Neolithic Turkey: The Cradle of Civilization, Ancient Anatolian Civilizations Series: 3. Arkeoloji ve Sanat Yayinlari: Istanbul.

Peltenburg, E., S. Colledge, P. Croft, A. Jackson, C. McCartney and Mary Anne Murray 2000
Agro-pastoralist colonization of Cyprus in the 10th millennium BP: initial assessments. *Antiquity* 74: 844–53.

Peltenburg, E., S. Colledge, P. Croft, A. Jackson, C. McCartney and M. Murray 2001a
Neolithic Dispersals from the Levantine Corridor: a Mediterranean Perspective. *Levant* 33: 35–64.

Peltenburg, E., P. Croft, A. Jackson, C. McCartney, and M. Murray 2001b
Well-Established Colonists: *Mylouthkia* 1 and the Cypro-Pre-Pottery Neolithic B. Pp. 61–93 in S. Swiny (ed.) *The Earliest Prehistory of Cyprus: From Colonization to Exploitation.* Cyprus American Archaeological Research Institute Monograph Series 12. American Schools of Oriental Research: Boston.

Peltenburg, E., *et al.* 2003
The Colonisation and Settlement of Cyprus. Investigations at Kissonerga-Mylouthkia, 1976–1996. (Lemba Archaeological Project, Cyprus III.1). Studies in Mediterranean Archaeology 70:4. Åströms Förlag: Sävedalen.

Quintero, L.A. 1996
Flint Mining in the Pre-Pottery Neolithic: Preliminary Report on the Exploration of Flint at Neolithic 'Ain Ghazal in Highland Jordan. Pp. 233–242 in Kozlowski and Gebel 1996.

Quintero, L.A. and P. J. Wilke 1995
Evolution and Economic Significance of Naviform Core-and-Blade Technology in the Southern Levant. *Paléorient* 21/1: 17–33.

Quintero, L. A., P. J. Wilke and J. G. Waines 1997
Pregmatic Studies of Near Eastern Neolithic Sickle Blades. Pp. 263–286 in H.G. Gebel, Z. Kafafi and G. O. Rollefson (eds.) *The Prehistory of Jordan II, Perspectives from 1997.* Studies in Early Near

Eastern Production, Subsistence, and Environment 4. Ex Oriente: Berlin.

Schmidt, K. 1996
Nevali Çori: Chronology and Intrasite Distrigution of Lithic Tool Classes. Preliminary Results. Pp. 363–376 in Kozlowski and Gebel 1996.

Schofield, A.J. (ed.) 1995a
Lithics in Context: Suggestions for the Future Direction of Lithic Studies. Lithic Studies Society Occasional Paper no. 5: London.

Schofield, A. J. 1995b
Artefacts Mean Nothing. Pp. 3–8 in Schofield 1995a.

Simmons, A. 1996
Preliminary Report on Multidisciplinary Investigations at Neolithic Kholetria-*Ortos,* Paphos District. *Report of the Department of Antiquities, Cyprus:* 29–44.

Simmons, A. 1998
Test Excavations at Two Aceramic Neolithic Sites on the Uplands of Western Cyprus. *Report of the Department of Antiquities, Cyprus:* 1–16.

Simmons, A. 2000
A Brief Summary of the Chipped Stone Assemblage from Akrotiri-*Aetokremnos,* Cyprus. *NeoLithics* 1/00: 11–13.

Stekelis, M. 1953
Appendix I, The Flint Implements from Khirokitia. Pp. 409–414 in P. Dikaios, *Khirokitia.* Oxford University Press: Oxford.

Todd, I. 1987
Vasilikos Valley Project 6: Excavations at Kalavasos-Tenta 1. Studies in Mediterranean Archaeology 71: 6. Paul Åströms Förlag: Jonsered.

Todd, I. 2003
Kalavasos-*Tenta*: a Reappraisal. In J. Guilaine and A. Le Brun (eds.) 2003. *Le Néolithique de Chypre. Actes du colloque international organisé par le département des antiquités de Chypre et l'Ecole française d'Athènes, Nicosie 17-19 mai 2001 (Bulletin de Correspondance Hellénique* Suppl. 43).

Watkins, T. 1979
Kataliondas-*Kourvellos*: The Analysis of the Surface Collected Data. Pp. 12–20 in V. Karageorghis (ed.) *Studies Presented in Memory of Porphyrios Dikaios.* Lions Club of Nicosia: Nicosia.

10

Hill and vale: understanding prehistoric lithic use in Cyprus

Sarah Tyrrell Stewart

Abstract

The Idalion Survey Project (ISP) in central Cyprus and the Canadian Palaipaphos Survey Project (CPSP) in western Cyprus have identified a number of Aceramic Neolithic sites. The location and use of these sites reveal a consistent pattern of lithic procurement during this early period. Most sites are similarly located on prominent features overlooking river valleys and are close to the boundary between the igneous Pillow Lava Formation and the sedimentary chalk and limestone zones. They thus have ready access to the many high quality chert veins and outcrops within the surrounding hills. The ISP has discovered two Aceramic Neolithic sites: Alambra-Spileos, a cave site located on a saddle-shaped hill above the Ammos River Valley; and Perachorio-Moutti, on a prominent outcrop overlooking a bend in the Yialias River. The CPSP has discovered four sites: Kannaviou-Kochina on a terrace and Kritou Marottou-Ais Yiorkis on a tributary above the upper Ezousas River; Kholetria-Ortos on a prominent hill overlooking the lower Dhiarizos River; and Kedhares-Yero Vasili on a terrace above the upper Khapotami River. Both the location and distinctive lithic assemblages of these sites can tell us much about prehistoric settlement patterns and lithic resource extraction and manufacture. The lithic assemblages reflect their differing needs and functions and the assessment of related isolated finds linking them to each other and the region will paint a picture of the prehistoric settlement and subsistence behaviour in these regions of linked valley systems.

Introduction

The focus of this paper will be a discussion of the relationships between Aceramic Neolithic sites in the Canadian Palaipaphos Survey Project (CPSP) and the Idalion Survey Project (ISP) study zones (Figure 10.1) and the chert sources within those regions. I will be examining the proportion of chert types at each site, how this is reflected in tool types and debitage, and their relationship to the apparent use of available chert sources. I will propose a simple method of determining cost of acquisition of the raw materials, based on distance and type of terrain between site and source. Using this method, I will then discuss the relationship between chert type, tools and debitage, and ease of acquisition.

For this discussion, tools are all chipped stone pieces with evidence of retouch or use and thus may exclude expedient tools where use is not visible to the eye. Primary debitage are cores, fragments, shatter and flakes with at least 75% cortex. Secondary debitage refers to all flakes with less than 25% cortex. Tests done previously on this material (Stewart 1987: 44; Rupp *et al.* 1992: 312) suggest that the samples obtained from the initial survey and later collections were comparable, so I will be using all these data sets in the following analyses. We should remember that survey material will not necessarily be proportionately comparable to the excavated collections. In the survey collections there will often be a higher ratio of formed tools to debitage, tools being generally more visible on the surface,

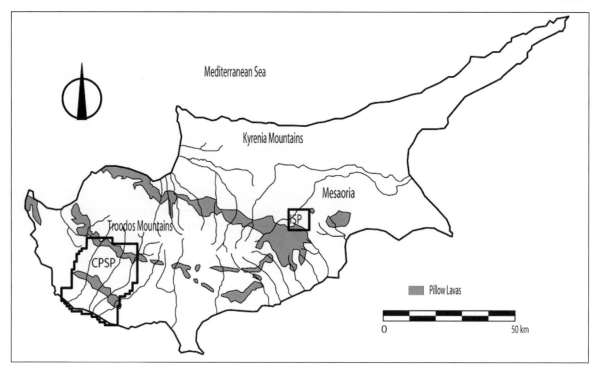

Figure 10.1 *CPSP (Canadian Palaipaphos Survey Project) and ISP (Idalion Survey Project) study zones in Cyprus*

while in excavation, screening and careful observation of the matrix will retrieve far greater numbers of small flakes, bladelets, microdebitage and shatter, as is seen at *Ortos* (Simmons 1996: 34, table 1). To address this problem, I plan a subsequent study of the material from *Ais Yiorkis* and *Ortos*. I will examine the collections from unsystematic survey, controlled survey, and excavation to compare the proportions of raw materials, tools and debitage to determine how and to what extent they differ.

Canadian Palaipaphos Survey Project

The CPSP discovered four Aceramic Neolithic sites in the course of the survey. From 1979–1991 this project undertook a series of judgemental and probabilistic surveys in three major drainage basins in the Paphos District (Rupp 1981, 1987b; Rupp *et al.* 1984, 1987). The study area is characterized by a varied topography ranging from a narrow coastal plain of alluvial clays, through a rolling interior plateau, to the foothills of the Troodos Mountain Massif. The area is rich in excellent quality chert, available in outcrop, veins and nodules along the Pillow

Lava/sedimentary zone interface and in cobbles in fields and the many ephemeral stream beds. We initially discovered the sites in the survey of randomly and judgementally selected 1 km. sq. units. Crew members were spaced at 100 m intervals and finds were collected unsystematically. The assemblage of chert tools and debitage recovered from the sites was obtained from several distinct collections: random, non-systematic collections when the sites were discovered; subsequent intensive, non-systematic collections; and intensive, systematic collections (Rupp in press). I will only be using the collections from the initial survey and subsequent non-systematic resurvey in this discussion, as only they are comparable to the ISP collections.

Chert sources

CPSP lithic analyst Bill Fox identified a number of chert sources and classified them by formation and colour during his research in 1980 and 1982 (Fox n.d.; Rupp *et al.* 1984). Subsequently I identified additional chert sources in 1983 and 1984 (Stewart 1987). In total we identified 20 sources, 10 from the Moni Formation, mostly located in the central plateau area of the study zone, and 10 from the Lefkara Formation, mostly

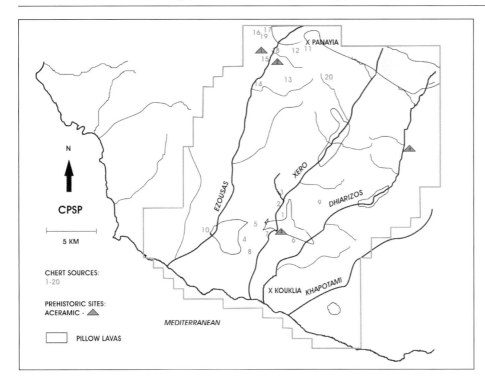

Figure 10.2
CPSP (Canadian Palaipaphos Survey Project) sites and sources.
X = modern village

in the upper foothills of the Troodos (Figure 10.2). We could readily identify chert types by colour and lustre. The Moni cherts were opaque and ranged from mottled and banded black through deep blue to grey. The Lefkara cherts were either translucent or opaque and ranged in colour from deep red through pink, brown, tawny and cream. While we could identify and classify ten grades of Lefkara chert and five grades of Moni chert, the data on the majority of the chert sources indicate that it is only reasonable to distinguish three chert grades that can be assigned to distinctive sources. These are the Lefkara basal (LB), Lefkara translucent (LT) and the Moni cherts (M). The distinctive colours and lustre gradation of these cherts permit accurate separation of the artefacts into these three groups.

To supplement our own discoveries, in 1982 Fox had interviewed a number of local informants in the Paphos district concerning historic chert knapping activities. These interviews produced data on chert sources and chert types used historically in the *Dhoukani* (threshing sledge) industry (Fox 1984; Fox and Pearlman 1987; Pearlman 1984). While this information was of great interest, it must be used with caution. We have no means of establishing

whether a preferred chert type in the *Dhoukani* industry was similarly prized by the Neolithic craftsmen, or whether the *Dhoukani* and the prehistoric craftsmen were using the same sources. Additional research on this problem would involve intensive examination of sources, with petrographic analyses, to attempt to distinguish prehistoric and historic acquisition strategies. Nevertheless, an examination of historic lithic technology can aid in our understanding of possible sources, preferred chert types and acquisition behaviour. Notably, aspects of the distribution of artefacts in relationship to the sources suggest that modern and prehistoric behaviours were indeed comparable.

Aceramic sites

Kritou-Marottou-*Ais Yiorkis* (*Ais Yiorkis*) was found in 1980 and initially assessed as being about .4 hectares in size. Recent test excavations indicated that it maybe somewhat larger (Simmons 1998). It is situated on a slope about 1 km from the river, in the upper Ezousas drainage. Finds consisted of a chipped stone industry of predominantly Lefkara Formation cherts, a ground stone industry of chalk and igneous stone, a single obsidian bladelet (Çiftlik source), bone fragments

Artefact/ Site	Ais Yiorkis N=239		Kochina N=153		Ortos N=239		Yero-Vasili N=70		Moutti N=72		Spileos N=215	
LB	145	60%	81	53%	90	38%	26	37%	16	22%	113	53%
Tools	47	32%	36	44%	34	38%	4	15%	5	31%	41	36%
Primary	15	10%	18	22%	16	18%	6	23%	1	6%	37	33%
Secondary	83	58%	27	34%	40	44%	16	62%	10	63%	35	31%
LT	76	32%	66	43%	44	18%	25	36%	56	78%	102	47%
Tools	13	17%	20	30%	11	25%	2	8%	16	29%	18	18%
Primary	6	8%	11	17%	9	20%	5	20%	2	4%	29	28%
Secondary	57	75%	35	53%	24	55%	18	72%	38	67%	55	54%
Moni	18	8%	6	4%	105	44%	19	27%	0	0%	0	0%
Tools	4	22%	1	17%	23	22%	0	0%	0	0%	0	0%
Primary	4	22%	1	17%	27	26%	7	37%	0	0%	0	0%
Secondary	10	56%	4	66%	55	52%	12	63%	0	0%	0	0%
Tools	64	27%	57	37%	69	28%	6	9%	21	29%	59	27%
LB	47	79%	36	63%	34	50%	4	68%	5	24%	41	69%
LT	13	20%	20	35%	11	16%	2	32%	16	76%	18	31%
Moni	4	6%	1	2%	23	34%	0	0%	0	0%	0	0%
Primary	25	10%	30	20%	52	22%	18	26%	3	4%	66	31%
LB	15	60%	18	60%	16	31%	6	33%	1	33%	37	56%
LT	6	24%	11	37%	9	17%	5	28%	2	67%	29	44%
Moni	4	16%	1	3%	27	52%	7	39%	0	0%	0	0%
Secondary	150	63%	66	43%	119	50%	46	65%	48	67%	90	42%
LB	83	55%	27	41%	40	34%	16	35%	10	21%	35	39%
LT	57	38%	35	53%	24	20%	18	39%	38	79%	55	61%
Moni	10	7%	4	6%	55	46%	12	26%	0	0%	0	0%

Table 10.1 *Distribution of artefacts by site*

and a tiny sample of carbonised seeds (Fox 1987: 27–28). The Lefkara cherts, both translucent and basal are the preferred type (Table 10.1), with only a tiny sample (N=18, 8%) of the Moni chert. Of the 239 artefacts collected, 145 (60%) are of the basal chert, 47 (32%) being tools and 98 (68%) debitage and 76 (32%) of the translucent, 13 (17%) being tools and 63 (83%) being debitage. Of all chert types, 64 (27%) of the collection are tools, 25 (10%) are primary debitage and 150 (63%) are secondary debitage. The Lefkara basal chert is preferred over the translucent and Moni. The fairly low proportion of primary debitage suggests that primary reduction occurred elsewhere but final tool preparation and maintenance in all chert groups occurred on site. Dates obtained from the Simmons test excavations date the site to *ca.* 7900–7500 BP (Simmons 1998: 13).

Kannaviou-*Kochina* (*Kochina*) was also found in 1980, and estimated to be about 1.4 hectares in size, although recent test excavations question this size (Simmons 1998). It is situated some 1.5 km southeast of *Ais Yiorkis* on low terraces along the Ezousas River. The chipped and ground stone industry is similar to *Ais Yiorkis*, although the proportions of materials used in the ground stone differ (Fox 1987: 30). As at *Ais Yiorkis*, Lefkara basal is the preferred chert although not to the same extent. Of the 153 artefacts, 81 (53%) are Lefkara basal, 66 (43%) are translucent and only 6 (4%) are Moni. Of the basal chert artefacts, 36 (44%) are tools and 45 (56%) are debitage. In the translucent group, 20 (30%) are tools and 46 (70%) are debitage. Of the Moni chert only 1 (17%) is a tool and 5(83%) debitage. In considering artefacts in all chert groups, 57 (37%) are tools, 30(20%) are primary debitage and 66 (43%) are secondary debitage. Certain trends are evident here, as at *Ais Yiorkis*. Lefkara basal chert is the preferred type, and there is a low proportion of Moni chert. In contrast to *Ais Yiorkis*, though, there is a slightly higher proportion of tools to debitage. The proportion of primary to secondary debitage is not as great, although it is clear again that most primary production occurred off site.

Kholetria-*Ortos* (*Ortos*) was found in 1983 and subsequently excavated by Simmons (Simmons and Corona 1993; Simmons 1994, 1996). Dates for the site range from *ca.* 7,500–6,500 BP (Simmons 1996: 40). It is some 2.4 hectares in size. The site is located on the top and slope of a prominent hill in the middle Xeropotamos River Drainage (Fox 1987: 31–34; 1988). Finds consist of a chipped stone industry of Moni and Lefkara cherts, and a ground stone industry of chalks and igneous stones. The presence of architecture was originally thought to be indicated by numerous igneous river cobbles, although this was not born out in the subsequent excavations. Of the 239 artefacts recovered in the survey, 90 (38%) are of basal chert, 44 (18%) are of translucent chert and 105 (44%) of Moni. In the basal group, 34 (38%) are tools and 56 (62%) are debitage. In the translucent group, 11 (25%) are tools and 33 (75%) debitage. In the Moni group, 23 (22%) are tools and 82 (78%) debitage. In considering all chert types, 68 (28%) are tools, 52 (22%) are primary debitage and 119 (50%) secondary debitage. In contrast to both *Ais Yiorkis* and *Kochina*, at *Ortos* Moni chert is clearly preferred, but interestingly, not in the tools found, where again the Lefkara basal cherts are preferred. As at the other sites, primary debitage is low, indicating that primary tool production occurred mostly off site.

Kedhares-*Yero Vasili* (*Yero Vasili*), found in 1986, is only about 1 hectare in size. It is located on a slope next to the river in the upper Dhiarizos drainage. Finds consist of chipped stone tools and debitage and a very small ground stone industry. Of the 70 artefacts recovered in survey, 26 (37%) are Lefkara basal, 25 (36%) are translucent and 19 (27%) are Moni chert. In the basal group, 4 (15%) are tools and 22 (85%) are debitage. In the translucent group, 2 (8%) are tools and 23 (92%) are debitage. In the Moni group, 0 are tools and 19 are debitage. In considering all chert types, 6 (9%) are tools, 18 (26%) are primary debitage and 46 (65%) are secondary debitage. As at *Ais Yiorkis* and *Kochina*, Lefkara basal is the preferred chert, but only by a small margin. There is a much lower tool to debitage proportion than at the other sites,

and as at *Ortos*, despite a fairly large proportion of Moni chert, it is not preferred for tool manufacture. As at all sites there is a low primary to secondary debitage ratio, consistent with the notion that most primary production occurred off site.

Numerous small finds and scatters of prehistoric lithic artefacts (at least 58) may be connected to the distribution of Aceramic Neolithic sites in the study zone. While the lack of diagnostic finds does not permit a definitive association with the Aceramic sites, initial analysis suggests a similar pattern to the ISP scatters, notably, their association with rivers and streams, prominent features and chert sources. While only *Ais Yiorkis* and *Ortos* have dates placing them firmly in the Aceramic Neolithic period, all four sites were initially identified as Aceramic based solely on the characteristics of their assemblages, especially the blade component.

Idalion Survey Project

We began the ISP in 1995, both as an archaeological training programme and to address various research goals. I was particularly interested in locating chert sources in the area as a preliminary to understanding their relationship with both the prehistoric and historic (*Dhoukani*, or threshing sledge) industries. The study zone of the ISP covers an 8 km^2 area around the ancient Iron Age city of Idalion (Morden and Stewart n.d.). The study zone is located at the interface between the pillow lava and sedimentary zones, and is rich in numerous outcrops of top quality chert. Our work in this area has located nine chert sources, two probable Aceramic Neolithic sites and several enigmatic prehistoric lithic scatters. All finds were located in the extensive survey, with crew members spaced at 100m intervals and finds collected unsystematically. We subsequently revisited both Aceramic sites and made additional unsystematic collections.

Chert Sources

All of the chert sources were located at the interface between the pillow lava and sedimentary zones and are primary outcrops providing cherts from vein and nodule (Figure 10.3). All are a source of the Lefkara (Lapithos) basal or translucent cherts. There are apparently no Moni

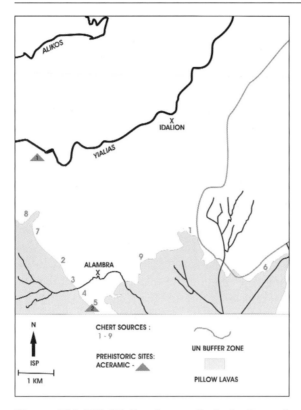

Figure 10.3 *ISP (Idalion Survey Project) sites and sources. X = modern village*

formation cherts in this area of Cyprus. In light of these finds, the large amounts of chert in the associated fields and archaeological evidence of *Dhoukani* (threshing sledge) manufacture and use, we decided to investigate whether there was any memory of the industry in the Dhali area. Interviews (Morden and Stewart n.d.: 20–22) with informants in the village of Alambra indicated that there had been a thriving industry of Dhoukani chert blade manufacture in the village up until the mid 1970's and that the last remaining *Athkiakadhes* (craftsman) had just recently died. The chert for this industry had been obtained from a local source, just south of the village at the hill of Alambra-*Mouttes*, one of the chert sources identified in our survey. We had investigated this location and found it to be a rich source of Lefkara basal and translucent chert. Evidence of Dhoukani manufacture was discovered on the hill slope, including an excellent example of an *in-situ* and virtually undisturbed knapping floor. We asked about *Athkiakadhes* in the village, and were informed that there had been several, all local men who

just repaired the *Dhoukanes*, which had been ready made elsewhere. For these repairs they obtained their chert locally from Alambra-*Mouttes* as well as Alambra-*Athkiakonas*, south of the village. While this information may not have a direct bearing on prehistoric activities, it can aid in helping us understand preferred sources and acquisition behaviour patterns that may also have had relevance in the past.

Aceramic sites

Perachorio-*Moutti* (*Moutti*) is located on the gentle eastern slope of a prominent hill some 300 m south of the Yialias River. A scatter of chert tools and debitage is concentrated around a small depression about 2 m in diameter. The lithic assemblage is dominated by excellent quality Lefkara translucent cherts, which are available about 3 km to the north, near the modern village of Alambra. There is an obvious contrast between the carefully made, retouched smaller flakes and blades and the patinated and weathered Lefkara basal cherts, which have been fashioned into heavy scrappers and retouched flakes. There are a number of diagnostic pieces, including a fragment of point base (Byblos type), a core and bladelet, and several blades typical of Aceramic assemblages. Of the 72 pieces we collected (Table 10.1), 56 are of the fine translucent chert and 16 of the opaque basal chert. In the translucent group, 16 are tools, or retouched pieces and 40 are debitage. The debitage is primarily small flakes and two small core fragments, suggesting that smaller pieces of this finer quality chert were brought in limited amounts to the site for secondary maintenance and repair. In the basal group there were only 5 tools and 11 pieces of debitage, including one core fragment, suggesting that fewer of these tools were highly curated and maintained.

Alambra-*Spileos* (*Spileos*) is located on a large, saddle-shaped ridge, which slopes gently down to the north towards a seasonal tributary of the Kalamoulia River, and drops sharply to the south into the deeply dissected ravines of the Pillow Lavas. The area is an excellent source of both the translucent and basal Lefkara formation cherts, in outcrops, veins and nodules (Figure 10.3). The site itself is located around a large cave some 10 x 10 m in size and 2 m in height. The major chert quarry is located about 200 m downslope from the cave. This was clearly an area of lithic extraction and tool manufacture. Of the artefacts we recovered from the survey (Figure 10.4), 102 are of the fine grained translucent chert, 18 of these are tools and 84 are debitage, including 29 cores and fragments. There are 113 artefacts of the opaque basal chert, 41 of which are tools and 72 debitage, including 37 cores and fragments. This site likely functioned primarily as a lithic extraction and tool production area, but could also have served as a hunting lookout. Based on the large amount of lithic material found, the site was probably occupied for brief periods, perhaps seasonally, and often reused.

In addition to these two important sites, we found a number of small lithic scatters in the study area. The finds at these locations are clearly prehistoric, and not from the recent *Dhoukani* industry, but unlike the two larger sites it is impossible to link then conclusively to the Aceramic Neolithic Period. Two of these are located beside rivers, four in areas offering strategic views and lookouts, and four at chert sources. Perachorio-*Kanajin* and Potamia-*Yerokolymbos* are located on terraces above the Yialias River. They could have been sites for hunting, fishing, plant collection and a source of perennial water. Dhali-*Paradhisha*, Lymbia-*Jimistron*, Dhali-*Ayiasmata* and Dhali-*Kamini* are all located on prominent hills or passes above rivers and tributaries in the study zone and could have served both as hunting lookouts and as routes between habitation sites and chert sources. Alambra-*Nostos*, Alambra-*Mouttes*, Lymbia-*Plaja* and Ayia Varvara-*Throumberka* are all located in major chert sources, overlooking rivers and tributaries and could thus be both sites of chert extraction and lookouts. These latter small scatters could also help substantiate that certain sources were used prehistorically.

As in the CPSP, I have initially identified the sites as Aceramic, based on their distinctive blade and core characteristics (as was also done by McCartney 1998 at the nearby Ayia Varvara site). Subsequently, a number of researchers specializing in the Aceramic Neolithic of Cyprus have concurred with my identifications (Fox, pers. comm. 2003; McCartney, pers. comm. 2002; Simmons, pers. comm. 2000; Watkins, pers. comm. 2000). While such a general consensus

among experts in the field is encouraging, we must continue to explore alternate methods of establishing chronology when conventional dates are not available. This should be based not only on the extensive analysis of formed tools, but on understanding reduction sequences, and the resulting debitage patterns.

Cost relationships between sites and sources

Previously (Stewart 1987), I had used a simple transportation model to demonstrate patterns of chert acquisition at three Aceramic Neolithic sites in the CPSP. The model defined the most efficient means of moving supplies (chert) from the supplier (source) to the consumer (site) based on minimizing costs (Croucher 1980: 123–162). I based the costs for the model on the assumption that the prehistoric chert knappers were minimizing acquisition difficulty, and established this through distance to source, type of terrain and type of source (Stewart 1987: 44, 45). I obtained a unit cost figure for acquiring chert from each source by multiplying distance in km by a scalar representing type of terrain and source acquisition difficulty (Table 10.2). Type of terrain from site to source was rated on a scale of 1–3, based on elevation change. Source acquisition difficulty was also rated on a scale of 1–3, based on availability and ease of extraction (field source being the most readily available, stream source being readily available but restricted somewhat by location and season, and outcrop source, having the most restricted access and greatest difficulty in acquisition). The optimal solution for the model was obtained by multiplying the demands for each site (N) by the lowest feasible cost unit for moving chert from source to site. While this model worked extremely well for the CPSP sites, I have had to modify it somewhat for this study. In the ISP, all the sources we identified were outcrop, yet none of these offered either limited access or difficulty in acquisition. Chert was readily available in veins and boulders, but also scattered in small, easily worked and transported nodules across these source sites. As a result, I have eliminated this category from the analysis, and obtained costs by examining distance and terrain alone.

Site	Chert Type	Source	Distance	Terrain	Cost
Ais Yiorkis (1)	LB/T	*Pano Panayia* (11)	7.0	3.0	21.0
Ais Yiorkis	LT	*Asproyia* (12)	5.0	3.0	15.0
Ais Yiorkis	Moni	*Statos* (13)	6.0	3.0	18.0
Ais Yiorkis	LT	*Vathyrkatchi* (14)	4.0	3.0	12.0
Ais Yiorkis	LB	*Ayios Dhimitrianos* (15)	2.0	3.0	6.0
Ais Yiorkis	LB/T	*Phiti* (16)	3.0	3.0	9.0
Ais Yiorkis	LT	*Anadiou* (17)	3.0	3.0	9.0
Ais Yiorkis	LB/T	*Kannaviou* (18)	1.0	2.0	2.0
Ais Yiorkis	LB	*Kritou Marottou* (19)	1.0	2.0	2.0
Ais Yiorkis	LB	*Kilinia* (20)	7.5	3.0	22.5
Kochina (2)	LB/T	*Pano Panayia*	5.5	3.0	16.5
Kochina	LT	*Asproyia*	4.0	3.0	12.0
Kochina	Moni	*Statos*	4.0	3.0	12.0
Kochina	LT	*Vathyrkatchi*	3.5	2.0	7.0
Kochina	LB	*Ayios Dhimitrianos*	3.0	3.0	9.0
Kochina	LB/T	*Phiti*	4.5	3.0	13.5
Kochina	LT	*Anadiou*	4.0	3.0	12.0
Kochina	LB/T	*Kannaviou*	0.5	1.0	0.5
Kochina	LB	*Kritou Marottou*	2.5	3.0	7.5
Kochina	LB	*Kilinia*	7.0	3.0	21.0
Ortos (3)	Moni	*Argakin tou Ayiou* (1)	0.5	1.0	0.5
Ortos	Moni	*Nata-Skales* (2)	2.0	2.0	4.0
Ortos	LB/T	*Nata-Yeratses* (3)	2.0	2.0	4.0
Ortos	Moni	*Argakin tis Athkias* (4)	5.0	3.0	15.0
Ortos	Moni	*Argakin tou Beys* (5)	4.0	3.0	12.0
Ortos	Moni	*Ayia Irini* (6)	2.5	3.0	7.5
Ortos	Moni	*Phinikas* (7)	2.0	1.0	2.0
Ortos	Moni	*Anarita* (8)	6.0	2.0	12.0
Ortos	Moni	*Stavrokono* (9)	3.5	3.0	10.5
Ortos	Moni	*Argakin tou Karkoti* (10)	8.0	3.0	24.0
Yero Vasili (4)	Moni	*Argakin tou Ayiou*	16.0	3.0	48.0
Yero Vasili	Moni	*Nata-Skales*	16.0	3.0	48.0
Yero Vasili	LB/T	*Nata-Yeratses*	15.5	3.0	46.5
Yero Vasili	Moni	*Ayia Irini*	16.0	3.0	48.0
Yero Vasili	Moni	*Stavrokono*	12.5	3.0	37.5
Yero Vasili	LB	*Kilinia*	11.0	3.0	33.0
Yero Vasili	Moni	*Statos*	13.0	3.0	39.0
Yero Vasili	LB/T	*Pano Panayia*	13.5	3.0	40.5
Yero Vasili	LT	*Asproyia*	15.0	3.0	45.0
Yero Vasili	LT	*Vathyrkatchi*	17.5	3.0	52.5
Moutti (1)	LB/T	*Syrkani* (1)	5.0	3.0	15.0
Moutti	LB	*Laxia* (2)	3.0	3.0	9.0
Moutti	LB	*Nostos* (3)	3.5	3.0	10.5
Moutti	LT	*Mouttes* C (4)	4.0	3.0	12.0
Moutti	LB	*Spileos* D (5)	4.3	3.0	12.0
Moutti	LB	*Plaja* (6)	7.3	3.0	21.9
Moutti	LB	*Konnies* (7)	2.0	2.0	4.0
Moutti	LB	*Throumberka* (8)	1.5	2.0	3.0
Moutti	LB	*Athkiakonas* (9)	4.3	3.0	12.9
Spileos (2)	LB/T	*Syrkani*	3.5	2.0	7.0
Spileos	LB	*Laxia*	1.3	2.0	2.6
Spileos	LB/T	*Nostos*	1.5	2.0	3.0
Spileos	LT	*Mouttes* C	0.8	1.0	0.8
Spileos	LB	*Spileos* D	0.3	1.0	0.3
Spileos	LB	*Plaja*	4.5	3.0	13.5
Spileos	LB	*Konnies*	2.5	3.0	7.5
Spileos	LB	*Throumberka*	3.0	3.0	9.0
Spileos	LB	*Athkiakonas*	1.8	3.0	5.4

Key: Distance = km; Terrain - 1= 0–49 m, 2=50–100 m, 3=100 m+

Table 10.2 *Cost tables*

In the CPSP, the optimal chert sources for *Ais Yiorkis* and *Kochina* would be Kannaviou (site 18 in Fis. 10.2) for the Lefkara basal and translucent cherts and Statos (13) for the small amounts of Moni chert. The optimal sources for *Ortos* would be Nata-*Yeratses* (3) for Lefkara basal and translucent cherts and Argakin tou Ayiou (1) for Moni chert. Clearly costs could be further reduced by exploiting only the lowest cost source, so why would *Ortos* not use the Moni cherts exclusively, and the other two sites the Lefkara exclusively? There are probably a variety of technological and social reasons that might explain this. Firstly, there could be a desire to afford risk avoidance by exploiting different sources. In addition, social relationships between sites might be reinforced through exchange or using sources with more difficult access. Or, as was clear from our interviews with the Athkiakadhes, certain craftsmen preferred specific sources and chert types, even if their acquisition was more difficult. Finally, technological factors may have played a role. At this stage of the analysis I had lumped all retouched pieces into the tool category, thus making it difficult to determine if certain chert types were preferred for certain tasks. A more detailed analysis might reveal this. As we have seen, at all sites Moni cherts were not preferred for formal tool types, but they may have played an important role in an, as yet unidentified, expedient technology.

Yero Vasili was not included in the original study, and I have included it with reservation here as I have not adequately examined the Dhiarizos River for chert sources, which would certainly be more accessible to the site than those in the Xeropotamos and Ezousas drainages. Based on the current available source information, the optimal sources for *Yero Vasili* would be Stavrokono (9) or Statos (13) for Moni chert and Pano Panaya (11), Asproyia (12) or Kilinia (20) for the Lefkara cherts. I am particularly convinced that other sources would be available to the knappers of *Yero Vasili*, as it has, relative to the other sites, the highest proportion of primary debitage and the lowest proportion of tools. Clearly, though, the relatively smaller sample size may also have a bearing on the interpretation of this site.

In the ISP, the optimal model for chert exploitation was rather more straightforward. *Spileos* is located in the midst of prime sources for both Lefkara basal and translucent cherts. Clearly, *Mouttes* C (4) and *Spileos* D (5), both within 1 km of the site along the ridge would be the obvious choices (see Figure 10.3 for numbered locations). Indeed, the large amount of primary debitage at *Spileos* would suggest that all stages of reduction took place here. *Moutti* is slightly more problematic. Excellent sources of Lefkara basal chert are available at Konnies (7) and Throumberka (8) just to the north across fairly even terrain, but the translucent chert would have to be obtained from either Nostos (3) or *Mouttes* C (4). Again, the choice to exploit a variety of sources when only one would reduce costs, could be for any of the social or technological reasons discussed above. Certainly the low amounts of primary debitage to tools at this site is a reflection of the greater costs of chert acquisition, and hence primary reduction occurring off site.

Conclusions

In the CPSP, at all sites, the Lefkara cherts are the preferred type, despite source location, although the Moni cherts make up a large proportion of artefacts at *Ortos* and *Yero Vasili*, in contrast to their almost complete absence at *Ais Yiorkis* and *Kochina*. The Lefkara basal cherts are consistently preferred over the translucent variety, with the exception of *Yero Vasili*, where proportions are almost identical. The sample size at *Yero Vasili* is much smaller, though, and this could well have some bearing on any interpretation. At all sites secondary debitage greatly outnumbers primary, indicating that most initial reduction occurred elsewhere, likely at the source, while secondary flakes and blades were transported to the site for final tool preparation. Proportions of retouched pieces were quite high, with the exception of *Yero Vasili*. This may in part be due to the survey process which might favour the collection of tools over small and obscure pieces of debitage. There does not appear to be any obvious selection of certain chert types for specific tool types, or a preference for more locally available types for expedient tools.

In the ISP, quite a different pattern can be observed. At *Moutti* the preferred chert type is Lefkara translucent chert, while at *Spileos* there

are about even amounts of Lefkara basal and translucent. There is no Moni chert at either site, which is not surprising as there is no local source. This absence might also indicate that there was no contact between the ISP and CPSP areas. At *Moutti*, the tools are mostly Lefkara translucent, mirroring the trend in chert preference, while at *Spileos*, the tools are predominantly Lefkara basal, a trend that is not reflected in the overall chert assemblage. Could it be that the Lefkara translucent chert is reduced at the *Spileos* site, and then removed for tool production elsewhere in secondary form, while the Lefkara basal cherts are fashioned on site as expedient tools? This supposition is born out by the proportions of tools to debitage at each site. At *Moutti*, there is an extremely low amount of primary debitage to high amounts of tools and secondary debitage, indicating primary reduction elsewhere, and final tool manufacture on site. Conversely, at *Spileos*, there are fairly even amounts of tools and primary and secondary debitage, consistent with an extraction and manufacturing site.

Results from the sites in the ISP and CPSP suggest the following similar patterns. In all cases, as is seen consistently in the Dhoukani industry, good quality chert sources are readily available, and it seems clear that the most easily accessible sources would have been utilized. Nevertheless, in all cases, the most accessible source did not apparently supply all the needs of the site. Cost was not the only factor in source selection, as at all sites in both areas, the optimal solution did not provide all needs. It is clear that there were not just specific superior grades of chert that would require the exploitation of sources less accessible. Based on the choices made in tool selection, all grades were used. Therefore, I would assume that a number of social and technological factors influenced source selection, notably risk reduction, social and economic interaction with other groups, personal preference of individual knappers and a variety of technological factors. While these behaviours are difficult to identify in the past, they are certainly to be observed in the modern Dhoukani industry and further research may indeed allow a more precise accounting of prehistoric behaviour.

While this paper focuses on the Aceramic (Khirokitian), there are a number of ways in which it might be relevant to a more pan-eastern

Mediterranean perspective. Most importantly, the differences between Levantine and Aceramic lithic acquisition and use patterns (notably the changes in raw material preferences and specific core technologies [Guilaine and Briois 2001: 47; Peltenburg *et al.* 2001: 78–84]) may suggest the extent of loss of contact between the two areas. This could be articulated by tracing these changes from the earlier Cypro-PPNB through the later Khirokitian Aceramic periods. In addition, it may be possible to distinguish between PPNB sites from survey (such as Ayia Varvara and *Ais Yiorkis*), and the Khirokitian by focussing on the presence of lustrous cherts, bi-directional core technology, burins, micro-blades and Byblos point types. This could help demonstrate that the PPNB in Cyprus was not restricted to a few primary sites, such as Shillourokambos, but scattered throughout the island in a variety of locales.

References

Croucher, J. S. 1980
    Operations Research. A First Course. Pergamon Press: Sydney.
Fox, W. A. 1984
    Dhoukani Flake-Blade Production in Cyprus. *Lithic Technology* 13: 62–67.
Fox, W. A. 1987
    The Neolithic Occupation of Western Cyprus. Pp. 19–42 in Rupp 1987a.
Fox, W. A. 1988
    Kholetria-*Ortos.* A Khirokitia Culture Settlement in Paphos District. *Report of the Department of Antiquities, Cyprus:* 29–42.
Fox, W. A. n.d.
    Research on Chert Knapping, Chert Sources, Slag and Ore Deposits in the Paphos District.
Fox, W. A. and D. A. Pearlman 1987
    Threshing Sledge Manufacture in the Paphos District of Cyprus. Pp. 227–234 in Rupp 1987a.
Guilaine, J. and F. Briois 2001
    Parekklisha-*Shillourokambos*: An Early Neolithic Site in Cyprus. Pp. 37–53 in Swiny 2001.
McCartney, C. 1998
    Preliminary Report on the Chipped Stone Assemblage from the Aceramic Neolithic Site of Ayia Varvara-*Asprokremnos*, Cyprus. *Levant* 30: 85–90.
Morden, M. E. and S. T. Stewart n.d.
    The Idalion Survey Project, Cyprus 1995–1998.
Pearlman, D. A. 1984
    Threshing Sledges in the East Mediterranean. M.A., University of Minnesota.
Peltenburg, E., P. Croft, A. Jackson, C. McCartney and M. A. Murray 2001
    Well Established Colonists: *Mylouthkia* 1 and the Cypro-Pre-Pottery Neolithic B. Pp. 61–93 in Swiny 2001.
Rupp, D. W. 1981
    The Canadian Palaipaphos Survey Project. Preliminary Report of the 1979 Season. *Report of the Department of Antiquities, Cyprus:* 251–268.
Rupp, D. W. (ed.) 1987a
    Western Cyprus: Connections. Studies in Mediterranean Archaeology 77. Paul Åströms Förlag: Göteborg.
Rupp, D. W. 1987b
    The Canadian Palaipaphos Survey Project: An Overview of the 1986 Field Season. *Echos du Monde Classique/Classical Views* 6(2): 217–224.
Rupp, D. W. in press
    Evolving Strategies for Investigating an Extensive terra incognita in the Paphos District by the Canadian Palaipaphos Survey Project and the Western Cyprus Project. In M. Iacovou (ed.) *Archaeological Field Surveying in Cyprus. Past History, Future Potential.* British School at Athens Studies: London.
Rupp, D. W., L. W. Sørensen, R. H. King and W. A. Fox 1984
    The Canadian Palaipaphos (Cyprus) Survey Project: Second Preliminary Report, 1980–1982. *Journal of Field Archaeology* 11: 133–159.
Rupp, D. W., L. W. Sørensen, W. A. Fox, R. H. King, T. E. Gregory, J. Lund and S. T. Stewart 1987
    The Canadian Palaipaphos (Cyprus) Survey Project: Third Preliminary Report, 1983–1985. *Acta Archaeologica* 67: 27–45.
Rupp, D.W., J.T. Clarke, C. D'Annibale and S. T. Stewart 1992
    Canadian Palaipaphos Survey Project: 1991 Field Season. *Report of the Department of Antiquities, Cyprus:* 285–318.
Simmons, A. 1994
    Preliminary Report on the 1993 Test Excavations at Kholetria-*Ortos*, Paphos District. *Report of the Department of Antiquities, Cyprus:* 39–44.
Simmons, A. 1996
    Preliminary Report on the Multidisciplinary Investigations at Neolithic Kholetria-*Ortos*, Paphos District. *Report of the Department of Antiquities, Cyprus:* 29–44.
Simmons, A. 1998
    Test Excavations at Two Aceramic Neolithic Sites in the Uplands of Western Cyprus. *Report of the Department of Antiquities, Cyprus:* 1–16.
Simmons, A. and R. Corona 1993
    Test Excavations at Kholetria-*Ortos*, A Neolithic Settlement near Paphos. *Report of the Department of Antiquities, Cyprus:* 1–10.
Stewart, S. T. 1987
    A Model for Prehistoric Chert Acquisition in the Paphos District, Cyprus. Pp. 43–52 in Rupp 1987a.
Swiny, S. (ed.) 2001
    The Earliest Prehistory of Cyprus: From Colonization to Exploitation. Cyprus American Archaeological Research Institute Monograph Series 12. American Schools of Oriental Research: Boston.

11

Flint workshops of the Southern Beqa` valley (Lebanon): preliminary results from Qar`oun*

Maya Ha dar-Boustani

Abstract

In Lebanon several flint workshops are concentrated in the Southern Beqa` valley. They are only known by surface finds collected mainly by the Jesuit priests. Most of these open sites have been frequented during the Palaeolithic and the Neolithic. We choose to deal with the shaping process of the heavy Neolithic tools such as axes, adzes and chisels. This paper presents the preliminary results obtained from Qar`oun I and II.

Introduction

In the inventories of the prehistoric sites of Lebanon, some sites are identified as flint workshops (Copeland and Wescombe 1965, 1966; Besançon and Hours 1970, 1971; Marfoe 1995; Copeland and Yazbeck 2002). They are located in three regions: the coast, South Lebanon and the Southern Beqa` valley. Most of them have been frequented during the Palaeolithic, particularly in the Lower and Middle Palaeolithic, and the Neolithic periods. The Neolithic industry is called "Heavy Neolithic," translated from French "Gros Néo-lithique," an expression invented by the Jesuit priest H. Fleisch (1954). It is characterized by hundreds of flakes strewn over the surface and many roughouts of heavy tools, such as axes.

All the "Heavy Neolithic" industries of Lebanon are known from open sites, except in one case, the Bezez Cave (Kirkbride 1983), where the material extracted from the upper layers is disturbed. Whether the context of the finds is on the surface or in stratified deposits, the dating of the "Heavy Neolithic" is still problematic. According to Mellaart (1965), the "Heavy Neolithic" or "Gigantolithic" could be earlier than the Pottery

Neolithic of Byblos. Some years later, J. and M. -C. Cauvin (1968) related this industry to the Pottery Neolithic of Byblos.

We must emphasize that the Neolithic period of Lebanon is not well known compared to other countries of the Levant. The only available stratigraphy is in Byblos where three stages were discovered: the "Néolithique ancien," "Néolithique moyen" and "Néolithique récent." They were identified on the basis of architecture, lithic industry and pottery (Cauvin 1968; Dunand 1973). J. and M. -C. Cauvin compared the roughouts of axes with rounded and straight bits with the same type of tools that are associated during the "Néolithique moyen" of Byblos. This stage corresponds to "period 7" (7,000–6,500 BP) of the chronology of the French team of the University of Lyon (Aurenche *et al.* 1981; Hours *et al.* 1994).

The typology alone is, of course, not a sufficient criterion for dating. In the present state of research, we keep the "Néolithique moyen" as a hypothesis. This chronological problem needs to be discussed in future when reliable data will be forthcoming. Recent studies on the flint workshops of the Levant (e.g. Barkai 2001; Taute 1994) will hopefully enable us to fit the "Heavy

---

* In the bibliography, the orthography of the Beqa` valley (Beqaa, Bekaa...) and of Qar`oun (Karaoun, Qaraoun) varies according to the authors. In this paper, we propose the exact transliteration from Arabic.

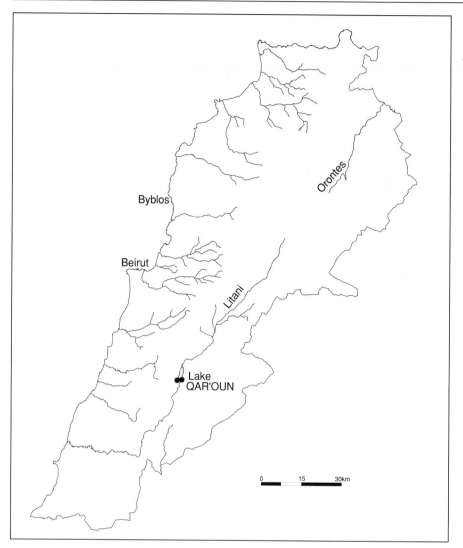

Figure 11.1 *Location map of the Qar`oun sites, Lebanon*

Neolithic" of Lebanon into a general context. We will deal with regional comparisons after the results of our current study on the flint workshops of the Beqa` are available[1].

The workshops of the Southern Beqa` valley are known only from surface material, collected mainly by the Jesuit priests. At the time when the priests used to circulate in Lebanon, scientific methods applied to surface collections didn't exist yet. So, we should keep in mind that these collections are the result of non-systematic work. We don't have any record or scale drawings that would give us indications on the space management and toolkit management.

Previous articles by H. Fleisch (1954) and J. and M. -C. Cauvin (1968) present a general view of the "Heavy Neolithic." In this paper, we deal with the "Heavy Neolithic" as attested in the lithic

material of Qar`oun I and II in the Southern Beqa` valley. We propose a dynamic approach for the shaping process of heavy Neolithic tools.

Qar`oun

Sites and setting

Qar`oun is situated in Southern Beqa` valley on the floor of the dam on the Litani River. The material comes from two stations separated by 800 meters. The first one, Qar`oun I, is on the left bank of the Litani. The second one, Qar`oun II, is on the right bank (Figure 11.1). These two stations[2] were very damaged by cultivation and by the construction of new houses (Copeland and Wescombe 1966: 38). As for the whole Southern Beqa` valley, Qar`oun lies in the Mediterranean

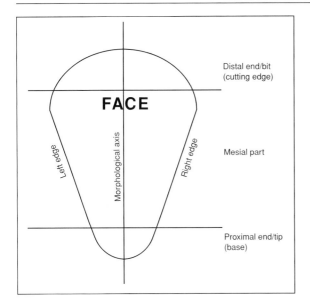

Figure 11.2 *Sketch of bifacial Neolithic tool parts*

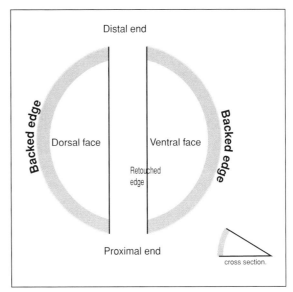

Figure 11.3 *Sketch of "orange slice" parts*

climatic zone, with wet winters and dry summers. The annual mean rainfall is about 800 mm. The outcrops, from which the flint was collected by prehistoric knappers, are abundant around Qar`oun (Besançon and Hours 1971).

The collections

The geologist L. Dubertret discovered both stations, Qar`oun I and II, at the beginning of the 20th century. Based on the marking of pieces, we found out there had been many surface collections since then (1952, 1954, 1958, 1959, 1961, 1963, 1964, 1966, 1968 and 1970). Most of the material is in the storeroom of the "Musée de préhistoire libanaise" (Université Saint-Joseph, Beirut-Lebanon), some in France, and others in Sarajevo and Zagreb Museums (Copeland and Wescombe 1966: 37-38). Only Saint Joseph's collection is dealt with in these preliminary results. In this paper, we examine separately the material of the two stations.

State of surface alterations

Since their manufacture, lithic artefacts were abandoned on the surface of the soil. They were affected by natural alterations and human activities. Most of the artefacts have a patina. Its colour is pale-pinkish at Qar`oun I and pale-greyish at Qar`oun II. Traces of oxidation on the surfaces of the pieces are very frequent at both stations. They are the result of a contact with modern agricul-

tural implements. Due to the trampling of both humans and animals on the artefacts, and the impacts that occur between them, some post-depositional removals exist on the artefacts.

Methodology

The sorting of artefacts

Surface material collected at Qar`oun I and II is very mixed, as in most of the flint workshops of the Beqa` valley. The typology of the lithic artefacts demonstrates that Qar`oun I and II have been frequented during the Palaeolithic and the Neolithic periods. We exclude from this study the characteristic pieces of the Palaeolithic: cores, bifaces and retouched tools. The flakes resulting from a shaping process, which are retouched at Qar`oun I and II, are also excluded because it is very difficult to link them to a precise morphology and then to a specific period. It is nearly impossible to differentiate between a flake resulting from a preparation of a core and a flake resulting from a biface and from an axe. We must add that the typical blade productions of the Neolithic, as in the Naviform technology, are not testified at Qar`oun I and II. In this way, we limit our study to the shaping process of heavy Neolithic tools, such as axes, adzes and chisels. The risk of mixing up the artefacts of different periods is dismissed and the phenomenon of the "Heavy Neolithic" is privileged.

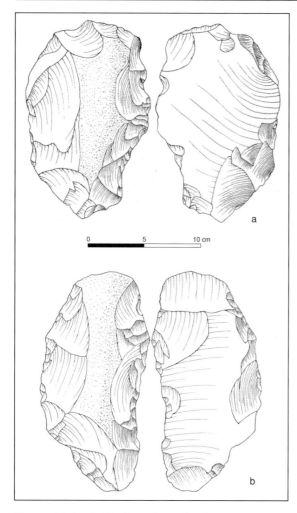

Figure 11.4 a, b *Qar`oun I roughouts*

Shaped by broad removals, the rough-outs can be bifacial or unifacial when the ventral face of the blank is unretouched. In general, the shape of the tool required is perceptible. At the second stage of manufacture, the preform stage, the piece becomes more regular. The regularity concerns the whole outline or a part: the distal end (cutting edge), the lateral edge(s), or the proximal end (base) (Figure 11.2). A shaped tool is finished from the moment it can be used. Polished tools are of course finished tools, because polishing is the last stage of manufacturing. It takes place after the shaping. In the case of used tools in the workshop context, it can be re-sharpened or even re-flaked. The polishing of the cutting edge makes it more solid and durable, but it is not a necessary operation; axes and chisels can be functional even having been polished.

In the case of axes and adzes, tools used in "percussive activity", like "chopping" and "adzing", two parameters must be taken into account: the distal end, or the cutting edge and the proximal end, or the base. When the edge-on-profile is regularized and the base is shaped for the haft, we consider the tool as finished. But, of course, the degree of the finish of these two ends could vary. In the case of non-hafted tools like the plane or the heavy end-scraper, only the first parameter is important.

Method of analysis

A techno-morphological analysis is the only approach applicable to this kind of material, which is collected on the surface and not homogeneous. It allows us to reconstruct the different stages of heavy tool production, from the roughout to the finishing. In order to make the classification easier, we begin our study from the final stage: the finished tool, toward the first stage: the roughout. In this way, we recognise the tools desired and the determination of the previous stages becomes less difficult. However, in the presentation of the analysis of the shaping pro-cess, we start with the first stage, the roughout.

Definitions of the stages

The roughout is the earliest stage of manufacture. It is knapped on nodules or massive flakes.

The finished tools

The finished tools are classified according to the position of the cutting edge and its shape. A tool with an axial cutting edge is one that is made on the longer axis of the piece (axe, adze, pick, chisel, end-scraper and plane). The cutting edge is convex, straight or pointed. In the case of axial tools, it is not always easy to distinguish between convex or straight cutting edges. We consider that a cutting edge is convex when the outline continues without interruption into the lateral ridges. It is straight; but sometimes slightly convex, when there is a right angle between the working edge and the lateral edges. There are also heavy tools with a lateral cutting edge. These are shaped on one or two edges (side-scraper, notch and denticulate).

The Neolithic heavy tools are already defined in the literature (e.g. Brézillon 1968) and are very well documented on many Neolithic sites of the Levant (e.g. Crowfoot-Payne 1983;

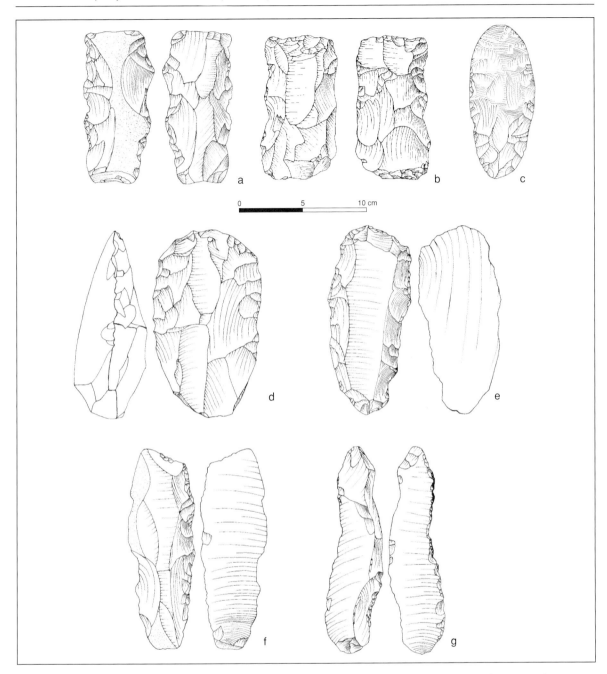

Figure 11.5 a–g *Qar`oun I: a) preform; b) axe; c) polished axe; d), e) heavy end-scrapers; f) heavy side-scraper; g) "orange slice"*

Lechevallier 1978), except one special morphology called by J. Hamal-Nandrin and J. Servais (1928) "quartier d'orange", translated as "orange slice." The shape of this flint artefact reminds one of an "orange slice." J. and M. -C. Cauvin (1968: 106) give a more recent definition. According to the authors, the "orange slice" is shaped on a massive blade. The intersection of the dorsal and ventral faces is very often retouched and it is pre-

sumed to be the cutting edge, while the second one is shaped by broad removals, which create a thick edge (Figure 11.3). Sometimes the distal end is worked by multiple burin blows, which round the section and facilitate the hafting. Qar`oun II is the only flint workshop of Lebanon where these pieces were found in large quantities. The summary description below demonstrates variability among the "orange slice" artefacts.

The shaping process of the heavy Neolithic tools at Qar`oun I
(Table 11.1)

Roughouts

Five roughouts are made on massive flakes and only one is worked on a nodule. Bifacial flaking shapes the faces of these coarse pieces but the flaking extent varies. Two shapes are recognizable: oval and rectangular. The choice of the end on which the cutting edge will be shaped, is done at this stage of manufacture (Figure 11.4 a). Only one roughout, which is made on a big flake, has a transversal blow on the ventral face of the distal end, the future cutting edge (Figure 11.4 b).

Preforms

We recognized two preforms of chisel and adze (Figure 11.5 a); the two others are discarded because of failure in shaping the body.

Finished tools

Axes and adzes are the most important classes in terms of quantity. Six specimens have a straight working edge (Figure 11.5 b) and four have a convex one, among which one axe is polished (Figure 11.5 c). Chisels and picks are scarce. There is one chisel with a convex working edge and one pick with a triangular cross-section. The eight heavy end-scrapers (Figure 11.5 d) and planes are partially shaped on the ventral face of the massive flakes. In many cases, the cutting edge is made on the distal end of the flake. It can also be on the proximal end. In one case, it is made on the edge of the flake (Figure 11.5 e). Five side-scrapers (Figure 11.5 f) and five notches represent tools with lateral cutting edges. They are shaped on big flakes, which still have cortex remnants. Among the five "orange slices" (Figure 11.5 g), four pieces still have the butt, which is flat. The ventral face is unretouched and the bulb is large. The dorsal face is shaped in one case. All the "orange slices" are retouched on one edge. The retouches are very often irregular. The opposite edge is worked by broad removals. The shape of the backed edge is irregular, except in two cases, where it is convex. The most massive piece, which is broken at the proximal end, has a backed edge of about 7.2 cm thick.

Categories	Totals	Frequencies
Hammerstone	1	0. 12
Small nodule	1	0. 12
Cores	128	16
Bifaces	2	0. 25
Chopping-tool	1	0. 12
Retouched tools:		
Notches/denticulates	462	57. 75
Side-scrapers/		
end-scrapers	67	8. 37
Backed pieces	2	0. 25
Retouched flakes:		
Completes	62	7. 75
Fragments	22	2. 75
Shaped pieces:		
Roughouts	6	0. 75
Preforms	4	0. 5
Finished tools	35	4. 37
Converted pieces	2	0. 25
Unidentifiables	5	0. 62
Total	**800**	

Table 11.1 *Counts of Qar`oun I lithics*

Converted pieces

One bifacial and one unifacial piece have a breakage on the working edge. The shape of this edge was convex. The retouch carried out after the breakage, indicates that these tools were converted into other tools.

Unidentifiables

Four unclassified shaped pieces can't be fitted into any of the mentioned categories.

The shaping process of the heavy Neolithic tools at Qar`oun II
(Table 11.2)

Roughouts

Most of the 41 coarse pieces are made on massive flakes with cortex remnants. Three principal shapes are recognizable: oval, rectangular and triangular. The future cutting edge is prepared by centripetal removals (Figure 11.6 a), by

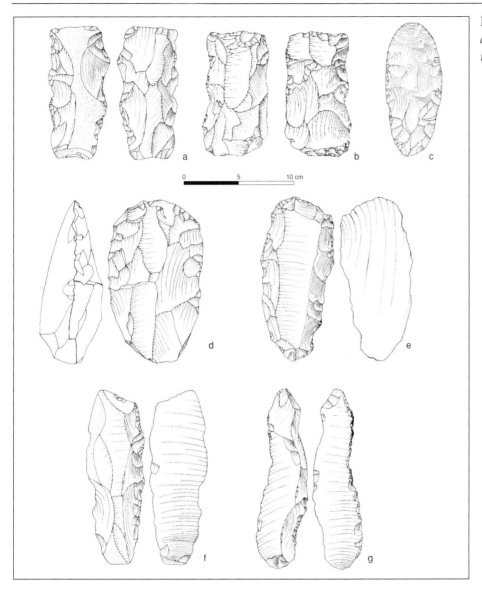

Figure 11.6
*a – d Qar`oun II
roughouts*

an axial blow (Figure 11.6 b) or by one or two transversals blows on the ventral face (Figure 11.6 c, d). Some of the roughouts have been discarded because of unsuccessful shaping of the body. The tools required are axes, adzes and picks.

Preforms

The blanks on which these 44 preforms are shaped can be determined in many cases. They are flakes with cortex remnants. Some of the preforms are partially shaped on both faces and some others are unifacial. This could mean that the prehistoric knapper has selected the flakes according to the morphology of the future tool. Among the preforms, the pieces with a straight working edge are more numerous than the

pieces with a convex working edge. These unfinished pieces are axes, adzes and chisels.

Finished tools

Whatever the extent of the shaping, overall bifacial, partial bifacial or unifacial, the most numerous pieces are the tools with a convex cutting edge. These are 43 heavy end-scrapers and planes knapped on massive flakes with cortex remnants, 17 axes and adzes (Figure 11.7 a, b) and only two chisels. The tools with a straight cutting edge are: 22 axes and adzes (Figure 11.7 c-f), five heavy end-scrapers and planes and three chisels. The pointed tools also occurred in the collection of Qar`oun II. They include 17 picks (Figure 11.8 b, c), some of which are unifacial, and

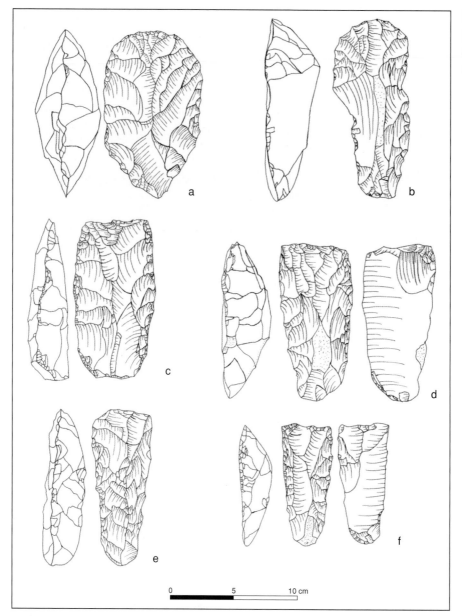

Figure 11.7 a–f
*Qar`oun II axes and
adzes with convex and
straight cutting edge*

0   5   10 cm

only one heavy burin (Figure 11.8 a). The tools with a lateral cutting edge are five side-scrapers and five notches shaped on massive flakes, most of which have cortex remnants.

Qar`oun II is the only workshop in Lebanon where the pieces called "orange slices" (Figure 11.9. a-d) have been produced in large quantities. Among the 44 specimens, only 10 are complete. The others are broken on the distal end (14 cases), on the proximal end (18 cases) or on both (two cases). Even when broken, the "orange slices" could reach 19 cm in length; the smallest and most complete one has 11.1 cm in length. It is difficult to specify if the breakage happened

during the manufacture or during the utilization. Some pieces are retouched after the breakage. Direct percussion detaches these thick blades. The butt is flat and the bulb is very often large. The edge is backed mostly by crossed flake-removals detached by direct percussion. In some cases, the shaping of the back extends partially on the ventral and dorsal faces of the blade. The backed edge can be convex, concave, straight or irregular, the retouched edge has also the same shapes. It is presumed to be the working edge. Not all the "orange slices" are necessarily hafted; they could be hand-held by using the thick backed edge.

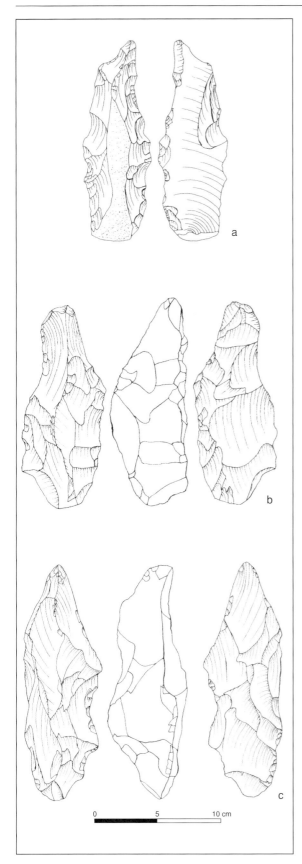

Figure 11.8 a–c *Qar`oun II : a) heavy burin; b), c) picks*

Categories	Totals	Frequencies
Cores	36	4. 29
Bifaces	7	0. 83
Retouched tools:		
Notches/denticulates	159	18. 95
Side-scrapers/		
end-scrapers	121	14. 42
Backed flakes	5	0. 59
Burins	2	0. 23
Retouched flakes:		
Completes	172	20. 50
Fragments	27	3. 21
Unretouched flakes	25	2. 97
Shaped pieces:		
Roughouts	41	4. 88
Preforms	44	5. 24
Finished tools	130	15. 49
Broken pieces	46	5. 48
Unidentifiables	24	2. 86
Total	**839**	

Table 11.2 *Counts of Qar`oun II lithics*

Broken pieces

Among the 46 broken pieces, we recognized 34 "orange slices" mentioned above, one axe and two elongated tools that could be chisels or picks. The degree of finishing and the patina indicates that these pieces have been broken at the end of the manufacture process or maybe during the utilization.

Unidentifiables

There are 24 pieces in the collection of Qar`oun II that can't be fitted into any of the stages or categories mentioned above.

Conclusion

On the basis of these preliminary results, Qar`oun I and II can be considered as contemporary workshops where the prehistoric knappers used the same raw material and produced the same industries during the Palaeolithic and the Neolithic periods. However, the high numbers of the "orange slice" found at Qar`oun II, situated

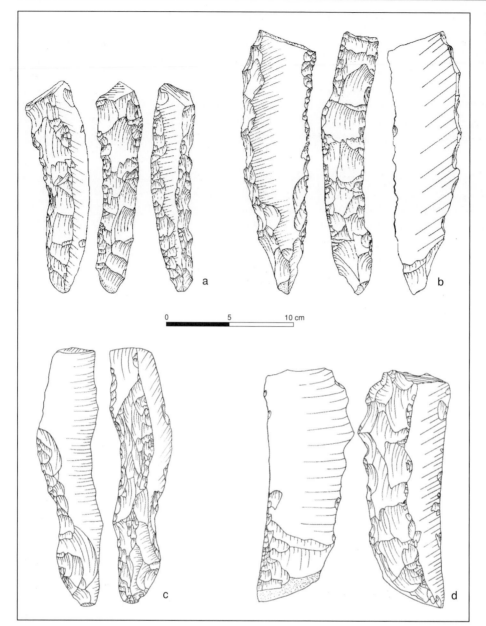

Figure 11.9 a–d
Qar`oun II
"orange slices"

on the right bank of the Litani, could be explained by the presence of a specialized zone within the workshop. We need more elements to be able to restore the production system of "orange slice" and to resolve the chronological problem. This specific morphology has not yet been found in a stratified site in Lebanon or generally in the Levant. So, these tools could be Neolithic or more recent.

Artefacts are very abundant at Qar`oun. Prehistoric knappers exploited the flint from nearby outcrops. The analysis of the heavy Neolithic tools of Qar`oun reveals that all the manufacture stages were done on the same site. Nodules and mainly massive flakes are used to make the heavy Neolithic tools. The roughouts were shaped on both faces by removals, which are generally broad. The shape of the future tool is generally perceptible, but it becomes more precise in the second stage of manufacture. In fact, in the preform stage the dimension and the outline of the piece are more precise. Usually the edges and the base are shaped before the cutting edge, which is retouched at the end of the process.

The classes of tools demonstrate that Qar`oun was specialized in the manufacture of heavy tools, such as axes, adzes, chisels, heavy end-scrapers and planes, most probably used for woodworking. Whatever the chronological attribution of the "orange slice" is, these heavy tools, retouched on one edge, could be hand-held with the thick backed edge and used to peel the wood. While the picks are not necessarily related to woodworking, they could be used for land working.

Usually in a flint workshop, all the products are discarded because of unsuccessful shaping, and the finished tools are absent or scarce because they have been transported to be used elsewhere. The same cannot be said of Qar`oun, where many tools in usable condition were found. The reason of abandonment of the finished tools in not clear. It is difficult to affirm whether the production of heavy Neolithic tools was merely intended for local purposes or for exchange with other regions.

Acknowledgements

We are most grateful to Ms. Lorraine Copeland for reading and commenting on this paper. Also we would like to thank the anonymous reader for his useful comments.

Notes

1   The study of the flint workshops of the Beqa` valley is the subject of my Doctoral thesis, part of a wider interest in the Neolithic period in Lebanon, and one that needs a revival of prehistoric excavations.

2   A third one, Qar`oun III, an Acheulean site discovered by J. Cauvin, disappeared beneath the water of the Litani. Recently, in February 2003, the showers falling on Lebanon, especially on the Southern Beqa` valley, raised the water level of the Litani River and the lake of Qar`oun, possibly damaging the sites close to the banks. Fieldwork is necessary to examine the condition of the sites.

References

Aurenche, O., J. Cauvin, M. -C. Cauvin, L. Copeland, F. Hours and P. Sanlaville 1981
Chronologie et organisation de l'espace dans le Proche-Orient de 12,000 á 5,600 avant J.-C. Pp. 571–601 in J. Cauvin and P. Sanlaville (eds.) *Préhistoire du Levant.* Éditions C.N.R.S.: Paris.

Barkai, R. 2001
Make my axe: flint axe production and resharpening at EPPNB Nahal Lavan 109. Pp. 73-92 in I. Canneva, C. Lemorini, D. Zampetti and P. Biagi (eds.) *Beyond tools Proceedings of the Third Workshop on PPN chipped lithic industries.* Departement of Classical and Near Eastern Studies Ca'Foscari University of Venice, 1st-4th November 1998. Studies in Early Near Eastern Production, Subsistence and Environment 9. Ex Oriente : Berlin

Besançon, J. and F. Hours 1970
Préhistoire et géomorphologie: les formes du relief et les dépôts quaternaires dans la région de Joubb Jannine (Béqaa méridionale - Liban). Première partie. Hannon, Revue libanaise de géographie 5 : 63-95.

Besançon, J. and F. Hours 1971
Préhistoire et géomorphologie: les formes du relief et les dépôts quaternaires dans la région de Joubb Jannine (Béqaa méridionale-Liban). Deuxième partie. Hannon, Revue libanaise de géographie 6 : 29-135.

Brézillon, M. 1968
La dénomination des objets de pierre taillée, IV. Supplément à Gallia Préhistoire. Editions du C.N.R.S. : Paris.

Cauvin, J. 1968
Les outillages néolithiques de Byblos et du littoral libanais. Fouilles de Byblos, IV. Maisonneuve : Paris.

Cauvin, J. and M.-C. Cauvin 1968
Des ateliers "campigniens" au Liban. Pp. 103-116 in M. Maziéres (ed.) *La préhistoire problème et tendances.* Hommage á Raymond Vaufrey. Éditions C.N.R.S. : Paris.

Copeland, L. and P. J. Wescombe 1965
Inventory of Stone Age sites in Lebanon. Part one: West-Central Lebanon. Mélanges de l'Université Saint-Joseph 41: 30-175.

Copeland, L. and P. J. Wescombe 1966
Inventory of Stone Age sites in Lebanon. Part two: North, South and East-Central Lebanon. Mélanges de l'Université Saint-Joseph 42: 1-174.

Copeland, L. and C. Yazbeck 2002
Inventory of Stone Age Sites in Lebanon. Part three. Mélanges de l'Université Saint-Joseph 45.

Crowfoot-Payne, J. 1983
The flint industries of Jéricho. Pp. 622-759 in K. M. Kenyon and T. A. Holland (eds.) *Excavations at Jericho. Volume V. The pottery phases of the Tell and other finds.* British School of Archaeology in Jerusalem. Oxford University Press: Oxford.

Dunand, M. 1973
L'architecture, le matériel domestique des origines néolithiques à l'avènement urbain. Fouilles de Byblos V. Librairie d'Amérique et d'Orient, J. Maisonneuve : Paris.

Fleisch, H. 1954
Nouvelles stations préhistoriques au Liban. *Bulletin de la Société Préhistorique Française* 51 : 564-568.

Hamal-Nandrin, J. and J. Servais 1928 Instruments à section triangulaire ou quadrangulaire et dont une ou deux faces sont retouchées. *Bulletin de la*

Société Préhistorique Française 25 : 505-517.

Hours, F., O. Aurenche, J. Cauvin, M.-C. Cauvin, L. Copeland and P. Sanlaville 1994
Atlas des sites du Proche-Orient (14,000–5,700 B.P.). Travaux de la Maison de l'Orient Méditerranéen 24. Maison de l'Orient Méditerranéen : Lyon.

Kirkbride, D. 1983
The Neolithic of Bezez Cave. Pp. 367-388 in D. A. Roe (ed.) *Adlun in the Stone Age. The excavations of D.A.E. Garrod in the Lebanon, 1958-1963.* British Archaeological Reports, International Series, 159 (ii): Oxford.

Lechevallier, M. 1978
Abou Gosh et Beisamoun. Deux gisements du VIIème millénaire avant l'ère chrétienne en Israël. Mémoires et Travaux du Centre de Recherches Préhistoriques Français de Jérusalem, 2. Association Paléorient : Paris.

Marfoe, L. 1995
Kamid el-Loz 13. The Prehistoric and Early Historic context of the site. Saarbrücker Beiträge zur Altertumskunde 41. Dr. Rudolf Habelt GMBH: Bonn.

Mellaart, J. 1965
The earliest civilizations of the Near East. Thames and Hudson: London.

Taute, W. 1994
The Pre-Pottery Neolithic flint mining and workshop activities southwest of the Dead Sea, Israel (Ramat Tamar and Mesad Mazzal). Pp.495-509 in H. G. Gebel and S. K. Kozlowski (eds.) *Neolithic chipped stone indsutries of the Fertile Crescent. Proceedings of the First Workshop on PPN chipped lithic industries. Free University of Berlin, 29th March-2nd April 1993.* Studies in Early Near Eastern Production, Subsistence and Environment 1. Ex Oriente : Berlin.

12

Geometric patterns on pebbles: early identity symbols?

Anna Eirikh-Rose

Abstract

Geometric ornamented pebbles first appeared in the Near East during the Upper Palaeolithic period and were widespread in Neolithic times, when they became an integral part of the material culture. It is pertinent to mention that the earliest seals, which appeared in the Near East during the Neolithic period, bear the same types of geometric designs. Chronologically the pebbles appeared first, and after a period of coexistence they disappeared and the seals became widespread. Similarity of geometric patterns may point to similarity of symbolic meaning; this assumption and the consecutive rise of two classes of artefacts imply similarity of function. It seems that the pebbles can be considered the predecessors of the seals. Seals mark ownership and indicate personal property; thus the geometric patterns on the seals and pebbles may represent specific entities, persons or families.

Introduction

The beginnings of agriculture and a sedentary way of life were accompanied by important economic and social processes, notably the accumulation of wealth and the rise of individuation in society. These processes are reflected in the archaeological data by the appearance of various new groups of artefacts, like permanent structures, new types of houses, flint tools, pottery and art objects. In this article I have chosen to discuss a group of these finds, a neglected category which has not so far received the attention it deserves: pebbles with geometric incisions. Geometric ornamented pebbles first appeared in the Levant during the end of the Palaeolithic period and were widespread by Neolithic times, when they became an integral part of material culture in the Near East. Despite their presence at many Late Prehistoric sites throughout the region, no comprehensive research on these enigmatic artefacts has been carried out. I will first present the relevant data and then discuss their implications.

The terminology used in the present article is that established specifically for the area of the Southern Levant. Thus sites from other parts of the Near East are arranged here according to parallel time spans. For comparative tables of periods and dates for the Near East, see, for example, Bar-Yosef and Meadow (1995: Figure 3. 2) and Cauvin (1994: Table 1).

The data

Pebbles bearing geometric incisions appeared for the first time in the Levant at the end of the Palaeolithic period (see Table 12.1). In the Palaeolithic period geometric ornamented pebbles are very rare, with only a few examples in the region. During the Natufian period the number of incised pebbles increased. Similar engraved pebbles became widespread in the Neolithic era, when they appeared throughout the Near East, from Eastern Anatolia to the Zagros, and from the Northern Euphrates to the Negev Desert. They have also been found at Cypriot Neolithic sites (see Table 12.1 and Figure 12.1).

During the Pre-Pottery Neolithic period, both the number of engraved pebble appearances and

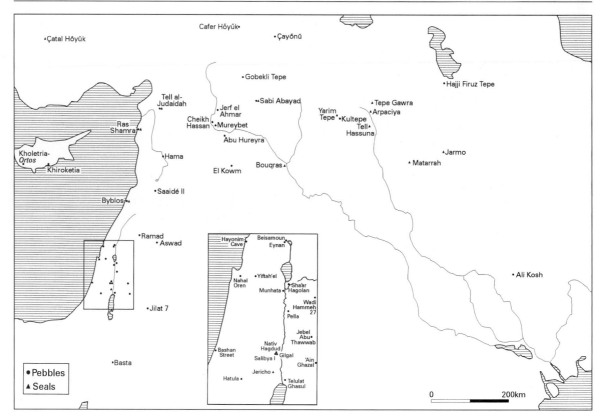

Figure 12.1 *Map of the Near East, showing sites mentioned in the text*

the number of pebbles per site continue to increase (in proportion to sites excavated per period).

In the Pottery Neolithic period (7,600–7,000 BP), engraved pebbles are common, not only from a geographic perspective but also in quantity; large numbers of these pebbles have been reported from several sites. From Sha`ar Hagolan, close to 40 such items are known, 3 from the excavation and the others collected on the site's surface over a 60-year period (examples were published in Stekelis 1972; Garfinkel 1999b). Another significant assemblage of geometric incised pebbles comes from two contemporary Neolithic sites on Cyprus: 106 items from Khirokitia (Dikaios 1953; Cluzan 1984) and more than 51 engraved pebbles from Kholetria-*Ortos* (Fox 1988; Simmons and Corona 1993; Simmons 1995; Stewart and Rupp, this volume).

After the eighth millennium BP, the number of geometric engraved pebbles dramatically decreased. Such pebbles are almost completely absent after the Neolithic/Early Chalcolithic.[1]

The incisions on geometrical engraved pebbles are made on different kinds of stone, including, among others, limestone and basalt.

The choice of raw material seems mainly to be determined by what could be found close to the site. At Sha`ar Hagolan, we observe a specific choice of raw material: most of the pebbles consist of hard basalt stone, in contrast to the incised figurines from the area that were made of softer raw material, namely limestone. A similar choice of hard volcanic raw material was noticed at other sites: Munhatta (Gopher and Orrelle 1995), Khirokitia (Dikaios 1953; Le Brun 1984) and Kholetria-*Ortos* (Fox 1988: 36).

The engraved items are round, oval or rectangular. The size varies from a few cm to 10–15 cm in diameter, suitable for holding in the palm of the hand.

The pebbles can be classified in three groupings, according to the means of manufacture:

1. *Natural pebbles*. The incisions are made on a natural pebble without any additional modification.
2. *Worked (ground and polished) pebbles*. Usually only the incised face was flattened, but in some cases the whole pebble was modified–for example, conical stones at Cypriot sites (Diakios 1953: 291).

Time Span (C¹⁴, BP)	Southern Levant	Syria and Lebanon	N. Mesopotamia (inc. E. Turkey and N. Syria)	Other regions
ca. 42,000–20,000	**Upper Palaeolithic:** Hayonim Cave (layer D, Belfer-Cohen and Bar-Yosef 1981: Figure 7. 4)			
ca. 20,000–12,250	**Epi-Palaeolithic:** Urkan e-Rub II (Hovers 1990: Figures 3, 4)			
ca. 12,500–10,200	**Natufian:** Salibiya I (Crabtree *et al.* 1991), Wadi Hammeh 27 (Edwards 1991), Eynan (Perrot 1966), Nahal Oren (Noy 1991)	Saa dé II (Schroeder 1991)	Shanidar B1, Zawi Chemi Shanidar B (Singh 1974: Figure 45; Matthews 2002:32), Abu Hureyra 1 (Moore *et al.* 2000)	
10,300/10,000–9600	**PPNA:** Netiv Hagdud (Bar-Yosef and Gopher 1997), Ein Suhun (Nadel *et al.* 2000)		Sheikh Hassan (Cauvin 1994), Göbekli Tepe (Beile-Bohn *et al.* 1998), Jerf el Ahmar (Stordeur 1988; 1998), Mureybet III (Cauvin 1994)	
9600–8100	**PPNB:** Basta (Nissen *et al.* 1991), Beisamoun (Lechevallier 1978), Jilat 7 (Garrard *et al.* 1994), Shaqarat Mazyad (Rehhoff –Kaliszan, pers comm.), Munhata 3, 4 (Gopher and Orrelle 1995)	Aswad II (de Contenson 1995), Ramad I (de Contenson 2000)	El Kowm 2, AV (Stordeur 1989), Cayönü, Phase I (Davis 1982), Cafer Höyük (Cauvin *et al.* 1999)	Ali Kosh (Hole *et al.* 1969)
8100–7600	**PPNC:** Atlit Yam (Galili *et al.* 1993), Tel Ali (Garfinkel 1993b)	Ras Shamra VB (de Contenson 1992), Ramad II (de Contenson 2000)	Kultepe, Level I (Bader 1993)	
7600–7000	**PN:** Bashan St. (Kaplan 1954), Pella (McNicoll, *et al.* 1982: 87.5), Ain Ghazal, Yarmoukian (Rollefson and Simmons 1986: 161), Jebel Abu Tawwab, LNI (Quadi 2000), Yiftah'el III (Braun 1994), Munhata, 2 (Gopher and Orrelle 1995: 64), Sha'ar Hagolan (Stekelis 1972, Garfinkel 1999b), Site 83 in Negev (Burian and Fridman 1973: 3.1), Wadi Chazeh (Site D: Rashwalb 1981: 152)	Byblos-Néolithique Ancien (Dunand 1973: 88), Tell al-Judaidah B (Braidwood and Braidwood 1960), Ras Shamra VA (de Contenson 1992),	Sabi Abyad 5 (Collet and Spoor 1996), Dja'de el Mughara, pre-Halaf level (Coqueugniot 1998), Hajji Firuz Tepe, A3 (Voigt 1983)	Khirokitia Ib, II, III (Dikaios 1953; Cluzan 1984), Kholethria-*Ortos* (Fox 1988; Simmons and Corona 1993; Simmons 1995; Stewart and Rupp, this volume),
7000–6000	**PN/Chalcolithic:** Munhata 1 (Gopher and Orrelle 1995), Tuleylat Ghassul 2B (Blackham 1999)	Byblos, Néolithique Récent (Dunand 1973: 160), Hama, K1, K6, L2 (Fugmann 1958), Ras Shamra VI, IIIC (de Contenson 1970; 1992)		

Table 12.1 *Chronological and geographical distribution of geometric engraved pebbles*

Design type/Subtype	Examples
1) Linear design 1a.Vertical lines	Saa dé II (Schroeder 1991: Fig. 10.4–6), Salibiya I (Crabtree *et al.* 1991: Fig.2), Göbekli Tepe (Beile-Bohn *et al.* 1998: Fig. 27.3), Basta (Nissen *et al.* 1991: Pl. V), Pella (McNicoll, *et al.* 1982: 87.5), Sha`ar Hagolan (Stekelis 1972: Fig. 57.1–4,8; Garfinkel 1999b: 89), Munhata (Gopher and Orrelle 1995: Fig. 45.2), Ras Shamra IIIC (de Contenson 1970: Fig. 21.2).
1b.Horizontal lines	Wadi Hammeh 27 (Edwards 1991: Fig. 8. 14), Beitsamoun (Lechevallier 1978: Fig. 107.7), Yiftah'el (Braun 1994: Fig. 20.1.6), Munhata (Gopher and Orrelle 1995: Fig. 45.5–7,9), Sha`ar Hagolan (Stekelis 1972: Fig. 57.5–7,9; Garfinkel 1992: Fig. 134.3), Jebel Abu Tawwab (Quadi 2000: Fig. 11.6), Tell al-Judaidah (Braidwood and Braidwood 1960: 93, Fig. 66.8).
1c.Combined horizontal and vertical lines	Jilat 7 (Garrard *et al.* 1994: Fig. 10a), Kholetria-Ortos (Fox 1988: Fig. 6.2), Khirokitia (Cluzan 1984: Fig. 74.3).
1d. A central line crossed by diagonal lines.	Hayonim Cave (Belfer-Cohen and Bar-Yosef 1981: Fig. 7.4), Wadi Hammeh 27 (Edwards 1991 Fig. 8.1–2 5–7), Eynan (Perrot 1966: Fig. 21.15), Jerf el Ahmar (Stordeur 1988: Fig. 1), Göbekli Tepe (Beile-Bohn *et al.* 1998: Fig. 27.2), Bashan Street (Kaplan 1954: Fig 7.13), Sha`ar Hagolan (Stekelis 1972: Fig. 57.10), Kholetria-Ortos (Simmons 1996: Fig. 2.1), Khirokitia (Dikaios 1953: Pl. CXXXVIII. 914; CXLI. 920), Hama (Fugmann 1958: Fig. 46), Byblos (Dunand 1973: Fig. 102).
2) Grid (criss-cross) design 2a. Straight	Nahal Oren (Noy 1991: Fig. 2.5–6), Beitsamoun (Lechevallier 1978: Fig. 107.6), Aswad (de Contenson 1995: Fig. 111.15), Ramad (de Contenson 2000: Fig. 89.1), Yiftah'el (Braun 1994: Fig. 20.1:5), Kultepe (Bader 1993: Fig. 4.5), Ras Shamra VB (de Contenson 1992: Fig. 126.6–7, 13, Pl. LXXXIX. 2, Pl. XC, Pl. XCI.4), Munhata (Gopher and Orrelle 1995: Fig. 44.7,9,11), Ain Ghazal (Rollefson, Kafafi and Simmons 1991: Fig. 4.3), Sha`ar Hagolan (Stekelis 1972: Fig. 59.2,5; Garfinkel 1992: Fig. 135.1–6; 1999b: 89), Kholetria-Ortos (Simmons 1996: Fig. 2.2), Khirokitia (Dikaios 1953: Pl. CXXXVIII. 14, 1153, 1074, 827, 1193b, 12, 1161, 1005, 115, 958, 1240a, 1046, 821; Cluzan 1984: Fig. 97; 98.2–3; 99.3).
2b.Diagonal	Haluza (Noy 1978a), Sha`ar Hagolan (Stekelis 1972: Fig. 59.3–4; Garfinkel 1992: Fig. 135.9), Munhata (Gopher and Orrelle 1995: Fig. 44.10), Khirokitia (Dikaios 1953: Pl. CXXXVIII. 23, 739, 95), Kholetria-Ortos (Fox 1988: Fig. 7.1), Sabi Abyad (Collet and Spoor 1996: Fig. 7.7. 16).
2c. Grid with straight and diagonal lines	Abu Hureira (Moore *et al.* 2000: Fig. 7.16.e), Cafer Höyük (Cauvin *et al.* 1999: Fig. 32), Sha`ar Hagolan (Garfinkel 1992: Fig. 135.10), Khirokitia (Dikaios 1953: Pl. CXXXVIII. 1152, 145)
3) Cruciform design 3a. Plain cross	Sha`ar Hagolan (Stekelis 1972: Fig. 61.3,5; Garfinkel 1992: Fig. 136.1–3,5), Munhata (Gopher and Orrelle 1995: Fig. 39.1), Ras Shamra IVB (de Contenson 1992: Pl. XCIX .2).
3b.Complex cross	Kholetria-*Ortos* (Fox 1988: Fig. 6).
4) Radiating/ star design	Ras Shamra VA (a mixture of radiating and grid lines (de Contenson 1992: Fig. 126.14), Sha`ar Hagolan (Stekelis 1972: Fig. 61.2; Garfinkel 1992: Fig. 135.4,6), Khirokitia (Dikaios 1953: Pl. CXXXVIII. 1071), Kholetria-Ortos (Simmons and Corona 1993: Fig. 7), Tulaylat Ghassul (Blackham 1999: Fig. 18.22).
5) Concentric design	Sha`ar Hagolan (Cauvin 1972: Fig. 32.1; Garfinkel 1992: Fig. 137.1).
6) Chevrons 6a. Zigzag lines	Ras Shamra IVC (de Contenson 1992: Pl. XCIV. 5), Khirokitia (Dikaios 1953: Pl. CXLI. 515), Ain Ghazal (Rollefson and Simmons 1986: 161), Mureybet (Cauvin 1994: Fig. 19. 2, 5,6), Haji Firuz Tepe (Voigt 1983: Fig. 118.2), El Kowm (Strodeur 1989: Fig. 5.4).
6b.Chevrons enclosed within lines	Sheikh Hassan (Cauvin 1994: Fig. 43.6), Cayönü (Davis 1982: Fig. 3.12.10, 3.13.1–2), Mureybet (Cauvin 1994: Fig. 19.2–3,6).
7) Drilled design	Nahal Oren (Noy 1991: Fig. 2.1), Sha`ar Hagolan (Stekelis 1972: Fig. 61.6).
8) Combined designs and miscellaneous	Urkan e-Rub II (Hovers 1990: Figs. 3–4), Netiv Hagdud (Bar-Yosef and Gopher 1997: frontispiece) and Ein Suhun (Nadel *et al.* 2000: Fig. 8), Tell al-Judaidah (Braidwood and Braidwood 1960: Fig. 66.7–6), Basta (Nissen *et al.* 1991: Fig.5.1. 8), Munhata (Gopher and Orrelle 1995: Fig 44.6, 8).

Table 12.2 *Geometric design types and their distribution*

3. *Flat slabs.* Though these are not pebbles, because their size and geometric pattern fit into the category of "incised pebbles" I have decided to include this group here, though technically some of them are limestone flakes.

In some cases geometric patterns were incised on tools such as whetstones, celts, pendants or net weights. In such cases it is not clear whether this comprises secondary use of these implements as raw material for creating engraved pebbles, or if we are dealing with ornamented tools.

This study does not include pebbles that have a single groove in the middle, although some scholars (e.g. Stekelis 1972; Gopher and Orrelle 1995) have included these in the category of geometric incised pebbles. I believe that such items are tools rather than a symbolic representation. From our examination of the stone tool assemblage of Sha`ar Hagolan, it appears that the grooves on items with a single groove are much deeper and broader than those on pebbles with geometric incisions, and we therefore consider the former to be whetstones.

While some scholars have concentrated on the shape of the pebbles (Cluzan 1984; Astruc 1994), my typological framework is concerned more with the geometric patterns themselves. The classification basically uses the typology proposed by Garfinkel (1992: 167–170; 1993a), with certain modifications based on re-examination of both the Sha`ar Hagolan material and material from other sites.

There are seven major types of design: *linear, grid, cruciform, radiating, concentric, chevron* and *drilled* (see Table 12.2). *Miscellaneous and combined patterns* form an eighth category. Further sub-types were noted as well. Some of the pebbles bear incisions on both sides. I treat the two sides as two different designs, though it appears from the way the stone is manufactured and the nature of the designs that the intended design is the result of the combination of the two sides.

The author is aware of the fact that all the objects derive from different periods and regions (see Figure 12.1 and Table 12.1). But since the goal of this paper is to explore the links between the appearance of the various objects and since the main research tool of this paper is the tracing of the design characteristics, in the following description all the incised pebbles are arranged according to their design without consideration of their provenance. Furthermore, in many field reports these items are published without their context and at other sites they are surface finds. The study of the context of the items is an issue for further research. The present framework, therefore, is concerned with pebble design regardless of provenance, though the design examples are organized chronologically in Table 12.2 from the earliest to the latest.

1. *Linear design.* These patterns are composed of different combinations of parallel straight lines, of a line crossed and lines on both sides, and irregular lines. The number of lines incised on these pebbles varies from 3 to 19. Variations include: vertical lines (subtype 1a, lines incised along the pebble, Figure 12.2. 1–2), horizontal lines (1b, lines incised across the pebble, Figure 12.2. 3–6), combined horizontal and vertical lines (1c, parallel lines that are horizontal on part of the pebble and vertical on another part, Figure 12.2. 10–11), and a central line crossed by diagonal lines (1d, Figure 12.2. 7–8). The final design group consists of horizontal parallel lines crossed by one central vertical line. It includes specimens in which the lines are incised not perpendicular to, but rather at an angle to the central line, thus creating a "leaf" or "tree" pattern.

2. *Grid (criss-cross) design.* This design includes incised lines crossing each other at different angles. Variations include a straight grid (2a, Figure 12.3. 1–4), a diagonal grid (2b, Figure 12.3. 5–6,9), and a grid with both straight and diagonal lines (2c, Figure 12.3. 7–8).

3. *Cruciform design.* This design is composed of intersecting lines forming a cross (Figure 12.4.1–3). On some pebbles the space between the lines was filled in with additional designs (dots or lines). This category includes plain cross (3a, two crossed lines, Figure 12.5. 1–2) and complex cross (3b, several crossed lines, Figure 12.5. 3).

4. *Radiating/star design.* Here the lines are arranged in a design radiating from the centre of the pebble. The centred design is usually composed of straight or irregular lines, but criss-cross lines also appear (Figure 12.4. 4–6).

5. *Concentric design.* This pattern is composed of several geometric figures, each enclosed within the other (Figure 12.4. 7–8). Concentric

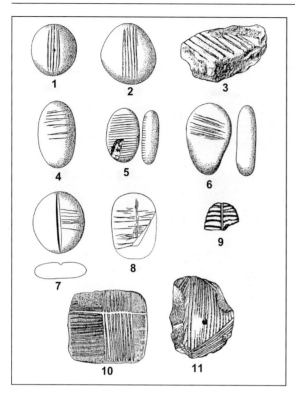

Figure 12.2 *Engraved pebbles with linear designs. 1–2, 4–7. Sha`ar Hagolan; 3. Tell Judaidah (Braidwood and Braidwood 1960: Figure 66. 8); 8. Byblos (Dunand 1973: Figure 102. 30304); 9. Bashan Street (Kaplan 1954: Figure 7. 13); 10. Jilat 7 (Garrard et al. 1994: Figure 10a); 11. Kholetria-Ortos (Fox 1988: Figure 6. 2)*

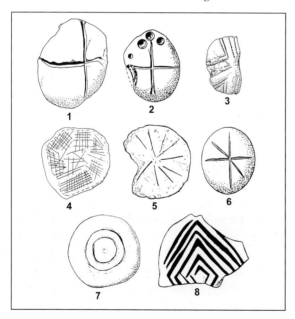

Figure 12.4 *Engraved pebbles with cross, radiating and concentric designs. 1–2, 6–8. Sha`ar Hagolan; 3– 5. Kholetria-Ortos (3: Fox 1988: Figure 6. 1; 5. Simmons and Corona 1993: Figure 7); 4. Ras Shamra (de Contenson 1992: Figure 126. 14)*

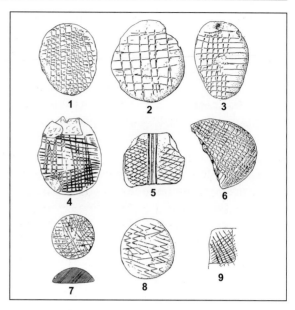

Figure 12.3 *Engraved pebbles with grid designs. 1–3,7. Khirokitia (1–3: Cluzan 1984: Figure 73. 6, 7, 4; 7: Dikaios 1953: Plate CXXXVIII. 1152); 4. Ras Shamra (de Contenson 1992: Figure 126. 13); 5. Sabi Abyad (Collet and Spoor 1996: Figure 7. 7. 16); 6, 8. Kholetria-Ortos (6: Fox 1988: Figure 7. 11; 8: Fox 1988: Figure 7. 1); 9. Munhata (Gopher and Orelle 1995: Figure 44. 10)*

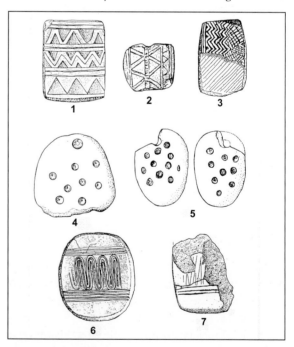

Figure 12.5 *Engraved pebbles with chevron, drilled and combined designs. 1 Sheikh Hassan (Cauvin 1994: Figure 43. 6); 2 Mureybet (Cauvin 1994: Figure 19. 2); 3 Hajji Firuz Tepe (Voigt 1983: Figure 118. 2); 4 Sha`ar Hagolan; 5 Nahal Oren (Noy 1991: Figure 2. 1); 6 Netiv Hagdud (Bar-Yosef and Gopher 1991: frontpage); 7 Ein Suhun (Nadel et al. 2000: Figure 8)*

circles are prevalent in this group, but other geometric figures, such as rectangles or diamonds, appear. The early examples of the concentric diamonds design have been discussed by Beck (1993). While only a few pebbles have been found bearing this design, this pattern is quite popular on prehistoric seals.

6. *Chevrons.* This design is composed of one or more zigzag lines or triangles. The zigzag lines are sometimes bordered by parallel lines. This category includes zigzag lines (6a, Figure 12.5. 3) and chevrons enclosed within lines (6b, Figure 12.5. 1–2).

7. *Drilled design.* This group includes pebbles that are ornamented by drilled depressions rather than by incisions (Figure 12.5. 4–5). Some researchers assume these objects to be anvils, but since this design appears on pendants/weights and on seals, artefacts of this kind may be considered as geometric ornamented pebbles rather than utilitarian objects.

8. *Combined designs and miscellaneous.* This group includes geometric designs that are composed of assorted elements, for example wavy or curved lines between horizontal lines (Figure 12.5. 6–7).

The most common designs are parallel lines and grids. At most sites in the Levant, the linear design is prevalent (for example, at Sha`ar Hagolan, 16 out of 41 pebbles are incised with parallel lines, and 13 bear grid designs). At Khirokitia, like other Cypriot sites, the grid design is prevalent (Figure 12.6).

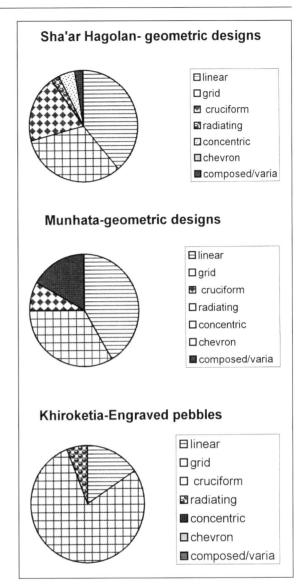

Figure 12.6 *Occurrence of different designs at three sites: Sha`ar Hagolan, Munhata and Khirokitia. Munhata (Gopher and Orelle 1995), Khirokitia (Astruc 1994: Table 11)*

Discussion

Various suggestions have been raised over the years concerning the meaning and function of the pebbles engraved with geometric patterns.

Dikaios (1953: 291), according to an analogy offered by stone stamps from Brak (Mallowan 1947: 40), suggested that at least some of the engraved pebbles from Khirokitia represented models of bread loaves and may have been used as bread stamp seals. Cauvin (1972: 91) agreed that geometric engraved pebbles were used for some kind of stamping and proposed that they were used as textile stamps.

According to Niklasson (1991: 95), who studied the same Khirokitia assemblage as did Dikaios, the significance of conical stones may be more complex, involving interpretations of both functional and symbolic nature (i.e. as seals, weights, models of female breasts or models of buildings). She prefers to see conical stones as models of circular buildings. Cluzan (1984) proposed that some pebbles from Khirokitia were used as gaming pieces.

Another explanation for the use of incised pebbles was a "hot stamp" theory, according to which the pebbles were heated in a fire and then pressed against the skin of young boys in initiation rituals (Bar-Yosef 1989: 38) or were used for branding animals (Lindelfeld pers comm.). However, viewing incised pebbles as branding implements seems to be problematic, since most of the incisions are shallow and thin and most of them could not have created a pattern of scars. Moreover, such pebbles show no signs of burning.

Wreschner (1996) has a theory that the pebbles were used in rain-calling rituals, and that the geometric incisions depict rain falling. This theory is not relevant to the whole range of designs and five types (cross, radiating, concentric, chevron and combined) are not appropriate to his subjective suggestion.

Marshack (1972) sees incised stones as lunar calendars, each incised line recording one appearance of the moon. This refers mostly to incised bones and stones from the European Palaeolithic, but in a separate article (Marshack 1998) he includes an engraved pebble from Jilat 7 (Figure 12.3. 10) in his theory. Marshack's explanation, even if acceptable for this particular pebble, does not seem be applicable to the whole category of finds under consideration, simply because most geometric designs engraved on pebbles consist of finished forms. Most of the designs (for instance crosses or concentric circles) are difficult to see as tallies. Furthermore, most designs seem to have been made with regard to the general shape of the pebble, and it seems that the maker was more interested in the overall result.

Stekelis (1972: 44), and later Gopher and Orrelle (1996: 267), regard the incised pebbles as representations of female pudenda. This explanation applies mostly to whetstones and the geometric symbols engraved on them. Stekelis sees in the whetstone incisions (type 1d in present typology) depictions of pubic hair, whereas Gopher and Orrelle proposed that these indicate women at different ages and reproductive stages, the grid designs indicating the childbearing history of women. For a rejection of these theories, see Garfinkel (1999a).

From the relatively very small quantity of engraved pebbles from each site proportional to other artefacts, and from the variety of incisions, it appears that these pebbles must be more than simple utilitarian objects. An explanation of the phenomenon of geometric incised pebbles throughout the Near East must consider a combination of symbolic and functional aspects.

In our estimation, most of the above explanations fit only some cases of the incised pebbles and do not explain the whole group. I propose that a better understanding of the whole phenomenon and its significance can be accomplished by comparing the engraved pebbles with another group of artefacts, the earliest seals. Dikaios (1953: 291), Cauvin (1972: 91, footnote) and Garfinkel (1992: 170) have already pointed out that geometric designs on pebbles resemble the designs on the earliest seals appearing in the Near East (around the Neolithic period). But these scholars have not investigated whether a functional connection exists between these two categories of finds. Understanding this issue may help us to solve the enigma of geometric signs on pebbles, and o reach some new conclusions regarding their significance and function.

The first seals appeared in the PPNB, in the 10th millennium BP (Tsuneki 1983; von Wickede 1990).[2] They are made of baked clay or stone and bear incised ornaments in a great variety of geometric shapes. The dominant form is flat-faced: a round (or elliptical) base with a conical or rounded apex (sometimes pierced) as a handle. These seals appeared at such Neolithic sites as: Jarmo (Broman Morales 1983: Figure 170. 1), Jericho (Kenyon and Holland 1982: Figure 227. 1), Ras Shamra (de Contenson 1992: Figures 125. 14-16; 126.1; 133.15–19; 140.12–17), Byblos (Dunand 1973: Figures 48, 49, 51, 52; Plates 115, 118), Tell al-Judaidah (Braidwood and Braidwood 1960: Plates 15–17, 20, 22), Çatal Höyük (Mellaart 1967: Figure 41. 6, 9), Tell Hassuna (Lloyd and Safar 1945: Figure 11. 2), Bouqras (Akkermans *et al.* 1981: Figure 11; Plate 42), Sabi Abyad (Duistermaat 1996: Figure 5. 1) and Mattarah (Braidwood *et al.*: 1952: Figure 20. 10). The prehistoric seals have been studied and classified by different scholars: Tsuneki (1983), Buchanan and Moorey (1984) and von Wickede (1990).

The similarity between the designs engraved on both groups (seals and pebbles) is immediately apparent. All seven groups of geometric designs that appear on pebbles have parallels in patterns found on seals (Figures 12.7–10). Not

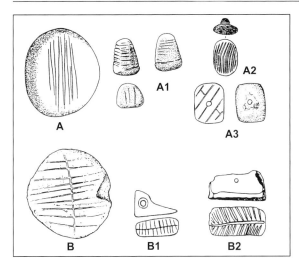

Figure 12.7 *Seals and pebbles: linear designs. A. Sha'ar Hagolan; A1. Hatoula (Lechevallier and Ronen 1994: Figure 2); A2. Byblos (Dunand 1973: Figure 49. 32145); A3. Mattarah (Braidwood et al. 1952: Figure 20. 10); B. Kholetria-Ortos (Simmons 1996: Figure 2. 1); B1. Byblos (Dunand 1973: Figure 52. 33119); B2. Ras Shamra (Schaeffer 1962: Figure 74)*

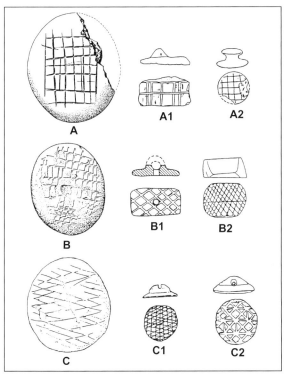

Figure 12.8 *Seals and pebbles: grid designs. A. Sha'ar Hagolan; A1. Qminas (Masuda and Sha'ath 1983: Figure 8. 17); A2. Byblos (Dunand 1973: Figure 75. 22759); B. Khirokitia (Astruc 1994: Figure 96. 3); B1. Hassuna (Lloyd and Safar 1945: Plate 11. 2); B2. Byblos (Dunand 1973: Figure 111. 26540); C. Kholetria-Ortos (Fox 1988: Figure 7. 1); C1. Sabi Abyad (Duistermaat 1996: Figure 5. 1. 1); C2. Tell Judeidah (Braidwood and Braidwood 1960: Figure 68. 2)*

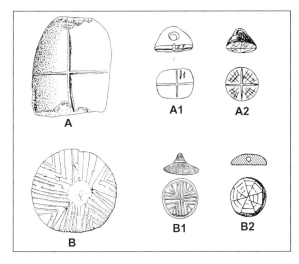

Figure 12.9 *Seals and pebbles: cross and radiating designs. A. Sha'ar Hagolan; A1. Ras Shamra (de Contenson 1992: Figure 125. 14); A2. Arpachiyah (Mallowan and Rose 1935: Figure 50. 18); B. Khirokitia (Cluzan 1984: Figure 73. 3); B1. Byblos (Dunand 1973: Figure 76. 29564), B2. Arpachiyah (Mallowan and Rose 1935: Figure 50. 18)*

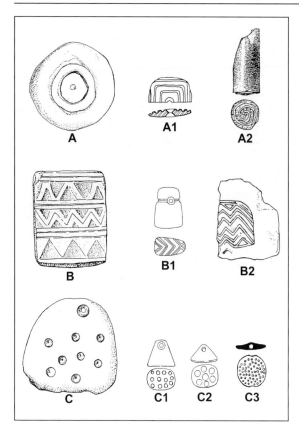

Figure 12.10 *Seals and pebbles: concentric, chevron and drilled designs. A. Sha`ar Hagolan; A1. Bouqras (de Contenson 1985:, Figure 19. 11) ; A2. (Broman Morales 1983: Figure 170. 1); B. Sheikh Hassan (Cauvin 1994: Figure 43. 6); B1. Bouqras (de Contenson 1985: Figure 19. 3); B2. Bouqras (Akkermans et al. 1982: Figure 11. 11); C. Sha`ar Hagolan; C1–3. Byblos (Dunand 1973: Figure 110. 34862, 30370, 32482)*

only do the seals bear the same types of geometric designs, but the first seals that appeared in the Near East generally bear mostly geometric symbols that are parallel to those found on engraved pebbles.

The following chronology is particularly worth noting: the pebbles appeared first, and after a period of coexistence with seals, they disappeared and seals became widespread. As mentioned above, incised pebbles initially appeared in the Near East at the end of the Palaeolithic period, and disappeared after the Neolithic period, the climax being the sixth millennium BC. Seals, on the other hand, started to appear during the Neolithic period. As noted above, the

earliest seals can be attributed to the late Pre-Pottery Neolithic, and they began to be popular after the Neolithic era. Three stages of pebble/seal appearance can be distinguished:

1. Palaeolithic period (42,000–10,200 BP). Exclusive appearance of pebbles in various scattered sites.
2. Neolithic and Early Chalcolithic (10,200–6,000 BP). Coexistence of pebbles and seals. While pebbles were prevalent, seals first appeared then and they began to be widespread throughout the sites.
3. Late Chalcolithic and following periods (post 6,000 BP). Exclusive appearance of seals. Seals were prevalent, while pebbles had disappeared from archaeological complexes.

In some cases, seals and pebbles were found in the same context, though usually not in equal numbers. At sites where engraved pebbles appeared in large numbers, only a few seals were unearthed, and vice versa. For example, at Sha`ar Hagolan around 40 engraved pebbles and only two seals were found, and from Ras Shamra over a dozen seals and only few incised pebbles were reported.

From both the chronological and symbolic points of view, it seems that the pebbles can be considered the predecessors of the seals, or even as proto-seals. Pebbles were invented first, and after a period of coexistence seals replaced them. The similarity of patterns on seals and pebbles points to a similarity of symbols and social function between the two.

This point makes even more significant the appearance of hybrid types between seals and pebbles, such as the mushroom-shaped stones found at Khirokitia. Dikaios (1953: 291) calls them "en champignon." These objects are made of similar stone, are similar in size to engraved pebbles and have the same geometric patterns; the only difference is their shape. The mushroom shape resembles that of seals, and conical stones that appear at the same site seem to be a link between seals and engraved pebbles. It is worth noting that at Khirokitia, out of 106 incised pebbles only 7 are of the mushroom type.[3] This proportion is similar to the proportions between seals and pebbles at sites where pebbles are prevalent. A similar pebble of hybrid type appeared at the Late Natufian site of Hatula (Figure 12.8. A1).

At Jerf el-Ahmar geometric signs on similar pebbles were sometimes found with pictograms depicting different animals like serpents, scorpions and whole scenes. According to the excavators, these scenes were intended to transmit a global message, showing the ability of the inhabitants to register messages in the form of pictograms (Stordeur 1988, 1998). Geometric incisions appear on the reverse of these scenes and could have served as the indicator of the message.

At this stage it is difficult to establish whether these artefacts were actually used as seals or were simply identifying symbols. Whatever the function of incised pebbles, it seems that it was later taken over by seals. Although no traces of clay were found in the incisions (Le Brun 1984: 123) and no clay bullae have been found that correspond with the incised pebbles, this evidence does not prove that the incised pebbles were not used for sealing. The same situation exists with the first seals: the earliest evidence of the actual use of seals is the discovery of bullas in burnt levels of Sabi Abyad (Duistermaat 1996) in the eighth millennium BP. At many earlier sites seals lacked any correspondence with clay sealing, but they were designated as seals by the application of form/function analysis and by analogy with later bullae. The strong parallel between seals and engraved pebbles may lead us to a possible interpretation of the meaning of the geometric incisions appearing on both groups of artefacts.

One common use of seals is to mark ownership and to indicate personal property (see, for example, Esin 1994: 79). From the very beginning, seals were used for marking and closing various containers (for detailed description of different ways using prehistoric seals see, for example, von Wickede (1990: 29–37). Traces of sealings were recovered at some Neolithic sites, such as Sabi Abyad, where more than 300 sealings made by 67 different seals were found (Duistermat 1996); other examples come from Bouqras (Akkermans *et al.* 1981) and Arpachiyah (Mallowan and Rose 1935). Stamping the goods and sealing them claimed both ownership and control of the goods. As indications of ownership, geometric patterns on seals possibly represented specific units in society (e.g. a person, a family, or some distinguishable group).

A number of scholars who have discussed similar incisions, for example Stewart and Rupp (this volume) and Schmandt-Besserat (1992) in her research on tokens, claim that these markings refer not to ownership but rather to the number of items in an invoice, the place of origin of goods being traded, or the quality of a commodity. This assumption seems to be doubtful because the same geometric patterns appear on pendants or amulets. Such pendants/seals were found at many Halaf sites, such as Arpachiyah (Mallowan and Rose 1935: Figure 50), Yarimtepe II (Merpert and Munchaev 1987: Figure 13. 4, 8), Tepe Gawra (Tobler 1950: Plates 172–173) and Chagar Bazar (Mallowan 1936: Figure 7. 4, 12, 33). These kinds of artefacts were supposedly worn on clothing, so it is likely that symbols on them indicate private ownership, as opposed to the quality of goods.

The archaeological context of some of the geometric engraved pebbles further supports this assumption. At Khirokitia, the engraved pebbles found in burials had all been buried with adults of both sexes. Each burial yielded only a single pebble, though in one instance an incised pebble and a conical stone with the same pattern were found together (tholos XIX) (Dikaios 1953; Niklasson 1991: 95). At Sha`ar Hagolan two excavated buildings each yielded an incised pebble, each with its own pattern (Figure 12.11): in Building I, a cross pattern and in Building II, a vertical line. Each pebble was discovered on the living floor of one of the storage rooms of the house (Garfinkel 1999b: 88). This could well serve as an indication of two distinct and separate units (households, persons, etc.).

The archaeological evidence indicates the importance of these items, which are very rarely found in large numbers in excavations. In the excavation of Sha`ar Hagolan, for instance, more than 86 clay and pebble figurines and only 3 engraved pebbles were unearthed (Garfinkel 2001).

Unfortunately in most cases, incised pebbles are published without their archaeological context, though the context could provide valuable information for understanding how these objects might have been used. Nevertheless, the few cases of known archaeological contexts give an indication of the importance of incised pebbles, thought they cannot point to any symbolic context. At Netiv Hagdud an incised

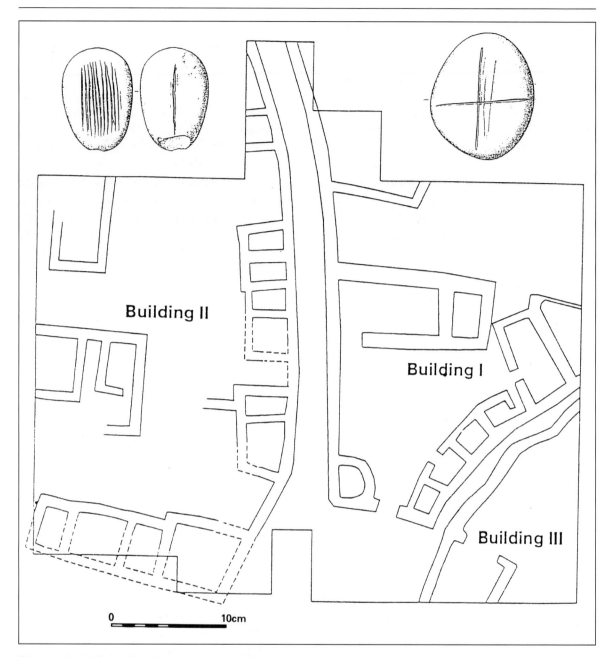

Figure 12.11 *Sha`ar Hagolan: engraved pebbles in two buildings*

pebble was found in a cache of several stone implements (shaft straighteners and a few polished pebbles) under a floor (Bar-Yosef and Gopher 1997: 51). At Ein Suhun a pebble shows traces of intentional breakage (Nadel *et al.* 2000).

In the Neolithic period the greatest numbers of pebbles occur in large, fully sedentary, agricultural communities. Large numbers of engraved pebbles were found at two megasites: Khirokitia (the largest Neolithic site on Cyprus) and Sha`ar Hagolan, the largest Neolithic site in

the Levant, comprising *ca.* 20 hectares according to survey results (Miller 2001).

The above observation makes it clear that geometric incisions were in fact an early code-system of lines that provided some kind of encoded information about the owners. Each pattern carried a unique meaning; the information was specific and intelligible to other members of the community and, eventually, to outsiders. This explains the occurrence of symbols that are similar (but not identical) at various sites in the Near East. For example, all the grid-engraved pebbles of Khiroki-tia differ in number of lines, size of squares, and the position of the grid on the pebble. The fact that similar objects with similar symbols appeared throughout the Levant supports the suggestion that peoples in this area shared a common symbolic world or had common origins. The geometric symbols found on pebbles on Cyprus may be remnants of an initial settlement and may indicate the possible origins of a founding population.

That geometric incisions served as a system of encoding information about private entities is also shown by the appearance of similar incisions on "complex tokens," clay objects that according to Schmandt-Besserat (1992) were used as counters to keep records of goods.

The appearance and distribution of engraved pebbles accompanied changes that took place in human society of the Near East. A sedentary way of life emerged in the Early Natufian period, and during the Pre-Pottery Neolithic we see for the first time the appearance of large agricultural communities (Belfer-Cohen and Bar-Yosef 2000). The transition from a nomadic hunter-gatherer socioeconomic system to that of sedentary early agriculturists involved more than a change in the way that food was accumulated. This change affected the fundamental basis of society and marked the recognition of persons/individuals within the new society. Social change appears to have accompanied the transition to a sedentary way of life. One of the aspects of being settled in one place is the accumulation of personal property. The ownership of personal property gives rise to a need for self-definition of individual units of society and for marking one's own goods to divide me/mine from all/everybody's.

The appearance of geometrically ornamented pebbles and seals thus accompanied social transformation. In fact, stages of pebble/seal distribution can be seen as corresponding to the development of society, in the stages of social evolution proposed by Service (1962). For further comments see, for example, Renfrew, (1984) and Flannery (1972; 1995).

1. The first occurrence engraved pebbles can be found within late hunter-gatherer bands that lacked marked economic differences and had open and shared food storage. The end of this stage, however, in the Natufian and

early PPNA periods was characterized by the rise of sedentary life and the appearance of permanent settlements. The institution of permanent structures as a living environment divided members of society from each other and created unit privacy. Such privacy, made universally possible by dwellings, provided both protection and concealment for people and their property (Wilson 1988: 99). This allowed the accumulation of private property even within a close-knit community and created a need for marking symbols. The consistent appearance of engraved pebbles after the Natufian period coincided with the beginning of sedentary life and all its consequent processes.

2. Pebbles and seals appeared together within communities of settled farmers whose economy was based on agriculture. Permanent settlements, villages and a permanent food supply based on agriculture/animal domestication encouraged property accumulation. At this stage, the individual household became the basic unit of production and each such house had its own storage facilities. Consequently, the self-definition and distinction of such units from other similar units within society increased.

3. Seals characterized a far more developed and formalized society, based on the principle of ranking–the social and property differentiation of members. Such societies completed the process of differentiation of personal property accumulation and social units. In a hierarchical society, the need not only for privacy markers but also for status symbols increased. Therefore, it seems that seals, in addition to serving as identity symbols, became markers of rank and authority in a newly developed society, replacing relatively simple markers like engraved pebbles.

As society changed, so may the function and meaning of these markers have evolved. Doubtless the social context of Early Neolithic society was drastically different from that of the Late Chalcolithic. According to these changes, the social meaning of the artefacts may also have changed. Nevertheless, I wish to emphasize the observable cultural continuity between these phenomena. On this assumption, we can assume that the roots of property/identity started to appear in the Natufian period and developed during the Neolithic. Institutional social inequality is also reflected by other archaeological finds at any given site: houses of different size, the appearance of rare and/or costly materials (Price 1995: 104). With the development of society and personal property came an increase in the need for identifying markers such as pebbles, until they were replaced by seals.

Conclusions

1. Geometric engraved pebbles are common phenomena in the Late Prehistoric Middle East. They became widespread on Cyprus as well as on the mainland, so demonstrating that the inhabitants of Neolithic Cyprus shared a common symbolic world with the mainland.

2. Engraved pebbles are strongly connected with the earliest seals. The connection is reflected in the similarity of geometric patterns on both, the chronological and spatial overlapping of the two and the appearance of hybrid types between seals and incised pebbles.

3. This connection leads us to the conclusion that the symbols on pebbles and seals alike represented individual units (persons or families) and were a symbol of identity.

4. Geometric incised pebbles played a specific social role and accompanied the process of transition to the new way of life, until they were totally replaced by seals.

Acknowledgments

My deepest gratitude to Dr. Y. Garfinkel, who provided invaluable support and inspiration at every step of this research and this article, from its inception to its publication. My thanks to the Institute of Archaeology of the Hebrew University of Jerusalem and to the Organization of the Neolithic Conference on Cyprus for its financial support and for enabling the publication of this article. My deep appreciation to Z. Matzkevich for listening and support. Technical support was provided by S. Halbreich for the figures and J. Rosenberg for the map.

Notes

1   It is sometimes difficult to determine the date of pebbles, especially those found in multi-layered sites.

2   Although T. Noy presented one stamp seal that came from the Natufian period of Kebara Cave (1978b:, Figure 1), this stamp was a surface find and its date is uncertain.

3   It worth noting that incised pebbles with a U-shaped depression on the reverse (non-engraved) occur at Parekklisha-Shillourokambos (Jean Guilaine, pers. com.). Seals of similar shape (a deep depression on the reverse) appear at the same site and other Cypriot sites (for example, at Kholetria-*Ortos*: Simmons and Corona, pers. com).

References

Akkermans, P. A., H. Fokkens and H. T. Waterbolk 1981
    Stratigraphy, Architecture and Layout of Bouqras. Pp. 485–501 in J. Cauvin and P. Sanlaville (eds.) *Préhistoire du Levant.* Éditions du CNRS: Paris.

Akkermans, P. A., M. N. van Loon, J. J. Rodenberg, and H. T. Waterbolk 1982
    The 1976–1977 Excavations at Tell Bouqras. *Annales d'Archéologique Arabes Syrienne* 32: 45–57.

Astruc, L. 1994
    L'outillage en pierre non taillée et les petits objets. Pp. 215–289 in A. Le Brun (ed.) *Fouilles récentes à Khirokitia (Chypre) 1988–1991.* Éditions Recherche sur les Civilisations: Paris.

Bader, N. O. 1982
    Nektorie rezultati rabot na rannezemledelcheskom poselenii Kultepe v severnom Irake. Pp. 50–58 in N. Y. Merpert (ed.) *Archeologia Starogo I Novogo Sveta.* Akademia Nauk: Moskva. (Rus.).

Bader, N. O. 1993
    The Early Agricultural Settlement of Tell Sotto. Pp. 41–58 in N. Yoffee and J. J. Clark (eds.) *Early Stages in the Evolution of Mesopotamian Civilization.* University of Arizona Press: Tucson and London.

Bar-Yosef, O. 1989
    The Neolithic Period. Pp. 10–39 in A. Ben-Tor (ed.) *Introduction to Archaeology of Eretz Israel in the Biblical Period.* Open University: Tel Aviv (Hebrew).

Bar-Yosef, O. and F. R. Valla (eds.) 1991
    The Natufian Culture in the Levant. International Monograph in Prehistory Archaeology Series 1: Ann Arbor, Michigan.

Bar-Yosef, O. and A. Gopher (eds.) 1997
    An Early Neolithic Village in the Jordan Valley. Part I: The Archaeology of Netiv Hagdud. American School of Prehistoric Research 43. Peabody Museum of Archaeology and Ethnology: Cambridge, Mass.

Bar-Yosef, O. and R. H. Meadow 1995
The Origins of Agriculture in the Near East. Pp. 39–94 in T. D. Price and A. B. Gebauer (eds.) *Last Hunters First Farmers: New Perspectives on the Prehistoric Transition to Agriculture*. School of American Research Press: Santa Fe, New Mexico.

Beck, P. 1993
A Note on a Neolithic Stamp Seal from Sha'ar Hagolan. *Mitekufat Ha'even* 25: 189–191 (Heb.).

Beile-Bohn, M., C. Gerber, M. Morsch and K. Schmidt 1998
Neolithische Forschungen in Obermesopotamien. Gürcütepe und Göbekli Tepe. *Istanbuler Mitteilungen* 48: 5–78.

Belfer-Cohen, A., and O. Bar-Yosef 2000
Early Sedentism in the Near East: A Bumpy Ride to Village Life. Pp. 19–38 in I. Kuijt (ed.) *Life in Neolithic Farming Communities*. Kluwer Academic Press: New York.

Blackham, M. 1999
Tulaylat Ghassul: An Appraisal of Robert North's Excavation (1959–60). *Levant* 31: 19–64.

Braidwood, R. J. and L. S. Braidwood 1960
Excavations in the Plain of Antioch, I. Oriental Institute Publications 61. University of Chicago Press: Chicago.

Braidwood, R. J., L. S. Braidwood, J. G. Smith and C. Leslie 1952
Mattarah: A Southern Variant of the Hassuna Assemblage, Excavated in 1948. *Journal of Near Eastern Studies* 11: 1–75.

Braun, E. 1994
Yiftah'el. Israel Antiquities Authority Report No. 2: Jerusalem.

Broman Morales, V. 1983
Jarmo Figurines and Other Clay Objects. Pp. 369 in L. S. Braidwood, R. J. Braidwood, B. Howe, C. A. Reed and P. J. Watson (eds.) *Prehistoric Archaeology along the Zagros Flanks*. The Oriental Institute Publications 105. University of Chicago Press: Chicago.

Buchanan, B. and P. R. S. Moorey 1984
Catalogue of Ancient Near Eastern Seals in the Ashmolean Museum II: The Prehistoric Stamp Seals. Clarendon Press: Oxford.

Burian, F. and E. Fridman 1973
Prehistoric Hunters in Halutza Dunes. *Mitekufat Ha'even* 11: 27–34 (Heb.).

Cauvin, J. 1972
Religions Néolithiques de Syro-Palestine. Maisonneuve: Paris.

Cauvin, J. 1994
Naissance des Divinités Naissance de l'Agriculture. La Révolution des Symboles au Néolithique. Éditions du CNRS: Paris.

Cauvin, J., O. Aurenche, M. -C. Cauvin and N. Balkan-Atli 1999
The Prepottery Site of Cafer Höyük. Pp. 87–103 in M. Özdogan and N. Basgelen (eds.) *Neolithic in Turkey*. Ancient Anatolian Civilization Series: 3.

Arkeoloji ve Sanat Yayainlari: Istanbul.

Cluzan, S. 1984
L'outillage et les petits objects en pierre. Pp. 111–124 in Le Brun 1984.

Collet, P. and R. N. Spoor 1996
The Ground Stone Industry. Pp. 415–438 in P. M. M. G. Akkermans (ed.) *Tell Sabi Abyad, the Late Neolithic Settlement*. Nederlands Historisch-Archaeologisch Instituut: Istanbul.

Contenson, H. de 1970
Sondage Ouvert en 1962 sur l'Acropole de Ras Shamra, Rapport Préliminare sur les Résultats Obtenus de 1962 à 1968. *Syria* 47: 1–23.

Contenson, H. de 1985
La Campagne de 1965 à Bouqras. *Cahiers de l'Euphrate* 4: 335–371.

Contenson, H. de (ed.) 1992
Préhistoire de Ras Shamra: 1. Éditions Recherche sur les Civilisations: Paris.

Contenson, H. de 1995
Aswad et Choraife, Sites Néolithiques en Damascène (Syrie) aux VIII et VII milléniaires avant l'ère chrétienne. Institut Français d'Archéologie du Proche Orient: Beyrouth and Paris.

Contenson, H. de 2000
Ramad- Site Néolithique en Damascène (Syrie) aux VIII et VII milléniaires avant l'ère chrétienne. Institut Français d'Archéologie du Proche Orient: Beyrouth.

Coqueugniot, E. 1998
Dja'de el Mughara (Moyen-Euphrate), un village néolithique dans son environnement naturel à la veille de la domestication. Pp. 109–114 in M. Fortin and O. Aurenche (eds.) *Espace Naturel, Espace Habité en Syrie du Nord (10è-2è millénaires av. J.-C*. Canadian Society for Mesopotamian Studies Bull. 33/ Publications de la Maison de l'Orient (TMO 28): Toronto/Lyon.

Crabtree, P. J., P. V. Campana, A. Belfer-Cohen and D. E. Bar-Yosef 1991
First Results of the Excavations at Salibiya I, Lower Jordan Valley in the Natufian Culture. Pp. 161–172 in Bar-Yosef and Valla 1991.

Davis, M. K. 1982
The Çayönü Ground Stone. Pp. 73–175 in R. J. Braidwood and L. S. Braidwood (eds.) *Prehistoric Village Archaeology in South-Eastern Turkey*. British Archaeological Reports, International Series 138: Oxford.

Dikaios, P. 1953
Khirokitia. Oxford University Press: Oxford.

Dornemann, R. H. 1986
A Neolithic Village at Tell El Kowm in the Syrian Desert. Studies in Ancient Oriental Civilizations 43. Oriental Institute Publications: Chicago.

Duistermaat, K. 1996
The Seals and Sealings. Pp. 339–401 in P. M. M. G. Akkermans (ed.) *Tell Sabi Abyad, the Late Neolithic Settlement*. Nederlands Historisch–Archaeologisch Instituut: Istanbul.

Dunand, M. 1973
  Fouilles de Byblos V. Maisonneuve: Paris.
Edwards, P. C. 1991
  Wadi Hammeh 27: An Early Natufian Site at
  Pella, Jordan. Pp. 123–149 in Bar-Yosef and Valla
  1991.
Esin, U. 1994
  The Functional Evidence of Seals and Sealings of
  Degirmentepe. Pp. 59-86 in P. Feroli, E. Fiandra,
  G. G. Fissore and M. Frangipane (eds.) *Archives
  before Writing.* Proceedings of the International
  Colloquium Oriolo Romano, October 23–25, 1991.
  Scriptorium: Rome.
Flannery, K. V. 1972
  The Origins of the Village as a Settlement Type in
  Mesoamerica and the Near East: a comparative
  study. Pp. 23–55 in P. J. Ucko, R. Tringham and G.
  W. Dimbleby (eds.) *Man, Settlement and Urbanism.*
  Duckworth: London.
Flannery, K. V. 1995
  Prehistoric Social Evolution. Pp. 3–25 in C. R.
  Ember and M. Ember (eds.) *Research Frontiers in
  Anthropology.* Prentice-Hall: Englewood Cliffs,
  New Jersey.
Fox, W. A. 1988
  Kholetria-*Ortos*: A Khirokitia Culture Settlement
  in Paphos District. *Report of the Department of
  Antiquities, Cyprus:* 29–43.
Fugmann, E. 1958
  *Hama: Fouilles et Recherches 1931–1938 II.1 : L'archi-
  tecture des périodes pré-héllenistiques.* National-
  museet: Copenhague.
Galili, E., M. Weinstein-Evron and I. Hershkovitz,
  1993
  A Prehistoric Site on the Sea Floor of the Israeli
  Coast. *Journal of Field Archaeology* 20: 133–158.
Garfinkel, Y. 1992
  *The Material Culture of the Central Jordan Valley in
  the Pottery Neolithic and Early Chalcolithic Periods.*
  Unpublished Ph.D. dissertation, The Hebrew
  University: Jerusalem. (Heb).
Garfinkel, Y. 1993a
  Tel 'Ali. Pp. 53–55 in E. Stern (ed.) *The New Ency-
  clopedia of Archaeological Excavation in the Holy
  Land.* Israel Exploration Society and Carta:
  Jerusalem.
Garfinkel, Y. 1993b
  The Yarmukian Culture in Israel. *Paléorient* 19/1:
  115–134.
Garfinkel, Y. 1999a
  Facts, Fictions and Yarmukian Figurines. *Cam-
  bridge Archaeological Journal* 9(1): 130–132.
Garfinkel, Y. 1999b
  The Yarmukian– Neolithic Art from Sha'ar Hagolan.
  Bible Lands Museum: Jerusalem.
Garfinkel, Y. 2001
  The Neolithic Art Assemblage from Sha'ar
  Hagolan. Pp. 47–61 in A. M. Maeir and E. Baruch
  (eds.) *Settlement, Civilization and Culture.* Proceed-
  ings of the Conference in Memory of David Alon.

Bar-Ilan University Press: Ramat-Gan. (Heb)
Garrard, A., D. Baird, S. Colledge, L. Martin and K.
  Wright 1994
  Prehistoric Environment and Settlement in the
  Azraq Basin. *Levant* 26: 73–109.
Gopher, A. and E. Orrelle 1995
  The Ground Stone Tool Assemblage of Munhata. Les
  Cahiers des Missions Archéologiques Françaises
  en Israël 7: Paris.
Gopher, A. and E. Orrelle 1996
  Another Interpretation of Material Imagery of the
  Yarmukians. *Cambridge Archaeological Journal* 6(2):
  255–279.
Hole, F., K. Flannery and J. A. Neely 1969
  *Prehistory and Human Ecology of the Deh Luran
  Plain. An Early Village Sequence from Khuzistan.*
  Memoirs of the Museum of Anthropology 1. Uni-
  versity of Michigan: Ann Arbor, Michigan.
Hovers, E. 1990
  Art in the Levantine Epi-Paleolithic: An Engraved
  Pebble from a Kebaran Site in the Lower Jordan
  Valley. *Current Anthropology* 31(3): 317–322.
Kaplan, J. 1954
  *The Neolithic and Chalcolithic Settlement in Tel Aviv
  and Neighborhood.* Unpublished Ph.D. disserta-
  tion, The Hebrew University: Jerusalem. (Heb).
Kenyon, K. and T. Holland, 1982
  *Excavation at Jericho, Vol. IV: The Pottery Type Series
  and Other Finds.* British School of Archaeology in
  Jerusalem: London.
Le Brun, A. (ed.) 1984
  Fouilles récentes à Khirokitia (Chypre) 1977–1981.
  Éditions Recherche sur les Civilisations: Paris.
Lechevallier, M. 1978
  *Abou Gosh et Beisamoun, deux gisements du VIIe mil-
  lénaire avant l'ére chrétienne en Israel.* Association
  Paléorient: Paris.
Lechevallier, M. and A. Ronen 1994
  Le Gisement de Hatoula en Judée Occidentale, Israël.
  Association Paléorient: Paris.
Lloyd, S., and F. Safar 1945
  Tell Hassuna. *Journal of Near Eastern Studies* IV(4):
  255–248.
Mallowan, M. E. L. 1936
  The Excavations at Tell Chagar Bazar, and an
  Archaeological Survey of the Habur Region. *Iraq*
  3: 1–86.
Mallowan, M. E. L. 1947
  Excavations at Brak and Chagar Bazar. *Iraq* 9:
  1–259.
Mallowan, M. E. L. and J. C. Rose 1935
  Excavations at Tell Arpachiyah. *Iraq* 2: 1–178.
Marshack, A. 1972
  Roots of Civilization. McGraw Hill: New York.
Marshack, A. 1998
  Space and Time in Pre-Agricultural Europe and
  the Near East, the Evidence for Early Structural
  Complexity. Pp. 19–63 in M. Hudson and B. A.
  Levine (eds.) *Urbanization and Land Ownership in
  the Ancient Near East.* Series by the International

Scholars Conference on Ancient Near East Economics Vol. II. Peabody Museum of Archaeology and Ethnology: Cambridge.

Masuda, S. and S. Sha'ath 1983
Qminas. *Annales d'Archéologique Arabes Syrienne* 33: 1–56.

Matthews, R. 2000
The Early Prehistory of Mesopotamia. *Subartu V.* Brepols: Turhout.

McNicol, A., R. H. Smith and B. Hennessy 1982
An Interim Report on the Joint University of Sydney and the College of Wooster Excavation at Pella. Australian National Gallery: Sydney.

Mellaart, J. 1967
Çatal Hüyük. A Neolithic Town in Anatolia. Thames and Hudson: London.

Merpert, N. Y. and R. M. Munchaev 1987
The Earliest Levels at Yarim Tepe I and Yarim Tepe II in Northern Iraq. *Iraq* 49: 1–36.

Miller, M. 2001
Archaeological Survey in Sha'ar Hagolan. Pp. 35–46 in Y. Garfinkel and M. Miller (eds.) *Sha'ar Hagolan: The Neolithic Art in Context.* Oxbow: Oxford.

Moore, A. M. T., G. C. Hillman and A. J. Legge 2000
Village on the Euphrates, from Foraging to Farming at Abu Hureyra. Oxford University Press: Oxford.

Nadel, D., A. Tsatskin, A. Zertal and T. Simmons 2000
Ein Suhum—a PPNA/B Settlement in Eastern Samarian Hills. *Mitekufat Haeven* 30: 73–88 (Heb).

Niklasson, K. 1991
Early Prehistoric Burials in Cyprus. Studies in Mediterranean Archaeology 96. Paul Åströms: Jonsered.

Nissen, H. J., M. Muheisen, and H. G. Gebel 1991
Report of the Excavation at Basta 1988. *Annual of the Department of Antiquities of Jordan* 35: 13–40.

Noy, T. 1978a
Two Large Stone Pendants from the Haluza Dunes. *Israel Museum News* 13: 109–111.

Noy, T. 1978b
Two Natufian Objects from Kebara Cave. *Israel Museum News* 13: 111–113.

Noy, T. 1991
Art and Decoration of the Natufian at Nahal Oren. Pp. 557–569 in Bar-Yosef and Valla 1991.

Perrot, J. 1966
Le Gisement Natoufien de Mallaha (Eynan), Israël. *L'Anthropologie* 70: 437–484.

Price, D. T. 1995
Social Inequality at the Origins of Agriculture. Pp. 129–155 in D. T. Price and G. M. Feinman (eds.) *Foundations of Social Inequality.* Plenum Press: New York and London.

Quadi, N. 2000
The Ground Stone Industry. Pp. 155–184 in Z. A. Kafafi (ed.) *Jebel Abu Thawwab (Er-Rumman), Central Jordan.* Bibliotheca Neolithica Asiae Meridionalis et Occidentalis and Yarmouk University, Monograph of the Institute of

Archaeology and Anthropology 3: Berlin.

Rashwalb, A. F. 1981
Protohistory in the Wadi Chazeh: A Typological and Technological study based on the McDonald excavations. Unpublished Ph.D. dissertation. University of London: London.

Renfrew, C. 1984
Approaches to Social Archaeology. Edinburgh University Press: Edinburgh.

Rollefson, G. O., Z. A. Kafafi, and A. H. Simmons 1991
The Neolithic Village at 'Ain Ghazal, Jordan. *Bulletin of the American School of Oriental Research* 27: 95–116.

Rollefson, G. O. and A. H. Simmons 1986
The 1985 Season at 'Ain Ghazal: Preliminary Report. *Annual of the Department of Antiquities of Jordan* 30: 89–126.

Schaeffer, C. F. A. 1962
Mission de Ras Shamra XV, Ugaritica IV. P. Geuthner: Paris.

Schmandt-Besserat, D. 1992
Before Writing: From Counting to Cuneiform, A Catalogue of Near Eastern Tokens. University of Texas Press: Austin.

Schroeder, B. 1991
Natufian in the Central Beqaa Valley, Lebanon. Pp. 43–80 in Bar-Yosef and Valla 1991.

Service, E. R. 1962
Primitive Social Organization. W. W. Norton: New York.

Simmons, A. H. 1996
Preliminary Report on Multidisciplinary Investigation at Neolithic Kholetria-*Ortos. Report of the Department of Antiquities, Cyprus:* 29–41.

Simmons, A. H. and R. F. Corona 1993
Test Excavations at Kholetria-*Ortos,* a Neolithic Settlement near Paphos. *Report of the Department of Antiquities, Cyprus:* 1–10.

Singh, P. 1974
Neolithic Cultures of Western Asia. Seminar Press: London and New York.

Stekelis, M. 1972
The Yarmukian Culture of the Neolithic Period. Magness Press: Jerusalem.

Stordeur, D. 1989
El Kowm 2 Caracol et le PPNB. *Paléorient* 15/1: 102–110.

Stordeur, D. 1988
Jerf el Ahmar et l'horizon PPNA en Haute Mesopotamie: Xe-IXe millenaire avant J. C. *Subartu* IV/1: 13–29.

Stordeur, D. 1998
Jerf el Ahmar. Pp. 93–107 in M. Fortin and O. Aurenche (eds.) *Espace Naturel, Espace Habité en Syrie du Nord (10è- 2è millénaires J. C.).* Maison de L'Orient Méditerranéen: Lyon.

Tobler, A. J. 1950
Exavations at Tepe Gawra II. University of Pennsylvania Press: Philadelphia.

Tsuneki, A. 1983

Some Notes on the Neolithic Stamp Seals in Western Asia. *Bulletin of the Ancient Orient Museum* 5: 153–173.

Voigt, M. 1983
Haji Firuz Tepe, Iran: The Neolithic Settlement. University Museum Monographs: University of Pennsylvania.

Von Wickede, A. 1990
Prähistorische Stempelglyptik in Vorderasien. Profil-verl: München.

Wilson, P. J. 1988
The Domestication of the Human Species. Yale University Press: New Haven and London.

Wreschner, E. E. 1976
The Potential Significance of the Pebbles with Incisions and Cupmarks from the Yarmukian of Sha'ar Hagolan, Israel. *Bulletin de la societé royale belge d'Anthropologie et de Préhistoire* 87 : 157–165.

13

Tools and toys or traces of trade: the problem of the enigmatic incised objects from Cyprus and the Levant

Sarah Tyrrell Stewart and David W. Rupp

Abstract

*The finds of incised pebbles and figurines from specific Aceramic Neolithic sites suggest parallels with contemporaneous sites in the Levant, which may indicate contact between the regions. Survey and excavation at the Cypriote sites of Khirokitia-*Vouni *and Kholetria-*Ortos *have recovered a number of these pebbles and a single figurine that are remarkably similar to pieces from the Levantine sites of Munhata, Byblos and Sha'ar Hagolan. A number of studies have suggested the possibility of limited trade during the early Neolithic in the Aegean and Levant (see notably Mellaart 1975; Renfrew 1977; Runnels 1985; Runnels and Van Andel 1988 and Perlès 1992). We propose to use models derived from this research to explain the patterns of distribution of these artefacts. While the objects are easily made of locally available material, their distinctive characteristics and limitation to specific yet wide-ranging sites suggest that they were more than generic utilitarian objects. There are a number of possible scenarios that may account for their presence and distribution and each would exhibit distinctive artefact patterning. Most simply, these artefacts may be common utilitarian items, such as food graters, or children's toys. Except for an original common origin, they would not indicate contact of any kind. Alternatively, they may be remnants from an initial settlement, which would not imply current contact but might indicate possible origins of a founder population. Finally, these items could be linked with some sort of exchange, from occasional, isolated contact up to limited directional trade between Cyprus and the Levant. To offer the most plausible explanation, we will explore the mechanics of these contacts by examining the nature of production, site consumption and regional distribution of goods.*

Introduction

Recent research has dramatically altered our understanding of relationships between Cyprus and the Levant during the Aceramic Neolithic Period (Figure 13.1). This is particularly true of the Cypro-PPNB culture now identified at a number of sites on the island. While the similarities between the two regions during this period are extensive (Peltenburg *et al.* 2001), notably in features of settlement structure, ideology and technology, similarities during the later Khirokitia,

Period (8,000–6,000 BP) are perhaps less evident. We would like to address the question of one small body of objects, which, although limited in number, appears only at specific sites in Cyprus and the Levant and may suggest some significance beyond a common regional heritage.

These objects are incised igneous pebbles and schematically incised figurines that appear and co-occur at specific yet far ranging sites, notably at Khirokitia-*Vouni* (Khirokitia) and Kholetria-*Ortos* (*Ortos*) in Cyprus and Byblos, Munhata and Sha'ar Hagolan in the Levant.

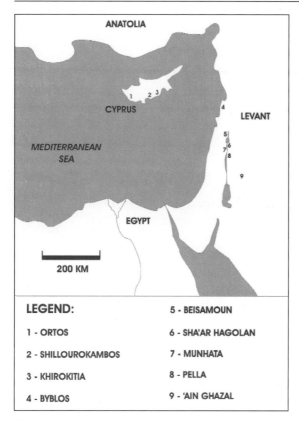

Figure 13.1 *Cyprus and the Levant*

Figure 13.2 *Schematic models of incised pebble types*

The incised pebbles (Figure 13.2)

These are natural pebbles about 8–10 cm in length, usually of an igneous stone, often andesite, basalt or occasionally gabbro. They have been carefully incised on a flat, slightly convex or conical surface with a variety of geometric designs, notably hatched, linear or star burst patterns. These objects could have a number of possible uses. Stekelis (in Dikaios 1953: 291) notes that they may have been a kind of stamp seal, similar to those found at Tell Brak, and perhaps used for stamping bread. Garfinkel suggests they could be cult objects, or tools for textile dyeing or animal branding (Garfinkel 1993: 125 and Figure 13). Gopher and Orrelle also offer a symbolic interpretation, arguing that the various designs on the pebbles represent female genitalia at specific life stages (Gopher and Orrelle 1996: 255–279). Similar motifs appear on contemporaneous stamp seals in the northern Levant at Amuq A and B sites (Braidwood and Braidwood 1960: Figure 37), Ras Shamra (de Contenson 1977: Figures 11, 14,

17), Qwinas (Masude and Sha'ath 1983: 201), further east at Tell Chagar Bazar (Mallowan 1936: Figure 7) and Tell Arpachiyah (Mallowan and Cruickshank Rose 1935) and on the so-called clay 'pintaderas' from Byblos Ancien (Dunand 1973: 84–88). Interestingly, there are no clay sealings that might correspond with the incised pebbles, nor any dye in the incisions (Le Brun 1984: 123). Microscopic wear analysis of a specimen from *Ortos* suggests that it had been rubbed against a soft (perhaps vegetable) material (Fox 1987: 23).

The number, decoration and distribution of the incised pebbles indicate some interesting patterns (Table 13.1). The possible interpretations are limited though, as for some sites, the preliminary reports give no exact descriptions or illustrations of design distribution.

Cyprus

At *Ortos*, survey and excavation found 51 incised pebbles: 18 in the initial Canadian Palaipaphos Survey Project (CPSP) (Fox 1988: 36–38); nine in the subsequent Western Cyprus

Site/Type	a	b	c	d	eI	eII	Unknown	Total
Ortos	0	4	4	3	2	1	37	51
Khirokitia	0	0	21	11	1	2	18	53
Byblos	0	0	1	0	0	0	0	1
Beisamoun	0	0	1	0	0	0	0	1
Sha'ar Hagolan	4	11	4	2	1	8	0	30
Munhata	4	1	3	1	1	1	0	11
Pella	0	1	0	0	0	0	0	1
Ain Ghazal	0	0	1	0	0	0	1	2

Table 13.1 *Distribution of incised pebbles*

Project (WCP archive); and 24 in the Simmons excavations (Simmons 1994: 42; 1996: 37; Simmons and Corona 1993: 6–7). At Khirokitia 53 were recovered: 21 in the Dikaios excavations (Dikaios 1953:290–291); 13 in the initial Le Brun excavations (Cluzon 1984: 120–124); and 19 in the subsequent excavations (Astruc 1994: 236–243).

Levant

At Munhata, the excavations recovered 11 incised pebbles (Perrot 1964; Zori 1954: Plate 11.1; Gopher and Orrelle 1995: 64), and at Sha'ar Hagolan, 30 (Stekelis 1951: 10–12; 1972) (Garfinkel 1999: 88). A few other examples come from nearby sites: one from Beisamoun (Lechevallier 1978: Figure 107.6), one from Pella (McNicoll *et al.* 1982: 87 5), and two from 'Ain Ghazal (Rollefson and Simmons 1986: 161)

In discussing decoration, we have used the typology proposed by Garfinkel (Garfinkel 1993: 125 and Figure 13), (Figure 13.2) with some modification and expansion of one type. These types are: a) incisions with horizontal lines (along short axis); b) incision with vertical lines (along long axis); c) square hatching or net pattern (oriented to axis); d) rhomboid hatching or net pattern (at 45° angle to axis); and e) central line crossed by perpendicular short lines. We have further subdivided this group into: eI) a star burst or radiating line pattern; and eII) a straight centre line crossed with a perpendicular line, or several perpendicular lines rising above or below the centre line.

While all these types are represented throughout the region, there is an obvious difference between the proportions in Cyprus and the Levant. There appears to be a stronger favouring of the net or hatch design at the Cypriot sites, while the simple line combination or crossed lines are more common in the Levant. A feature found only at the Cypriot sites is the inclusion of a carved conical or domed reverse on a few examples, which in both shape and design are markedly similar to the pintaderas from Byblos. We have identified five different designs used in these: a) net or hatch; b) radiating line; c) chevron; d) star burst; and e) pitted. With such a small number represented (Table 13.2), it is difficult to say much about their distribution, save that they are apparently unique to Cyprus. Some of these tops are perforated, presumably for suspension. Again, this feature appears only in Cyprus, and in too few examples to see any obvious patterns.

The designs themselves, although simple, are neither rudimentary nor easily produced. The motifs are consistently repeated, with little spatial variation, and are deeply and precisely etched into the very hard igneous pebbles of basalt, andesite or gabbro. All motifs appear in both areas, but with some difference in distribution, as mentioned above. This could be as much due to sampling errors as function. It may be particularly true of the finds from Cyprus, where

Sites/Type	a	b	c	d	e	Total
Ortos	1	2	1			4
Khirokitia	1	5	4	2	3	15

Table 13.2 *Distribution of conical tops*

the number of unknowns makes any final conclusions on motif distributions difficult. What seems clear, though, is that the substantially larger number of finds from Cyprus, and the use of the more complex domed tops and perforations, suggest that there may be differences in manufacture and use between the two areas.

Unfortunately, we did not conduct petrographic studies, primarily due to problems in accessing the samples and obtaining permission for destructive analysis. Astruc (1994: 236), though, notes that the pebbles from Khirokitia had a local source, although she does not explain what analyses determined this. Certainly a firm knowledge of the raw material source for the pebbles and figurines would make any interpretations more convincing, and this problem will be considered in greater detail below.

Contextual evidence from most sites was similarly disappointing. In Cyprus, there is detailed spatial information on the distribution of the pebbles at Khirokitia, but none from *Ortos*, where unsystematic survey or the preliminary excavation reports do not provide distributional information. At Khirokitia, the incised pebbles seem to be distributed both within and between the tholoi. Astruc (1994: 241–242) mentions that there is generally a greater complexity in design and shape of the pebbles in the eastern half of the site. The pebbles are often incorporated into walls, floors and hearths, and even in one case a grave. In most cases, these were secondary contexts. Clearly, an understanding of context could aid in interpreting these pieces, but even at Khirokitia, where there is a great deal of contextual evidence, there is apparently no distinct patterning in distribution. This also seems to be true at Munhata, where again there appears to be a fairly even distribution of these artefacts across the site (Gopher and Orrelle 1995: 152–155; 160–163). With little contextual evidence from the other sites, it is impossible to compare distributions either between the Cypriot sites or Cyprus and the mainland.

Incised pebble figurines (Figure 13.3 and Table 13.3)

These figurines are fashioned from unworked limestone pebbles about 8–15 cm in length and

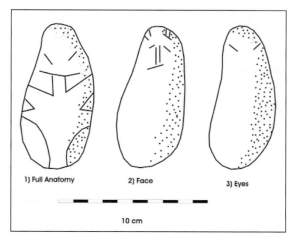

Figure 13.3 *Schematic models of pebble figurines*

are schematically incised with eyes and less frequently mouths, noses and clothing (Garfinkel 1993: 125). As with the incised pebbles, we have used the design typology proposed by Garfinkel (1993: 125) for analysing these pieces. He identifies three types: I) those with anatomy and clothing indicated; II) those with full face incised; and III) those with only the eyes incised.

Cyprus

Ian Todd found a single incised figurine at *Ortos* in a 1991 survey of the site (WCP archive). It is apparently the first identified on Cyprus. This find from 1991, only now recognized, could mean that other similar pieces might yet be identified. It was made of hard, white limestone and belongs to type II. The carefully incised parallel lines indicating the nose are almost identical to a specimen from Byblos (Dunand 1973: no. 23083).

Levant

At Byblos, excavations recovered 16 pebble figurines (Dunand 1973: Plates CX, CXI). Six of these belong to type II and ten to type III. The largest collection in the Levant, about 105 figurines, comes from Sha'ar Hagolan (Garfinkel 1999: 70; Stekelis 1952). About 28 of these belong to type I, 39 to type II and 38 to type III (Garfinkel 1993: 125). The use of the convention of parallel lines indicating the nose, seen also on the *Ortos* example, is rare, but it does occur at Sha'ar Hagolan (Garfinkel 1999: 76). The excavations at Munhata produced 14 incised pebble figurines (Gopher and Orrelle 1995: 61 and

Sites/Type	I	II	III	Total
Ortos	0	1	0	1
Khirokitia	0	0	0	0
Byblos	0	6	10	16
Beisamoun	0	0	0	0
Sha`ar Hagolan	28	39	39	10
Munhata	3	1	10	14
Pella	0	0	0	0
Ain Ghazal	0	0	0	0

Table 13.3 *Distribution of pebble figurines*

Figures 44, 41). Most are defined by simple eye incision, but a single surface find also exhibits the parallel nose lines seen in the *Ortos* example (Gopher and Orrelle 1995: Figure 41. 10). Of this group, 3 belong to type 1, 1 to type II and 10 to type III.

We can make several observations based on the distribution of these figurines. By far the largest number comes from Sha'ar Hagolan. There is a slight preference for types II and III at Byblos and Munhata. While only one figurine, of type II, has been found on Cyprus, the distinctive execution of the incised nose links it firmly to the mainland sites.

As discussed above in reference to the incised pebbles, we have done no petrographic studies, and there is little contextual evidence to allow a spatial comparison of sites or areas. It is important to note, though, that although the designs themselves are relatively simple, the execution is precise and consistent.

Interpretation

1) Utilitarian

What then do these objects mean? The first and simplest explanation is that they were locally made, simple and utilitarian. The figures were perhaps merely children's toys, the incised pebbles vegetable graters, laundry scrubbers, bread stamps or the like. That they are found at diverse sites in Cyprus and the Levant would be no more remarkable than would be the presence of pottery or stone tools. The similarity in the objects would relate more to their utilitarian

nature, and except for an original common origin, would not indicate any obvious contact between sites. If this were the case though, one would expect the following; i) a more random, diverse distribution of objects throughout the region, with no apparent co-occurrence; ii) less consistency in the design elements, such that one should not expect the canonical adherence to the facial characteristics of the figurines (slash eyes, horizontal line nose, round mouth) or the specific geometric incisions on the pebbles. With these objects, neither of the conditions has been met. The objects appear to be limited to specific yet far ranging sites, and their execution is remarkably canonical and precise.

2) Cultural origins

Alternatively, the figurines and pebbles, again locally made, may be remnants from an initial settlement, which would not imply current contact, but might indicate possible origins of a founder population. If this were the case, one would expect other aspects of the society to reflect this, possibly in vessel manufacture, lithic technology, subsistence, architecture and so on. In other words, if the origin of the Aceramic Neolithic (as distinct from the PPNB) in Cyprus could trace its roots to a specific region in the Levant, around the area of Sha'ar Hagolan, Pella and Munhata, one should see these similarities in both areas. In fact, this does tend to be born out in some aspects, notably burials, architecture and stone vessels.

There is very little evidence for burials from this area of the Levant during this period but one from Munhata and one from Sha'ar Hagolan (Garfinkel 1993: 127) show close parallels with burials from Khirokitia and other Aceramic Neolithic sites from Cyprus. In each case, all were intramural, single, primary, flexed, with intact skull. Further convincing evidence can be found from contemporaneous levels at Byblos (Dunand 1973: 29–32). Here again we see simple sub-floor inhumations in stone cists or pits. The bodies are flexed and grave goods, if present, usually consist of pottery vessels.

The classic examples of architecture at Khirokitia (Dikaios 1953; Le Brun 1984: 23–30; 1989. 22–127) are round structures, approximately 3 m in diameter, with stone foundations and internal benches, hearths and pillars. At Munhata during this period, there are also circular structures with stone foundations, also about 3 m in diameter (Garfinkel 1993: 128). Other Yarmukian sites with round architecture are Megiddo and Jebel Abu Thwab, the latter with 2 m round structures, plastered floors and central post holes (Kafafi 1993: 108).

Cypriot stone bowls are characterised by distinctive spouts, handles and relief decoration consisting of vertical lines, zigzags, notches, knobs and chevrons (Dikaios 1953: 232–264; Le Brun 1984: 97–109; 1989: 137–175; Lehavy 1989: 207). It is interesting to note that these characteristics not only occur on stone bowls from the Levant, notably at Byblos (Dunand 1973: 38, 42–61), and Sha'ar Hagolan (Garfinkel 1993: 120, 123), but that contemporary pottery from these sites exhibit similar motives.

The major stumbling block to this argument, of course, is the recent discovery of several sites in Cyprus that predate the Khirokitian Aceramic Neolithic, and can be convincingly related to the PPNB of the mainland (Peltenburg *et al.* 2001). Aspects such as subsistence, technology, settlement organization, ideology and exchange indicate strong connections with the PPNB cultures of the Levant, and specifically to areas north and east of the area under consideration here. We could argue that sites such as *Ortos* and Khirokitia were settled later, by groups from the areas around Munhata and Sha'ar Hagolan by way of Byblos, and that these people were gradually integrated into the original PPNB settler population in Cyprus. There would be a number of weaknesses to this proposition, though. There is such a paucity of Yarmukian burials that it would be risky drawing parallels with the material on Cyprus. Circular architecture can also be found in earlier PPNA and PPNP contexts at various places in the Levant, which could certainly have influenced the Cypriot examples (Peltenburg *et al.* 2001: 41–42), rather than any later, direct migration from the Sha'ar Hagolan area. Similarities in vessel shape and decoration can also be seen at more northerly mainland sites, notably Amuq A and B (Braidwood and Braidwood 1960: 46–55, 57; Mellaart 1975: 130). Finally, when looking specifically at the incised pebbles and figurines, if their presence in Cyprus was the result of founder populations, with no current contact, one should

not see the retention of specific motifs so exactly (the 6 pebble types and the canonical execution of facial features on the figurines). These would surely have been adapted or altered over time. At least three incised pebbles and one pebble figurine, however, come from the PPNB site of Shillourokambos in Cyprus (Guilaine *et al.* 2000: 589–594). The pebbles are made of picrolite, limestone and serpentinite, and are decorated with either cross (N=2) or rhomboid lattice (N=1). The picrolite pebble figurine is most like the later type 1 examples, with firm incisions indicating the anatomy, and with eyes and nose similar to the *Ortos* specimen. The fact that these pieces are found in a PPNB context in Cyprus, and are clearly earlier than the finds from the mainland sites, may indicate continuity between the PPNB and Aceramic periods in Cyprus. In addition, this, along with the larger number and greater complexity of incised pebbles found in Cyprus, might indicate that the influence of these objects moved from Cyprus to the Levant, rather than the reverse. A more in depth analysis of this hypothesis would be well beyond the scope of this paper, although it would offer interesting possibilities for further research.

3) Exchange

Finally, these items could be linked with some sort of exchange, from occasional, isolated contact up to limited directional trade between Cyprus and the Levant.

We would like to briefly discuss evidence for neolithic trade in the eastern Mediterranean and the probable mechanics of how that trade might have operated by looking at such aspects as the nature of goods production, site consumption and regional distribution.

Of particular interest for our analysis is Renfrew's discussion of directional trade (Renfrew 1977: 85), trade that supplies some places preferentially (for whatever reasons), even if they are further away from more accessible "markets." Unfortunately, this and other exchange systems may produce identical fall-off curves (Knapp 1985: 3). To deal with this problem, one must identify sources of raw material and centres of production and then consider the possible mechanisms with respect to patterns of distribution, which will prove difficult for the Cypriot and Levantine material.

Runnels notes that in the early Neolithic, andesite was imported from the Greek islands to the mainland, but he observes that the method of exchange was uncertain (Runnels 1985: 41). Others also concur with a model of Neolithic trade represented by simple reciprocal exchange and fairly direct access (Cherry 1985: 14–15). Trade may not have been formally organized as such, yet would have gone beyond single episodes, being persistent yet intermittent (Renfrew *et al.* 1968: 330). Runnels and Van Andel (1988: 95) suggest that early Neolithic trade was probably a mix of essential commodities with gift exchange and social networking.

Perhaps the research most applicable to the problem at hand is that of Perlès (1992). She looks at aspects of production, site consumption and regional distribution of various categories of goods in the Greek Neolithic. She determined that three distinct systems of production and exchange were in place:

1) economic, being utilitarian goods widely distributed both geographically and socially;
2) intergroup alliances, exhibited by goods of high stylistic visibility and social function, with a restricted geographic range; and
3) trade in prestige goods, which were wide-ranging but limited in social access (Perlès 1992: 115).

She argues that research in the past has been limited, as it assumes that all forms of exchange were conducted in the same fashion, with a single socio-economic basis and single distributional network (Perlès 1992: 118). She maintains that by ignoring geographical (availability of resources and means of communication) and sociological factors (social organization and product demand) one cannot draw a direct link between fall-off patterns and modality of distribution. In order to understand exchange patterns, it is necessary to consider all commodities in circulation, looking in particular at procurement of raw material, commodity production, site consumption and regional distribution (Perlès 1992: 119). In addition, in order for trade across an expanse of water to operate, maritime navigational skills would have been necessary, probably in the form of specialized rather than *ad hoc* seafaring (Perlès 1990). In specific reference to stone vessels and

ornaments, of particular interest here, Perlès states that the more exotic an item, the more valuable and prestigious it was. This in itself can explain the circulation of such objects, without invoking shortages of raw materials. One would expect these objects would often be for symbolic or ritual use, have specialised production, and be distributed in small quantities, but over very long distances (Perlès 1992: 149). Distribution could be the result of down-the-line trade, or of systems controlled by elite groups. Much of the prestige of an item would be due in part to its remote origin (Perlès 1992: 149).

Based on the above research, the following points are suggestive in understanding the possibility of exchange of specific goods between Cyprus and the Levant:

1) supply would be based on patterns of procurement of raw materials, manufacture and site consumption;
2) distribution would vary greatly according to the nature of the object (utilitarian, social or prestige), but essential commodities might be combined with gift exchange and social networking;
3) a variety of mechanisms of distribution could have been in place, including simple reciprocal exchange and fairly direct access, down-the-line exchange, and especially directional trade, in which specific objects may have been targeted for specific places;
4) exchange would likely be persistent yet intermittent;
5) demand for certain objects (e.g. prestige) would be reflected in number and use at destination sites;
6) trade in prestige goods would be wide-ranging but limited in access; and
7) the prestige of an item would be due in part to its remote and exotic origin, rather than its material or execution.

So, bearing all this in mind, what evidence have we for exchange between specific sites in Cyprus (*Ortos* and Khirokitia) and the Levant (Byblos, Munhata and Sha'ar Hagolan)? How would such a system have operated and what was being exchanged?

If the incised pebbles and figurines were locally made, they would obviously not be the items of exchange themselves. Nevertheless, the identical repetition of the designs in both areas certainly suggests some form of contact. The pebbles and figurines may represent some practical, business aspect of exchange, where other, possibly perishable objects (food, textiles) were the actual items traded. The incised pebbles could be stamps used on these perishable items, or some sort of accounting tools in the business of exchange. The single figurine might also denote a business connection with specific mainland sites. Alternatively, the pebbles and figurines may have been imitations of foreign items, copied at home for prestige, symbolic value or pure exotica, similar to the Levi's and Rolex knockoffs found in today's market. The numbers of these objects might suggest the direction of influence, the incised pebbles from Cyprus to the Levant, and the figurines from the Levant to Cyprus. The Cypriote repertoire of incised pebbles includes a wider range of shapes, notably the conical and mushroom shaped tops, some with perforations, which are not found in the Levant and which may have influenced the 'pintaderas' from Byblos. In addition, the incised pebbles and figurine found at PPNB Shillourokambos indicate that this tradition appears earlier on Cyprus than on the mainland.

If the pebbles and figurines were not locally made, we would be dealing more probably with non-utilitarian, potentially prestige items. Perlès' research indicated that such items would exhibit markedly different patterns of production, distribution and consumption than would either utilitarian items (obsidian, for example) or social indicators (such as specific pottery types). She notes that the exotic nature of the object itself may encourage trade, even if local sources are available. As is the case here, one should expect such objects to be used in symbolic or ritual use, with specialised production, and the distribution of small quantities over large distances. The larger number of incised pebble figurines from Sha'ar Hagolan and the possible movement of these items to specific sites in the Levant and Cyprus (as yet only one identified example, and the possibly related PPNB piece) would indicate a highly specialised market, conducted on a small scale. Again, it is not the nature of the raw material, as local limestone and basalt are readily available at all sites, but rather the

unique and specialised nature of the items that would suggest the attraction. Although these pieces could be easily imitated locally, the attraction would lie in their exotic origin and probable symbolic or ritual purpose (Perlès 1992: 147). Interestingly, there appears to be a preference for type II and III figurines in this system. Garfinkel notes that type I are the least schematic, while those in type III are the most, with only the more important symbolic details being retained (Garfinkel 1993: 125). This could explain why only the most abstract (types II and III), hence the most symbolic pieces would enter the exchange system.

The incised pebbles could also have served a symbolic or ritual purpose, perhaps linked in some way with the figurines. Or, conversely, as suggested above, these were stamps, possibly for textiles, or were for accounting of some kind. Both these latter suggestions could be appropriate in an exchange model. Either they were stamps for textiles or other goods, which were the actual trade items, or these pieces were connected with the actual business of exchange itself. The various designs could indicate number of items, place of origin and so on. Possibly this could be seen in the apparent preference for type c) and d) in Cyprus and a/b) and e) in the Levant. This might also help explain the exclusive use of the decorated 'conical tops' in Cyprus. The flat, incised reverse surface would be the 'business' end, linked with its counterparts in the Levant, while the decorated tops would be unique to Cyprus, serving either a symbolic, economic or purely decorative function, and possibly influenced by the pintaderas of Byblos. While a model of exchange in purely symbolic or prestige items, such as this, would not require an association with any essential commodities, certain items could be connected with this exchange. Stone bowls from Cyprus might well figure into this system. If raw materials of good quality were available in the Levant, why would Cypriote vessels be imported? At this time in the Levant, most standard vessel production had shifted to ceramic wares, which was not the case in Cyprus. Therefore, highly specialised and finely crafted stone vessels might be desired on a limited basis as the craft died out on the mainland. As a result, we should expect to see only the finest materials and the most ornately decorated pieces as imported items. Mellaart (1975: 130) notes such a stone bowl of Cypriot origin in Amuq A.

How could such an exchange model have operated? We know that with the presence of definite imports such as obsidian and Mediterranean shells at all these sites (Garfinkel 1993: 129; 1999: 42; Renfrew 1966; Renfrew *et al.* 1968), long distance trade networks were already in place. In the case of the items under consideration here, all would have been manufactured from locally available materials, and, especially in the case of the stone bowls, technical input, production knowledge and regional variation would be high, suggesting at least part-time independent specialists. Output could be expected to be low. All these trends were identified in the Neolithic Greek trade (Perlès 1992: 125–135) and should be applicable to the Cyprus-Levant situation. One would expect evidence of workshops, as may indeed be the case at *Ortos*, where at least eight pieces found in the survey appear to represent items broken and rejected during manufacture (Fox 1988: 39). Nevertheless, it is difficult to determine to what extent manufacture was for local use rather than surplus for export. Furthermore, sites that lack evidence of manufacture may be the recipients of imports or simply those whose manufacturing areas have yet to be identified.

The actual mechanics of exchange of these goods are difficult to determine with such small numbers, but Renfrew's model of directional exchange may be appropriate here. In this model, specific "markets" are targeted for specific social reasons, regardless of proximity. While occupation of Cyprus had clearly begun some 2000 years prior to the Aceramic Neolithic, there may be reasons to link sites such as *Ortos* and Khirokitia with specific mainland sites such as Byblos, Munhata and Sha'ar Hagolan. This can be seen not only in the incised figurines and pebbles, but possibly in other culturally significant traits such as architecture, burial patterns and vessel decoration. There may have been ongoing links between these sites, established perhaps by an original immigration to the island, which was then maintained through specific, directional trade of rare, prestige goods (stone vessels), symbolic items (figurines and incised pebbles), and possibly perishables such as printed textiles or skins.

Conclusions

A number of factors limit the strength of these models. Most importantly, for sites such as *Ortos* that have not yet been fully published, exact figures for stone bowls and incised pebbles are not yet available. Furthermore, although raw materials are locally available at all sites, petrographic analyses might help determine whether the vessels, pebbles and figurines were locally made. If this were true, it would alter the nature of possible exchange. Clearly contact of some kind would be indicated, due to the similarity of the items, but these pieces as items of exchange would be questionable. Local manufacture could support the model of initial founder populations, or, conversely, that they were markers of business rather than symbolic items of trade itself. In addition, site consumption rates are impossible to determine.

To what extent might objects be purely for local consumption? Can one ever determine from the artefacts how many would be needed and for over what time period? Do other sites, as well as *Ortos*, exhibit evidence of manufacture? Might *Ortos* and Khirokitia share some special status, not seen at the other Aceramic Neolithic sites, and were they connected in some way to contact or exchange with the Levant? Although no architecture has been found at *Ortos*, the quality of other finds, notably the number and quality of stone bowls, links the two sites. Not all the incised pebbles are illustrated, so it is impossible to determine the exact ratio of various designs and what might be their significance. Also, exact provenience is not available for many of the finds, especially those from survey, so context within the site and relationships to each other and other artefacts are impossible to determine. Finally, in light of the fact that we recognized the single identified Aceramic Neolithic pebble figurine in Cyprus some nine years after its recovery, there might well be others ignored or misidentified. Further research must address these problems, as well as pursue the apparently strong correlation between incised pebbles and figurines at specific sites in Cyprus and the Levant.

References

Astruc, L. 1994
L'outillage en pierre non-taillée et les petits objets. Pp. 215–289 in A. Le Brun (ed.) *Fouilles*

récentes à Khirokitia (Chypre) 1988–1991. Editions Recherche sur les Civilisations ADPF : Paris.

Braidwood, R. J. and L. S. Braidwood 1960
Excavations in the Plain of Antioch 1 The Earlier Assemblages. Phases A-J. Oriental Institute Publication 61. University of Chicago Press: Chicago.

Cherry, J. F. 1985
Islands out of the Stream: Isolation and Interaction in Early East Mediterranean Insular Prehistory. Pp. 12–29 in Knapp and Stech 1985.

Cluzon, S. 1984
L'outillage et les petits objects en pierre. Pp. 111–124; 134–144 in Le Brun 1984.

de Contenson, H. 1977
Le néolithique de Ras Shamra VA et VB. *Syria* 54: 1–23.

Dikaios, P. 1953
Khirokitia. Oxford University Press : Oxford.

Dunand, M. 1973
Fouilles de Byblos V. Maisonneuve : Paris.

Fox, W. A. 1987
The Neolithic Occupation of Western Cyprus. Pp. 19–42 in D. W. Rupp (ed.) *Western Cyprus: Connections*. Studies in Mediterranean Archaeology 77. Paul Åströms Förlag: Göteborg.

Fox, W. A. 1988
Kholetria-*Ortos*. A Khirokitia Culture Settlement in Paphos District. *Report of the Department of Antiquities, Cyprus*: 29–42.

Garfinkel, Y. 1993
The Yarmukian Culture in Israel. *Paléorient* 19/1: 115–134.

Garfinkel, Y. 1999
The Yarmukians. Neolithic Art from Sha'ar Hagolan. Bible Lands Museum: Jerusalem.

Gopher, A. and E. Orrelle 1995
The Ground Stone Assemblages of Munhata. Les Cahiers des Missions Archéologiques Françaises en Israel 7. Association Paléorient: Paris.

Gopher, A. and E. Orrelle 1996
An Alternative Interpretation for the Material Imagery of the Yarmukian, a Neolithic Culture of the Sixth Millennium B.C. in the Southern Levant. *Cambridge Archaeological Journal* 6(2): 255–279.

Guilaine, J., F. Briois, J.-D. Vigne, I. Carrère, G. Willcox and S. Duchesne 2000
L'habitat néolithique précéramique de Shillourokambos (Parekklisha, Chypre). *Bulletin de Correspondance Hellénique* 124: 589–594.

Kafafi, Z. 1993
The Yarmukians in Jordan. *Paléorient* 19/1: 101–114.

Knapp, A. B. 1985
Production and Exchange in the Eastern Mediterranean: An Overview. Pp. 1–11 in Knapp and Stech 1985.

Knapp, A. B. and T. Stech (eds.) 1985
Production and Exchange. The Aegean and the Eastern Mediterranean. Institute of Archaeology Monograph XXV. University of California: Los Angeles.

Le Brun, A. 1984
Fouilles récentes à Khirokitia (Chypre) 1977–198. Éditions Recherche sur les Civilisations ADPF: Paris.

Le Brun, A. 1989
Fouilles récentes à Khirokitia (Chypre) 1983–1986. Éditions Recherche sur les Civilisations ADPF: Paris.

Lechevallier, M. 1978
Abou Gosh et Beisamoun, deux gisements du VIIe millénaire avant l'ére chrétienne en Israel. Association Paléorient : Paris.

Lehavy, Y. M. 1989
Dhali-Agridhi: The Neolithic by the River. Pp. 203–243 in L. Stager and A. Walker (eds.) *American Expedition to Idalion, Cyprus 1973–1980*. The American Schools of Oriental Research: Cambridge, MA.

Mallowan, M. E. L. 1936
The Excavation at Tell Chagar Bazar, and an Archaeological Survey of the Habur Region. *Iraq* 3: 1–86.

Mallowan, M. E. L. and J. Cruickshank Rose 1935
Excavations at Tell Arpachiyah 1933. *Iraq* 2: 1–178.

Masuda, I. and S. Sha'ath 1983
Qwinas, The Neolithic Site near Deinit Idlib. *Annales Archéologiques Arabes Syriennes* 33(1): 199–231.

McNicoll, A., R. H. Smith and B. Hennessy 1982
Pella in Jordan 1. Australian National Gallery: Canberra.

Mellaart, J. 1975
The Neolithic of the Near East. Thames and Hudson: London.

Peltenburg, E., S. Colledge, P. Croft, A. Jackson, C. McCartney and M. A. Murray 2001
Neolithic Dispersals from the Levantine Corridor: A Mediterranean Perspective. *Levant* 33: 35–64.

Perlès, C. 1990 L'outillage de pierre tailée néolithique en Grèce: Approvisionment et exploitation des matières premières. *Bulletin de Correspondance Hellénique* 114: 1–42.

Perlès, C. 1992
Systems of Exchange and Organization of Production in Neolithic Greece. *Journal of Mediterranean Archaeology* 5(2): 115–164.

Perrot, J. 1964
Les deux premières campagnes de fouilles Munhata. *Syria* 41: 323–345.

Renfrew, C. 1966
Obsidian and Early Cultural Contact in the Near East. *Proceedings of the Prehistoric Society* 32: 30–72.

Renfrew, C. 1977
Alternative Models for Exchange and Spatial Distribution. Pp. 71–90 in T. K. Earle and T. K. Ericson (eds.) *Exchange Systems in Prehistory*. Academic Press: London.

Renfrew, C., J. E. Dixon and J. R. Cann 1968
Further Analysis of Near Eastern Obsidian. *Proceedings of the Prehistoric Society* 34: 319–333.

Rollefson, G. and A. Simmons 1986
  The Neolithic Village at 'Ain Ghazal, Jordan: Pre-
  liminary Report of the 1984 Season. *Bulletin of the
  American Schools of Oriental Research Supplement*
  24: 145–164.
Runnels, C. N. 1985
  Trade and Demand for Millstones in Southern
  Greece in the Neolithic and the Early Bronze Age.
  Pp. 30–43 in Knapp and Stech 1985.
Runnels, C. N. and T. H. Van Andel 1988
  Trade and the Origins of Agriculture in the
  Eastern Mediterranean. *Journal of Mediterranean
  Archaeology* 1(1): 83–109.
Simmons, A. 1994
  Preliminary Report on the 1993 Test Excavations
  at Kholetria-*Ortos*, Paphos District. *Report of the
  Department of Antiquities, Cyprus*: 39–44.
Simmons, A. 1996
  Preliminary Report on the Multidisciplinary

Investigations at Neolithic Kholetria-*Ortos*,
  Paphos District. *Report of the Department of Antiq-
  uities, Cyprus*: 29–44.
Simmons, A. and R. Corona 1993
  Test Excavations at Kholetria–*Ortos*, A Neolithic
  Settlement near Paphos. *Report of the Department
  of Antiquities, Cyprus*: 1–10.
Stekelis, M. 1951
  A New Neolithic Industry: The Yarmukian of
  Palestine. *Israel Exploration Journal* 1: 1–19.
Stekelis, M. 1952
  Two More Yarmukian Figurines. *Israel Exploration
  Journal* 2: 216–217.
Stekelis, M. 1972
  The Yarmukian Culture of the Neolithic Period.
  Magnes Press: Jerusalem.
Zori, N. 1954
  Survey of the Beth Shan Basin. *Bulletin of the Israel
  Exploration Society* 18: 78–90.

14

"Néolithique" and "Énéolithique" Byblos in Southern Levantine Context

Yosef Garfinkel

Abstract

The site of Byblos in Lebanon is of unparalleled importance to the study of late prehistory as it yielded one of the most comprehensive stratigraphic sequences of the 9th to 6th millennia BP in the Levant. The following five phases of occupation, from virgin soil upwards, were identified: "Néolithique Ancien", "Néolithique Moyen", "Néolithique Récent", Énéolithique Ancien" and "Énéolithique Récent." Since no other site in the Levant uses this terminology, it is not obvious how to relate the various "Néolithique" and "Énéolithique" phases of Byblos to the general chronological sequence of the area. This study re-evaluates Byblos according to the stratigraphic sequence and ceramic typology which I have recently established for the southern Levant.

The site of Byblos is situated on the Mediterranean Coast in Lebanon. It is well known for its impressive remains of the Early and Middle Bronze Ages. But beside its unique contribution to historical periods, the site is of unparalleled importance to the study of late prehistory. It has yielded one of the most comprehensive stratigraphic sequences of the 9th to 6th millennia BP in the Levant. It is also the only extensively excavated protohistoric site between Israel and the Amuq Plain, thus bridging between the southern and northern Levant.

M. Dunand, who conducted large-scale excavations during the 1940s and early 1950s, unearthed the late prehistoric layers. He published his results in 1973 in a two-volume final report (Dunand 1973). J. Cauvin (1968; 1972) studied the flint and some of the art objects. The following five phases of occupation at the bottom of the site, from virgin soil upwards, were identified (Table 14.1): "Néolithique Ancien", "Néolithique Moyen", "Néolithique Récent", Énéolithique Ancien" and "Énéolithique Récent." The next phase represents the first urban city of the Early Bronze Age II. Since no other site in the Levant uses this terminology,

it is not obvious how to relate the various "Néolithique" and "Énéolithique" phases of Byblos to the general chronological sequence of the area.

In addition, as often happened in those early days of research, the methods of excavation and recording were not very accurate. The main problem is that absolute elevations were used and every 20 cm unit was declared a "layer." A few such layers at Byblos constitute a "settlement phase." However, as is well known today, the thickness of archaeological debris varies, and various pits or heaps make absolute elevations meaningless. Thus, the stratigraphy of Byblos is seriously mixed, and in each so-called settlement phase one can find items from different periods placed together.

Since during the years the sequence of late prehistory, the so-called "Pottery Neolithic" in the southern Levant, had also not been very clear, there was no solid point of departure for the re-evaluation of prehistoric Byblos. Aside from some general attempts (Perrot 1962, 1969; Kirkbride 1969; Aurenche *et al.* 1981; Joukowsky 1997), it has usually been overlooked. The purpose of this presentation is to re-evaluate

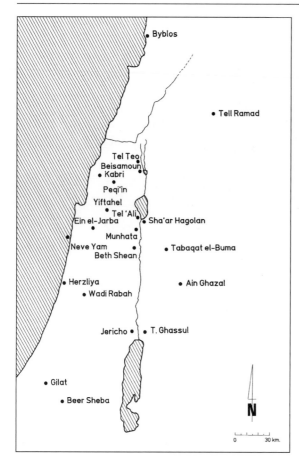

Figure 14.1 *The location of Byblos and other major sites mentioned in the text (drawn by R. Bonfil)*

Byblos according to the stratigraphic sequence and ceramic typology which I have recently established for the southern Levant (Garfinkel 1999a). There are obviously various differences between Byblos and the southern Levant during these periods, but this is not the subject of the current presentation.

Early "Néolithique Ancien" – the Pre-Pottery Neolithic B

This is the thickest phase, and its accumulation reaches 160 cm. It seems to me that two different periods have been mixed together here: Pre-Pottery Neolithic B (hereafter PPNB) and Pottery Neolithic (Yarmukian tradition). The PPNB is characterized by rectangular houses and plastered floors (Figure 14.2). This type of architecture is known in the Levant only in the PPNB, at sites like Jericho (Kenyon 1981), Yiftahel (Garfinkel 1987a), Ain Ghazal (Rollefson 1990), Beisamoun (Lechevallier 1978), Tell Ramad and Ugarit (de Contenson 1983). Various studies have been devoted to the usage of plaster for floor construction (Balfet *et al.* 1969; Gourdin and Kingery 1975; Garfinkel 1987b; Kingery *et al.* 1988; Malinowski and Garfinkel 1990; Rollefson 1990; Goren and Goldberg 1991), a type that is not known in periods before or after the PPNB. Thus, the rectangular houses with the plastered floors at Byblos represent a PPNB settlement and the site was first occupied during the 9th millennium BP. This point can be proven in further research, by direct ^{14}C datings of plaster samples from these floors.

Other typical PPNB elements can be noted in the material culture of the "Néolithique Ancien." The flint assemblage bears typical PPNB technological and typological characteristics. The knapping technology includes naviform cores and elongated naviform blades (Figure 14.3.1, 2). The elongated arrowheads of the Byblos and Amuq types (Figure 14.3.3–6) clearly characterize the late PPNB (Gopher 1994). Another aspect which should be connected to the PPNB of Byblos is the

Phases	"Layers"		Thickness in cm	Traditional terminology (after Kenyon)	Terminology of southern Levant (Garfinkel 1999a)
Néolithique Ancien	LIII–XLVI	(53–46)	160	PPNB PNA	PPNB Pottery Neolithic
Néolithique Moyen	XLV–XLIV	(45–44)	40	PNB	Early Chalcolithic
Néolithique Récent	XLIII–XL	(43–40)	80	—	Middle Chalcolithic
Énéolithique Ancien	XXXIX–XXXVIII	(39–38)	40	Chalcolithic	Late Chalcolithic
Énéolithique Récent	XXXVII–XXXIII	(37–33)	80	Proto-urban	Early Bronze I

Table 14.1 *The phases of occupation, layers and thickness of debris at Byblos, and the equivalent periods in the southern Levant*

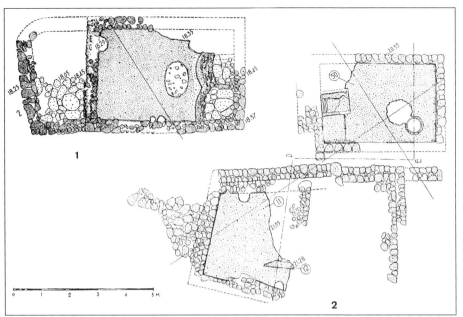

Figure 14.2
Pre-Pottery Neolithic
B houses with
plastered floors from
"Néolithique
Ancien" Byblos
(Dunand 1973:
Figures 8, 10)

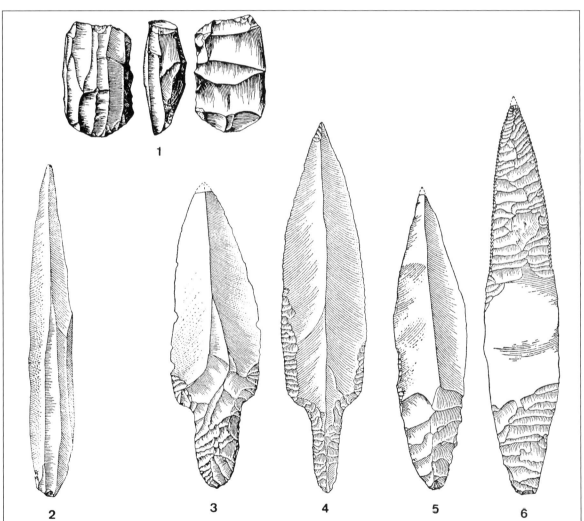

Figure 14.3 *Typical Pre-Pottery Neolithic B flint artefacts from "Néolithique Ancien" Byblos (Cauvin 1968:*
Figures 7, 13, 33)

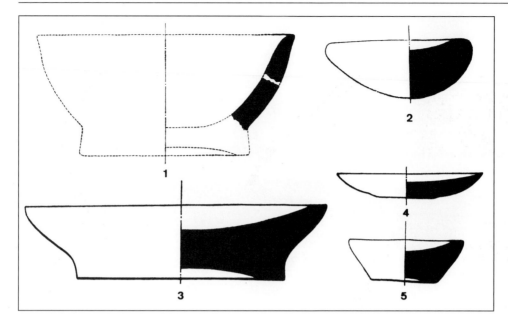

Figure 14.4
*White Ware
vessels from
"Néolithique
Ancien" Byblos
(Dunand 1973:
Figures 11–13)*

large number of portable containers made of lime plaster (Figure 14.4). These, known as "White Ware" or "vaisselles blanches," are reported from PPNB sites (Rollefson 1990).

The data presented above clearly contradicts the information given in the Oxford Encyclopedia of Archaeology in the Near East: "Although Byblos has been occupied since the Neolithic Period (6,000 BC), there are no early architectural remains. In about 4,500 BC small monocellular houses appear with crushed-limestone floors" (Joukowsky 1997). The earliest occupation of Byblos took place in the 7th millennium BC, in the PPNB period. It was a typical village-type settlement that flourished on the Mediterranean coast, an integral part of the so-called "Levantine corridor" (Bar-Yosef and Belfer-Cohen 1989).

Late "Néolithique Ancien" – the Pottery Neolithic (Yarmukian)

The second period clearly incorporated into the "Néolithique Ancien" is a Pottery Neolithic settlement with Yarmukian material culture. The Yarmukian culture flourished mainly in the Mediterranean parts of Israel and Jordan (Garfinkel 1993). Byblos is the most northern site known with this material culture, indicating its geographical extension into Lebanon and the central Levant. The Yarmukian of Byblos is

clearly visible in various aspects: pottery, flint and art objects.

Typologically the following pottery vessels appear at Byblos: bowls (Figure 14.5.3), spoons (Dunand 1973: Plate XLVIII, lower row, right), pots and holemouth jars with two opposing lug handles (Figure 14.5.6), jars with rounded body and two handles extending from the neck to the shoulder (Figure 14.5.4) and "Byblos jars" (Figure 14.5.5), as defined in the Munhata report (Garfinkel 1992: 51; 1999a: 50, 51).

The typical incised decoration of the Yarmukian pottery, as defined at Munhata, was found at Byblos in large quantities. This includes the typical herring bone incisions inside a frame (Figure 14.5.1, 2), frame incisions without the herring bone pattern (Figure 14.5.3) and various schematic incisions (Figure 14.5.4). In addition, Byblos presents quite a number of items decorated with incised parallel lines in triangles (Figure 14.5.7, 8). Such decoration is quite rare in the southern Levant, but some examples have been reported from Sha'ar Hagolan, Munhata and Megiddo (Garfinkel 1999a: 62, 63). The flint industry also displays typical small arrowheads (Figure 14.6.1–6) and deeply denticulated sickle blades (Figure 14.6.7–11).

Another typical aspect of the Yarmukian Culture is the rich assemblage of art objects discovered at these sites (Stekelis 1972; Garfinkel 1995, 1999b). At Byblos, a typical Yarmukian clay

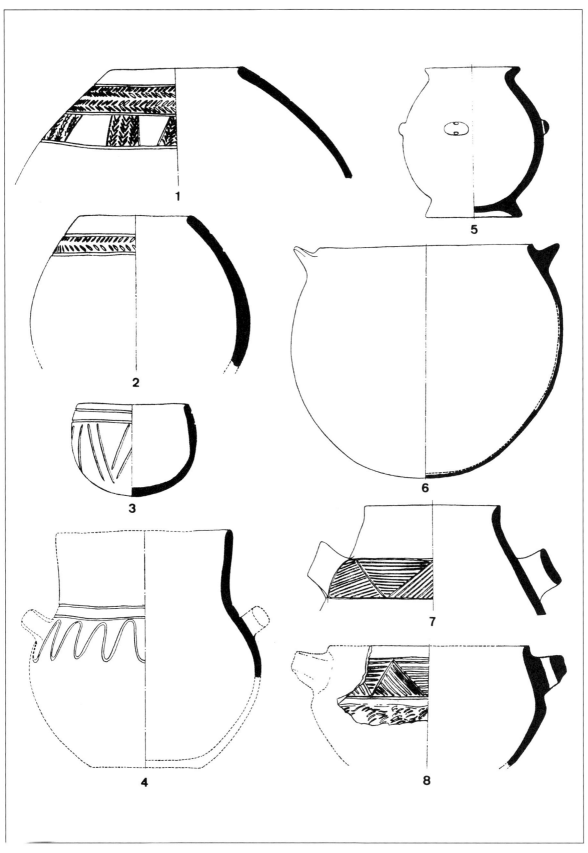

Figure 14.5 *Typical Yarmukian pottery from "Néolithique Ancien" Byblos (Dunand 1973: Figures 17, 20, 23, 25, 62)*

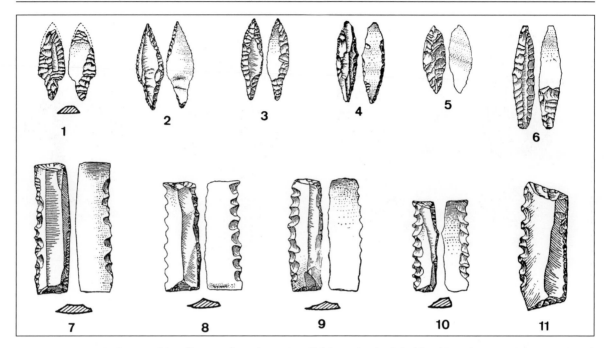

Figure 14.6 *Typical Yarmukian flint artefacts from "Néolithique Ancien" Byblos (Cauvin 1968: Figures 20, 21)*

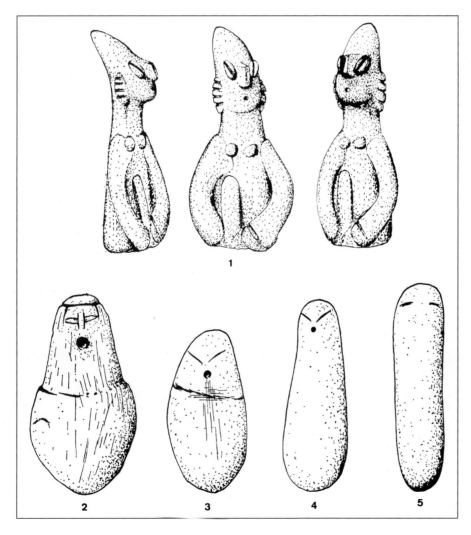

Figure 14.7
*Typical Yarmukian
figurines from
"Néolithique Ancien"
Byblos (Cauvin 1972:
Figures 20, 28)*

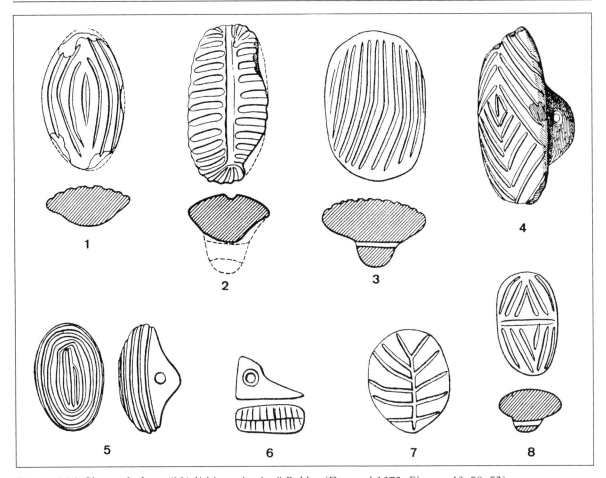

Figure 14.8 *Clay seals from "Néolithique Ancien" Byblos (Dunand 1973: Figures 48–50, 52)*

figurine with an elongated head and "coffee-bean" eyes was found (Figure 14.7.1). This is the first male figure reported from a Yarmukian site. Another male with such a head was found at Sha'ar Hagolan (Stekelis 1972: Plate 49. 3; Garfinkel 1999b: 58, 59). Byblos also presents about a dozen schematic figurines incised on limestone pebbles (Figure 14.7.2–5). Such pebble figurines were found in large quantities at Sha'ar Hagolan and Munhata (Garfinkel 2001; Gopher and Orrelle 1995: Figures 40.1, 2, 41.2–10). Also, quite a number of clay seals bearing various geometric designs were found (Figure 14.8). Similar patterns have been found at Yarmukian sites such as Sha'ar Hagolan and Munhata (Stekelis 1972: Plates 55.4, 5, 56, 58; Gopher and Orrelle 1995: Figures 39.1, 44.6–11, 45; Garfinkel 1999b: 88, 89).

Stylistically, the Yarmukian figurines from Sha'ar Hagolan bear more similarities to those of Byblos (*ca.* 200 km away) than to the figurines of nearby Munhata (*ca.* 10 km away). This is evident in the following aspects:

1. Depiction of a mouth on clay figurines is usually rare, but known on items from Sha'ar Hagolan and Byblos. No clay figurines with a mouth were found at Munhata.

2. Depiction of a mouth on pebble figurines is known at Sha'ar Hagolan and Byblos. No pebble figurines with a mouth were found at Munhata.

3. Depiction of large male clay figurines is known only from Sha'ar Hagolan and Byblos. No such figurine was found at Munhata.

4. Usually the pebbles on which the pebble figurines were depicted were not worked. One worked example is reported from Byblos and another such item is known from Sha'ar Hagolan.

5. Usually the ears of the clay figurines are depicted by a large, rounded lump of clay. The male figurine from Byblos is depicted

Phase	Jericho	Byblos	Byblos Finds	Calibrated dates (Garfinkel 1999a:6)
PPNA	PPNA	–	–	*ca.* 9400–8800 BC
PPNB	PPNB	Néolithique Ancien (early phase)	Plastered floors, points, naviform technology	*ca.* 8800–7000 BC
PPNC	–	–	–	*ca.* 7000–6400 BC
PN (Yarmukian)	PNA (Jericho IX)	Néolithique Ancien (late phase)	Pottery, small points, sickle blades, clay and pebble figurines	*ca.* 6400–5800 BC
E. Chalcolithic (Wadi Rabah)	PNB (Jericho VIII)	Néolithique Moyen	Pottery	*ca.* 5800–5300 BC
M. Chalcolithic (Beth Shean)	–	Néolithique Récent	pottery, stone vessels, seals, silos, chamber tombs	*ca.* 5300–4500 BC
L. Chalcolithic (Burial sites in Coastal Plain)	Garstang's pits (Ghassulian)	Énéolithique Ancien	churn, pierced flint, violin figurine, cemetery (jar burials)	*ca.* 4500–3600 BC
Early Bronze I	Proto-urban	Énéolithique Récent	pottery, architecture, cylinder seal impressions	*ca.* 3600–3100 BC

Table 14.2 *Correlation between Jericho and Byblos*

differently, with denticulate ears. One pillar figurine from Sha'ar Hagolan bears the same type of ear (Garfinkel 2001: Figure 5. 4). No figurine with such ears was found at Munhata.

We can conclude that, based on the pottery, flint and art objects, Byblos clearly represents a Yarmukian settlement, and should be dated to the second half of the 8th millennium BP. One ^{14}C date from Byblos (GrN-1544: 7360±80 BP) fits well into this chronological frame (Garfinkel 1999c; Garfinkel and Miller 2002: 30). The excavator associated this settlement with PPNB architecture. Similar observations were made about Jericho by Garstang, who worked there in the 1930s. His Layer IX included PPNB rectangular plastered houses and Neolithic pottery (Garstang *et al.* 1935; 1936). It became apparent only during Kenyon's excavations that the pottery and houses at Jericho are not related to one another (1957; 1981). The houses are dated to the PPNB, while the pottery came from later Pottery

Neolithic A pits, which were cut down into the PPNB remains. It seems to me that a similar mistake is evident at Byblos, since many of the PPNB houses are badly damaged by later activities (Dunand 1973: Figure 5. 7–10). Thus the excavator combined in his "Néolithique Ancien" two periods: PPNB and Pottery Neolithic.

What was the character of the Pottery Neolithic settlement at Byblos? As no architecture can be safely related to it, it may have been another Yarmukian site comprised mainly of pits, like Hamadya, Habashan Street and Munhata (Kaplan 1993; Kaplan and Ritter-Kaplan 1993; Perrot 1993).

"Néolithique Moyen"

This phase is only 40 cm thick. Its pottery consists of quite a number of items with classical "Wadi Rabah" typological characteristics, as recorded at Munhata and other sites in the

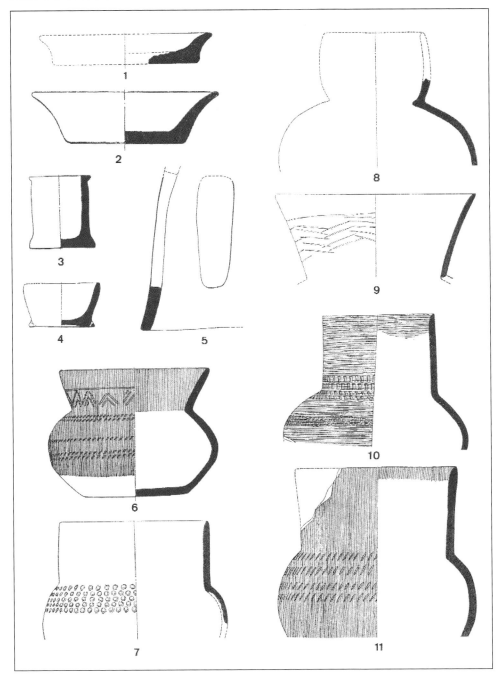

Figure 14.9
Typical Wadi Rabah pottery fraom "Néolithique Moyen" Byblos (Dunand 1973: Figures 57, 58, 60, 62, 64, 66, 82, 88)

southern Levant (Garfinkel 1992; 1999a: 104–152). These include shallow platters (Figure 14.9.1–2), lids with a base wider then the vessel body (Figure 14.9.3, 4), fenestrated stands (Figure 14.9.5), flaring-rim deep carinated bowls (Figure 14.9.6), bow-rim jars (Figure 14.9.8), flaring-necked jars (Figure 14.9.9) and straight-necked jars (Figure 14.9.7, 10). The "Néolithique Moyen" pottery of Byblos is also decorated with the typical incised decoration of the Wadi Rabah

pottery (Figure 14.9.6, 7, 9–11). This phase corre-lates to the Early Chalcolithic (Pottery Neolithic B Jericho) of the southern Levant (Table 14.2).

"Néolithique Récent"

This phase is characterized by a large number of rounded silos. They are paved with large rounded stones at the bottom and their circumference is

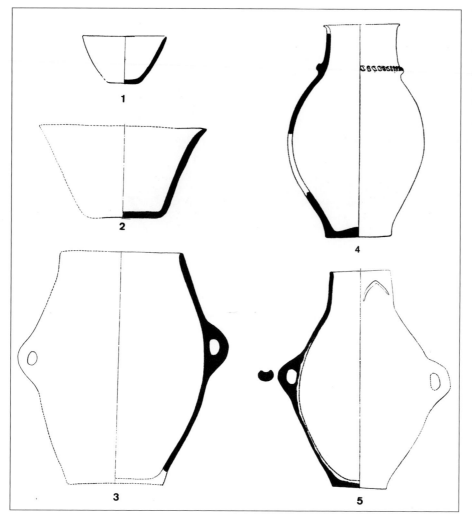

Figure 14.10
*Typical Middle
Chalcolithic pottery
from "Néolithique
Récent" Byblos
(Dunand 1973:
Figures 85, 91)*

lined with large flat stones standing on their narrow side (Dunand 1973: Plates XXXIII. 1–3, XXXIX.2). Similar silos have been found at various Middle Chalcolithic sites of the southern Levant, including Tel Ali layer 1b, Beth Shean Layer XVIII, Tell Shunah, Kabri, Tel Teo, Layers VIII–X, Tell Qiri, Ein el-Jarba, Hayonim Cave Terrace, Kefar Galim and Kefar Gil'adi (Garfinkel 1999a: 155–158).

The typically simple-shaped pottery of this phase consists of v-shape bowls (Figure 14.10.1, 2), large holemouth jars with large handles at the centre or lower part of the body (Figure 14.10.3) and various large jars (Figure 14.10.4, 5). Also included in this phase are flat strap handles that widen considerably where they meet the jar body (Dunand 1973: Plate LXXX). In this stage, the applied rope decoration appears on pottery for the first time (Dunand 1973: Plate LXXX. 26999). These features characterize the pottery of

the Middle Chalcolithic in the Southern Levant (Garfinkel 1999a: 153–199).

The flint industry of "Néolithique Récent" Byblos is characterized by transversal arrowheads (Figure 14.11). These are known from other Middle Chalcolithic sites such as Herzliya (Prausnitz *et al.* 1970; Bar-Yosef *et al.* 1970). This phase also yielded stone chalices, which are bowls with a high pedestal (Dunand 1973: Plate LXXIX). Similar items, usually made of basalt, have been reported from quite a number of Middle Chalcolithic sites in the southern Levant: Beth Shean, Tel Ali, Kabri, Tel Dan, Kefar Galim, and Tel Teo (Garfinkel 1999a: 155–158).

The burial customs of the "Néolithique Récent" include a number of chamber tombs lined with stones (Dunand 1973: Plate XLII). Similar cist tombs were reported from Layer 16 at Tabaqat el-Buma, which, according to my analysis, should be dated to the Middle Chalcolithic

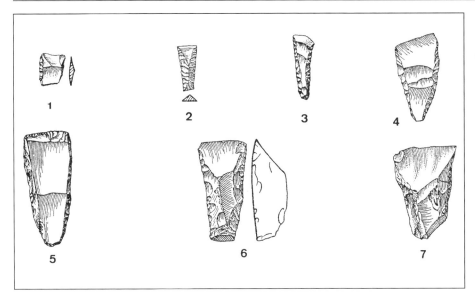

Figure 14.11
Transversal flint arrowheads from "Néolithique Récent" Byblos (Cauvin 1968: Figure 49)

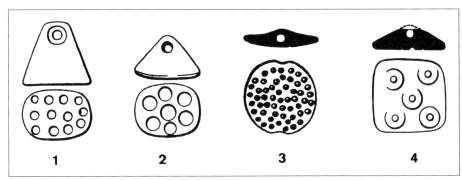

Figure 14.12
Seals from "Néolithique Récent" Byblos (Dunand 1973: Figure 110)

(Garfinkel 1999a: 158), at Kabri (Prausnitz 1969) and the underwater site of Neveh Yam (Galili *et al.* 1996).

Byblos also produced a number of seals (Figure 14.12). One of the seals is decorated with five concentric circles (Figure 14.12.4). A similar pattern has been found at the site of Herzliya near Tel Aviv, also located near the Mediterranean Sea shore (Garfinkel *et al.* 1992). At Herzliya, similar jars and transversal arrowheads were also found. The location of Byblos on the Mediterranean probably testifies to some marine activity as early as the fifth and fourth millennia BC, which is well attested by the third millennium BC in connections with Egypt.

"Énéolithique Ancien"

This phase is characterized by 1,675 jar burials. I personally believe that the few jar burials related in Byblos to "Néolithique Ancien," "Néolithique Moyen" and "Néolithique Récent" were actually

dug down from this phase. It seems that "Énéolithique Ancien" Byblos was not a settlement but only a cemetery. The pottery consists of v-shaped bowls (Figure 14.13.1), pedestal bowls (Figure 14.13.2), churns (Figure 14.13.3) and large storage jars (Figure 14.13.4, 5). In the flint industry one can find pierced flat scrapers (Figure 14.14.1) which characterized Late Chalcolithic sites in the Golan Heights (Epstein and Noy 1988), the Jordan Valley (Perrot *et al.* 1967), Peqi'in (Gal *et al.* 1997) and elsewhere.

"Énéolithique Ancien" Byblos also produced a violin figurine made of stone (Figure 14.14.2). Such figurines are known from various Late Chalcolithic sites like Gilat, Ghassul and Peqi'in (Alon 1990: Figure 1; Lee 1973: 279; Gal *et al.* 1997: Figure 10).

The material culture of "Énéolithique Ancien" Byblos bears many similarities to the pottery, flint and figurines of the Late Chalcolithic, the Classical Chalcolithic of the southern Levant: Ghassul-Beer Sheba-Golan cultures. The recently excavated site of Peqi'in, in Upper

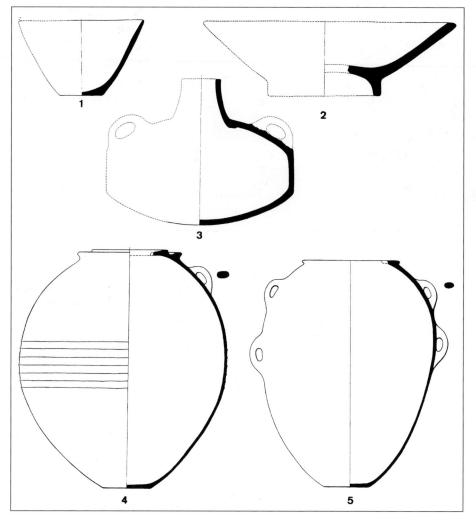

Figure 14.13
Late Chalcolithic pottery from "Énéolithique Ancien" Byblos (Dunand 1973: Figures 120, 127, 170)

Galilee, may open knew horizons on the connections between Byblos and the Southern Levant.

In the coastal plain of Israel, burial caves with special rectangular ossuaries and jar burials characterize the Late Chalcolithic (Perrot and Ladiray 1980). Byblos is different in that it displays primary burials in the ground without secondary treatment. However, we have a similar phenomenon of a large cemetery with jars as containers for the deceased.

"Énéolithique Récent"

This phase has been treated in detail by A. Ben-Tor (1989) and it correlates to the Early Bronze Age Ia and Ib of the southern Levant. This is apparent from a comparison of the pottery, oval architecture and cylinder-seal impressions found at Byblos and various sites in Israel, Palestine and Jordan.

Conclusion

Despite great difficulties caused by the method of excavation and the terminology used by the excavator of Byblos, the early settlement history of the site corresponds in many aspects to the picture known from the southern Levant:

1. Byblos was first inhabited during the Pre-Pottery Neolithic B (PPNB) of the 9th millennium BP. It was a village with rectangular buildings and plastered floors.
2. The next phase is dated to the Pottery Neolithic. Byblos was a Yarmukian site with the typical pottery, flint and artistic expressions.
3. Byblos presents a full sequence of the Chalcolithic period: Early, Middle and Late.
4. During the Late Chalcolithic the site functioned mainly as a cemetery.

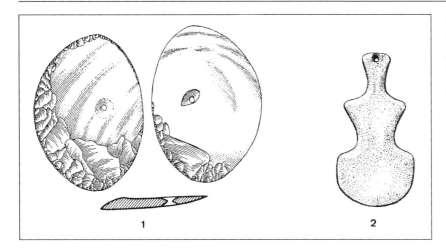

Figure 14.14 *Late Chalcolithic flint scraper and a violin figurine (Dunand 1973: Figure 180 and frontispiece)*

References

Alon, D. 1990
  Cult Artifacts from Gilat and Relations with Northern Edom in the Chalcolithic Period. *'Atiqot* 10 : 1–12 (Hebrew).

Aurenche O., J. Cauvin, M.-C. Cauvin, L. Copeland, F. Hours and P. Sanlaville 1981
  Chronologie et organisation de l'espace dans le Proche Orient de 12,000 à 5600 av J.C. Pp. 571–601 in P. Sanlaville and J. Cauvin (eds.) *Préhistoire du Levant.* Association Paléorient: Paris.

Balfet, H., H. Lafuma, P. Longuet and P. Terrier 1969
  Une invention néolithique sans lendemain. *Bulletin de la Société Préhistorique Française* 66: 188–192.

Bar-Yosef, O., F. Burian and E. Friedman 1970
  Transversal Arrowheads from the Coastal Plain. *Mitekufat Ha'even* (Journal of the Israel Prehistoric Society) 10: 22–24.

Bar-Yosef, O. and A. Belfer-Cohen 1989
  The Levantine "PPNB" Interaction Sphere. Pp. 59–72 in I. Hershkovitz (ed.) *People and Culture in Change.* Proceedings of the Second Symposium on Upper Palaeolithic, Mesolithic and Neolithic Populations of Europe and the Mediterranean Basin. British Archaeological Reports, International Series, 508: Oxford.

Ben-Tor, A. 1989
  Byblos and the Early Bronze Age I of Palestine. Pp. 41–52 in P. de Miroschedji (ed.) *L'urbanisation de la Palestine à l'âge du Bronze ancien.* British Archaeological Reports, International Series 527: Oxford.

Cauvin, J. 1968
  Fouilles de Byblos IV: Les outillages néolithiques de Byblos et du litoral libanais. Librairie d'Amerique et d'Orient, Adrien Maisonneuve: Paris.

Cauvin, J, 1972
  Religions Néolithiques de Syro-Palestine. Librairie d'Amerique et d'Orient, Adrien Maisonneuve: Paris.

Contenson, H. de 1983
  Early Agriculture in Western Asia. Pp. 57–74 in T. C. Young, P. E. L. Smith and P. Mortensen (eds.) *The Hilly Flanks and Beyond: Essays on the Prehistory of Southwestern Asia Presented to R.J. Braidwood.* Oriental Institute Publications: Chicago.

Dunand, M. 1973
  Fouilles de Byblos. Vol. V. Librairie d'Amerique et d'Orient, Adrien Maisonneuve: Paris.

Epstein, C. and T. Noy 1988
  Observations concerning Perforated Flint Tools from Chalcolithic Palestine. *Paléorient* 14/1: 133–141.

Gal, Z., H. Smithline and D. Shalem 1997
  A Chalcolithic Burial Cave in Peqi'in, Upper Galilee. *Israel Exploration Journal* 47: 145–154.

Galili, E., Y. Sarvit and A. Nagar 1996
  Neve Yam, Underwater Survey. *Hadashot Arkheologiyot* 106: 54–56 (Hebrew).

Garfinkel, Y. 1987a
  Yiftahel: A Neolithic Village from the Seventh Millennium B.C. in Lower Galilee, Israel. *Journal of Field Archaeology* 14: 199–212.

Garfinkel, Y. 1987b
  Burnt Lime Products and Social Implications in the Pre-Pottery Neolithic B Villages of the Near East. *Paléorient* 13/1: 68–75.

Garfinkel, Y. 1992
  The Pottery Assemblages of Sha'ar Hagolan and Rabah Stages from Munhata (Israel). Association Paléorient: Paris.

Garfinkel, Y. 1993
  The Yarmukian Culture in Israel. *Paléorient* 19/1: 115–134.

Garfinkel, Y. 1995
  Human and Animal Figurines of Munhata, Israel. Association Paléorient: Paris.

Garfinkel, Y. 1999a
  Neolithic and Chalcolithic Pottery of the Southern Levant. Institute of Archaeology (Qedem 39): Jerusalem.

Garfinkel, Y. 1999b

The Yarmukians, Neolithic Art from Sha'ar Hagolan. Bible Lands Museum: Jerusalem.

Garfinkel, Y. 1999c
Radiometric Dates from Eighth Millennium B.P. Israel. *Bulletin of the American Schools of Oriental Research* 315: 1–13.

Garfinkel, Y. 2001
The Neolithic Art Assemblage from Sha'ar Hagolan. Pp. 47–60 in A.M. Maeir and E. Baruch (eds.) *Settlement, Civilization and Culture. Proceedings of the Conference in Memory of David Alon.* Bar-Ilan University: Ramat Gan (Hebrew).

Garfinkel, Y., F. Burian and E. Friedman 1992
A Late Neolithic Seal from Herzliya. *Bulletin of the American Schools of Oriental Research* 286: 7–13.

Garfinkel, Y. and A. M. Miller 2002
Sha'ar Hagolan 1, Neolithic Art in Context. Oxbow: Oxford.

Garstang, J., J. P. Droop and J. Crowfoot 1935
Jericho: City and Necropolis (Fifth Report). *Liverpool Annals of Archaeology and Anthropology* 22: 143–173.

Garstang, J., I. Ben-Dor and G. M. Fitzgerald 1936
Jericho: City and Necropolis (Report for Sixth and Concluding Season). *Liverpool Annals of Archaeology and Anthropology* 23: 67–90.

Goren, Y. and P. Goldberg 1991
Petrographic Thin Sections and the Development of Neolithic Plaster Production in Northern Israel. *Journal of Field Archaeology* 18: 131–138.

Gopher, A. 1994
Arrowheads of the Neolithic Levant. Eisenbrauns: Winona Lake.

Gopher, A. and E. Orrelle 1995
The Ground Stone Assemblages of Munhata, A Neolithic Site in the Jordan Valley, Israel. A Report. Association Paléorient : Paris.

Gourdin, H. W. and W. D. Kingery 1975
Beginnings of Pyrotechnology: Neolithic and Egyptian Lime Plaster. *Journal of Field Archaeology* 2: 133–150.

Joukowsky, M. 1997
Byblos. Pp. 390–394 in E.M. Meyers (ed.) *The Oxford Encyclopedia of Archaeology in the Near East.* Oxford University Press: New York.

Kaplan, J. 1993
Hamadya. Pp. 560–561 in E. Stern (ed.) *The New Encyclopedia of Archaeological Excavations in the Holy Land.* Israel Exploration Society: Jerusalem.

Kaplan, J. and H. Ritter-Kaplan 1993
Tel Aviv. Pp. 1451–1457 in E. Stern (ed.) *The New Encyclopedia of Archaeological Excavations in the Holy Land.* Israel Exploration Society: Jerusalem.

Kenyon, K. M. 1957
Digging Up Jericho. E. Benn: London.

Kenyon, K. M. 1981

Excavations at Jericho. III. British School of Archaeology in Jerusalem: London.

Kingery, W. D., P. B. Vandiver and M. Prickett 1988
Beginnings of Pyrotechnology, Part II: Production and Use of Lime and Gypsum Plaster in the Pre-Pottery Neolithic Near East. *Journal of Field Archaeology* 15: 219–244.

Kirkbride, D. 1969
Ancient Byblos and the Beqa`a. *Mélanges de l'Université Saint Joseph* 45 : 46–53.

Lechevallier, M. 1978
Abou Gosh et Beisamoun: deux gisements du VIIè millénaire avant l'ère chrétienne en Israël. Association Paléorient: Paris.

Lee, R. 1973
Chalcolithic Ghassul: New Aspects and Master Typology. Unpublished Ph.D. Thesis, The Hebrew University of Jerusalem: Jerusalem.

Malinowski, R. and Y. Garfinkel 1990
Prehistory of Concrete. *Concrete International* 13/3: 62–68.

Perrot, J. 1962
Palestine – Syria – Cilicia. Pp. 147–164 in R. J. Braidwood and G. R. Willey (eds.) *Courses toward Urban Life.* Edinburgh University Press: Edinburgh.

Perrot, J. 1969
Le "Néolithique" du Liban et les récentes découvertes dans la haute et moyenne vallée du Jourdain. *Mélanges de l'Université Saint Joseph* 45: 46–53.

Perrot, J. 1993
Minha, Horvat. Pp. 1046–1050 in E. Stern (ed.) *The New Encyclopedia of Archaeological Excavations in the Holy Land.* Israel Exploration Society: Jerusalem.

Perrot, J. and D. Ladiray 1980
Tombes à ossuaires de la région cotière palestinienne au IVè millénaire avant l'ère chrétienne. Association Paléorient: Paris.

Perrot, J., N. Zori and I. Reich 1967
Neve Ur, un nouvel aspect du Ghassoulien. *Israel Exploration Journal* 17: 201–232.

Prauznitz, M. W. 1969
The Excavations at Kabri. *Eretz-Israel* 9: 122–29 (Hebrew).

Prausnitz, M. W., F. Burian, E. Friedman and E. Wreschner 1970
Excavation in the Site Herzliyah, 1969. *Mitekufat Ha'even* (Journal of the Israel Prehistoric Society) 10: 11–16.

Rollefson, G. O. 1990
The Uses of Plaster at Neolithic `Ain Ghazal, Jordan. *Archeomaterials* 4: 33–54.

Stekelis, M. 1972.
The Yarmukian Culture of the Neolithic Period. Magnes Press: Jerusalem.

Edinburgh University Library

Books may be recalled for return earlier than due date;
if so you will be contacted by e-mail or letter.

Due Date	Due Date	Due Date
2 1 OCT 2009		

University of Edinburgh

30150   024465517